A Philosophical Introduction to Human Rights

While almost everyone has heard of human rights, few will have reflected in depth on what human rights are, where they originate from and what they mean. *A Philosophical Introduction to Human Rights* – accessibly written without being superficial – addresses these questions and provides a multi-faceted introduction to legal philosophy.

The point of departure is the famous 1948 Universal Declaration of Human Rights, which provides a frame for engagement with western legal philosophy. Thomas Mertens sketches the philosophical and historical background of the Declaration, discusses the ten most important human rights with the help of key philosophers, and ends by reflecting on the relationship between rights and duties. The *basso continuo* of the book is a particular worldview derived from Immanuel Kant. 'Unsocial sociability' is what characterizes humans: the tension between the individual and social nature. Some human rights emphasize the first, others the second aspect. The tension between these two aspects plays a fundamental role in how human rights are interpreted and applied.

Thomas Mertens is a specialist on the relationship between law and morality. He has published extensively on human rights, Kant's moral and legal philosophy, the just war tradition and law and morality in Nazi-Germany. He teaches at Radboud University Nijmegen and has also held adjacent positions at Leiden University and Catholic University Leuven.

The Law in Context Series

Editors: Kenneth Armstrong (University of Cambridge)
Maksymilian Del Mar (Queen Mary, University of London)
Sally Sheldon (University of Kent)

Since 1970, the Law in Context series has been at the forefront of a movement to broaden the study of law. The series is a vehicle for the publication of innovative monographs and texts that treat law and legal phenomena critically in their cultural, social, political, technological, environmental and economic contexts. A contextual approach involves treating legal subjects broadly, using materials from other humanities and social sciences, and from any other discipline that helps to explain the operation in practice of the particular legal field or legal phenomena under investigation. It is intended that this orientation is at once more stimulating and more revealing than the bare exposition of legal rules. The series includes original research monographs, coursebooks and textbooks that foreground contextual approaches and methods. The series includes and welcomes books on the study of law in all its contexts, including domestic legal systems, European and international law, transnational and global legal processes, and comparative law.

Books in the Series

Acosta: *The National versus the Foreigner in South America: 200 Years of Migration and Citizenship Law*
Ali: *Modern Challenges to Islamic Law*
Alyagon Darr: *Plausible Crime Stories: The Legal History of Sexual Offences in Mandate Palestine*
Anderson, Schum & Twining: *Analysis of Evidence, 2nd Edition*
Ashworth: *Sentencing and Criminal Justice, 6th Edition*
Barton & Douglas: *Law and Parenthood*
Baxi, McCrudden & Paliwala: *Law's Ethical, Global and Theoretical Contexts: Essays in Honour of William Twining*
Beecher-Monas: *Evaluating Scientific Evidence: An Interdisciplinary Framework for Intellectual Due Process*
Bell: *French Legal Cultures*
Bercusson: *European Labour Law, 2nd Edition*
Birkinshaw: *European Public Law*
Birkinshaw: *Freedom of Information: The Law, the Practice and the Ideal, 4th Edition*
Broderick & Ferri: *International and European Disability Law and Policy: Text, Cases and Materials*
Brownsword & Goodwin: *Law and the Technologies of the Twenty-First Century: Text and Materials*
Cane & Goudkamp: *Atiyah's Accidents, Compensation and the Law, 9th Edition*
Clarke: *Principles of Property Law*
Clarke & Kohler: *Property Law: Commentary and Materials*

Collins: *The Law of Contract, 4th Edition*

Collins, Ewing & McColgan: *Labour Law, 2nd Edition*

Cowan: *Housing Law and Policy*

Cranston: *Commercial Law from the Nineteenth Century: Law as Backcloth*

Cranston: *Legal Foundations of the Welfare State*

Darian-Smith: *Laws and Societies in Global Contexts: Contemporary Approaches*

Dauvergne: *Making People Illegal: What Globalisation Means for Immigration and Law*

David: *Kinship, Law and Politics: An Anatomy of Belonging*

Davies: *Perspectives on Labour Law, 2nd Edition*

Dembour: *Who Believes in Human Rights?: Reflections on the European Convention*

de Sousa Santos: *Toward a New Legal Common Sense: Law, Globalization, and Emancipation*

Diduck: *Law's Families*

Estella: *Legal Foundations of EU Economic Governance*

Fortin: *Children's Rights and the Developing Law, 3rd Edition*

Garnsey: *The Justice of Visual Art: Creative State-Building in Times of Political Transition*

Garton, Probert & Bean: *Moffat's Trusts Law: Text and Materials, 7th Edition*

Ghai & Woodman: *Practising Self-Government: A Comparative Study of Autonomous Regions*

Glover-Thomas: *Reconstructing Mental Health Law and Policy*

Gobert & Punch: *Rethinking Corporate Crime*

Goldman: *Globalisation and the Western Legal Tradition: Recurring Patterns of Law and Authority*

Haack: *Evidence Matters: Science, Proof, and Truth in the Law*

Harlow & Rawlings: *Law and Administration, 3rd Edition*

Harris: *An Introduction to Law, 8th Edition*

Harris, Campbell & Halson: *Remedies in Contract and Tort, 2nd Edition*

Harvey: *Seeking Asylum in the UK: Problems and Prospects*

Herring: *Law and the Relational Self*

Hervey & McHale: *European Union Health Law: Themes and Implications*

Hervey & McHale: *Health Law and the European Union*

Holder & Lee: *Environmental Protection, Law and Policy: Text and Materials, 2nd Edition*

Jackson & Summers: *The Internationalisation of Criminal Evidence: Beyond the Common Law and Civil Law Traditions*

Kostakopoulou: *The Future Governance of Citizenship*

Kreiczer-Levy *Destabilized Property: Property Law in the Sharing Economy*

Kubal: *Immigration and Refugee Law in Russia: Socio-Legal Perspectives*

Lewis: *Choice and the Legal Order: Rising above Politics*

Likosky: *Law, Infrastructure and Human Rights*

Likosky: *Transnational Legal Processes: Globalisation and Power Disparities*

Lixinski: *Legalized Identities*

Loughnan: *Self, Others and the State: Relations of Criminal Responsibility*

Lunney: *A History of Australian Tort Law 1901–1945: England's Obedient Servant?*

Maughan & Webb: *Lawyering Skills and the Legal Process, 2nd Edition*

McGlynn: *Families and the European Union: Law, Politics and Pluralism*

Wells & Quick: *Lacey, Wells and Quick: Reconstructing Criminal Law: Text and Materials*, 4th Edition

Zander: *Cases and Materials on the English Legal System*, 10th Edition

Zander: *The Law-Making Process*, 6th Edition

International Journal of Law in Context: A Global Forum for Interdisciplinary Legal Studies

The *International Journal of Law in Context* is the companion journal to the Law in Context book series and provides a forum for interdisciplinary legal studies and offers intellectual space for ground-breaking critical research. It publishes contextual work about law and its relationship with other disciplines including but not limited to science, literature, humanities, philosophy, sociology, psychology, ethics, history and geography. More information about the journal and how to submit an article can be found at http://journals.cambridge.org/ijc

A Philosophical Introduction to Human Rights

THOMAS MERTENS

Radboud University Nijmegen (Netherlands)

CAMBRIDGE
UNIVERSITY PRESS

University Printing House, Cambridge CB2 8BS, United Kingdom

One Liberty Plaza, 20th Floor, New York, NY 10006, USA

477 Williamstown Road, Port Melbourne, VIC 3207, Australia

314–321, 3rd Floor, Plot 3, Splendor Forum, Jasola District Centre,
New Delhi – 110025, India

79 Anson Road, #06–04/06, Singapore 079906

Cambridge University Press is part of the University of Cambridge.

It furthers the University's mission by disseminating knowledge in the pursuit of
education, learning, and research at the highest international levels of excellence.

www.cambridge.org
Information on this title: www.cambridge.org/9781108416313
DOI: 10.1017/9781108236287

© Boom uitgevers Amsterdam 2020

First published 2020

Printed in the United Kingdom by TJ International Ltd, Padstow Cornwall

A catalogue record for this publication is available from the British Library.

ISBN 978-1-108-41631-3 Hardback
ISBN 978-1-108-40282-8 Paperback

Contents

Contents

Preface

Readers of recent literature on human rights could easily come to the conclusion that we are approaching what one commentator has called 'the end of human rights', and another, 'the endtimes of human rights'. The heyday of human rights seem to be over and courts, such as the European Court of Human Rights, now attract fierce criticism from across the political spectrum when they find that acts of national governments violate human rights. Contrary to this trend, this book argues that the age of human rights need not be over, certainly not when they are understood in line with the Universal Declaration of Human Rights.

This very important 1948 document does not, as critics of human rights often argue, focus exclusively on civil and political rights. It does not deny the importance of human duties. Neither does it invoke an implausible view of the human being as primarily an egoistic being, nor, as Marx once formulated it, as an individual separated from the community and solely concerned with self-interest. Moreover, the Universal Declaration includes no role for activist courts.

In addition to enriching our understanding of the human rights debate, the Universal Declaration encapsulates an attractive philosophy of law. Not all aspects of the long and rich tradition of legal philosophy can be discussed when analysing the text of this Declaration, but much of this tradition can be accessed through it and thereby given context: the validity of positive law, the role of individual rights, the just claims by communities and states, and the place of morality within the life of the law. An earlier, Dutch edition of this book, *Mens & Mensenrechten* (beautifully published in 2012 by Boom Publishers Amsterdam) has introduced large numbers of students to the ancient and modern worlds of legal philosophy. While this book is designed as an introductory text for all readers, it has been created for teaching purposes and has served this goal well over the last several years. For this English edition, all chapters of the book have been thoroughly revised and updated. Yet the hope remains the same: that it will serve the same goal of introducing an audience of students of law and philosophy, in an accessible yet not superficial manner, to the fascinating and important world of legal philosophy by means of reflecting on human rights.

I am grateful not only to the generations of students that I have had the privilege to teach, but also for the support given to me by Boom Publishers in Amsterdam and by Cambridge University Press. I have been helped in preparing this book by Jill Bradley and Steven van Gool. Over the years, I have received excellent feedback on the thinking that forms the basis of this book, and on the texts themselves, by many colleagues. Here I single out Morag Goodwin, Corjo Jansen, Stanley Paulson and Ronald Tinnevelt for particular thanks.

1

Legal Philosophy and Human Rights

This chapter is an introduction to legal philosophy. Legal philosophy combines two academic disciplines – philosophy and law – and therefore it is necessary to say something about these two disciplines. Subsequently we deal with how they are connected to each other, that is, with what the philosophical approach to law is. This means that two common philosophical views of the law, natural law and legal positivism, are discussed. Finally, we consider why the subject of human rights is a good starting point for engaging with legal philosophy's important themes.

Philosophy

Originally philosophy meant 'science' or 'love of knowledge', and that is why classical philosophers such as Aristotle wrote about practically everything, ranging from what we would now consider to be in the realms of biology and physics, by way of logic and rhetoric, to politics, and from the good of a human being to metaphysical issues such as the world or God. More recent philosophers such as Immanuel Kant still covered a wide range of topics, as varied as geography and epistemology. With the passage of time, and particularly since what we call the scientific revolution of the sixteenth and seventeenth centuries, the various constituents of 'science' have gradually gained independence, so that in a certain sense, philosophy has 'shrunk'.

Nowadays philosophy concerns itself, on the one hand, with theoretical matters, and considers such questions as the possibility of knowledge and science; on the other hand, it deals with practical matters like the possibilities for the well-being of the human being and human society. The term 'practical philosophy' is a good expression of what it is all about – philosophy of the practices in which human beings are involved, the philosophy of human actions in the broadest sense of the word. Practical philosophy is often called 'ethics'. That term is justified too. The word 'ethics' comes from the Greek word *ethos* and today we would translate that word as habit or custom. With regard to habit, it is significant that the word *ethos* also indicates living or dwelling. In this way ethics has to do with the way we conduct ourselves and interact with each other – in our own home, in a university or business, but also in the political institutions to which we belong. Ethics, then, says which of all these ways are (morally) good and which are not, and establishes the criteria by which it is possible to make such a distinction. That is why we associate ethics with questions of good and evil, with justice and injustice, even with virtue and vice. Ethics, in the sense of 'custom', is to be found in the expression 'customs and traditions', in the somewhat old-fashioned concept of morality and in the legislation of morals and public decency. In regard to the latter the obvious association is with punishable offences in connection with sexuality, prostitution and pornography.

As part of practical philosophy or ethics, legal philosophy focuses on the questions concerning the juridical organization of society. While practical philosophy in general deals with the well-being of human beings both as private individuals and as citizens in the public sphere, in legal philosophy the latter aspect is paramount. In a certain sense, however, the distinction between human beings as private individuals and human beings as citizens is itself artificial. From time immemorial some philosophers have maintained that one could only be a good person if one is part of a good society. According to Plato this connection is so intrinsic that you can only know what a good person is by looking at a good society. Even if one holds that the connection is less intimate, it remains a fact that the possibilities for a person to lead a good and successful life are determined to an important degree by the social environment and political society into which they are born. The private human being and the public citizen cannot be fully separated. Take, for example, the profession of the notary or the legal advocate: anyone wishing to occupy such a profession must meet certain professional conditions and have certain competences. In order to function properly, such a professional should not merely be 'good' in the technical, legal sense of the word, but also in the moral sense: they must serve society as a whole.[1] The same applies to the judiciary: judges have an important role in society, and how well they function not only depends on their knowledge of the law, but also on their qualities as human beings, notably their integrity.

Along these lines legal philosophy then would concern the morally good *legal* organization of society; in this way it is close to political philosophy.[2] Both are concerned with the question of when a political order is 'just'. This question – as history has made clear – can be answered in various ways. The answer can have to do with relatively minor things, such as a particular tax rate or a certain criminal penalty, but it can also concern relatively major matters,

---

[1] Obviously, some might argue that the common good can only be reached if such a professional focuses solely on the interest of their client. However, this is not what most professional codes state.

[2] Obviously, this is a particular take on legal philosophy. Not all legal philosophers would agree. Analytic legal philosophy is mainly interested in the conceptual analysis of central legal categories such as the concept of law itself, or authority. Legal positivists sometimes argue that there is no final answer to the question what a 'just' or a 'good' legal organization is. Variations of (German) legal positivism will be discussed in Chapter 11.

such as the question as to whether there is really any justification for such institutions as taxation or a penal system. With this we indeed touch on political philosophy, because it concerns the good organization of the 'polis' too. Nowadays, neither political philosophy nor legal philosophy wishes to give an unequivocal or final answer to such minor or major questions; what both attempt to do is to bring together various opinions and views on these matters into a systematic and coherent unity.

In a certain sense, therefore, practical philosophy is of all times. One could even say that humans are 'ethical beings'; not because they continually do what is good and just, but because they continually judge themselves and especially others on moral grounds. Often, they do that hastily and without much reflection, but all these judgements have in common that they contain both the personal and the institutional element. Guiding concerns are questions such as 'How should I behave towards other people and (especially) how should others behave towards me? How should society be organized and what institutions are to be promoted and what to be rejected?' Such questions and opinions are unavoidable: they impose themselves on humans precisely because we are 'ethical beings'.

Since the institutions of society are nowadays to an important degree determined by law, and because the law consequently determines how individuals can organize their lives, both for themselves and together with others, it is obvious that an important part of practical philosophy is concerned with law. Legal philosophy is thus, in this understanding, 'practical philosophy' about law; law regarded not from the internal, but from an external, philosophical point of view. Legal philosophy does not content itself with establishing what the law is at a particular moment, but examines the law from the perspective of good and evil, of justice and injustice. It strives to give an evaluative judgement, even if it does not claim any monopoly on the moral 'value' of the law. Legal philosophy primarily articulates the values that inevitably play a role in law. In this sense it is not prescriptive, but descriptive. To 'do' legal philosophy is to filter the specific moral values regarding the law, to order them and examine them for their coherence, whilst being always aware of the demands of justice.

Despite the fact that the search for moral value(s) is certainly not always a priority for lawyers, they cannot avoid legal philosophy. Because every lawyer is involved in the organization of society, on a big or a small scale, in a certain sense every lawyer harbours within themselves a legal philosopher. Since nowadays the value of the law and the criterion for determining the justice of the law is often sought in human rights, these rights are central in this book.

Law

Anyone who thinks that everything will become clear now that we have finished dealing with the notoriously vague definition of philosophy and can start considering a definition of law is sadly mistaken. If anything, there may even be more disagreement about what exactly 'law' is than there is about the precise nature of practical philosophy. That should not come as a surprise, because law often concerns conflicting claims in which a great deal is at stake. How such conflicting claims should be resolved often depends on different views on how the law has to be interpreted. For example, is the freedom of assembly and association – to be found both in many constitutions and in Article 20 of the 1948 Universal Declaration of Human Rights – more important than 'the Elimination of all Forms of Discrimination against Women', as enshrined in a 1979 International Convention? Is it permitted for political parties, based, for example, on the different roles given to men and women according to the Bible, to claim priority of the former over the latter and legitimize their restricting of their electoral lists of candidates for public office to men only? Such a claim by a Dutch political party, however, was rejected in 2010 by the highest court in the land. Law deals not only with conflicting claims but also with conflicting values. For instance, is it within the competence of judges, sitting in national or in international courts, to set aside domestic laws that have been decided in a democratic manner because they are considered to be in conflict with human rights? Which value should prevail: the democratic decision-making process or the individual human right (as interpreted by such judges)? What is the proper relationship between legislative and judicial powers? Finally, law has to deal not only with conflicting claims and values, but sometimes also with conflicts between what a particular law demands from a person as a citizen, and what this person considers as their moral duty. Here one finds a conflict between the citizen's duty of obedience to the law and the person's duty to follow one's moral judgement. To put it more elegantly, this is a conflict between heteronomy and autonomy. This raises the following question: from what source does the law derive the authority by which it claims priority over the personal moral convictions and judgements of those who are subjected to the law? This question will be explored further in Chapter 17.

Due to these and related difficulties many scholars are inclined to accept a rather limited and apparently simple definition of law: the entirety of promulgated, regulatory and enforceable rules that apply within a particular territory. According to such a definition it is better not to speak of law in general, but of 'positive law', or posited law, from the Latin *ponere*. Positive law is, then, the law that is posited or in place at a particular time and within a particular territory.

This apparently simple definition has at least four problematic components. First, since promulgating a law is not an arbitrary act, but one that is carried out by a person or body that has the competent authority to do so, this concept of law immediately raises the issue of competence. Someone who, with the threat of a gun, robs me of my wallet, also sets a rule ('your money or your life'), but no one would acknowledge this to be a lawful rule. It is not issued by a competent authority.[3] The best-known body that is considered competent to promulgate legal rules is the legislative power. Obviously, the question that then arises is who has authorized the legislator to issue such legal rules? This question cannot easily be answered on juridical grounds only. The present legislator can certainly point to earlier legislators or legislative bodies and finally to an original or constitutive legislator, but from where did this original legislator derive its competence? Did it simply declare itself to be competent, but if so, on what grounds? Did it simply assume or take the power to declare itself competent, or was it based on societal acceptance or a social compact? If the first option was the case, does the law ultimately stem from (political) power? If the second, how broad must such societal acceptance be for a legal system to be valid?

Secondly, according to the simple definition, the law consists of rules, of general regulations that must be applied to concrete cases. Of course, it is possible to imagine a legal system in which the person or instance that issues the rule also applies the rule. Consider, for instance, a simple legal system in which a monarch is both legislator and judge. In modern complex societies, however, this is impossible and there exists a division of (legal) labour. The legislator issues general rules and delegates the competence to apply these rules to the judiciary. In applying, the judiciary has a certain room for interpretation because rules can only be formulated in general terms and the cases that must be adjudicated are always concrete. In daily life cases can always arise that are not foreseen by the legislator. One might then ask what really determines the law in a particular case: the rule or its application. On the basis of such considerations, Oliver Holmes, a famous former judge in the United States Supreme Court, offered a daring thesis.[4] He defended the thesis that the law was basically nothing more than a prediction of what judges will decide in a concrete case. In other words, the outcome of a particular legal case is not (at least not fully) determined by the rule, but by the way in which that case is interpreted by a judge given certain concrete circumstances. Holmes's thesis appears to be exaggerated, but it indeed happens often that, on the basis of existing positive law, it is not clear beforehand what the outcome of a particular legal case will be.

Third, the simple definition of the law speaks of the difference between regulatory and enforceable rules. This indicates an important distinction within the law. Some rules regulate the voluntary interaction between citizens: if two persons wish to make a contract with each other, they must do so in a certain way in order to make the contract legally binding. Whoever wants to marry or make a labour contract must follow certain rules. Other rules deal with what can be called 'involuntary' interaction between citizens. A clear case

---

[3] This is Herbert L. A. Hart's famous gunman example in his well-known article, 'Positivism and the Separation of Law and Morals', *Harvard Law Review* (1958) 71: 593–629.

[4] In his 'The Path of the Law', *Harvard Law Review* (1897) 10: 457–78.

of such involuntary interaction is when a citizen, either deliberately or not, damages or injures another, such as in a traffic accident. The law wants to prevent such occurrences by means of enforceable rules and it sanctions the person who breaks such a rule. It is beyond doubt that the law is a system of rules that entail coercion, and that is true also of rules that regulate. If I ignore such rules, then no marriage or labour contract has been established.[5] The law, however, cannot be reduced to mere coercion, because some of its rules merely regulate relations between citizens. In short, the law 'does' different things.

This leads to a fourth and final difficulty. It is held that all the rules of the law form a 'unity' that is valid within a certain territory. Anyone with even a rudimentary understanding of modern law knows of the multiplicity of rules that are ascribed to various legal domains – civil law, constitutional and administrative law and criminal law. The question as to how these heterogeneous rules can possibly form a single unity seems to have an obvious answer. The law is a hierarchically ordered set of rules, whereby the validity of a lower rule can be 'deduced' from a higher rule, which itself in the end can be deduced from an ultimate legal rule. Yet, what is the status of this ultimate rule? Does this ultimate rule belong to positive law or is it only a quasi-rule that simply stipulates or presumes that all other rules are legally binding? Is this ultimate rule 'merely' the result of the exercise of political power or must it reflect some societal acceptance? Furthermore, the 'unity' of such legal rules that are valid within a particular territory suggests that law is tied up with the existence of a particular sovereign state: no law without a state. These days, however, no state is governed by its internal legal rules only, but by external legal rules as well, coming from bodies such as the European Union or the World Trade Organization, to name but two 'transnational' legal systems. Is 'law' still a unity if it is constituted by legal rules stemming from such heterogeneous sources?

Still, the 'simple' definition of law is useful in legal practice. Anyone studying law is chiefly concerned with the law as it is posited in rules and statutes; anyone consulting a lawyer about a concrete juridical problem wants an answer to what one can expect from the law, and in many cases it is possible to give such an answer. However, in the case of more complex questions, often concerning conflicting claims and values, or from a theoretical perspective, this positivist definition is not satisfactory due to problems, as we saw, of authority, interpretation, coercion and unity. Therefore, it is now necessary, albeit briefly, to pay attention to the classical perspectives on law that have dominated legal philosophy for centuries. On the one hand, one finds positivist thinking that regards the law chiefly in terms of statutory law and the political power whence it derives its 'authority'. On the other hand, one finds the

---

[5] Whether this lack of validity can then be considered a 'sanction' is discussed among legal philosophers. See, for example, Herbert Lionel Adolphus Hart, *The Concept of Law* (Oxford: Oxford University Press, 1994), 33–5.

natural law position that declares that in the last instance, the authority of the law is (also) a moral issue.

Two Schools of Legal Philosophical Thinking

It may raise eyebrows to pay attention now to a centuries-old discussion between two opposing perspectives on law. Has no progress been made on this question? In any case, these views and the concepts and contradictions that ensue from them are still current. They are still part of the present-day discourse on law. At the same time, they are found not only in abstract debate, but can also be recognized in positions taken by judges in 'difficult cases', albeit not often explicitly: this will become apparent in Chapter 8 which discusses the well-known Berlin Wall shooting cases. Precisely because this discussion took place over the centuries, many specific versions of these two perspectives have emerged and many efforts have been made to find a middle ground. It is better, therefore, to speak of schools of thought rather than strict and well-defined views. Moreover, it is frequently the case that there is something to say in favour of each point of view: we need not choose one or other of the 'camps'.

The tension between the two views is apparent in Sophocles's classic tragedy *Antigone*. This tragedy hinges on Antigone's refusal to obey an explicit prohibition, in the form of a (legal) rule issued by her monarch (and uncle) Creon, that her brother, who had been slain on the battlefield, was 'not to be buried, not to be mourned'. Following her conscience, she chooses not to obey this law and to fulfil the religious and familial duties that she derives from natural law. She gives priority to religious duty to bury her brother over the duty to obedience. For this, Antigone has received, over the centuries, a great deal of sympathy, but there are good reasons for Creon's position as well. The city of Thebes was just emerging from a period of civil war, and the establishment of a stable legal system would be of great benefit to all citizens. This would demand that one's duty as a citizen outweighs one's personal duties of religion or natural law.

Over time, various values can lie behind both legal positivism and natural law. For instance, during the Weimar Republic in Germany between 1919 and 1933 positivism stood for loyalty to the newly established republican legal order, while at the same time positive law (and the Weimar legislator) were undermined by an appeal to a conservative (higher) 'Law'. Eventually this appeal and the undermining of positive law contributed to the dissolution of Weimar and the rise to power of the Nazis. The defeat of Germany in 1945 was followed by a renaissance of Christian natural law which led to a central place in the new German constitution being given to (the inviolability of) human dignity.

Before 'defining' these two perspectives, it is important to recall the kind of questions they want to answer. First and foremost, the question of the origins of the law: is law merely a set of conventional rules established by human beings on the basis of their particular standards and values, or does law (also) consist of (moral) values that have a validity independent of human beings and that can be found in God, nature or reason? Is law exclusively the result of a human act of the will, such as the will of a legislator, so that any content can become 'the law'? Or is it rather a matter of knowing or discovering (moral) values and standards that, so to speak, exist beyond human will? In other words, are there sources of the law other than the mere 'fact' that a certain legal rule is posited, so that the possibility of a conflict between a posited legal standard and a higher standard exists? Is the law established arbitrarily, or subject to a higher standard and value? Linked to this question is that of whether the law is a closed system of values and standards in their own right, or rather whether a continuum exists between legal and moral values.

We must be cautious here because there is always a certain relationship between the moral opinions of society and the law. The law always reflects to a certain extent the prevailing moral views current in society: that is a sociological fact. The law's dependence on the views of society is made clear by a simple example. The fact that nowadays the law in various lands makes same-sex marriages possible is a reflection of the changed views on what marriage means and (gender) equality demands. Some people, however, hold, and here we approach a natural law claim, that marriage is an institution ordained by God between a man and a woman only and may not be extended to couples of the same sex (this subject is discussed thoroughly in Chapter 13). Positive law is, according to these people, subject to a higher religious norm and if one of its rules violates that higher norm (as in the case of enabling same-sex marriage) it should lose its validity. Therefore, the discussion between legal positivism and natural law is of greater importance than the mere sociological observation of the actual relationship between legal rules and prevailing moral opinions. That the Jewish part of the German population were declared to be second-class citizens – on the basis of the Nuremberg race laws of 1935 – was also the result of certain 'moral' opinions. Others held then that these 'laws' should never have been part of positive law in (Nazi) Germany. Partly because of these laws and its consequences the Universal Declaration of Human Rights declares that discrimination on the basis of race is strictly prohibited.

The difference between positivism and natural law concerns, in short, the question whether there is a necessary link between the legal system and certain moral values. It concerns the question of whether the law can be valid even if it does not satisfy certain minimum moral conditions. Nowadays these minimum standards are often located in human rights.

Legal Positivism

Despite the many varieties of legal positivism, its general view is that there is no necessary or intrinsic connection between law and morality; it acknowledges only a contingent sociological link. The validity of the law does not depend on prevailing moral views. Law should be regarded as the totality of valid rules established and upheld by competent institutions and persons. In other words, the validity of the law and the demands of justice or the standards of moral decency are different issues. According to positivism there is a sharp distinction between the law as it is and the law as one would perhaps want it to be based on one's morality. The question of justice has therefore no place in establishing what counts as law.[6] According to some positivists, the reason for this separation lies in the fact that humans cannot agree on what justice requires: myriad answers are given to the question of what justice really is. These positivists emphasize the importance of posited law on the basis of moral scepticism: no unequivocal, clear answer to the question of justice exists. Take as an example the classic definition of justice that 'everyone should get what they deserve'. That may sound convincing, says the sceptical positivist, but how can one decide who gets what? Is 'merit' the criterion for dividing up resources or should it be 'need'? Other positivists emphasize the importance of legal certainty: the authority of the law would be impaired if citizens were encouraged to take into consideration (moral) standards of behaviour that are not set by a competent authority. Basically, this is the position of Creon we have seen. Still others advocate positivism because a scientific approach to law is only possible with a well-defined 'object'. Therefore, it is necessary to distinguish law from other standards of behaviour.

Given that positivism maintains that moral considerations play no part in determining what the law is, the question of the validity of the law cannot be answered with reference to morality. A different answer is given, namely by looking at whether a certain legal standard is posited in a correct manner and whether that standard is in fact followed by those to whom it is addressed. In short, whether some rule is considered 'legal' is not decided on the basis of its (moral) content or some moral source, but on the basis of whether this norm is generally obeyed and effectively sanctioned. Effectiveness of the law must be understood here in a broad sense. It means that a legal rule is not only (generally) externally enforced, for example by means of making sanctions available, but also that this rule has been internalized in the sense that the person to whom the legal rule is addressed is also, as it were from an internal perspective, willing to accept that rule as a standard of behaviour.[7] The definition given in the early years of the twentieth century by the sociologist Max Weber still fits this view rather well: law is a system of rules – issued by a particular group of persons – whose existence is guaranteed by the

---

[6] Therefore, Kelsen, the proponent of the pure theory of law, describes his task as 'to unfetter the law, to break the connection that is always made between the law and morality'. See Hans Kelsen, *Introduction to the Problems of Legal Theory*. Translated by Stanley L. Paulson and Bonnie Litschewski Paulson (Oxford: Clarendon, 1996), 15.

[7] On this internal aspect of law, see Hart, *The Concept of Law*, 89–91.

possibility of physical and psychological coercion whenever the law is broken.[8] Put in a different way, law is a particular social order within a centrally organized society based on a monopoly of (political) power. The central elements of this definition are a social system and the existence of a central institution that is authorized to enforce compliance with the existing legal rules. Obviously, this presupposes the statutory aspect of the law. After all, how can any order exist without rules that are issued and promulgated?

For this reason, the emphasis of positivism sometimes rests on the fact that the legal norm is issued. Hereof we find a classic definition in the nineteenth century command theory of John Austin[9] – the law is the totality of commands as they are promulgated or 'issued' by a sovereign and that are generally obeyed because they are backed up by sanctions. Accordingly, the law would (solely) consist of three components: (1) It is established by a person or a body that is competent to do so. (2) This person or body itself is not subject to these legal standards, but can enforce their compliance. (3) That which is promulgated has the character of an order that people obey; it is not merely an exhortation or recommendation. Precisely by emphasizing its commanding character and the obedience that follows from this, we find the element of social effectiveness in this definition too.

To summarize, according to a legal-positivist approach the law is statutory and judicial power. It is strongly connected with (societal) power because it must be effective, and this power is 'codified' because it is laid down in legal standards. Over the course of time refinements of this theory have emerged. It has been acknowledged that there are legal commands that are not always obeyed, but nevertheless do not lose their legal character. Since the legal philosopher Hart wrote his famous treatise on law, every contemporary positivist has defined law in terms of rules rather than commands. The heterogeneity of all the elements of which the law consists can be better encompassed by the broader concept of 'rule' than by 'command'.

Some claim that being issued or promulgated and being effective would in the end amount to the same thing, but the distinction is nonetheless useful. The second aspect of effectiveness has more to do with the perspective of the outsider or observer. If, as a scholar or as an outsider, I ask whether a particular standard in a certain legal system is 'law', then I look for whether it is being upheld. Being promulgated or issued reflects the perspective of the participant. Take for instance, the judge or the citizen seeking legal advice: they would first ask what is 'statutory' in law before considering the question of whether it is upheld.

---

[8] See Robert Alexy, *Begriff und Geltung des Rechts* (Freiburg/München: Alber, 1994), 32.

[9] John Austin, *The Province of Jurisprudence Determined* (Indianapolis: Weidenfeld & Nicholson, 1954), Lecture 1.

Natural Law

The opposite of a positivist view of the law is natural law. In general, the emphasis is here on the necessary, intrinsic link between positive law and morality, in particular justice.[10] Positive law as it is cannot be separated from law as it ought to be. The plausibility of such a non-positivist approach can easily be made clear by considering two very important arguments that can be made against legal positivism. In the first argument the question is raised whether a legal-positivist definition of the law is sufficient. According to positivism, the law consists of legal standards, of commands or of rules (depending on the version of positivism). Natural law stresses that law must be more than what is laid down in general terms. Consider for instance the 'application' of the law by a citizen, or more specifically by a judge: due to the general nature of the (legal) language, interpretation is necessary to know whether a particular case falls under a general standard, command or rule. Such an interpretation must lead to a juridical conclusion in which, so the supporter of natural law claims, certain principles, such as equality before the law or fairness or due care, play a major role. These principles are of a moral nature and can never be fully and clearly expressed in legal standards. In other words, the law does not consist of statutory general standards only. The need for interpretation of the law implies that moral categories play an important role in the life of the law. A clear separation between law and morality is impossible.

Sometimes this first argument is clarified by the concept of 'open texture'. Each set of standards, commands and rules has an open structure (what counts as a vehicle in a legal rule prohibiting taking a vehicle into a public park, to mention a famous example?[11]) so that there is a need for interpretation, especially by the judge. Another case occurs when on the basis of certain rights conflicting claims are made. Then a judge must decide on the basis of balancing these claims but he cannot do so – so the argument goes – on legal grounds only. In such cases of indeterminacy and conflicting claims, a judicial decision can never be reached on the basis of the legal standards issued by the law-giver alone. Some scholars have even argued that any judicial decision ultimately requires an appeal to moral conscience. In short, the positivist perspective on the law as a closed system of legal standards is not a satisfactory description of the (practice of the) law.

Of course, this argument does not leave the positivist speechless. This argument can be even countered relatively easily, argues the positivist, in the

---

[10] Thomas Aquinas formulates this connection as follows: 'Laws framed by man are either just or unjust. If they be just, they have the power of binding in conscience . . . laws may be unjust in two ways: first, by being contrary to human good. The like are acts of violence rather than laws . . . Secondly, laws may be unjust through being opposed to the Divine good; . . . of this kind must nowise be observed, because, as stated in Acts 5:29, "we ought to obey God rather than man".' (*Summa Theologiae*, Prima Secundae, Questio 96, Article 4.)

[11] Hart, 'Positivism and the separation of law and morals', 607.

following manner. It is certainly possible for those who issue legal standards – the lawgiver – to delegate the competence to adjudicate to the judiciary, and to subsequently prescribe that the application of the law is based on certain moral considerations such as fairness, good faith, due care or what is customary in social interaction. These moral considerations are then deliberately integrated into positive law so that they become part of the law. It is clear that 'moral' values can form part of the law: the protection of 'human dignity' as the duty of the government is now part of German law, as Article 1 of the Constitution; the American federal state must guarantee the equal protection of the law for all its citizens on the basis of the fourteenth amendment to the Constitution. Is this counter-argument enough to uphold the positivist view – that there is a clear separation of the realm of the law from that of morality?[12]

The second argument against positivism can be simply expressed in the Latin adage – *Lex iniusta non est lex*: an unjust law is no law at all – extreme injustice cannot form part of any positive legal system. Instead, the very nature or essence of law does not allow such injustice. This argument has taken many forms. In historic periods in which religion played a dominant role in society, it was held that the law should not contain any provisions that would be in conflict with core religious rules. Sometimes, human nature plays a crucial role: what is deemed contrary to human nature cannot be law. Along these lines, some have argued that the legal (and medical technological) provisions enabling women to bear children long after they have ceased to be fertile violate human nature and should therefore be considered invalid. Another variant of this argument has been formulated by the American legal scholar Lon Fuller. He argued that provisions must always fulfil a number of minimum formal conditions in order to become law, such as that the law should always be made known, that the law must contain only obligations that humans are able to fulfil and that the law must not be internally contradictory. It might well be possible that some (dictatorial) political power enforces on a population some specific rules retrospectively, that is before they were promulgated, but these rules would then not qualify, according to Fuller, as legal rules.[13] Applying (unknown) standards first and promulgating them later violates the nature of the law. The contention is that certain obvious injustices can never be part of the positive law.

Is this a valid or convincing argument against positivism? There are many examples of extremely unjust legal rules, such as those in place during the Nazi period in Germany or during the Apartheid regime in South Africa. Or think

---

[12] This question forms part of the interesting debate between hard, exclusive and soft, inclusive positivism, a debate which need not be addressed here.

[13] Lon Fuller, *The Morality of Law* (London: New Haven, 1964). The prohibition on retroactive laws is in particular relevant and important with regard to criminal law; in other instances, it is quite common that legal rules change the status of citizens status retrospectively, see, for example, Hans Kelsen, 'The rule against Ex Post Facto laws and the prosecution of the axis war criminals'. *The Judge Advocate Journal* (1945) II: 8–12.

of the provisions that made and, in many countries, still make homosexuality a punishable offence. Should a natural-law approach not simply be considered irrelevant or 'untrue' given the fact that such unjust legal rules are or were (considered) valid despite their immorality? Those who are in favour of a natural law approach would perhaps answer that such 'rules' give only the 'semblance' of law, but that in reality they are not law and therefore people should contest them or refuse to obey them. But how then to establish a clear criterion by which to distinguish between 'true' law and 'false' law? Some have located this criterion in the will of God, as has been mentioned, others in human nature, still others, like Fuller, in what he calls the 'internal morality' of law. Nowadays, many argue that human rights play a crucial role in determining what proper 'law' is and what 'false' law. Injustice consists of a violation of these rights.[14] It is now often defended that positive law must fulfil the minimum moral requirements found in human rights.

Therefore, this introduction to legal philosophy takes human rights as its reference point. Human rights are of great importance because on the one hand they make moral claims on the law, but on the other hand they (very often) form part of the law. This enables us to study the relationship between law and morality not so much in the abstract, but in rather specific domains. The focus will be not so much on the idea of human rights but on how human rights functions within and in relation to the law. Obviously, a philosophical reflection on human rights is not the same as legal philosophy broadly understood. Yet, since human rights are often considered the contemporary embodiment of justice, they not only deserve a careful investigation, but they also enable us to focus on many important issues within legal philosophy.

Human Rights as the Modern Form of Justice

In order to appreciate that human rights can be regarded as the contemporary embodiment of the idea of justice, let us turn for a moment to the well-known classical Roman definition of justice: *suum cuique tribuere*. Here justice means that everyone should have or should be given his due. This definition, which will be examined further in Chapter 18, appears to say that justice is, first, something which is due everyone (*cuique*) and, secondly, that this is what he or she deserves, or merits, or in some sense already has (*suum*). According to this definition, justice is linked to both universality and to 'goods' that are relevant and important to everyone. These important 'goods' must therefore be the kind of goods that can be 'held' universally, in the sense that when one person 'owns' such a good no other person is therefore automatically deprived or excluded of that good. Human rights claim to meet these criteria.

---

[14] Human rights are considered by many as the contemporary moral *lingua franca*, see, for example, Joseph Raz, 'Human Rights without Foundations,' in *The Philosophy of International Law*, ed. Samantha Besson and John Tasioulas (Oxford: Oxford University Press, 2010), 321–38.

the chair of the meeting, US President Truman, declared that there was hope that an international treaty on human rights could be realized within the framework of the United Nations and its Charter. This would then be a document in which the rights of every human being on earth would be enumerated – a universal bill of rights. The idea was the following: since many (national) constitutions contain a bill of the rights of their citizens, should not, in a similar way, the bill of (human) rights be part of the 'constitution of mankind'? This initiative did not lead, at the time, to a treaty with enforceable rights, but merely to a 'Declaration'. Still, this Declaration became very famous and is now regarded as perhaps the most influential document of the twentieth century and one of the most important 'legal' documents in the history of mankind. On its basis, international treaties on human rights were established quite a few years later, in 1966. They came into force in 1976 – after sufficient ratifications.[6] In a sense, the Declaration was a precursor of these treaties, but it remained important of itself.

In order to understand the origin of the Declaration a little better, it is relevant to know that the Charter led to the establishment of various institutions. One of these was the already mentioned Security Council; another was the Economic and Social Council. Within the ambit of this Council, a Commission on Human Rights was set up, under the chairmanship of the widow of the much-admired US President Franklin Delano Roosevelt, who had died in April 1945. At what was the perhaps darkest moment of the war, in 1941, Roosevelt delivered a speech in which he had advocated a world based on 'four freedoms' – freedom of expression, freedom of belief, freedom from want and freedom from fear. This speech was an important source of inspiration for the later Declaration and, relevant for this book, 'anticipated' a well-known distinction, which is a red thread of this book, namely that between negative and positive freedom (as further explicated in Chapter 5). Indeed, according to the first two of Roosevelt's four freedoms, a person can only be 'free' if they are in no way hindered by others in expressing their views and in following their religion. These freedoms require governments to refrain from acting. The other two freedoms, however, do not focus on the absence of hindrance or interference, but aim at establishing the conditions under which human beings need no longer live in fear or in suffering. They require active involvement of others, i.e. of governments. The two latter freedoms demand that states and the world at large are organized in such a manner that people do not have to be fearful, nor suffer deprivation. Thus, Roosevelt's speech as an important source of inspiration for the Universal Declaration proclaims not only the then well-known human rights regarding civil and political freedoms, but also the less well-regarded social and economic rights.

---

[6] Within the European context a human rights treaty emerged much earlier. The European Convention on Human Rights was signed in 1950 and came into effect in 1953.

Many organizations and prominent persons representing a wealth of national and religious backgrounds, under the leadership of the formidable Eleanor Roosevelt, were involved in the drafting process of the Universal Declaration of Human Rights. Of course, there was the task of drawing up a list of rights, which in itself was difficult enough, but also of determining the foundation for these rights. When considering the 'ordinary' rights of citizens of a state, it is not difficult to establish their basis: these are rights called into being by the state, granted to a particular category of persons – those recognized as citizens of that state.[7] However, rights that are independent of a person's citizenship and are thus supposed to apply to all human beings, even to those who are stateless, cannot derive their validity from a body similar to the state: no political body that embraces all human beings exists. It is often stated that those rights are natural rights, but what would that mean? Can rights be derived from 'nature'? If it should be a natural law that decrees the respect of universal human rights, what is the basis of the authority of that law? Surely, the commission with the task to formulate a list of universal rights did not itself have such authority? Where then to find such a higher authority? Should not 'God', as the ultimate law-giver, be the foundation for universal human rights? This idea was indeed considered by the members of the Roosevelt commission, but it was rejected because human beings throughout the world have quite different ideas about God and the divine. When drawing up a list of fundamental rights with universal validity, an appeal to God would immediately give rise to particular associations and thus undermine the universality of the document. For this reason, during the process of drawing up and finalising the Universal Declaration, no reference to the divine was mentioned and the question of the foundation of the rights was deliberately left open. When studying the final text of the Declaration, one might argue that the concept of 'human dignity' functions very much as a foundation (see Chapter 4).

Another important discussion point during the drafting of the list of human rights was the question of whether those rights should (or could) be legally enforceable and, if they were, who should ensure their observance. Rights granted to every individual and then applied and enforced internationally, would at the very least require a supranational body such as an international court and this would constitute a violation of the sovereignty of the member states who had already agreed – in Article 2 of the Charter – that the United Nations would respect 'matters which are essentially within the domestic jurisdiction of any state'. Therefore the work of the Roosevelt commission led to a 'Declaration', and not an enforceable treaty. This Declaration was adopted by the General Assembly of the United Nations without a single

[7]   Although the eighteenth-century declarations of human rights solemnly declared that these rights were 'inalienable' or 'natural and imprescriptible', they were in fact the rights of citizens, as Hannah Arendt (in *The Origin of Totalitarianism* (London: New Edition, 1973), 295) correctly notes.

dissenting vote on 10 December 1948. Still, eight of the then forty-eight member states abstained – the Communist countries had little sympathy for the enterprise from the start; South Africa disliked the Declaration's stance against discrimination, and Saudi-Arabia disagreed with the clause on freedom of religion and on the right to change one's religion.

A First Encounter with the Universal Declaration

It has already been mentioned that the Preamble to the Universal Declaration mentions 'barbarous acts'. This Preamble contains some other important elements, such as a reference to the four freedoms. This refutes the sometimes expressed view that preambles to constitutions or treaties have little impor- tance: that they are nothing but pious wishes or good intentions without much legal significance. Such downplaying of preambles seems wrong. Whereas the practical relevance of preambles may seem insignificant, they often indicate the values and aims for which these constitutions and treaties are established. 'We, the People' in the American Constitution has the meaning of invoking the unity of the American people[8] and is even the act by which the unity of that state was established. The Lisbon Treaty, which forms at present the basis of the European Union, mentions in its preamble the now highly disputed aim of 'creating an ever closer union among the peoples of Europe'.[9] The preamble of the German Constitution invokes the responsibility to mankind and God. Its first Article refers to human dignity – the reference to the history of World War II could hardly be clearer.

Something similar is the case with the Preamble to the Universal Declaration. The first element the Preamble mentions is the importance of the recognition of human dignity and the equal and inalienable rights of all members of the human family. It is clear that the Declaration emphasizes that all political, cultural and religious differences between human beings notwithstanding, they form one community, even a family, and that this community can only attain freedom, justice and peace by respecting equal rights for all. The Preamble does not explain the relationship between dignity and equal rights, but often dignity is now considered as the foundation for those rights (see also Chapter 4). Another element prominent in the Declaration is its emphasis on the supremacy of law. For bringing 'freedom, justice and peace in the world' it is crucial that everyone is equal before the law and is protected by the law. In other words, the Declaration endorses the importance of what it calls the 'rule of law'.[10] The

---

[8] US Const. Preamble.

[9] European Union, Treaty of Lisbon Amending the Treaty on European Union and the Treaty Establishing the European Community, 13 December 2007, 2007/C 306/01, www.refworld.org/docid/476258d32.html. The so-called Constitutional Treaty, rejected in 2005 and then replaced by the Lisbon Treaty, mentions not only the 'cultural, religious and humanist traditions' on which the European integration is based, but also (correctly, it seems to me) the 'bitter experiences' that have plagued Europe in the past.

[10] An excellent introduction is Tom Bingham, *The Rule of Law* (London: Penguin Books, 2006).

idea here is the following: if somebody is punished or somebody's property is taken away, as by taxation, this may only happen on the basis of a legal rule. Another aspect of the rule of law is that legal rules apply equally to all, regardless of rank or status and of race or religion: no one stands above the law. This also implies that legal disputes should be adjudicated by a judiciary which is impartial with regard to the parties in front of it and independent from the other branches of government. Therefore, it is possible to read into this preamble the separation of the three branches of state power. This mentioning of the rule of law is not astonishing, given the immediate political context of the Declaration. The 'barbarous acts', both in Nazi Germany and elsewhere, were the result of the rule of men, who used the law and the judiciary as an instrument of their perfidious polities.[11]

Articles 1 and 2 of the Declaration develop further the idea of equality and reject the ideology of racism. This ideology was found not only in the Axis countries such as Germany and Japan, but in quite a few Allied countries also, where equal rights for all citizens did not exist. Still, the Declaration rejects distinctions based on race, religion and other characteristics. Article 3 stresses everyone's right to life, important in the aftermath of an era in which many human beings were deprived of their life simply because of their membership of a particular race, nation or religion. Direct references to this immediate past cannot be found in the formulation of these Articles, but when they formulated the prohibition on torture in Article 5, some of the drafters may have been thinking of the extremely cruel manner in which Hitler had tortured and executed those involved, both directly and indirectly, in the attempt on his life on 20 July 1944. Freedom of expression and assembly were considered important mechanisms to counterbalance fascist regimes that had ruled without the legitimacy of formal procedures. Upbringing is a matter for parents, not the state, Article 26 states. Mothers and children (whether legitimate or illegitimate) deserve special protection and support. This is an interesting 'detail', as it makes clear that the Declaration, just like Roosevelt's four freedoms approach, does not merely emphasize negative rights against interference by the state, but also imposes positive duties on the state. The Declaration thus enumerates both first-generation, as they are called, negative rights and second-generation positive rights: social, cultural and economic rights. Therefore, the Declaration can be considered a major step forward in comparison with the first human rights declarations developed in the eighteenth century. It not only emphasizes rights that impose restrictions on the state, but also rights that require the active involvement of the state. The Declaration is not a mere liberal tract.

This is further confirmed by two other elements. The first is that the Declaration not only enumerates 'rights' but also formulates duties. Article

---

[11] See, for example, Ingo Müller, *Hitler's Justice: The Courts of the Third Reich*, trans. Deborah L. Schneider (Cambridge, MA: Harvard University Press, 1992).

29, along with Article 30, states that everyone has duties to the 'community'. For many commentators, imposing duties certainly towards an unspecified 'community', may sound strange and perhaps even dangerous within the context of a declaration of human rights. Imposing a duty is the opposite of what the purpose of human rights seems to be, namely enabling human beings to be free. Can human rights be reconciled with duties? Part IV will argue that this is indeed possible. In short: surely, the rights enumerated in the Universal Declaration aim at establishing a legal order in which the freedom of the one person is compatible with the rights of all others. This objective can only be reached when citizens simultaneously have the duty to respect the rights of others and to obey a legal order based on these rights. Suppose I invoke the human right of expression or assembly. This implies the duty of others to respect my expression and my getting together with others, but it obviously also obliges me as the holder of that right to respect that others have the same right. My right to freedom of expression is thus not unlimited, and it may not be abused by rallying for war or for the extinction of a certain group of human beings that I consider inferior. This indeed fits well with Articles 29 and 30 of the Declaration, which prohibit the use of the rights and freedoms of the Declaration to the detriment of the principles and purposes of the United Nations or of the human rights and freedoms mentioned in the Declaration.

The second aspect of the Declaration that confirms that it is not a liberal tract is Article 28 on the basis of which everyone is entitled to 'a social and international order in which the rights and freedoms set forth in this Declaration can be fully realised'.[12] This is a remarkable 'right', in that it is a right to a specific societal order in which human rights can be fulfilled. As a meta-right it stresses that human rights imply an (international) order that can be collectively inhabited. Since no one can 'have' a societal order on their own, this right clearly has a collective dimension: it is the right to live in a society in which the human rights of all can be fully realized. It thus seems that the Universal Declaration indeed calls for an international organization such as the United Nations which should enable the realization of human rights. In a sense then, the absence or the failure of such an organization can be seen as the reason why 'barbarous acts' were possible. The Declaration holds that human rights cannot be separated from a decent social and international order and in a sense urges the newly established Organization of the United Nations to provide that infrastructure in order that barbarous acts, such as those committed during World War II, will definitively belong to the past. The promise of Article 28 includes a 'social' order that guarantees to everyone the reasonable standard of living to which everyone is entitled on the basis of Article 25. According to the Declaration, then, human rights violations occur when people suffer from political persecution as well as when they are unable

---

[12] My understanding here has been influenced by Thomas Pogge, *World Poverty and Human Rights* (Cambridge: Polity, 2002), 52–70.

to meet their basic needs. It is thus clear that the Declaration raises questions concerning war and peace and global well-being (Chapters 15 and 14 will discuss these questions). It has a utopian dimension. It envisions a peaceful world order based on law, in which 'barbarous acts' belong to the past and in which the basic needs of all human beings, both political and social, are met.[13]

The Universal Declaration did not stand alone in this utopian dimension. Another utopian development of those days was the prosecution and the conviction of (some of) the perpetrators of the 'barbarous acts' of World War II. This development in criminal law was utopian, since it meant the removal of an important legal defence of those state criminals: the principle of the *par in parem non habet jurisdictionem*. According to this principle, states and their representatives cannot adjudicate each other before a court, because they stand vis-à-vis each other in a horizontal relationship of equality. Thus the veil of state sovereignty, behind which those Nazi leaders wanted to hide, was suddenly removed by new principles of international criminal law. The General Assembly of the United Nations had already formally endorsed these so-called Nuremberg principles in December 1946 and had thus confirmed that human rights can be more important than state sovereignty.

The International Military Tribunal at Nuremberg

In the historical context of the drafting of the Universal Declaration of Human Rights, one finds one of the most important legal trials of the twentieth century: the International Military Tribunal established by the victorious Allies in order to have those who committed the most appalling crimes by commencing a war and during World War II adjudicated in front of a court of law.[14] Between 1945 and 1946, the remaining leadership of the Nazi regime faced a military tribunal in Nuremberg. This tribunal was later succeeded by various other trials of Nazi criminals both in Germany and in other countries. For the idea of universal human rights, this trial of the leadership of a state was immensely important.

The fact that Nazi leaders were put on trial, and Germany's state sovereignty set aside as a defence, was quite unique; because of the excellent juridical quality of the tribunal and its verdicts, 'Nuremberg' became famous as a major stepping stone in the development of international criminal law. Given the

---

[13] An important manner in which the Declaration can be understood is suggested by one of its drafters, René Cassin, who compared the Declaration to the portico of a temple. The preamble plus Arts 1 and 2 would then represent its foundation, with the principles of dignity, liberty, equality and brotherhood. The main body of the declaration would consist of four columns (concerning the individual: Articles 3–11; the individual in relation to others: Articles 12–17; the spiritual, public and political liberties: Articles 18–21; and economic, social and cultural rights: Articles 22–7). The pediment would then link the individual with broader society: Articles 28–30. See Glendon, *A World Made New*, 173–92.

[14] There exists a vast amount of literature on this subject. An excellent beginning would be James Owen, *Nuremberg: Evil on Trial* (London: Headline Review, 2006).

significance of this trial of major war criminals who earlier served as political leaders of the Nazi state, one would perhaps presume that the Allies had decided already during the war to criminally prosecute those responsible for the crimes that were taking place. But initially, it was far from decided that the top criminals of the Nazi regime would face criminal justice. The primary objective of the Allies was to defeat the Nazi enemy and its allies, the other Axis powers Italy and Japan. Prosecuting war crimes, including the crime of initiating war, was only a minor aim of the war. Notwithstanding the enormous prestige and impact of the International Military Tribunal, only a few 'top-level' Nazis were brought to court after the defeat of Nazi Germany. Middle-rank Nazis were often not prosecuted; some Nazis, like Adolf Eichmann, the architect of the Holocaust, escaped Germany in order to build a new existence in South America. Neither the Allied occupying forces nor the new German government felt an urgent need to prosecute all perpetrators of the atrocities of the Nazi era.

However, the fact that the International Military Tribunal stood rather alone in adjudicating the Nazi leadership immediately after Germany's defeat does not diminish its legal relevance. It established standards of procedural fairness; it raised public awareness of the evil of Nazism; it abolished the idea that a state and its representatives would have immunity for their acts and would thus stand so to speak above the law; it also refuted the legal defence of invoking superior order. In other words, it rejected in its judgements the two classical tenets of legal positivism, acts of state and superior orders, as prescribed by the Charter of London, the statute for the International Military Tribunal.[15] The Tribunal and its success contributed to the (re)birth of 'natural law' and to the concept of international criminal accountability for violations of human rights.

The importance of the Tribunal consisted first and foremost in the fact that it took place, despite these legal challenges of state immunity and the superior order defence, and despite the prosecutions not having political priority. Only when during the war it became clear that the Nazis had committed the most atrocious crimes against parts of Germany's own civilian population and against civilian populations in occupied territories, the need for criminal prosecution grew. These crimes, which are now generally known under the heading of the Holocaust, may have had relatively little to do with the actual war between the Axis powers and the Allied powers. Initially, these crimes against humanity received only little attention, partly perhaps because the Allies did not want to repeat the mistake of World War I, by exaggerating German atrocities, partly perhaps they could not believe the reports on the extent of the crimes that were taking place: was it really true that millions of Jews and others were being slaughtered in exterminations camps? When the full scale of the Nazi crimes became clear, it was not automatically concluded

---

[15] See Stanley L. Paulson, 'Classical Legal Positivism at Nuremberg,' *Philosophy and Public Affairs* 4 (1975): 132–58.

that legal proceedings against Nazi leaders had to be initiated, given the legal obstacles already mentioned. Perhaps also another problem played a role. After World War I it had been impossible to criminally prosecute the German Kaiser, who had fled to the Netherlands. Starting criminal proceedings against ordinary German soldiers was also difficult, because such proceedings had to take place in Germany, and German prosecutors were not keen on prosecuting the country's own veterans.

With the growing awareness of the scale of the atrocities, so the emphasis on punishing the perpetrators grew. But this did not yet mean the setting up of an international criminal court. Punishment could also mean 'getting rid of'. Churchill launched a plan to capture and summarily execute fifty prominent Nazis. According to him, their criminal guilt was too great to fit within the boundaries of a juridical process. The fate of the Nazi leaders should be a political matter and not a legal one. The US was not very enthusiastic about criminal trials either, some within the administration supporting the British plan of summary execution, and others supporting the idea of setting up a criminal tribunal. The latter view finally carried the day, partly because Stalin – for very different reasons, as he was used to show trials – was also in favour of a trial.

Thus, the International Military Tribunal and its trials were a novelty, both politically and legally. The first of the obstacles that had to be overcome was the lack of a proper basis for the Tribunal in law and the absence of a criminal code. This problem was 'solved' by the so-called 'Charter of London', signed by the Allies on 8 August 1945. This charter established the Tribunal, its code and its jurisdiction. On the basis of the Charter, the Tribunal was given jurisdiction over those (war) criminals that had acted on behalf of the Axis powers[16] and whose crimes were not limited to a particular territorial entity. Criminals whose offences were limited to a particular territory could be dealt with by the relevant state on the basis of the so-called territoriality principle. The Nuremberg Tribunal would be competent to adjudicate criminals for the following charges: conspiring against peace, initiating a war of aggression (crimes against peace), war crimes and crimes against humanity. Establishing these criminal offences in the Charter of London led to a specific problem: is it not a requirement of a fair trial that no one is prosecuted, let alone convicted for acts that were not criminal at the moment in which these acts took place? This is indeed even formulated as a human right in Article 11 of the Universal Declaration: no one shall be held guilty for any criminal offence which did not constitute a criminal offence at the time it was committed. Indeed, none of the charges mentioned in the Charter of London were unequivocally considered as criminal prior to World War II. Was

[16] Jurisdiction was not given over those war crimes that were committed by members of the Allied forces. This was an important element in the case of Vassili Kononov, a Latvian who was convicted in 1998 for war crimes committed during World War II. His defence revolved around the fact that he had been fighting as a member of the Allied forces. His conviction was nonetheless upheld by the European Court, see Chapter 8.

this Charter then not a piece of ex post facto legislation, making criminal what was not criminal at the time, and thus a violation of human rights and of the rule of law?

Of course, the legal defence teams repeatedly stressed this point and argued that Nuremberg was merely a matter of victor's justice, but in all fairness it should be acknowledged that this was not fully the case. With regard to the crime of commencing a war (the crime of aggression) regarding Germany's invasion of Poland on 1 September 1939 and other acts of aggression, the 1928 Kellogg-Briand Treaty – also known as the Pact of Paris[17] – could be invoked as the legal basis, even if the validity of this basis was not uncontested. The treaty was not acknowledged by all states as a part of international law. For example, the German legal scholar and Nazi jurist, Carl Schmitt, did not consider this pact as a legal step towards universal peace, as it was presented, but rather as a political expression of the imperialistic foreign policy of Western states. Moreover, it could easily be argued that one of the Allied forces and prosecuting parties had equally been guilty of the crime of aggression. On the basis of the secret Molotov-Ribbentrop Pact, the Soviet Union had attacked Poland in 1939 and some months later it attacked Finland, clearly a breach of that country's sovereignty.

With regard to war crimes, it is also not evident that the Charter of London constituted a violation of the prohibition of ex post facto legislation. War crimes were internationally established in the Hague Conventions, at the end of the nineteenth and beginning of the twentieth century in order to restrict the violence of war. The rules of these Conventions were widely recognized. The problem, however, was that not only the Axis powers had committed war crimes, but the Allied forces as well, so that the *tu quoque* defence would apply: how can you prosecute us, Germans, for crimes you also committed yourselves? Do not the firebombing of open German towns, the rape of German women and the use of atomic weapons without strict military necessity constitute 'war crimes'?

The final criminal charge in the Charter of London was indeed new: it made 'crimes against humanity' punishable. No historical precedent for this charge existed and therefore the ex post facto reproach would have full force here. Yet, this charge was hardly contested during the trial. Murdering large numbers of innocent human beings could indeed only be labelled as what it was: a crime against humanity.[18] This was so obviously criminal that no prior legal criminalization would appear to be needed. The extermination of large numbers of human beings is clearly an 'evil' in itself (*malum in se*) and not just an 'evil' because it is

---

[17] Recently an important monograph on this pact has been published. See Hathaway, Oona A. and Scott, Scapiro J., *The Internationalists. How a Radical Plan to Outlaw War Remade the World* (New York: Simon & Schuster, 2017).

[18] This crime could also be labelled as 'genocide'. In 1951, the Convention on the Prevention and Punishment of Genocide came into force. Whereas 'crimes against humanity' emphasizes the crimes committed on an individual, often in large numbers, the concept of 'genocide' – developed by Lemkin – focuses on the intent to destroy a particular group. See, for example, Philippe Sands, *East West Street: On the Origins of Genocide and Crimes against Humanity*

forbidden (*malum prohibitum*). Through the Charter of London, humanity itself became a legal category. The Nazi leadership was prosecuted and convicted for offences against 'humanity', committed on certain peoples, including Jews, before and particularly during the war. Could the Military Tribunal also prosecute such crimes that took place before the war? This is how the Charter of London formulates 'crimes against humanity' in its Article 6, clause c:

> '. . . murder, extermination, enslavement, deportation, and other inhumane acts committed against any civilian population, before or during the war, or persecutions on political, racial or religious groundes in execution of or in connection with any crime within the jurisdiction of the Tribunal, whether or not in violation of the domestic law of the country where perpetrated.'

Important to note here is the comma between 'during the war' and 'or persecutions'. In the original English and French versions of the text one finds at that point a semi-colon, whereas the Russian version of the text contains a comma. An amendment was made to follow the Russian comma instead of the semi-colon. This apparently minor detail proved to be important with regard to the reach of the concept of crimes against humanity: by adopting the comma, crimes against humanity could only occur 'in connection with' the other crimes mentioned in the Charter: crimes against peace or war crimes, whereas the semi-colon would have opened the possibility of an interpretation of crimes against humanity independent of the other offences or of the war as such.[19] The implication that states could commit international crimes (against humanity) without being in conflict with another state, would have fitted perfectly well with the spirit of the Universal Declaration: human rights are a matter of concern for the international community.

Let us conclude this short overview of the International Military Tribunal and elaborate a bit more in detail the two procedural obstacles that could have stood in the way of convicting the Nazi criminals, had they not been removed by the Charter and by the Tribunal. First, the defence that the accused had acted as representatives of the state and were immune from prosecution and thus beyond the reach of the law. As mentioned before, this objection stems from legal positivism, according to which the law finds its origin in a sovereign body that can promulgate and enforce laws, and that is a state. Actions of sovereign states cannot be prosecuted. The doctrine of acts of state and the concomitant doctrine of state immunity hold that one sovereign state cannot adjudicate the acts of another sovereign state. Since

(London: Orion Publishing, 2016). Around the same period, the Geneva Conventions were established. Together, the Geneva Conventions, the Universal Declaration and the Genocide Convention are sometimes called the 'human rights triptych'; see Robertson, *Crimes against Humanity*, 40.

[19] David Fraser, *Law after Auschwitz. Towards a Jurisprudence of the Holocaust* (Durham: Carolina Academic Press, 2005), 129; Sands, *East West Street*, 47.

law always implies a vertical relationship between the person or the body in power that issues legal rules and persons or bodies that are subject to these rules, no sovereign state can sit in judgement on another state. Article 7 of the Charter rejects this view emphatically: 'the official position of defendants, whether as Heads of State or responsible officials in Government Departments, shall not be considered as freeing them from responsibility or mitigating punishment'. In his opening statement the chief prosecutor, the American Robert Jackson, added that it is a fiction to believe that a state commits a crime. Crimes are committed by persons only and it would be an unacceptable 'legalism' to let the fiction of 'collective liability' become the basis of personal immunity.[20]

The second and related obstacle to finding those accused culpable was their claim that they were acting on superior orders. This obstacle was removed by the Charter's Article 8: 'the fact that the Defendant acted pursuant to an order of his Government or of a superior shall not free him from responsibility but may be considered in mitigation of punishment if the Tribunal determines that justice so requires'. The argument that those lower in rank could not be held accountable if they merely executed an order issued by a superior is thus no longer valid. Obviously, all those accused in Nuremberg, despite themselves having been in the position of a superior, wanted to point at their ultimate superior, Hitler, who was of course absent, in order to escape prosecution. This argument was rejected by the Tribunal, not merely on the basis of Article 8, but also because it is an accepted understanding of any military legal code that criminal military orders must not be obeyed. The superior order defence can only be successfully invoked if the accused could not reasonably have known the criminal nature of the order or if the accused was put under extreme pressure to execute the order. These exceptions obviously did not apply to those prosecuted in Nuremberg.

The International Military Tribunal proved a great success and contributed significantly to the development of international criminal law. Due to the fairness of the trials in terms of procedural justice, it was certainly not victor's justice. Some of the accused were acquitted by the Tribunal. The proceedings greatly contributed to our knowledge of the 'barbarous acts' that had taken place during those dark years. Just like the Universal Declaration, it was part of a revival of natural law thinking.

From Statutory Injustice to Supra-Statutory Law

The question of how to respond to the 'barbarous acts' that had taken place in World War II received attention at the international level, through the

---

[20] Find 'Opening Statement before the International Military Tribunal', at: Robert H. Jackson Centre, www.roberthjackson.org/speech-and-writing/opening-statement-before -the-international-military-tribunal/.

establishing of an International Military Tribunal and the international acceptance of the Universal Declaration. But obviously national responses were needed, especially from Germans, and one of these responses has proven to be important for legal philosophy.

Generally speaking, Germany's coming to terms with its past has taken a considerable amount of time. Immediately after the war, many Germans were unable and unwilling to acknowledge what had taken place in their name. A small group of citizens and scholars however addressed this issue openly soon after Germany's unconditional surrender. One of them was the philosopher and psychiatrist Karl Jaspers who addressed the question of guilt, in which he distinguished between four different types of guilt: criminal, political, moral and metaphysical.[21] Another response came from the legal philosopher and criminal law scholar Gustav Radbruch (1878–1949). The short essay that he published in 1946 under the title 'Statutory Injustice and Supra-Statutory Law'[22] is without doubt one of the most important texts in legal philosophy of the twentieth century. Until recently, the established view was that its importance lay in its call for a renewal of 'natural law' in Germany. The text emphasizes indeed the importance of human rights and presents a formula with which positive law could be 'measured'. Radbruch inaugurated therewith a renaissance of natural law in Germany, but his text is more than a mere theoretical argument.[23] Radbruch's plea for human rights and natural law is part of a discussion of a few difficult legal cases that can only be resolved in a satisfactory manner, according to Radbruch, when adopting a natural law perspective. The underlying problem of these cases is quite straightforward: during the Nazi era, the life of the law continued, but many criminal activities were not acknowledged as such and were given the pretext of legality. The question now was how to resolve these cases after the collapse of the Nazi regime. Is it possible that something that was 'legal' during the Nazi era suddenly became illegal or criminal because it was in fact 'wrong' already then? Is there a criterion, a sort of supra-statutory law, with which to evaluate past legislation and past judicial decisions? And if there is such a thing as a 'higher' law, is it possible to use this higher law to undo the legal consequences of past legal injustices? In short, Radbruch's text deals with the possibilities and impossibilities of the use of criminal law after a radical political transformation. Today one would perhaps categorize his essay under the rubric of 'transitional justice'.

---

[21] Karl Jaspers, *Die Schuldfrage: Von der politischen Haftung Deutschlands* (Zürich: Lambert Schneider, 1946).

[22] Gustav Radbruch, 'Gesetzliches Unrecht und übergesetzliches Recht'. *Süddeutsche Juristenzeitung* (1946) 1: 105–8; Translated by Bonnie L. Paulson and Stanley L. Paulson as 'Statutory Lawlessness and Supra-Statutory Law (1946)'. *Oxford Journal of Legal Studies* (2006) 26: 1–11. I follow this translation with one exception, translating 'Unrecht' as 'injustice' instead of 'lawlessness'.

[23] Here, I refer to Stanley L. Paulson, 'Lon L. Fuller, Gustav Radbruch and the "Positivist" Theses'. *Law and Philosophy* (1994) 13: 313–59.

When Radbruch published this now famous essay, he was a highly respected jurist. Shortly after World War I and during the Weimar Republic he became a member of the Reichstag, the national parliament, for the social democrats and for some period he acted as minister of justice, during which some important reforms of the criminal code took place. In 1926, he returned to his university until he was dismissed from his post by the Nazis in 1933 because of his political 'unreliability'. He upheld his moral integrity during the Nazi era; in 1945, after the collapse of the regime, he was quickly reinstated as a law professor and dean of the law faculty in Heidelberg. He was seen as a person of great importance for the (legal) rebuilding of Germany, but sadly he died already in 1949. In the short period between his rehabilitation and his death, he published many short essays, of which 'Statutory Injustice and Supra-Statutory Law' is the most important. As noted, this essay discusses the problem of how to deal with persons who committed crimes under the cloak of Nazi legality, a problem that also arose before the Nuremberg Tribunal. Radbruch's solution to this problem is the introduction of the concept of 'statutory injustice', that is: statutes or juridical decisions that appear to be legal, but are in fact unjust, like – to mention one example – those legal provisions on the basis of which Jews could be expropriated or deprived of their nationality. These provisions may have had the 'appearance' of 'law' but were in fact so thoroughly unjust that they cannot be considered law. Positive law and justice are, in Radbruch's view, not identical but they should not be radically separated from each other either, as legal positivism tends to do. To identify legality with justice is incorrect: in order to be legally valid, promulgated positive laws must fulfil a minimal criterion of justice, which is supra-statutory. Radbruch calls this criterion 'natural law', 'divine law' or 'the law of reason'. He admits that many specifics regarding what has been claimed under the rubric of 'natural law' are doubtful, but still holds that the work of many centuries has resulted in a relatively stable 'hard core' of 'natural law' in the declarations of human rights and of citizens.[24]

It is important to note that Radbruch holds legal positivism to a large extend responsible for the fact that so many involved with the life of the law during the Nazi era so easily acquiesced with statutory injustice. Radbruch described this development as follows: by means of two maxims, national socialism managed to bind its followers: 'an order is an order' and 'a law is a law' respectively. The dominance of positivistic legal thinking with its denial of a supra-statutory criterion contributed significantly to the dominance of Nazism. Turning away from the criminal past would thus require the embracing of a different, non-positivistic view on law.

However, since Radbruch's publication it has become clear that his allegations regarding positivism are not very accurate. There is no straightforward

---

[24] Remember that Radbruch wrote his essay before the Universal Declaration of Human Rights was drafted and accepted by the United Nations General Assembly.

connection between legal positivism and Nazism. Obviously, much depends here on how to understand positivism. Radbruch might have had a point if positivism were to have meant the identification of law with political power, but that is hardly a position defended by legal positivists. They would rather argue, like Hans Kelsen, that the normative spheres of law and of morality are distinct, which would, for instance, imply that the question of whether a particular prescription belongs to law has to be separated from the question of whether it ought to be obeyed. Whereas the former is a legal question, the latter is a moral one. For such positivists the proposition 'a law is a law' is no more than a tautology, without the implied message that it has to be obeyed because it is law. Carl Schmitt, the most prominent among the Nazi jurists, and a contemporary of Radbruch, rejected 'positivism' and enthusiastically supported the Nazi idea that the division between law and morality should be overcome. The popular sentiment (*gesundenes Volksempfinden*) should be recognized in law; instead of the maxim 'no punishment without a law', the maxim 'no crime without punishment' should be followed. Were we to define legal positivism in terms of the supremacy of the law and the prohibition of overcoming the law by means of invoking unwritten principles of justice (as understood in the Nazi ideology), then Radbruch was surely wrong. There is ample historical evidence to show that even during the years of the Weimar Republic many conservative jurists invoked principles of morality (under the heading of 'justice') in order to circumvent positive law. Many jurists felt little loyalty to the Weimar Republic and welcomed the 'national revolution' when the Nazis rose to power. Quite a few of those jurists contributed to the legal infrastructure of the Nazi state, either by writing authoritative commentaries to the racial laws decreed in 1935 or by happily contributing to the legal justification of Germany's expansionist policies.

However, as said, Radbruch was right in a particular sense, namely if positivism is understood as the identification of law and power. In Nazi Germany, indeed sufficient willingness existed to obey whatever was proclaimed and enforced by the state and to assume justification wherever one finds political power. After Hitler's seizure of power, Germany's positive law was quickly brought – mainly through extensive interpretation, promoted by a movement called 'German renewal of law' (*Deutsche Rechtserneuerung*) – into agreement with the ideology and the objectives of the Nazi movement. One might even say that the Nazis promoted a particular kind of national or popular natural law (*völkisches Naturrecht*) by making the sentiments of the people (as interpreted by the Nazis) a source of the law. 'Nature' in a quasi-biological sense was thus considered a source of law that could be interpreted in a very wide manner. It enabled some of the Nazi legal philosophers to justify a broad variety of malicious practices, ranging from concentration camps, the abolition of political parties and the federal structure of the state, to the lifting of the prohibition on the use of ex post facto legislation and analogous reasoning in criminal law.[25] Only if legal positivism were to mean 'might makes right': the identification of law with power, would Radbruch have been right.

Radbruch states that legal positivism so understood was the dominant mentality among the legal profession – even among the whole population – and that it rendered jurists helpless against laws with arbitrary and unjust content. Remarkably, this led Radbruch to exonerate those jurists. The significance of this becomes clear when examining Radbruch's solution to a case which would become famous in legal philosophy: the grudge informer case.[26] This is Radbruch's case: Puttfarken denounced Göttig during the war for having written that Hitler was a mass murderer and guilty for the war, for which Göttig was then sentenced to death. After the war, the question arose whether Puttfarken could or should be prosecuted for the death of Göttig. But Göttig was not killed by Puttfarken, but sentenced to death by a court of law. Therefore, the question arose whether the judges of this court during the Nazi era could or should be prosecuted as well, for their clearly unjust verdict. Radbruch describes the legal case as it played out before the post-war Nordhausen court as follows. Two legal constructions were applicable to Puttfarken: he could either be convicted for 'indirectly perpetrating' the murder on Göttig, or he could be convicted for 'complicity' in that murder. The choice between these constructions would have important implications for the (legal) position of the former judges. If the Nordhausen court decided for complicity (which in fact it did), the former judges, who sentenced Göttig to death, should by implication be considered as his murderers, just like Puttfarken. This would mean that these former judges, too, should be brought before a criminal court. In his alternative interpretation of the case, Radbruch opts for the other legal possibility: Puttfarken had the intention to kill Göttig, and he perpetrated this murder indirectly, by using the court as a means to this end. In this interpretation, the judges should not be held accountable for the murder of Göttig. It merely applied the prevailing, admittedly outrageous, legislation against defamation of Hitler, but it cannot be held responsible for applying this legislation because of its 'positivistic mentality' that a law is a law. Finding the former judges guilty of 'murder' while executing their judiciary task – under the alternative legal construction of 'complicity' – would presuppose that these judges had 'bent' or abused the law (*Rechtsbeugung*). According to Radbruch, this would be unreasonable. It might well be, writes Radbruch, that the application of the outrageous defamation law in the Göttig case entails a bending or an abuse of the law (because the applied law should have been considered statutory injustice) on the

---

[25] An excellent source of Nazi legal thinking now is Herlinde Pauer-Studer and Julian Fink, eds., *Rechtfertigungen des Unrechts. Das Rechtsdenken im Nationalsozialismus in Originaltexten* (Frankfurt am Main: Suhrkamp, 2014).

[26] This case is discussed by Hart (and by Fuller) and is often discussed in legal philosophy classes. See Thomas Mertens, 'Radbruch and Hart on the Grudge Informer. A Reconsideration'. *Ratio Juris* 15 (2002), 186–205.

basis of our principles. In an objective sense it is wrong to sentence someone to death for privately criticizing Hitler. Yet, because of their positivist mentality and training these former judges were unable to acknowledge any other law than positive law. Therefore, their judgement in the Göttig case did not constitute a bending of the law (in the subjective sense). Radbruch's interpretation of legal positivism as the dominant Nazi mentality thus led to the remarkable result of exonerating the judiciary for their unjust sentences during the Nazi regime. Given that they only acknowledged statutory law and considered the concept of 'statutory injustice' an inner contradiction, they were both defenceless against unjust laws and statutory injustice and unaccountable for applying these unjust laws.

This Göttig/Puttfarken case shows clearly how important and relevant legal philosophy is. Since Radbruch ultimately holds positivism responsible Göttig's conviction, it is understandable that he pleads for the reintroduction of natural law in post-war Germany. It even explains that Radbruch might have changed his view on the nature of the law because of the Nazi era. Some scholars argue that Radbruch's short post-war essays testify to a 'conversion' from positivism to natural law. In his pre-war writings, such as his *Rechtsphilosophie*, Radbruch does not seem to advocate or acknowledge the existence of 'supra-statutory law'. Still, even as early as 1934, he advocated respect for the separation of state powers, for democracy and for fundamental rights. Precisely the violation of these rights constitutes 'statutory injustice' in Radbruch's post-war essays and they become the heart of the so-called Radbruch Formula. This formula is Radbruch's criterion of identification of 'statutory injustice'. The law always needs to find a balance between three legal values, that of legal certainty which gives stability to society, that of legal purposiveness by which the law aims to reach certain beneficial objectives and that of justice, which seeks equality. Under normal circumstances, the value of justice should not have priority over the values of legal certainty and purposiveness, unless a sharp conflict arises:

> 'The conflict between justice and legal certainty may well be resolved in this way: The positive law, secured by legislation and power, takes precedence even when its content is unjust and fails to benefit the people, unless the conflict between statute and justice reaches such an intolerable degree that the statute, as "flawed law", must yield to justice. It is impossible to draw a sharper line between cases of statutory injustice and statutes that are valid despite their flaws. One line of distinction, however, can be drawn with utmost clarity: Where there is not even an attempt at justice, where equality, the core of justice, is deliberately betrayed in the issuance of positive law, then the statute is not merely "flawed law", it lacks completely the very nature of law. For law, including positive law, cannot be otherwise defined than as a system and an institution whose very meaning is to serve justice.'[27]

---

[27] Translation is taken from Paulson and Paulson, 'Statutory Lawlessness', 7. At one point, I have changed, as said, the translation, rendering 'gesetzliches Unrecht' into 'statutory injustice'.

This formula has attracted much attention, but it ultimately says that in case of a sharp conflict between what is required by some positive legal regulation on the one hand and what justice as equality requires on the other, the former must yield to the latter. According to Radbruch, the validity of a particular positive law is dependent ultimately not only on whether it is promulgated by some authority and whether it is effective, but also on whether it is not in an 'intolerable degree' unjust. The validity of a law depends not only on formal criteria but also on 'justice'. Thus, according to Radbruch, law and morality are connected. The last question that remains is that justice is indeed classically understood as equality, but what does equality mean? Radbruch acknowledges that equality can be understood in various ways and therefore justice as equality trumps legal certainty and legal purposiveness only in extreme cases. Such extreme cases can be of two kinds: when the law in its application turns out to lead to an intolerably 'unjust' result and, second, when the lawgiver makes no attempt to establishing equality or deliberately 'betrays' equality. For Radbruch, it was evident that the Nazi regime in many of its legislative acts deliberately 'betrayed' equality. These regulations therefore never attained the status of law. Radbruch mentions in this regard the 'legal' provisions by which the Nazi party laid claim to the whole of the state, by which some categories of persons were treated as of lesser worth and provisions by which the proportionality principle in criminal law was abolished (as was the case in sentencing Göttig to death). According to Radbruch, these are all examples of statutory injustice.

Today, we would perhaps be reluctant to apply the Radbruch formula, especially in its second meaning. After all, how is it possible to show that a lawgiver indeed lacked the 'intention' to realize the core of justice? Equality is an important legal concept, but it needs a criterion – equality with regard to what? The Radbruch formula has been used in German case law primarily in its first sense: intolerable tension between legal certainty and justice. When the application of a law violates fundamental human rights, the law may lose its validity. We will return to this formula in Chapter 8 when discussing the trials of former DDR (East German) soldiers who killed DDR citizens when these citizens tried to escape from the DDR in order to reach West Germany.

3

The Philosophical Context of the Universal Declaration

The topic of this chapter is a short outline of the development of the modern idea of human rights as found in legal history and philosophy. Before starting, some caveats must be made. In the first place, it is obviously impossible to give *the* history of the idea of human rights. Many different histories could be given and are given in the rich literature on human rights and its history. Presenting a succinct history will inevitably run the risk of suggesting that the (ideological) history of mankind is a progressive development in the direction of human rights.[1] Yet, it is difficult to defend the thesis that 'mankind' has reached the apex of moral thinking with the modern concept of human rights. Present day experiences with totalitarian and populist and autocratic regimes, and with the enormous gap between the rich and poor, should give us sufficient reason to hesitate. It is thus rather difficult to join in with the teleological reasoning of Enlightenment that the history of mankind is one of continuous moral progress. Nonetheless, it remains the case that 'human rights' have become the contemporary ethical *lingua franca*,[2] and therefore a historical overview of that idea is needed. Whereas the last chapter took the relatively short perspective of the context of the Universal Declaration, this chapter will adopt the long perspective and will progress with giant steps through the history of moral thinking. It will present the development of the idea of human rights as a, relatively late, product of western thinking, but this does not mean that other interpretations or other perspectives are not possible.

My second caveat concerns the use of certain concepts. When presenting a history of human rights, one inevitably makes use of the same concepts within different historical contexts, thereby suggesting that these concepts

---

[1] This is certainly suggested by Kant, who argues that we can 'discover a regular progress of improvement in the political constitutions of our continent (which will probably legislate eventually for all continents).' See Immanuel Kant, *Idee zu einer allgemeinen Geschichte in weltbürgerlicher Absicht*, AA VIII, 27, 28. An English translation can be found in *Kant, Political Writings*, ed. Hans Reiss (Cambridge: Cambridge University Press, 1991). Most recently, a similar idea has been defended by Francis Fukuyama in 'The End of History'. *The National Interest* (1989) 16: 3–18.

[2] See, for example, Joseph Raz, 'Human Rights without Foundation', in *The Philosophy of International Law*, ed. Samantha Besson & John Tasioulas (Oxford: Oxford University Press, 2010), 310.

have stable meanings. That is obviously not the case. It makes an enormous difference whether we discuss the concept of 'the state' defined, for example, as 'the sovereign power over a people on a particular territory' within a premodern context such as that of Thomas Aquinas's thirteenth century or within the contemporary context of the administrative state. The meaning of abstract concepts can only be clarified when they are contextualized and put in relationship with other concepts. With regard to the concept of the state, it matters who, in what way, to what extent and with what objectives is able to exercise sovereign power within a particular territory. It is in any case clear that the influence of the state on the lives of ordinary people in say the thirteenth century was far more limited than it is today. As regards the concept of property, which will be discussed extensively in Chapter 10, it is important that for some authors such as Locke and Kant property is considered to pre-date the state, thereby reducing the role of the state to that of a property protecting agency. This leads Marx to conclude that the state is a mere instrument in the hands of the property-owning capitalist class. However, because the production of goods is a societal matter, property – especially with regard to the means of production – should according to Marx never reside in the hands of a minority of individuals. Today, the discussion on the relationship between state and property remains important: some still assert that the state is a mere instrument to protect property – who owns what should solely be the outcome of the impartial working of market forces – and that the state should not redistribute societal wealth in order to divide it more evenly among all citizens. Others, however, refuse to believe in the fairness of the market – human beings enter into this world with either advantageous or disadvantageous starting positions – and therefore it isn't fair to limit the role of the state to merely reinforcing property positions.

These discussions have implications for how we understand the concept of law. One could define law in an apparently neutral manner as the sum total of valid norms within a particular territory, but obviously the question is which social order is established by that 'sum total': is it a fair and equitable order, or rather a dictatorial order which promotes the welfare of some and suppresses the interests of others? Legal norms are the expression of social choices, for example whether to protect employees by strict labour laws or to protect employers by making it relatively easy to hire and fire personnel; whether to protect innovative work through a regime of intellectual property or to ensure that information is freely shared among all those interested, as advocated by the supporters of the so-called 'open sources'; whether to privilege, for example through tax law, certain social configurations such as the traditional marriage or to focus on individuals irrespective of the social relationships in which they live; whether to conceive of the law as a means of educating citizens to become virtuous human beings or as a mechanism by which citizens are able to freely choose their own lifestyle, to mention just a few examples.

What is true for the concepts mentioned so far is also true for the concept of human being itself. When discussing 'human rights', the emphasis is often on rights and not on the human being who is supposed to be the bearer of those rights. But obviously, the anthropology underlying specific societies is of the utmost importance. Historically, human beings are conceived in at least two very different ways. Sometimes, man is primarily seen as a social being (even a social animal), as a member of a particular socio-economic group or national or religious community; however, sometimes man is primarily considered as an individual, whose social ties and contexts are the result of his own choosing. We will come back to this point.

As to the concept of 'human rights' itself, it is sometimes assumed that it has the same meaning in different historical and geographical circumstances, and to a certain extent that is not completely wrong. Many cultures and religions have in different periods embraced the principle of equality and that of the freedom of each human being. In another sense however, one should be hesitant to 'discover' the concept of human rights everywhere. Not every time when equality and freedom are mentioned, is it clear what is meant. It is safer to regard the concept of human rights as a rather modern attempt to make equality and freedom the basis of a legal system.

Some argue therefore that the first step towards this concept was made in modern history, roughly during the seventeenth and eighteenth centuries. Here emerged a new concept of the freedom and equality of human beings.[3] This meant a breach with the past in which these concepts often had a religious or philosophical dimension. In order to be make this historical thesis plausible and to appreciate both discontinuity and continuity, a sketchy outline of a few historical periods will be presented. We will have to look at the Bible – without doubt, one of the most important texts in human history – and at important (Greek and Roman) sources from Antiquity, as well as at a few important medieval legal documents, such as the Magna Carta from 1215. Important changes took place, as said, in what is called the era of the Enlightenment, broadly understood. These changes influenced the first bills and declarations of (human) rights that emerged out of the North American struggle for independence (and the 1776 Declaration of Independence) and the French Revolution (with its Declaration of the Rights of Man and Citizen from 1789). These declarations do not contain the broad spectrum of rights that are included today under the heading 'human rights' but are restricted to civil and political rights. In those days, it was also not considered evident that a judicial body would be authorized to adjudicate on these rights. These rights were primarily understood as constitutional principles that should guide the legislator. In the nineteenth century, due to all sorts of criticisms, the idea of human rights lost most of its appeal, only to regain prominence, as we saw in

---

[3] I am influenced here by Lynn Hunt, *Inventing Human Rights. A History* (New York: W.W. Norton & Company, 2007).

Chapter 2, after World War II. Since then, it has gained more and more adherence, although some say we are now witnessing its demise.[4]

The Idea of Human Rights

Because we have to be careful not to overestimate progress and continuity, it is worthwhile to look at the history and the sources of the idea of human rights. Today 'human rights' have become so 'normal' that one finds human rights everywhere: in the daily news, in the curricula of legal studies (as part of positive constitutional, criminal or civil law, or as a separate subject matter), in the judgements of important courts, such as the European Court of Human Rights, and in the rhetoric of our politicians. Because the focus here is on the philosophical aspects of human rights, in particular in relation to the 1948 Universal Declaration, it is important to pay attention to that history and its sources.

In Chapter 1 it was stated that the idea of human rights embodies today to a large extent the authority or legitimacy of the law. Whereas the concept of 'legality' is generally used to discuss whether a particular legal regulation or juridical decision is in conformity with valid law, the concept of 'legitimacy' refers to the social acceptance and moral acceptability. These are obviously not the same: there are some examples of laws and legal systems that were socially accepted by a large majority of the population, but are seen now as morally unacceptable, such as the 1930s anti-Jewish legislation in Nazi Germany. Today it is often claimed that the legitimacy of positive law or of a specific legal order, in the senses of both acceptance and acceptability, resides in human rights. The idea of human rights goes therefore beyond 'mere' positive law. Positive law alone cannot generate legitimacy, only certain values can. Therefore, a philosophical approach aims to reveal the moral values and principles that underlie the prevailing legal system. The coming chapters will at times discuss important legal cases, but they are always primarily concerned with these underlying values from which the law may (or may not) derive its authority. In the past, the values underlying positive law were situated in 'nature', hence the concept of 'natural law'. Sometimes these values were found in some other higher standard, often within a religious context.[5] At other times, the nature of mankind was conceived as the basis and the need of establishing positive law.[6] As regards the principles and values underlying positive law, one notices various changes over time.

---

[4] See, for example, Stephen Hopgood, *The Endtimes of Human Rights* (Ithaca: Cornell University Press, 2015).

[5] According to Thomas Aquinas, the precepts of natural law can be derived from the order of the natural inclinations of mankind (which are directed at preservation of human life, at procreation and education of offspring, and at knowledge of God and living in society). See Thomas Aquinas, *Summa Theologica*, Secunda Secundae, Questio 94, Article 2.

[6] According to Thomas Hobbes, human nature contains three principal causes of quarrel: competition, diffidence and glory, which makes a life without positive law 'solitary, poor, nasty,

Today, the principles and values underlying positive law are often located in human rights. The emergence of human rights as the foundation of positive law must be located in the seventeenth and eighteenth centuries. In that period, the use of the concept of natural law gradually fell from fashion and was replaced by the concept of 'natural rights', which was then replaced by the concept of 'human rights'. This concept became a central notion during the political upheavals of the American and French Revolutions, which were rightly conceived at that time as a major transformation in human history.

Obviously, this does not mean that no changes have taken place with regard to human rights since the American War of Independence and the French Revolution. These political transformations have been the subject of severe criticism from a variety of angles: from utilitarian, Marxist and nationalist perspectives, with profound effect on our view on human rights. It is now generally accepted that socio-economic rights should be added to civil and political rights in order to reach a comprehensive understanding of human rights. Even a cursory comparison between the 1789 French Declaration and the 1948 Universal Declaration of Human Rights makes this difference clear. Another development influenced the scope of human rights. Since 'human' rights are now no longer limited to the rights that citizens have within a state, as was the case with the French Declaration, but have acquired a universal dimension, violations of human rights are often considered a reason for concern for the international community as a whole. It is as if Kant's words have become reality, namely that 'a violation of rights in one part of the world is felt everywhere'.[7] If indeed violations of human rights are the concern of humanity, the implication might be that the international community has a responsibility to protect human rights across the globe. Does this give rise to a duty to militarily intervene in a sovereign state in order to stop grave violations of human rights? Chapter 15 will discuss the tension between human rights on the one hand and state sovereignty on the other. Another implication of this cosmopolitan dimension is the following. Not only violations of civil rights, such as the right to life or the right not to be tortured, are the concern of humanity as a whole, but also violations of socio-economic rights when humans do not have the possibility to live a life without 'want' due to lack of the most basic needs qua food and shelter. Is there a global duty based on human rights to make sure that wealth and prosperity are fairly distributed across the world? In the so-called global justice debate, discussed in Chapter 14, it is argued that the present gap between the small minority of the global rich and the large majority of the global poor is incompatible with the idea of human rights. This global justice debate is a very lively discussion at the moment and seems to have supplanted the debate that revolved around the

---

brutish, and short'. See Hobbes, *Leviathan*, 1.13. As in, for example, *Leviathan* (Adelaide: The University of Adelaide Library, 2016), https://ebooks.adelaide.edu.au/h/hobbes/thomas/h68l/.

[7] Immanuel Kant, *Zum ewigen Frieden: Ein philosophischer Entwurf*, AA VIII, 360.

opposition between a more liberal and a more socialist conception of human rights, which ended with the end of the Cold War in 1989.

Human Rights in Antiquity

Often the Biblical tradition and ancient philosophy are considered sources of the idea of human rights. Sometimes this argument is made in the context of underlining the supremacy of 'western' culture,[8] even though the eastern part of the Mediterranean Sea can hardly be labelled the west. Sometimes this background of human rights is used as an argument against the universality of human rights; precisely because of such sources, human rights are foreign to other cultures and civilizations.[9] This debate on how 'western' the idea of human rights is need not be decided here, even if looking at a few elements of these presumed old sources of the idea of human rights remains interesting.

Although human dignity has regularly been trampled underfoot in the name of religion, Christianity like many other religions cherishes, at least in theory, the dignity of every individual, just like the idea of human rights does. In the case of Christianity, the absolute value of the individual lies in the doctrine of the personal eschatology of eternal life. This builds on what the prophet Isaiah says in what Christians call the Old Testament, namely that the name of each person – the expression of individual life – is engraved on the palms of God's hand.[10] It is unmistakably the case that the Jewish prophets expressed themselves strongly against injustice and the oppression of the weak. The New Testament confirms this message, to such an extent that the teachings of Jesus Christ have been interpreted as being incompatible with any form of violence against another person. 'To anyone who slaps you on one cheek, present the other cheek as well; to anyone who takes your cloak from you, do not refuse your tunic.'[11] In the Greco-Roman culture, particularly with the Stoics such as Seneca and Cicero, one finds a similar emphasis on the equal value of individuals, irrespective of social status, and on the universal cosmopolitan brotherhood of all mankind.[12]

---

[8] See, for example, Roger Scruton, *The West and the Rest: Globalisation and the Terrorist Threat* (Wilmington: ISI Books, 2002).

[9] Mary Ann Glendon in *A World Made New: Eleanor Roosevelt and the Universal Declaration of Human Rights* (New York: Random House, 2001), 216, mentions this criticism, but rejects it on the basis of the history of the drafting of the Declaration which saw an input from a variety of backgrounds.

[10] Isa. 46:16. I make use of Henry Wansbrough, ed., *The New Jerusalem Bible: Reader's edition* (New York: Doubleday, 1990).

[11] Lk. 6:29. An effort to understand the importance of the Judaeo-Christian tradition on the idea of human rights can be found in Hans Joas, *Die Sakralität der Person: Eine neue Genealogie der Menschenrechte* (Frankfurt am Main: Suhrkamp, 2011).

[12] See, for example, Seneca's attitude towards slavery in Seneca, *Letters from a Stoic*, trans. Robin Campbell (London: Penguin Books, 1969), 70: 'he whom you call your slave sprang from the same stock, is smiled upon by the same skies, and on equal terms with yourself breathes, lives, and dies. It is just as possible for you to see in him a free-born man as for him to

Still, it seems incorrect to locate the origin of the idea of human rights in these traditions. Jewish and Christian thought is basically theological in nature and takes its basis from divine revelation. Dignity and equality have a religious meaning and need not be translated into legal and political principles. Certain forms of institutionalized injustices are certainly the subject of complaint but are not always addressed politically. For instance, the apostle Paul seems to have had no strong objection to slavery as an institution, but rather (infamously) advises slaves to be obedient to their masters.[13] This is part of St Paul's general instruction to obey the governing authorities, because – and this is contrary to the idea of human rights – 'there is no authority except from God and so whatever authorities exist have been appointed by God'.[14] Elsewhere it is emphasized that one must 'pay Caesar what belongs to Caesar – and God what belongs to God'.[15]

Although the importance of the classical philosophy of Antiquity cannot be denied, as will become clear, it is not the place to locate the origin of the idea of human rights. Plato's *Republic* – undeniably one of the major works in philosophy – has little sympathy for human freedom and equality: a just state gives to everyone what is his due, in accordance with *suum cuique tribuere*. But that does not mean that everyone will be given the same.[16] A just society consists of different categories of persons and is hierarchically organized, with those who are most fit for that role, the philosophers, leading the community. Nor is Aristotle – often called the founder of political science because of his empirical studies of politics – an advocate of the idea of human rights, despite his influential analysis of the different aspects of the concept of equality. Equality is trumped, so Aristotle holds, by a few natural differences that separate equals from unequals. He accepts as natural the difference between men and women, between free men and slaves, between Greeks and barbarians.[17] Neither does the idea of freedom as individual private choice – which will later be called 'negative freedom' – play an important role. Liberty has for Aristotle a public meaning: being able to participate in the decision-making of the polity and to sit in a court of law.[18] With regard to equality, a vast difference exists between Aristotle and the already mentioned Stoics, who emphasized the equality of all human beings as participating in the same 'logos'. But this emphasis on human equality had no genuine legal or political

see in you a slave'. See also Martha C. Nussbaum, 'Kant and Stoic Cosmopolitanism'. *The Journal of Political Philosophy* (1997) 5: 1–25.

[13] Ephes. 6:5.   [14] Rom. 13:1.   [15] Mt. 22:21.

[16] For Plato, democracy is a society in which freedom and equality reigns and therefore it will go to ruin because it is incompatible with authority. Democratic citizens 'cease to care even for the laws, written or unwritten; they will have no one over them' (*Republic*, 563a).

[17] Aristotle, *Politics*, 1252a–60b. Work is available from, for example, http://classics.mit.edu/Aristotle/politics.1.one.html.

[18] Benjamin Constant, 'The Liberty of the Ancients compared with that of the Moderns (1819)', in *Constant: Political Writings*, ed. Biancamaria Fontana (Cambridge: Cambridge University Press: 1988), 308–27.

consequences. The equality in dignity of all mankind with respect to 'logos' left the social and political life rather untouched. It only affected the way in which one should for example behave vis-à-vis one's slaves, as Seneca makes clear in his famous letter on 'Master and Slave',[19] but this equality was not understood as an imperative to abolish slavery. The Roman jurist Gaius argued that slavery was permitted under the *ius gentium*, the law that was customary under the peoples of the human race, although all persons are born free according to natural law (the *ius naturale*). The legacy of Stoicism is therefore not part of legal philosophy but is today very alive within what is called the philosophy of how to live one's life. One finds stoic advice on how to live well in the writings of persons as diverse as Emperor Marcus Aurelius, whose personal notes are still read in our days, and the slave Epictetus, Seneca's contemporary. Both were convinced Stoics, but this did not make them seek to reform the imperial regime or to abolish slavery. Stoic philosophy rather concerned the spirit of humanity in which each person has to undertake his task, but this task does not include the reformation of the legal and political world. The fundamental aim of stoicism is to teach how to live well, rather than to establish a world based on equal rights of all men. Freedom does not consist in having one's rights protected but in living in accordance with nature.

Although concepts of justice, dignity, equality and freedom play an important role in all these religious and philosophical schools, they cannot be considered direct precursors of the idea of human rights, precisely because it belongs to the idea of human rights in the modern sense that the dignity and equality of all men lies at the foundation of society.

Human Rights in the Middle Ages

Sometimes it is argued that the first traces of human rights can be found in documents from the Middle Ages. The argument goes as follows. One of the essential characteristics of classical human rights is the legal protection of the individual against the state. Well, such protection can be found, for example, in the Magna Carta of 1215, one of the most famous legal documents from the Middle Ages. It is disputed whether the Magna Carta is the actual origin of the so-called habeas corpus right, but the fact that it is part of this prestigious document helped its legal standing.[20] Roughly, habeas corpus is a protection against arbitrary imprisonment and arbitrary expropriation, because someone's freedom or property can only be taken on the basis of 'the lawful judgement of his equals or by the law of the land'.[21] Therefore, when someone

---

[19] Seneca, *Moral Letters to Lucilius*, Letter 47 (available from https://en.wikisource.org/wiki/Moral_letters_to_Lucilius).

[20] Tom Bingham, *The Rule of Law* (London: Penguin Books, 2006), 10–14. See also: Ed West, *1215 and All That. Magna Carta and King John* (New York: Skyhorse Publishing, 2017).

[21] 'English Translation of Magna Carta', The British Library, published 28 July 2014, www.bl.uk /magna-carta/articles/magna-carta-english-translation, cl. 39.

is arrested, he must quickly be brought before a court where good evidence should be provided for this detention. The Magna Carta is very highly regarded in legal history; it could even be argued that the habeas corpus right is an early version of the human right against arbitrary arrest, detention or exile, as formulated in the Universal Declaration, Article 11. Yet this famous document cannot be considered a human rights document for at least two reasons. First, the document forms part of a feudal judicial system, which means that these rights and privileges do not 'belong' to human beings as such but only to certain categories of persons, such as archbishops, bishops, abbots, priors, counts, barons and 'all free men of our kingdom'. Second, these rights are 'granted' by the king 'out of our free will' and are thus not seen as 'natural' rights.[22] In this charter, the king promises to respect its provisions 'in perpetuity', which can only mean that the king regards himself, at least in theory, as the sovereign and the sole source of the law from which any rights must be derived. What is granted in this document must be seen as privileges rather than as inherent rights.

This does not deny the importance of the Magna Carta in the development of European legal thinking. What counts for the Magna Carta also counts for a later document, important for the Low Countries – the so-called Joyous Entry of the Dukes of Brabant, originating in 1356. In this charter, too, certain privileges were granted to specific parts of the population in return for obedience and the right to collect taxes. In the feudal conception of political authority of those days, rights and freedoms originated in the sovereignty of the monarch, who was only answerable to God from whom he derived his authority. This feudal world is totally different from the context in which human rights in their modern form emerged. The transition from collective rights or privileges in the medieval documents to individual human rights did not occur overnight. This can be seen, for example, in the development of religious freedom. In the Middle Ages it was self-evident that all human beings were part of the same *res publica christiana*; only after the Reformation was this unity destroyed, which then led to horrific religious quarrels and civil wars. The Peace of Augsburg (1555) was an effort to bring these horrors to an end by adopting the principle that whoever held political power within a particular territory also decided on the religion of its inhabitants, under the slogan 'whose region it is, he decides on religion' ('*Cuius regio, eius religio*'). No individual right to religious freedom, therefore. This principle was still dominant in the 1648 Peace of Westphalia, where the principle of the equal sovereignty of individual states was definitely established and the overarching authority of the Roman Catholic Church came to a formal end. This separation of the realms of Church and state planted the seed for the later division between the private and the public spheres and for the freedom of religion which would belong to each and every individual. But it would still take some time before this individual

[22] Ibid., cl. 1.

right to religion was rigorously advocated by authors such as Locke and
Spinoza.[23]

Human Rights and the Doctrine of the Social Contract

The idea of human rights first emerged in the seventeenth and eighteenth
centuries with the political philosophy of the social contract. These were turbulent times in which Europe expanded its sphere of influence and gradually
became a dominating force in the world, through processes of colonialism and
imperialism. Turbulent also was the development of science, which we now
associate with names such as Copernicus, Galileo and Kepler. Was the fragmen-
tation of power between small European states in competition with each other
the reason for these developments, or did the appearance of extraordinary
scientists play a major role in Europe becoming dominant on a global scale?[24]
It is in any case possible to notice from the early sixteenth century a certain
emancipation of the individual person from restrictive social and religious ties.
This emancipatory tendency became manifest in the works of Descartes, often
marked as the beginning of modern philosophy. He aimed at building
a philosophical system solely on his own individual understanding, and in
order to do so, he developed what has become known as the method of
systematic doubt. Only by putting into doubt all received truths and worldviews,
could one hope, according to Descartes, to reach the unshakable foundation for
a true philosophical system. This foundation could only reside in the certainty of
self-understanding: 'I think, therefore I am'. The importance of Descartes's
approach resides here not in the metaphysical implications of his position, but
in his starting point: reflection no longer starts with the totality of being, as in
Thomas Aquinas, but in the individual human understanding.

This mentality of individual self-understanding also became the starting
point of political philosophy. Just as Descartes subjected the accepted philosophical worldview to the critique of methodological doubt, Hobbes no longer
accepted in a similar manner political authority based on tradition or religious
views.[25] The starting point for the legitimacy of any political authority should

---

[23] In his famous *A Letter concerning Toleration*, Locke denies this freedom to Catholics and
atheists, because the former would be loyal to 'another Prince' and the latter because 'promises,
covenants and oaths . . . can have no hold upon an atheist', because he denies the Being of a God
(John Locke, *A Letter concerning Toleration (1689)*, ed. Kerry S. Walters (Peterborough:
Broadview Editions, 2013), 81). In the famous last chapter of his *Tractatus Theologico-Politicus*
(1677) (see on this book Steven Nadler, *A Book Forged in Hell* (Princeton: Princeton University
Press, 2011), Baruch Spinoza praises the economic benefits that come with regarding religion as
having no importance for commerce and mentions how Amsterdam flourishes as a 'most
splendid city' as a result of this freedom (*Theological Political Treatise*, ed. Jonathan Israel
(Cambridge: Cambridge University Press, 2007)).

[24] See Hendrik Floris Cohen, *The Rise of Modern Science Explained: A Comparative History*
(Cambridge: Cambridge University Press, 2015).

[25] However, see for a critical reading of the social contract John Maxwell Coetzee, *Diary of a Bad
Year* (London: Vintage Publishing, 2007), 3–9.

be the consent of the individual person; only individual interests could justify the acceptance of political authority. Hobbes became the first representative of the modern doctrine of the social contract. The emergence of this doctrine was rather sudden; its novelty can easily be grasped by comparing Hugo Grotius's *De Jure Belli ac Pacis* (1625), with its wealth of classical, Biblical and juridical sources to underpin his political theory, with Hobbes's 1651 *Leviathan*. Only 25 years after Grotius, one finds a completely new political theory which is built on a few axiomatic assumptions concerning human nature.

Later philosophers, such as the Englishman John Locke and the Frenchman Jean Jacques Rousseau, who will play a role in the rest of the book, especially in Chapter 11, made use of the social contract as well. This theory contains the following elements: it adopts a kind of thought experiment, in which all existing political and legal structures are 'removed' or 'put into brackets' in order to determine which elements are absolutely crucial for thinking about political structures and political authority. Thus, one begins with a clean slate. Suppose indeed that all existing structures – government institutions, laws and those who enforce them – were no longer there. This would lead, most would agree, to an 'anarchical' situation in which only individual human beings exist: a plurality of human beings without any structure, organization or supervision; in short, without political authority. This situation could be called the 'natural condition' or the natural state or the state of nature. Considering this state, one quickly realizes that such an anarchical situation is far from ideal, given that human beings are not by nature benevolent and live in a situation of scarcity. They need external goods for their survival but these goods are not at hand in abundance. This natural condition, it is argued, is unsustainable, because it is a chaotic and extremely dangerous situation: every human being is after his own well-being at the cost of others. Because such competition would lead to a war of all against all, it is in the interest of all individual human beings to move away from this natural situation and to establish a society which is governed by rules. How could such a society be brought into existence, when there are only individuals? This transition from the natural state to the state of law must be brought about by these individuals by means of an agreement among them. An 'original contract' brings an end to the state of nature, in which each alone decides how to act, and establishes a situation in which they are collectively ruled by fundamental laws. The decision to do so is called the 'social contract'. It constitutes the state and this implies that a state is only legitimate if it is based on the collective will of its individual members. These individuals give up their 'wild' freedom, which is of little value in the state of nature, in exchange for a limited, regulated freedom in which their basic interests are met.

Since the anarchical state of nature is highly undesirable, it is a matter of rational self-interest to accept the existence of a political state. But what should such a state look like? It would obviously be foolish for them – in Locke's words – to 'take care to avoid what mischiefs may be done them by pole-cats, or foxes, but [to be] content, nay, think it safety, to be devoured by lions'.[26] Because the legitimacy of the state can only be based on the fact that it is beneficial for all individuals and therefore on their consent, it is obvious that this benefit must be reflected in the structure of the state. It must respect their natural rights; its laws should be based on their consent. One can easily recognize in these thoughts not only individual rights but also 'democracy'. Chapter 11 will examine this in detail. The most fundamental interests of the citizens of the state – they are called human rights – must be protected by that state. Its authority is not derived from some higher divine instance, as in the feudal view on the state, but can solely be based on the consent of the participating individual human beings. If one compares the view of the social contract with that of the Magna Carta – or, even earlier, with that of Plato – one notices a world of difference. Both in the medieval English document and in the classical Greek political philosophy, 'human rights' are absent. In the Magna Carta, all political authority is in theory in the hands of the monarch who 'benevolently' grants certain privileges to some of his subjects on the basis of certain qualifications. For Plato, a just society requires the recognition of fundamental differences between human beings and the granting of authority to rule to those who are most qualified for the 'job'? In contrast, the perspective of social contract theory is that political authority comes from below, so to speak, that is, from the consent of the participating human beings who are all considered equal in rights. Even if – historically – the central authority still resides with a monarch, his legitimacy can no longer be found in a divine right ('by the grace of God') but solely in the will of the people.

The First Declarations

As regards 'human rights', two 'waves' of declarations are to be distinguished. We have already discussed the second wave, with its main document: the Universal Declaration. The first wave of declarations grew out of the doctrine of the social contract; its main documents are the American Declaration of Independence (1776) and connected with this declaration the American Bill of Rights and the French Declaration of the Rights of Man and Citizen (1789).

In these eighteenth-century documents the idea of a social contract is easily recognizable. The American Declaration of Independence reads: 'We hold these truths to be self-evident, that all men are created equal, that they are endowed by their Creator with certain unalienable Rights, that among these are Life, Liberty and the pursuit of Happiness. That to secure these rights, Governments are instituted among Men, deriving their just powers from the consent of the governed.'[27] Article 1 of the French Declaration employs

[26] John Locke, *Two Treatises of Government*, 2.93, for instance in Peter Laslett, ed., *Two Treatises of Government* (Cambridge: Cambridge University Press, 1988).

[27] Declaration of Independence, Philadelphia, 4 July 1776, www.archives.gov/founding-docs /declaration-transcript.

a similar vocabulary: 'Men are born and remain free and equal in rights. Social distinctions may be founded only upon the general good.'[28] Particularly telling is Article 2 which states that 'the aim of all political association is the preservation of the natural and imprescriptible rights of man. These rights are liberty, property, security, and resistance to oppression.' The wording of this second Article reflects closely the idea of the social contract. First, these rights are called 'natural'. Therefore, they must exist prior to the state – they are not 'established' or 'granted' by the state and therefore they precede the existence of the state. Secondly, this is confirmed by the element of 'preservation'. Apparently, the sole task of the state consists in preserving or 'securing' these rights. It is apparently the aim of the state to uphold rights of individual human beings, who have a life 'before' the state comes into existence. Human beings are understood as isolated beings, who exist independently from any political community. Since they understand that their rights cannot be 'secured' without the power of the state and its legal system, they decide to transform their natural existence into an artificial political situation of coexistence. This understanding of the instrumental character of the state is perhaps expressed most clearly by the Italian philosopher Beccaria, whom we will meet later in this book. He described the 'origin' of the state in a similar negative phrasing:

> 'Weary of living in a continual state of war (i.e. the state of nature), and of enjoying a liberty which became of little value, from the uncertainty of its duration, they sacrificed one part of it to enjoy the rest in peace and security. The sum of all these portions of the liberty of each individual constituted the sovereignty of a nation; and was deposited in the hands of the sovereign as the lawful administrator.'[29]

It is clear that the unlimited freedom of the individual human being is seen here as the ideal and that this ideal must only be compromised because of the need for some kind of social regulation. The state is a necessary evil. This view is in stark opposition to the classical view, as perhaps expressed most clearly by Aristotle, that human beings are by nature social or 'political' beings. According to him, the state comes 'before' the individual; a person who is incapable of living in society or is self-sufficient, must either be 'a lower animal or a god'.[30] For Aristotle it is inconceivable that some human being could exist without society, because every human being is born in a state of helplessness within a particular familial, cultural and political environment. From an Aristotelian perspective, the concept of human rights would be one-sided by

---

[28] Declaration of the Rights of Man and Citizen, Paris, 26 August 1789, www.conseil-constitutionnel.fr/sites/default/files/as/root/bank_mm/anglais/cst2.pdf.

[29] Cesare Bonesana di Beccaria, *An Essay on Crimes and Punishments: By the Marquis Beccaria of Milan: With a Commentary by M. de Voltaire: A New Edition Corrected* (Albany: W.C. Little & Co., 1872), Ch. 1, http://oll.libertyfund.org/titles/beccaria-an-essay-on-crimes-and-punishments.

[30] Aristotle, *Politics*, 1253b25.

emphasizing solely the axis of the human being as an individual and by neglecting the axis of the human being as a social creature. Which of the two views accepted has direct implication on how society should be structured? Look at Article 17 of the French Declaration, which declares the individual right to property to be holy and inviolable, and thus implicitly rules out the existence of a system of collective property. Therefore, later criticisms of human rights, as formulated for example by Marx, become quite understandable: the idea of human rights is one-sided, in that it promotes the interests of property owners; it does not take into consideration the interests of those who don't own property or the interests of the political community as a whole.

Despite the undoubtedly positive point that the idea of human rights takes the individual human being as the focal point of the legal system, the question must be asked: which human beings in particular? Who are the human beings who benefit from the declaration of these rights? Certainly not all human beings. The American Declaration of Independence mentions that all 'men' are born equal and free. But we know that the concept of 'men' did not include women, slaves, coloured people or those without property. It would still take quite some time before slavery was formally abolished, despite declarations of 'natural rights'. The French Declaration mentions the rights of French citizens and does not proclaim universal rights of all human beings. The French Declaration has a particular national flavour. In other words, eighteenth-century 'human rights' certainly gave the lie to any claim of universality.

Reactions to Human Rights

The doctrine of the social contract was literally revolutionary. British rule of the American colonies came to an end with the Declaration of Independence and the ensuing war, and the French Declaration led to a change of royalist France into a republican direction. The idea of human rights acquired popularity among the reading public through a work that today is regarded as a classic – *Rights of Man* by Thomas Paine (1791). Many others, however, were less than pleased with the sudden and violent upheavals that took place in the Americas and in France, and a conservative counter-movement rapidly emerged. These conservatives argued that revolutions such as the French one aimed at making a complete break with the past and its traditions in order to install a new regime from scratch. But this, the conservatives held, is impossible; any attempt to radically depart from tradition is destined to fail and will inevitably lead to violence and catastrophe. This viewpoint was formulated for example by Burke, who became a well-known opponent of the French Revolution, as early as November 1790. In his famous *Reflections on the Revolution in France* he asserted that only the gradual, organic development of the state and its law is possible, and argued strongly against the idea of an artificial social contract that, in the spirit of Descartes, wants to break all ties with the past. Later Bentham joined in with this criticism, not from a conservative standpoint but rather because of his fear that the granting of all kind of 'natural' rights to individuals would disrupt the stability of society. If individuals were to constantly claim their rights, they would inevitably lose sight of the well-being of the social order as a whole. For this reason, Bentham labelled these rights 'anarchic'. Moreover, as a second element, it would be foolish to advocate rights without specifying who would bear the responsibility or duty correlated with these rights. In short, Bentham called human rights 'nonsense upon stilts' and as an alternative he presented utilitarianism as the basis for a legitimate societal order. A society would not become legitimate by accepting human rights, but by advancing and encouraging social utility, or happiness for society as a whole. If utility is indeed the aim for society, then in principle no individual rights should be recognized because they would create individual privileges that could easily clash with social utility.

Moving away from English reactions to the age of revolution, towards Germany, we find initially enthusiastic endorsements. The philosopher Kant and the composer Beethoven welcomed the French Revolution,[31] but when the revolutionary armies started to occupy large parts of German and other territories the mood quickly changed and many thinkers wanted nothing more to do with these 'French' ideas. Similar objections to those of Burke were supported by what is called the 'historical school'. Here it is argued too that law develops in a historical and gradual manner only, not by means of revolution. If an effort is made to revolutionize society – in line with the social contract doctrine – then this will inevitably lead to war and terror. Indeed, the concept of 'terrorism' stems from a period within the development of French Revolution, when terror was exercised by the French revolutionaries in the name of the state.[32] By the early nineteenth century little German enthusiasm remained for the French Revolution and for the rights of man.

One of the most illuminating 'German' criticisms was voiced by Hegel. He wrote that the theory of the social contract conceives of the citizens of the state only as private individuals who are solely after their own interests, and not after the well-being of the community as a whole. Hegel rejected this 'bour-geois' egocentrism and defended, in the line of Aristotelian thinking, another view on the human being and the state, according to which humans are primarily social beings whose flourishing can only be realized within the common life of the state. Rather than opposing the life of human beings to the state, Hegel sees the state as a reality that transcends the private interests of its citizens and makes a common life for them possible. As the synthesis between individual interests and common life – rather than a contract – the state is the embodiment of true freedom. Such criticism, initially voiced by

---

[31] According to Kant, this revolution was 'an occurrence in our times which proves the moral tendency of the human race'. Immanuel Kant, *Der Streit der Fakultäten*, AA VII, 85.

[32] One of the most illuminating accounts of terrorism is found in the chapter 'Absolute Freedom and Terror' in Georg Wilhelm Friedrich Hegel, *Phenomenology of Spirit*, ed. Terry Pinkard (Cambridge: Cambridge University Press, 2018), 339–48.

Hegel, Burke and the historical school, is still very much alive today. Today, 'communitarianism' opposes the social contract idea, as prominently formulated in a new, twentieth-century fashion in John Rawls's theory of justice, which will be discussed in later chapters. Whereas Rawls gives primacy to individual rights, communitarians argue that the community of the state is more than just the summation of individual interests. A true community, as often – but not always – embodied in the state, constitutes the individual, not the other way around. Who I am as an individual, is to a large degree formed by the (culture of the) community in which I am born and grow up.

Prominent in the nineteenth-century reaction to the early human rights declarations is Marx's criticism. In line with Hegel, he also attacked the abstract character of 'human rights', in particular as they were expressed in the French Declaration. His criticism, however, did not centre on a lack of historical continuity; it was grounded in what could be called a structural analysis of the text of the Declaration. Marx claims, not wholly unjustifiedly, that the rights claimed in this declaration had indeed (as the reading of its Article 2 confirms) the intention of maintaining, as far as possible, the natural condition of unrestricted individual freedom. This would inevitably lead to the legal protection of the rights of those with the strongest (economic) position. According to Marx, human rights are nothing other than the rights of individual egoists. He formulates this as follows:

> 'none of the so-called rights of man, therefore, go beyond the egoistic man, beyond man as a member of civil society – that is, an individual withdrawn into himself, into the confines of his private interests and private caprice, and separated from the community. In the rights of man, he is far from being conceived as a species-being; on the contrary, species-life itself, society, appears as a framework external to the individuals, as a restriction of their original independence. The sole bond holding them together is natural necessity, need and private interest, the preservation of their property and their egoistic selves.'[33]

Following up on this criticism, Marx argues that the classical individualistic human rights as formulated in the French Declaration should be complemented by social rights that strengthen the ties between human beings and that stimulate equality and solidarity within society. These rights would later become known as the socio-economic human rights of the so-called second generation. They were absent in the French Declaration but found their way into the Universal Declaration (in Articles 22–7). The importance of these rights was also acknowledged in political theory, most notably in the (social contract) philosophy of Rawls.

One could thus say that the Universal Declaration combines the human rights of the eighteenth century with those claimed in Marxist circles in the

---

[33] Karl Marx, 'On the Jewish Question' (1844), www.marxists.org/archive/marx/works/1844/jewish-question/.

nineteenth century. The inclusion of these socio-economic rights aimed at equality and solidarity changes the position of the state. According to the classic view, human rights are meant to keep the state as far away as possible, emphasizing that these individual rights, in particular the right to property, should not be infringed but merely protected. Human rights are understood to have the negative function of prohibiting interference; the state is conceptualized as a mere night-watchman or a property-protecting agency. The real, socio-economic life of individuals is left to the market. With the rise of a poor class of (in Marxist's vocabulary, proletarian) labourers and growing inequality, the nineteenth century led to a call for social human rights and a different role for the state, namely as an institution responsible for a fair distribution of well-being for all in society. Human rights of the second generation lead to positive obligations for the state; it has a duty to ensure that everyone's claims to specific goods (minimum income) or services (access to education) are fulfilled.

One final important difference between the eighteenth and the twentieth-century conceptions of human rights has so far only been alluded to. It needs mentioning here, but will be addressed further in Chapter 12. This concerns its claim to universality. The eighteenth-century rights were called 'the right of man', but they had legal consequences only for the citizens of the newly established United States and republican France (and not even for all those humans who lived on those territories). The precondition for having these rights was being a member, a citizen, of the national state. But what about residents, foreigners or stateless persons? Do they have human rights? Or are human rights merely a vehicle for the national state? It is no coincidence that the emergence of human rights occurred at the same time as the definitive rise of the nation state, in which citizenship matters and a distinction is made between those who are members of a particular state and those who are not. Belonging to a national state and having civic rights becomes far more important than having (abstract) human rights. What is relevant is not the 'abstract universality' of being human, but the concrete membership of a national state. If this is indeed the case, then a truly universal declaration of human rights must transcend the boundaries of the plurality of nation-states.

The Universal Declaration of Human Rights of 1948

It is no surprise that the human rights of the eighteenth century were amended and that the individualistic mentality in which they originated was abandoned. The Universal Declaration does not defend an individualistic view on human beings. It benefited from the criticisms of the nineteenth century and took into account the gradual inclusion of social rights in a number of national constitutions. After the 'barbarous acts' of World War I and particularly World War II, there was a clear need to re-emphasize the importance of human rights from an enriched anthropology. This is what the 1948 Universal Declaration of Human Rights delivered.

The difference between this declaration and its earlier predecessors can therefore be summarized as follows: social and economic rights now form an integral part of 'human rights'; human rights cannot fully be realized only by granting civil and political rights. The Universal Declaration acknowledges that human beings can only flourish within a society in which certain social conditions are met. The exclusive focus on the (inviolable) individual right to property is replaced by a formula according to which everyone has the right to own property, alone as well as in association with others. The emphasis on property is moderated by stressing the importance of other rights, such as everyone's right to a nationality and the acknowledgement that every human being is part of an international community. Human rights are no longer seen as merely negative rights, directed against the state, but they contain the utopian element of a truly cosmopolitan order in which human beings enjoy the full breadth of their human rights. This clearly resonates with the ancient Stoic idea that all human beings participate in Logos. But the Universal Declaration goes further: all human beings should be seen as part of one global community, even if this community does not take the shape of a world state. In this regard, it really is a *universal* declaration of human *rights*. One final difference has also been mentioned already. Whereas the French Declaration invokes the 'Supreme Being' and the American Declaration mentions a 'Creator' as the origin of the rights, the Universal Declaration lacks any reference to a God. The Universal Declaration was to be a secular document with which every human being on this earth, it was hoped, could identify. The foundation of human rights was sought no longer in God, but in something called 'human dignity', to which we turn in the next chapter.

anyone reasonably agree to being put permanently in a subordinate position, like when he is owned by another person. Article 4 of the Universal Declaration prohibits slavery.[24] Kant explicitly rejects slavery, which was in his time still a widespread practice. Despite the fine wording of the American Declaration of Independence about the self-evident truth that all men are created equal, the War of Independence against Britain was also waged by a number of slave-owners to protect their 'property'. Apparently, these people saw no contradiction between what they stated in theory and how they acted in practice. Later the Civil War was fought partly over this question and it was only in 1865 that slavery was formally abolished in the United States by means of adding amendment 13 to the US Constitution. An international formal prohibition on slavery came about only in 1885, with the Treaty of Berlin.

According to Kant, slavery is in contradiction with the principle of equality that is the core of human dignity. But what if someone should choose to become a slave of their own free will? According to Kant, it is 'logically' impossible that someone by means of their own legal act (a contract for instance) would cease to own themselves and enter into the 'class of cattle'. First, Kant denies that a person can reduce themselves to a slave: 'no one can bind himself to this kind of dependence, by which he ceases to be a person.'[25] Contrary to what one might perhaps expect, the fact that someone has dignity and is 'their own master' does not entitle them to enslave themselves. Being one's own master does not give rise to rights only, but also to duties, namely not to make oneself into a mere means to others, as in slavery. It is important to note that Kant uses the concept of 'can' in the moral sense: no one ought to deny their freedom in such a way that they are no longer free but a slave. Second, the principle of dignity and equality of all human beings weighs heavier than a possible voluntary agreement of someone to become the slave of another. Although it is obviously empirically possible to 'sell' oneself as a slave, this is 'logically' impossible: the contract on enslaving oneself would lose its validity at the moment it was concluded, because one of the two contracting parties would disappear as soon as the contract was concluded. The 'slave' would therefore not be bound by the terms of the contract. The moral depravity obviously resides in the refusal of the person consenting to slavery to acknowledge their own dignity. In Kant's view, dignity does not entitle a person to give up their freedom. The situation of slavery in which one person has only rights and the other person only duties is irreconcilable with equality and freedom. Therefore, not only the person who 'owns' a slave ignores the

---

[24] Obviously, criticism of slavery is much older than the Universal Declaration or authors of the modern era. A classic example here is Seneca's famous forty-seventh letter to Lucilius already mentioned. Seneca interestingly adds that in some sense every human being is a slave ('Show me a man who is not a slave; one is a slave to lust, another to greed, another to ambition, and all men are slaves to fear'). See Seneca, *Moral Letters to Lucilius*, 47.10.

[25] Immanuel Kant, *Metaphysik der Sitten*, AA VI, 330.

slave's dignity, but also the person who was prepared to accept for themselves such a status. Everyone should respect the dignity of others but also their own dignity. Dignity brings with it not only rights, but also duties to oneself.

The utilitarian philosopher John Stuart Mill emphasizes more strongly than Kant the principle that there can be no wrong when consent lies at the basis of one's treatment of another person. This is the old Roman adage *volenti non fit iniuria* (to a willing person, no injury is done). But Mill agrees with Kant with regard to the so-called voluntary slavery. According to Mill, it is not permissible to renounce one's freedom and such an engagement would be null and void, because it is not an act of freedom to abdicate one's liberty. Voluntarily entering into slavery conflicts with freedom itself.[26] The fact that humans are free does not mean that they can do whatever they like as long as they freely consent. The limit to freedom lies either in liberty itself or in human dignity. The formulation of Article 1 of the Universal Declaration that 'all human beings are born free and equal in dignity and rights' is thus not unproblematic. Freedom in the sense of arbitrariness and freedom in the sense of dignity are sometimes in conflict.

There are quite a few examples that show that human dignity limits what someone is at liberty to do with themselves. A famous case concerns Manuel Wackenheim, a dwarf who attempted to make a living by letting himself be tossed, while wearing a protective suit, in a French discotheque. This was then prohibited by a local mayor, who argued that such a practice was in violation of public order and safety. In a legal case, after appeals by Wackenheim against the decision of the mayor, a high court in France ruled that an attraction of this sort was to be regarded as 'infringing the dignity of the human person' and that the concept of maintaining the public order includes 'a conception of human beings for which public authority must require the proper respect'. Wackenheim's complaint that his dignity was infringed by the prohibition to take up the employment of his choice, was not accepted in further legal procedures before the European Court of Human Rights and the UN Human Rights Committee. According to these authorities and courts, a person can indeed infringe their own dignity and thus violate what Kant would call a duty to oneself. Obviously, Wackenheim did not see it that way.[27] We will see in Chapter 10 that many jurisdictions contain a prohibition on the sale of one's organs and commercial surrogate motherhood. These are also cases in which dignity limits what one can do with oneself.

An example of where dignity limits what one can do to others, is the following case in which the competence of the state was curtailed, under reference to Kant's imperative never to use human beings as a mere means. In 2006, the German Constitutional Court ruled that a law concerning the

---

[26] John Stuart Mill, *On Liberty* (1859), ch. 5, www.utilitarianism.com/ol/five.html.

[27] In my description of this case, I follow Michael Rosen, *Dignity: Its History and Meaning* (Cambridge, MA: Harvard University Press, 2012), 63–8.

security of air space (the Aviation Security Act), accepted by government and parliament was in conflict with the German Constitution, more particularly with the constitutional task of the state to protect human dignity and to guarantee the right to life. The circumstances of the case were the following. With the attack on the Twin Towers on 11 September 2001 fresh in mind, a law was made to authorize the Minister of Defence, in certain strictly specified circumstances, to shoot down a hijacked aeroplane that was threatened to be used as a bomb. The German Constitutional Court rejected the law as unconstitutional because it would treat the innocent crew and passengers of the hijacked plane as a mere means to save others. This would be a violation of their dignity. Many commentators disagreed with the decision. It would mean that the protection of the lives of possible innocent victims of such a terrorist attack, for example those in a fully packed football stadium, would weigh less heavily than the duty to respect the human dignity of crew and passengers in the aeroplane. But the court argued that this law would allow the state to dispose of their lives unilaterally. The innocent crew and passengers would be sacrificed and used as a mere means to prevent a possible disaster. But the state should respect their dignity categorically. The Court rejected emphatically the utilitarian approach according to which such a preventive strike could be legitimized on the grounds of a comparison between the numbers of casualities: innocent victims on the plane and estimated innocent victims if the plane was indeed successfully used as bomb. Such an act of the balancing of numbers would be in conflict with human dignity.[28]

Clearly, this decision of the German Constitutional Court was met with a lot of criticism. Kant's uncompromising ethics with the sole emphasis on good will and human dignity did play an important role in the decision, but should the Court not have acknowledged other considerations as well, even if these perspectives are incompatible? Many argued that utilitarian considerations are important as well. Some commentators say that once a certain threshold has been reached,[29] Kantian, deontological considerations based on human dignity and the right to life should give way to considerations concerning the harm to all innocent human beings that are possibly involved.[30] According to this position, human dignity cannot be the last word in a moral and legal decision. The worth of an individual human being cannot be the ultimate touchstone of legitimacy; the well-being of society as a whole should be taken into consideration.

---

[28] See BVerfG 1 BvR 357/05, www.bverfg.de/e/rs20060215_1bvr035705en.html.

[29] This position is sometimes called 'threshold deontology', which holds that certain moral or legal rules have a near-absolute status but should be abandoned when the consequences become so great that they pass a certain threshold. See for a discussion Jeremy Waldron, 'What Are Moral Absolutes Like?' *The Harvard Review of Philosophy* (2012) 18: 4–30.

[30] The case has been portrayed in Ferdinand von Schirach, *Terror: Ein Theaterstück und eine Rede* (München: Verlagsgruppe Random House GmbH, 2016), and in the 2016 movie *The Verdict*.

5

Intermezzo I

This short chapter marks the transition from a general introduction to the Universal Declaration to a description and a discussion of the most central rights it contains. Already a superficial reading of the Universal Declaration has indicated that it is a fairly comprehensive document so that introducing its central rights enables us to discuss the most pressing issues in legal philosophy. Although the chapters dedicated to these rights can be read independently, the order in which they are presented is not arbitrary: the Universal Declaration implies a certain anthropology which can be presented in relation to what I call two important axes.

In the Preamble we saw that human rights are considered to be the foundation of 'freedom, justice and peace in the world'.[1] Thus, the thirty Articles that follow the Preamble must indicate the way(s) in which this goal can be reached. If all these Articles are realized, then the world will consist of peace, justice and freedom. Whereas the Declaration does not say a great deal about 'peace' and 'justice', it considers 'freedom' in great detail, thereby suggesting that peace and justice would be the result of a world in which the freedoms and rights proclaimed in the Declaration are acknowledged and realized. Each of the following ten chapters therefore introduces and discusses one of these freedoms. The order in which these freedoms are examined is dictated largely by the Declaration itself; a further distinction is made between the first five rights discussed, generally brought under the heading of negative freedom, and the second five rights, under that of positive freedom.[2] This distinction reflects, or so I hold, the two axes, or aspects, according to which the human being is considered in the Universal Declaration.

Under the aspect of negative freedom, the human being is basically seen as an individual entity in need of protection against certain types of wrong, especially on the part of the state. Here, the human being needs to be 'free from' and to be allotted a certain sphere in which the state shall not intervene.

---

[1] Universal Declaration of Human Rights, 10 December 1948, www.ohchr.org/EN/UDHR/Documents/UDHR_Translations/eng.pdf.

[2] I will use in my own way the distinction introduced by I. Berlin between two concepts of liberty: see Isaiah Berlin, 'Two Concepts of Liberty', in *Four Essays on Liberty* (Oxford: Oxford University Press, 1969).

Positive freedom indicates that every human being is at the same time a member of a particular community as well; in this regard, one is entitled to certain provisions and facilities; claims can also be made on that person on behalf of the community, as will be discussed in Part IV on human duties. In this regard, human rights guarantee, so to speak, the 'freedom to', by ensuring certain provisions and facilities. This distinction is useful, but it will also turn out to be somewhat artificial, with aspects of positive freedom being present in the discussion of negative rights and vice versa. Nonetheless, it offers a useful framework for dealing with the rights of the Universal Declaration.

The Human Being as Individual and Social Being

Under the heading of negative freedom I will discuss five rights in which the human being is considered principally as an individual. In order to survive and to lead a good life, a number of conditions must be met. Life as the basis of being human and the physical integrity of the human being must be protected: humans must be free from attacks on their life and body. Further, a human being is a creature that wants to give their life a certain form. A human being is not someone else's property and is not to be robbed arbitrarily of the freedom of movement. Therefore, humans must be free from slavery and from the taking away of freedom due to an unjustified prosecution or punishment. In addition, a human being is a creature that needs a certain space in which to move freely. This private 'space' that a human being needs is larger than the mere physical boundaries of the body; the integrity of this space must be guaranteed too. This is not a new idea. Aristotle for example argued that humankind as a social animal is distinguished from all other animals because its voice not merely expresses feelings of pleasure and displeasure, but enables a true language whereby human beings are able to express themselves about the useful and the useless, and about justice and injustice.[3] Thus, the human being must be entitled to have the 'space' to make such judgements, about the useful and the just. A human must also have the right to make their own judgement about life as a whole and to develop or adhere to a specific world-view, be it religious or not. Finally, in order to lead a decent life, a human being must not only control matters of life and physical integrity, and qua mental and physical space, but must also be able to have access to material and non-material goods. A human should be able to own property, and this property should not be arbitrarily interfered with.

Part II of this book focuses therefore on a number of prohibitions that follow from human rights. These concern the prohibitions on taking a human life, on subjecting someone to torture or to a cruel and degrading treatment, on arbitrarily robbing someone of their freedom of movement by an unjust punishment, on invading someone's space without justification, and finally,

---

[3] Aristotle, *Politics*, 1253a7–1253a18.

on arbitrarily taking someone's property. What matters here is not to treat anyone in a way that is incompatible with these freedoms and thus with human nature in so far as they are an individual. According to the Declaration, the state in particular is the potential 'violator' that needs to be restrained. Therefore, negative freedom is linked to a limitation of action, chiefly on the part of the state. It is freedom from interference by the state. The state is prohibited from acting in ways that violate the rights of human beings in general and its citizens in particular: it must refrain from actions that invade the lives and integrities of human beings, their mental and physical space, and their freedom of movement or the enjoyment of their property.

Under the heading of positive freedom, Part III examines five rights as well. These do justice to the fact that a human being is always a member of a particular community. All human beings form a 'human family', according to the Preamble of the Universal Declaration. Indeed, a human being is not a Robinson Crusoe, and if they were, they would not need any rights. The rights discussed in this third part aim at guaranteeing access and membership to such human communities. At issue here are not rights that protect humans from some interference, but rights that offer and enable access. Because human beings belong to various communities, the subjects here are diverse. They include the right to participate in governing one's political community. Possibly even more fundamental is the right simply to be a member of a national community and the right to apply for such membership if the need arises. The Universal Declaration also aims to guarantee membership of communities other than the democratic nation state, on both 'lower' and 'higher' levels. The lower level entails membership of a family and a cultural entity within the state in which one can express one's identity; on the higher level, as indicated in Article 28 of the Universal Declaration, there figures prominently the right to be a 'member' of the international community. Even though this membership is not citizenship, it should nonetheless function as a sort of safety-net for the 'realization' of human rights. On the basis of this 'membership', every human being is entitled to sufficient basic goods to give them and their family a reasonable standard of living. On the basis of this article, the protection of the most fundamental rights of the individual, such as the right to life and freedom from slavery, is a matter of international concern.

Under the heading of positive freedom, therefore, a number of obligations, based on human rights, are assigned to the state and to international legal institutions. These obligations must ensure that access to participation and membership be granted and that certain means, services and facilities be provided. Here, the Universal Declaration is not prohibiting the state from acting in a specific manner, but urging the state to act in a specific manner. The state and the world community are being told that there should be, for example, an infrastructure to ensure that the will of the people reigns, that all human beings have access to citizenship, that family structures and cultural identities can develop autonomously, and that basic means of existence of every human being are supplied. Again, at issue here is that the human being is provided with what is needed for a being who is part of (several) communities. The Declaration obliges the 'actor' (primarily the state) to provide those means. Positive freedom is linked to the creation and guaranteeing of opportunities – not by omitting to act, but by acting.

In short, Part II of this book examines the negative rights and freedoms of the Universal Declaration, and Part III its positive rights and freedoms. However, an important caveat has to be added. Although it is common to distinguish between rights that entail an obligation not to act in a specific manner and rights that impose an obligation to act in a specific manner, this distinction is not watertight. In examining specific rights, it will become apparent that the so-called negative human rights sometimes involve the duty to act on the part of the state. Look at the simple example of the human right to life. This right not only implies that the state is prohibited from (arbitrarily) disposing of the lives of its citizens, but it must also actively protect the right to life. If a state does not act to dismantle existing death squads or against involuntary euthanasia, it violates the right to life. This follows from the doctrine of the social contract we have already seen. The state is consti-tuted, as it were, to guarantee the right to life because nobody's life was secure in the state of nature. Another example would be the right of expression. Everyone has the right to form and express their opinion, but that does not mean that it is prohibited to enact forms to regulate who may express an opinion at what time: otherwise there would be cacophony. The reverse is also true: some positive rights clearly imply a duty to abstain from action. Although positive rights are entitlements to specific services, the human right to family life or a cultural identity also requires a certain restraint on the part of the state. It should allow human beings to form their family life and to give expression to their cultural identity as they see fit.

Therefore, the distinction between negative freedom (in Part II) and positive freedom (in Part III) is to some extent an artificial one. These concepts of freedom provide the structure for ordering and discussing certain human rights. One should also add that all ten human rights discussed in Parts II and III deal with important aspects of human existence; it would be wrong then to prioritize the negative rights over the positive ones. In a final analysis, negative freedom and positive freedom could turn out to be two sides of the same coin.

Freedom: Negative and Positive

According to Benjamin Constant at the beginning of the nineteenth century,[4] if one should ask us moderns what we understand by liberty, the answer is

---

[4] Benjamin Constant, 'The Liberty of the Ancients compared with that of the Moderns', in *Political Writings*, ed. Biancamaria Fontana (Cambridge: Cambridge University Press, 1988), 309–28.

clear. It would perhaps not be the most trivial one – to be able to do whatever you like – but a more sophisticated one. Being free means not to be interfered with in leading one's own life, not to be arrested arbitrarily, not to be hindered in forming one's own opinion or in one's religion, etc. In short, 'modern' liberty seems to consist in being able to lead a life without interference from others. However, if one were to ask the ancients, say Aristotle or Cicero, the same question, one would get a completely different answer. What was important for them was not individual independence or self-determination, but the ability to participate in sovereign decisions. Only they are free who live under laws they together with others created, who participate in what we would now call the people's assembly where matters of how to rule the state are discussed, as well as questions of war and peace and who can sit as judge in law suits. While freedom for the modern human being is primarily a private matter and is accompanied by a certain neglect of the public domain, for the ancients – as Constant calls them – the opposite was true. Liberty can only be public freedom, which may entail a certain disregard for private matters. For a modern person, no one can be free unless they are able to develop their own preferences and organize their own life. For the classical person, a slave was the symbol of the unfree person, because without political status a slave had to live according to laws set by others. To be free certainly required a degree of prosperity, but when exercising freedom, the classical man had no objection to subordinating himself as an individual to the authority of the community.

In the twentieth century Isaiah Berlin reworked this distinction between the modern and classical views in an influential text, 'Two concepts of liberty'. Unlike Constant, who concentrated on explaining historically the transition from the one concept to the other, and on finding a manner in which the two forms of liberty could be integrated, Berlin's emphasis was on pointing out the dangers of the positive concept of liberty. When classical freedom is exercised primarily in a collective manner, individual liberty is under attack, as was the case in the totalitarian regimes of Nazi Germany and Soviet Russia. According to the concept of positive liberty, the domain in which the individual human being can lead their life should be determined completely by the political community, as it decides what is 'good' for everyone. This inevitably leads to the curtailment of individual freedom. Therefore, Berlin strongly advocates (negative) liberty, or the freedom not to be hindered by others. The 'freedom from' is considered to have much more value than the 'freedom to'. As a result of the present dominance of liberal philosophy, Berlin's appeal still enjoys a great deal of support. Nevertheless, it seems incorrect to interpret freedom only as the absence of coercion and interference, and thus to give, as regards human rights, priority to negative rights and to disregard positive rights. This becomes clear in the following argument.

Berlin defines being free as 'the degree to which no man or body of men interferes with my activity' and political liberty as 'the area within which a man can act unobstructed by others'. Indeed, negative freedom is concerned with absence of hindrances and obstructions – as we have seen. But Berlin readily admits that this definition is insufficient and incorrect. Consider physical disabilities. Suppose I enjoy playing tennis and would very much like to win the Wimbledon tournament. Is the fact that there are many more talented tennis players than me a sign of lack of freedom? After all they get in the way of me winning Wimbledon. This argument is obviously foolish. Coercion, as a limitation of my negative freedom, implies 'the deliberate interference of other human beings within the area in which I could otherwise act'.[5] My freedom is thus in jeopardy when other human beings create obstacles so that my options are restricted. However, this still does not seem quite right. Assume that the number of traffic lights in the United Kingdom is far greater than, for example, in North Korea where the limitations on free movement of traffic are far less. It would be absurd to say that because of this, human beings are freer in North Korea than in the United Kingdom. When discussing negative freedom and its obstacles the question must be raised as to what these obstacles are for. Is there a good reason for interfering with someone's negative liberty? Often there is: only by means of hindrances such as traffic lights and traffic regulations in general can freedom of movement for all become possible: the (positive) liberty to make use of the traffic infrastructure. It is certainly justified and good that negative liberty is curtailed here. In a democracy, such limits are often the result of a collective decision by those who have to live with the consequences of these limits, and that means that these limitations are the result of the positive freedom of those human beings. They live under their own laws. Many restrictions of negative freedom follow from the law. After all, the law encourages certain behaviour and sanctions other behaviour; and it would be absurd to argue that our freedom is limited by sanctions on risky or criminal behaviour. It would be truer to say that freedom is only possible by such means. This comes close to Kant's understanding of freedom within the state. Every free action is right, he writes, if it can coexist with everyone else's freedom in accordance with a universal law. In a just society, everyone is entitled to be as (negatively) free as is compatible with an equal 'amount' of freedom for everyone else.[6] The popular opinion that freedom is limited whenever the state intervenes in individual lives in order to regulate certain behaviour of acting is therefore certainly not always correct. Traffic lights and speed bumps and making the wearing of seat belts compulsory are all restrictions of the (negative) liberty of road users, but they serve the freedom to safely make use of the roads. The same argument applies in other areas: think of compulsory primary education, which is a clear limitation of the freedom of parents and children, but it stimulates the autonomy, positive freedom, of future adults. Autonomy is not possible without a good education.

---

[5] Berlin, 'Two Concepts of Liberty', 15–16.
[6] Immanuel Kant, *Metaphysik der Sitten*, AA VI, 230.

As regards freedom, it is important to focus not only on restrictions, but also on options and possibilities to choose. One might be inclined to hold that someone is freer the more options that person has. This too is less self-evident than may at first appear, because the quality of the options matters a great deal. The fact that the supermarket offers you the choice between various sorts of cereal does not make you a free human being in any profound sense of the word. Miller, on whose argument I rely here, gives the following example. Who is freer: someone who has to choose between two attractive jobs – say, as a barrister or a top post in the business world – or someone who must choose between four unattractive jobs, such as cleaner, rubbish collector, park keeper or fork-lift truck operator? The freedom to choose between options is more a matter of quality than quantity; and the quality of the options is determined by the opportunities offered by these options to lead an autonomous and meaningful life.[7] A true liberal who embraces negative freedom only and denies positive freedom, would argue that determining what is an autonomous and meaningful life is a purely individual matter. According to the ancient point of view this is not the case: someone can only be considered free when he lives with others under his own laws. Thus, there is an appealing view on human life in freedom that does not revolve around the individual human being alone. According to this view, choices that can be made on the basis of negative freedom must be such that they favour positive freedom and the leading of an autonomous life.

It is not easy to deny this positive dimension of freedom. Think of a motorist who comes to a cross-roads and chooses to turn right, while nobody forces him to do so. At the next junction he turns left, also of his own volition. But then it appears that he is on his way to a place where he can buy hard drugs, to which he is addicted. Is he free because he can choose his own route, or not free because he is addicted? Freedom does not consist only in the absence of obstacles and not even in qualitative good options, but concerns autonomy as well. Someone is free when he is able to make autonomous choices, independent of external pressure from others or internal pressure from, for instance, addiction. Such internal pressure also occurs when someone is so greatly under the influence of someone else or of a group that he continuously makes choices other than those he would have made had he been free from such pressure. At the same time, pressure by another person need not always be in conflict with freedom. Think of a talented student, who after doing brilliantly in his final school examinations chooses instead of going to university to work at the check-out of a large supermarket because of the money that would make the weekends so much more exciting. Certainly, this person's negative freedom would be violated if his parents pressurized him into abandoning this plan, but they would probably do so with an eye on his positive

---

[7] David Miller, *Political Philosophy. A Very Short Introduction* (Oxford: Oxford University Press, 2003), 57.

freedom, even if they accepted that there is nothing wrong with working in a supermarket.

Reflecting on negative freedom almost inevitably leads to a shift from seeing freedom as the absence of hindrances to choosing freedom as autonomy. Someone is free only when he can make choices on the basis of autonomously weighing the options. For this reason, Griffin sees as the basis of human rights not just *liberty,* but also *autonomy.*[8] Human rights exist not only to protect negative freedom, but also to increase positive freedom. Freedom does not consist in the complete absence of limits; frequently limits serve the cause of freedom. Therefore, it is incorrect to consider negative freedom as the only true form of freedom and to reject positive freedom as the prelude to objectionable paternalism and political despotism. The Universal Declaration, so it seems, does not make such a choice, but envisions a world of peace and justice as the result of a combination of negative and positive freedom.

[8] James Griffin, *On Human Rights* (Oxford: Oxford University Press, 2008), 149–51.

Part II
Negative Freedom

Everyone Has the Right to Life

Article 3 of the Universal Declaration of Human Rights concerns the right to life. This right is considered both the most fundamental and the most elementary of all human rights. After all, no other human right would exist without it. Life appears thus to be the most important basic good to which human beings can lay a legal claim. The right to life has a certain self-evident quality that, on closer examination, however, does not appear to be so simple. The right to life is a complicated right. This becomes clear when comparing the text of the Universal Declaration's Article 3, which includes the freedom and inviolability of the person as well as the right to life, with a number of other formulations of the right to life.

While the Universal Declaration speaks of the right to life in general terms and does not mention limitations to this right, Article 2 of the European Convention on Human Rights (ECHR) clearly states that this right has limitations. It starts with the stipulation that life must be protected by the law, but then adds that no one can be deliberately deprived of their life unless this is in execution of a sentence of a court for a crime for which the law provides the death penalty. Thus, according to the drafters of this convention, the death penalty as such was not a violation of the right to life. Nor is the right to life violated, according to Article 2 para. 2 of this convention, if someone dies as a result of defending life against unlawful violence: the right to life does not rule out the use of lethal force when a person defends themselves or others against unlawful violence. In such cases, the use of force must be an absolute necessity. Moreover, the right to life does not protect one from being killed as a result of resisting arrest or when being prevented from escaping from prison. If such use of force is absolutely necessary then the right to life is not violated. This is also the case when there are fatal casualties in an attempt to suppress – in accordance with the law – riot and rebellion: such violence too must be 'absolutely necessary'.[1]

The International Covenant on Civil and Political Rights (ICCPR) sets out similar limitations on the right to life.[2] Here too, the acknowledgement of that

---

[1] Council of Europe, Convention for the Protection of Human Rights and Fundamental Freedoms, 4 November 1950, ETS 5, www.coe.int/en/web/conventions/full-list/-/conventions/rms/0900001680063765.

[2] UN General Assembly, International Covenant on Civil and Political Rights, 19 December 1966, 2200A (XXI), www.ohchr.org/en/professionalinterest/pages/ccpr.aspx.

right does not exclude the death penalty, although conditions are placed on imposing this penalty, such as that it can be pronounced only for the most serious of crimes, and that the possibility of appeal against a death sentence and the opportunity to request a pardon must exist. The death sentence cannot be imposed on persons who have committed such serious crimes before the age of eighteen, nor on pregnant women.

It is remarkable that the right to life, which in a certain sense is a pre-condition of all other rights, is still subject to a number of exceptions. Unlike the right not to be tortured (see Chapter 7), the right to life is not an absolute right. When someone uses unlawful violence and dies as a result of someone else's necessary resistance, there is no violation of their right to life. When someone commits a very serious crime that incurs the death penalty (which still is the case in certain countries), and when, after a fair trial, they are convicted and executed, this does not constitute a violation of their right to life. Obviously, there are now many countries where the death penalty has been abolished and where it is regarded as being incompatible with the right to life, but that is not the international standard according to the original drafters of the ECHR (even if this has changed in the meantime as a result of its 1983 compulsory Protocol 6) or according to the ICCPR (in its Article 6, amended since 1983 by the Second Protocol). Simply because the Universal Declaration is silent on this issue, we cannot infer that it opposes the death penalty. After all, the Declaration was formulated and accepted by the representatives of the same states that were later involved in the two conventions mentioned. Therefore, these two conventions will be followed here when examining the right to life. We start with the death penalty.

The Right to Life and the Death Penalty

It may not happen very often, but occasionally discussion of the death penalty arises, even in countries where it has long been abolished.[3] When a particularly heinous murder takes place and the perpetrator is caught, any other sentence than the death penalty seems too lenient to quite a number of people. Despite its abolition, there exists in many countries a considerable minority within the population who are convinced that the death penalty is the (only) appropriate sentence in certain cases of homicide. Often they invoke the principle of equality: the death penalty is the only just punishment for those who know-ingly take the life of another person; someone can only make a valid claim to the right to life if they themselves respect the right to life of other persons. Sentencing a murderer to mere imprisonment (even for life) would imply giving them an (undeserved) advantage over the person who has been mur-dered. While the victim has absolutely nothing left, the imprisoned murderer

---

[3] In the Netherlands, for example, the death penalty was abolished in 1870. Article 14 of the present Dutch Constitution states that the death penalty shall not be imposed.

still has their life and the rights that (might) go with it – shelter, food, physical integrity and possibly even the right to a return to society. The inability to impose the death sentence is thus perceived as a violation of what justice as equality requires.

In countering this support of the death penalty, one might in the first instance start with the argument that any public authority must bear in mind a number of aims that punishment should serve when imposing punishments and sanctions. Not only do retribution or 'just deserts' matter, but also the prevention or deterrence of crime and possibly the rehabilitation of the criminal. Moreover, one might see the death penalty as a violation of human dignity. No one, no matter how serious the crime they have committed, is so evil that they must be permanently removed from society in the most extreme way possible.

While such an appeal to human dignity as standing in the way of the death penalty may be a current view in our days, the penalty was considered legitimate for a long time, as testified both by legal history and by important legal philosophers. The abolition of the death penalty in many countries is of a relatively recent date. The campaign for abolition has been very successful, given that the death penalty no longer exists in two-thirds of all the countries in the world. Contrary to the (original) texts of the ECHR and the ICCPR, a large part of the international community has moved away from the death penalty. Neither the special international criminal tribunals that were established by the UN after the Yugoslav wars and the Rwanda genocide (the ICTY and the ICTR), nor the (permanent) International Criminal Court established in 1998 by means of the Rome Statute adopted by many states, can impose the death penalty. At the same time, however, influential states continue to apply the death penalty, such as China and the United States (in the latter, the death penalty can be imposed in some states but not in others). In contrast, the death penalty has been almost completely abolished in Europe, within the framework of the Council of Europe, on the basis of Protocol 6 of the European Convention on Human Rights – mentioned before – which has been accepted by all the Member States of that Council and which now forms a non-negotiable part of both membership of the Council and the European Union. Protocol 6 prohibits the imposition of the death penalty during times of peace. This commitment has far-reaching consequences. It not only prohibits states from applying the death penalty, but it also implies a positive duty on these states, namely not to extradite persons to another state in which they are likely to face the death penalty. In the case of *Soering v. The United Kingdom*, the European Court of Human Rights ruled that Mr Soering, a German citizen who was arrested in the United Kingdom for a murder committed in the United States, could not be extradited to the United States because of the likelihood that he would face the death penalty. The very fact of being sentenced to death and the time one waits on death row with the knowledge of one's eventual execution constitute for the Court 'inhuman and degrading treatment'.[4]

Even though there is no global consensus on the death penalty, all kinds of international rules have been created whereby, as was already clear from the ICCPR, the death penalty is subject to strict limitations: it can only be applied in cases of the most serious crimes and after a fair trial. Legal provisions must be in place for a convicted person to appeal their sentence and to request pardon. Certain categories of people are excluded from the death penalty, such as the young, pregnant women and the mentally ill. Furthermore, the execution itself, unlike in earlier times, cannot be a public spectacle for the amusement or titillation of an audience, and must not be accompanied by any form of unnecessary suffering. This seems to follow from the respect that is due to life. In particular this last condition, in the opinion of some, deprives the death penalty of its most important function – the deterrent effect and the manifestation of the power of the state over life and death.

When we distance ourselves today from the death penalty, we also distance ourselves from important representatives of legal philosophy. Among them we find far more advocates of the death penalty than opponents. Plato, for instance, was horrified by the death sentence of his teacher Socrates, but this indignation arose less from the punishment itself than that it was given to Socrates, whom he considered a moral hero.[5] In modern times, Rousseau and Kant are the most prominent spokesmen for the death penalty. He who commits murder thereby declares, according to Rousseau, that he no longer wishes to be considered part of society; he breaks the social contract and thereby places himself in a state of war with society, which can therefore choose to condemn him to death.[6] According to Kant, punishment in general has nothing to do with the aim of promoting the well-being of society (by means of deterrence) or the improvement of the criminal, but solely with retribution. In Kant's view, there can be no exception from the rule that a crime must be punished, and therefore the law of punishment is 'a categorical imperative'.[7] As seen in Chapter 4, the concept of a categorical imperative, as the expression of a universal moral law to respect the dignity of every person, has many positive connotations. In the context of criminal law, however, Kant emphasizes that punishment categorically must be imposed whenever a crime has taken place. Notoriously, he writes that even the last murderer who sits in prison must be executed, even when the members of a particular society, for instance living on an island, decide to separate and disperse themselves

[4] *Soering v. The United Kingdom* (1989), ECHR, no. 14038/88. Interestingly, Article 3 of the European Convention which will be discussed in Chapter 7 also played a role in the case.

[5] See, for example, Plato, *Laws*, 871d, http://classics.mit.edu/Plato/laws.9.ix.html.

[6] Jean Jacques Rousseau, *The Social Contract or Principles of Political Right*, 2.5, in *The Social Contract and Other Later Political Writings*, ed. Victor Gourevitch (Cambridge: Cambridge University Press, 2012).

[7] Immanuel Kant, *Metaphysik der Sitten*, AA VI, 331.

throughout the world. The execution of the last murderer follows from the imperative that everyone experiences what their deeds are worth and so that – and this is clearly a second element which sounds odd coming from Kant – the blood guilt should not cling to a people for not having insisted upon this punishment.[8] The contemporary proponents of the death penalty and those who believe that the right to life is not an inalienable right have powerful advocates.

Nevertheless, convincing arguments against the death penalty were also developed and these have gradually prevailed. Important in this was *Of Crimes and Punishments* (1764) by the Italian Marquis Cesare di Beccaria, who repudiated the death penalty and was subsequently accused by Kant of false sentimentality. For Beccaria, this repudiation was closely linked with the rejection of retribution as the aim of punishment. The aim should instead be the protection of society and the prevention of crime.[9] According to Beccaria, the death penalty does not contribute to this aim. Empirically, Beccaria seems to have a point: for example, those states in the United States of America that impose the death penalty have a higher rate of criminality than those where this punishment does not exist.[10] According to Beccaria, there would be a clear reason for this: criminals weigh the advantages to be gained from their crimes against the disadvantages if they should be caught. If they knew that they could be sentenced to life imprisonment, then they would be more cautious than if their sentence were to be death. The punishment of death is very intense but brief, and it therefore makes little impression on those contemplating a life of crime. It is even counterproductive with regard to crime prevention. The prospect of the death penalty means that in certain circumstances the criminal has nothing to lose from further criminality – the severity of the punishment no longer acts as a deterrent. For this reason, according to Beccaria and based on his – not necessarily empirically correct – interpretation of a criminal's calculation, it is a punishment that is not proportionate; it is either too light (it lasts only a short moment), or too severe (it does not restrain a criminal from engaging in serious crimes). Therefore, Beccaria pleads for another form of punishment that is both proportionate and has preventive effect – and that is (life) imprisonment.[11]

Obviously, this is not a principled argument. The death penalty is only counterproductive if it is empirically true that criminals are neither deterred by such a punishment, nor restrained by it. If it could be shown that (a particular type of) death penalty does indeed have a preventive effect, under

[8] Ibid., AA VI, 333.
[9] Cesare Bonesana di Beccaria, *An Essay on Crimes and Punishments: By the Marquis Beccaria of Milan, with a Commentary by M. de Voltaire. A New Edition Corrected* (Albany: W.C. Little & Co., 1872), ch. 3, http://oll.libertyfund.org/titles/beccaria-an-essay-on-crimes-and-punishments.
[10] Many websites, such as the Amnesty International website, provide information on the death sentence and homicide rates in particular countries and states.
[11] Di Beccaria, *An Essay on Crimes and Punishments*, ch. XXVIII.

this type of argument, that would legitimate it. In order to make the case against the death penalty, arguments of a more principled nature are needed. Sometimes selectivity is presented as such an argument, because the death penalty is imposed more often on members of a particular group or ethnicity within the population than on others. The death penalty is thus discriminatory and violates the principle of equality under the law. But this cannot be a fully principled argument either. Because this fact impinges on its legitimacy in practice, it can relatively easily be countered by ending the discriminatory manner in which the death penalty is applied. Therefore, this is not the principled argument we are looking for.

Something similar can be said about the next argument, namely that the death penalty is irreversible. If serious mistakes are made during (or before) the criminal trial that subsequently led to the conviction and execution of a person who later turns out to be innocent, this mistake can never be rectified. Indeed, we know that judicial mistakes do occur. It would indeed be terrible if an innocent person was convicted and executed; these kinds of mistakes should never occur, and therefore the death penalty should never be imposed. Important as this argument may be, it could also be taken as a plea for the improvement of criminal investigation and procedure, rather than undermining the legitimacy of the death penalty. The conclusion would then merely be that mistakes in criminal procedures should be avoided as much as possible, and that one must be extremely cautious and certain when applying this penalty.

The argument on the possibility of mistakes in criminal procedure can therefore only count as a principled objection to the death penalty if it can be shown that mistakes are unavoidable for the simple reason that it is impossible to devise a criminal procedural system that does not make such mistakes. Criminal procedure is a form of what Rawls calls imperfect procedural justice. While one knows what the outcome of a criminal procedure should be, namely that only the guilty and none but the guilty are convicted and sentenced, it is impossible to develop a system that guarantees this outcome.[12] Perfect procedural justice exists in the following example: consider a bet on the outcome of a football match in which everyone stakes the same amount – the result is just, whoever wins. The criminal process, however, is not a form of perfect procedural justice, where the just outcome is the result of (following) a certain procedure. Due to difficulties with regard to evidence and the law, criminal procedure does not always lead to a just result. If mistakes are indeed always possible, we cannot – out of respect for the right to life – take the risk of an unjust death sentence. After all, a state cannot dispose of the lives of its citizens arbitrarily.

Obviously, one could still retort that one cannot make an omelette without breaking eggs. It appears that a certain percentage of those treated in hospitals

---

[12] John Rawls, *A Theory of Justice: Revised Edition* (Oxford: Oxford University Press, 1999), 74–5.

have contracted their illness in the hospital itself, but is that any reason to close hospitals? What should happen is that strenuous efforts are made to reduce the risk of infection in the hospital as much as possible. The advantages of having hospitals still far outweigh the incidental disadvantage of some persons being infected and catching a disease. But to this objection, the answer would be that what applies to hospitals does not apply to the death penalty. That people become sick in hospital is an unintentional and undesired effect of there being hospitals, while the death sentence is the conscious and intentional killing of individuals, rather than a by-product of the criminal system – and that is simply impermissible, in the opinion of those who oppose the death penalty.

We have now gradually reached the principled argument against the death penalty: that it is in conflict with the right to life. In the first instance, this does not appear to be a convincing argument: originally, the death penalty was not seen as a violation of the right to life, neither by some legal philosophers nor in the original understanding of Article 2 ECHR. Plus, there are many other rights, and often it is not unjustified that these rights are restricted. Take for example the right to freedom of speech: this does not mean that someone has the right to spread lies about the royal family or others in the public sphere or – as is the case in quite a few European countries – to deny that the Holocaust took place. Another example is the right to privacy. Police officers cannot simply walk into my house and start looking around; but if there is sufficient reason to suspect that I have a cannabis plantation in my attic, then, with a search warrant, the police can enter my house without my permission. Would something similar not be the case with the right to life, namely that it can be restricted in special circumstances? Surely no single right is absolute. Should the state not respect the right to life only of those who respect the lives of others? One could perhaps argue with Kant and others, that those who murder make an exception to the general rule that prescribes respect for life, and that such an exception cannot be tolerated? This even seems to follow from the 'golden rule': 'Therefore all things whatsoever ye would that men should do to you, do ye even so to them.'[13] This rule could be turned around: if you take the life of another, your life will be taken; in other words: if someone takes the life of another, he cannot expect that others will respect his right to life.[14] What you do to another, you do to yourself. The idea of retribution is simply the reverse of the golden rule. People must regard each other as equals, and if they do not do so then they will not receive equal treatment or respect.

---

[13] Matt. 7:12.

[14] In her endorsement of Eichmann's death penalty, Arendt echoes this reasoning: 'Just as you [Eichmann] supported and carried out a policy of not wanting to share the earth with the Jewish people and the people of a number of other nations . . . we find that no one . . . can be expected to share the world with you. This is the reason, and the only reason, you must hang.' See Hannah Arendt, *Eichmann in Jerusalem: A Report on the Banality of Evil* (London: Penguin Classics, 1992), 279.

According to Beccaria, such reasoning overlooks the most important argument against the death penalty, namely that the state does not have the right or the authority to impose this particular punishment. In his view, the state derives its powers from the (fictive) transfer or delegation – by means of a social contract – of the powers possessed by individuals ('portions of liberty') in a state of nature. What is crucial here is that individuals do not have the right to dispose of their (own) lives. In this, Beccaria joins a long tradition of philosophers who emphasize that suicide is absolutely forbidden, as it is in conflict with human dignity or with a duty to self or with the will of God. Life is not something that the living have freely at their disposal.[15] In Chapter 4 the tension between dignity on the one hand and freedom on the other has already been considered. Since individuals do not have the authority to dispose of their own life, according to Beccaria, they cannot transfer this power to the state. This leads to the conclusion that the state can never acquire the right to impose the death sentence. The right to dispose of life does not belong to the state because it does not belong to individuals in the first place.[16] According to Beccaria, the right to life is therefore not like other rights: the right to life cannot be transferred, whereas other rights such as the right to property can. Someone can dispose of his right to a particular book to someone else by giving it away or by selling it. While one can dispose of a book, one cannot dispose of one's life, even though it really is one's own life. The right to life is thereby special because the right holder does not have full power of disposal of it.[17] This is indeed a principled argument against the supposed right of the state to take the lives of its citizens when they commit a murder. It is the task of the state to protect life. This principled argument inevitably raises religious connotations, namely that humankind has been 'given' life (by God) and that life must be respected both by the one whose life it is as well as by all others.

The Scope of the Right to Life

Beccaria was not the first philosopher to point out the special significance of life. He forms part of a tradition in which the Christian idea of creation and the giftedness of life has played an important role. In this regard, Griffin – in a recent excellent monograph on human rights – highlights an interesting passage at the beginning of Locke's famous *Second Treatise of Government* (1690). Locke writes that all men are equal in the state of nature. In itself this is not very surprising, since in all versions of the social contract, as we saw in Chapter 3, equality in the state of nature plays a fundamental role. Remarkable,

---

[15] One of the oldest testimonies of this prohibition in philosophy is Plato, *Phaedo*, 61c–62c.

[16] Di Beccaria, *An Essay on Crimes and Punishments*, ch. XXVIII.

[17] With regard to suicide, Kant would agree that suicide is a violation of a strict duty to oneself. He formulates that a person is *sui iuris* with regard to his own life and body, but not *sui dominus*. See Immanuel Kant, *Metaphysik der Sitten*, AA VI, 270.

however, is what follows from this (original) moral equality, according to Locke. To begin, he cites approvingly the then famous author Hooker, who states:

> 'Things that are equal must be measured by a single standard; so if I inevitably want to receive some good . . . how could I expect to have any part of my desire satisfied if I am not careful to satisfy the similar desires that other men, being all of the same nature, are bound to have?'

Since I want my life to be respected, it follows, says Locke, not only that 'no one ought to harm anyone else in his life, health, liberty, or possessions', but also that everyone must do 'as much as he can to preserve the rest of mankind', when his own existence is not at stake.[18]

Thus, from the special status of life arises not only the negative duty not to take the life of others (nor that of oneself), but also the positive duty to preserve and protect the life of others (this issue will be further addressed in Chapter 14). According to Locke, this is how the right to life should be understood. It has frequently been said of the human rights of the first generation, the civil and political rights, that they are mere negative rights that require others, in particular the state, *not* to commit, or to abstain from, certain acts. The main aim of these rights would be to prevent the state from infringing them. This is not wrong: Beccaria's reasoning aims to show that the state is not authorized to impose the death penalty. But Locke indicates that these rights, and prominently the right to life, imply not only the absence of action; in his view, human beings, and thus the state constituted by them, have the positive duty to preserve life. This duty not to take life and to preserve it also applies to one's own life. For Beccaria that is crucial. Precisely because no one has the right to dispose of their own life, he infers that the state does not have that right either. The right to life does not include the right to end one's life. Indeed, for a long time and in many legal systems suicide was considered a punishable crime. Some may be tempted to argue that such a prohibition is meaningless: who is going to be punished for a successful suicide? But this rebuttal is too simplistic. Criminalization of suicide was meant to deter any attempts at suicide (and to deter encouraging and assisting suicide), and if a suicide succeeded, a criminal sentence could be carried out either on the dead body or the bereaved family, or a combination of the two.[19] On the basis of the right to life, the state has the positive duty to 'preserve' life. Since the days of Locke and Beccaria, things have changed, particularly because today the right to life is often understood from the viewpoint of self-determination. This concept, however, is not unproblematic, as will become clear.

Today it has become fairly self-evident that the right to life and the special status attributed to life, along with a prohibition on murder and manslaughter

---

[18] John Locke, *Two Treatises of Government*, 2.5–6; James Griffin, *On Human Rights* (Oxford: Oxford University Press, 2008), 213–14.

[19] See, for example, William Blackstone, *Commentaries on the Laws of England (1765–69)*, Bk IV, Ch. XIV, https://lonang.com/library/reference/blackstone-commentaries-law-england/bla-414/.

gives rise to the negative duty not to kill, but also to a great number of positive duties. An example of a negative duty concerns a not so recent case before the European Court of Human Rights, in which a state was found guilty of violating the right to life. The case was as follows: the state had given its security services the task of preventing a terrorist attack. The security forces did so by killing these terrorists, while – in the judgement of the Court – it had been possible during the whole operation to arrest these terrorists instead. The lethal force used was, in the terminology of the Court, 'not absolutely necessary'.[20] Instances of the positive duty for the state to actively preserve and protect life follow from two other cases before the same Court. In the first case, the state was found guilty because it had not taken seriously enough the threats issued against a journalist who was later murdered. In the second case, the same state was found guilty of violating the right to life because it had not paid sufficient attention to the enforcement of (public) safety regulations for a refuse dump located closely to a residential area.[21] Thus, on the basis of the right to life, a state has both negative and positive duties.

Where the precise boundaries lie of what is obligatory on the basis of the right to life is not completely clear. Locke writes that there is a duty to preserve the rest of humankind if one's own existence is not thereby threatened. What does that mean? To preserve life everyone needs some basic provisions. Can the right to food be inferred from the right to life, so that those who have more than sufficient food have a duty to share with those who have no food? That would not only seem quite demanding, but also raises the issue of what counts as more than sufficient and how to distribute this duty over 'the wealthy'. A number of other duties are less contentious: does the state not have the duty to ensure food and road safety? The duty to rescue someone in need is also fairly well accepted. When survivors of shipwrecks, or asylum-seekers in rubber dinghies, appear off our shores, it would seem that the right to life requires that they be saved. Perhaps even asylum should be given to them, if we follow Locke. After all, he writes that there is a duty to preserve humankind as long as one's own existence is not at stake. Taking in limited groups of persons in need certainly does not threaten the existence of the state or its citizens.

Right to Life and Right to Death

The perspective on the right to life of, among others, Locke and Beccaria is one in which life is considered a gift: those who live this life therefore cannot determine fully what to do with it. According to Locke, human beings are the work of 'one omnipotent, and infinitely wise maker; all the servants of one sovereign master, sent into the world by his order about his business; ... his property ... made to last during his, not one another's pleasure; everyone is

---

[20] Case 18984/91, *McCann and others v. The United Kingdom* [1995] 21 ECHR 97 GC.
[21] Case 2668/07, *Dink v. Turkey* [2010] ECHR; Case 48939/04, *Öneryildiz v. Turkey* [2004] ECHR.

bound to preserve himself, and not to quit his station wilfully'.[22] As a result of modernization and secularization such religious perspectives have lost ground. Nowadays, many hold the view that the right to life derives its meaning from the superior value of self-determination or autonomy. The right to life should be respected because it forms the basis on which each and every human being can express his own life. This shift from the religious perspective to one of self-determination is however not without problems.

This becomes clear when we look at the discussions about the beginning and the end of human life. It is clear that the interpretation of the right to life as part of or derived from a supposed 'right to self-determination' (which is not mentioned in the Universal Declaration) has nowadays more support than life as a gift that human beings have in trust. If human beings did not really 'own' their lives, then it is easy to imagine a role for the state: it should ensure that this 'trust' is well managed. It would be the duty of the state to protect 'life', especially at both the (natural) beginning and the (natural) end of life. *Abortus provocatus*, as a violation of the life of a foetus which is worthy of protection, must therefore be forbidden. However, in recent years, the categorical prohibition of abortion has been successfully challenged within many legal systems. As a result, now the right to abortion exists in many places. At least two powerful arguments played an important role here. First it has been argued that the scope of a constitutionally protected right to life does not automatically encompass the biological life of a foetus in the very early stages of a pregnancy. Second, the right to self-determination of the woman, in the form of her right to privacy, weighs more heavily than a possible right to life of a foetus in the early stage of a pregnancy.[23]

A juridical milestone in the establishment of the 'right to abortion' in the United States was the decision by its Supreme Court in the case of *Roe v. Wade* in 1973.[24] Briefly summarized, it was decided that certain laws that categorically prohibit abortion were in conflict with the US Constitution, more particularly with the woman's right to privacy, which would include the right to abortion. Obviously, the right to privacy is not absolute: it loses importance as the pregnancy progresses. At a certain point, the interests of the state in protecting life and also in maintaining medical standards weigh more heavily than the woman's right to privacy. Specifically, this has led to what is called the three months rule: during the first three months of pregnancy, a woman should be able to choose to have an abortion; while in the second three months this is not the case and the state can regulate this trimester by providing exceptions. In the last three months, abortion is prohibited. Today, *Roe v. Wade* is seen as one of the most controversial decisions made by the Supreme Court, and that is not surprising. Those who regard life as given by

---

[22] John Locke, *Two Treatises of Government*, 2.6.

[23] See, for example, Ronald Dworkin, 'The Morality of Abortion', in *Life's Dominion: An Argument about Abortion, Euthanasia, and Individual Freedom* (New York: Random House, 1993), 30–67.

[24] *Roe v. Wade*, 410 US 113 (1973).

God cannot accept a judicial decision that gives women the right to cut off lives. In those eyes, abortion is not so much a violation of the right to life as a violation of the Creator who is the source of life. This is the reason why the campaign against abortion is so strong and sometimes, astonishingly, violence has been used against doctors who perform abortions.

The conflicting views that life is a gift and that the right to life is part of the right to self-determination also play a major role with regard to the end of life. We do not need to immediately think of euthanasia here. Some time ago in Germany there was a gruesome case involving someone known as 'the cannibal of Rotenburg'. Two men came into contact via the internet and one expressed the wish to kill and eat another person while the other volunteered to fulfil this wish. Eventually they met and brought their wishes to fulfilment. In the criminal proceedings, the remaining man – the killer – defended himself by arguing that he had only done as the other desired and could at most be prosecuted for a form of assisted suicide. This claim, however, was dismissed and he was convicted of murder.[25] This case is interesting in at least two aspects. First, the boundaries seem to have been reached of the old Roman adage, *volenti non fit iniuria* (to a willing person, no injury is done). Normally, someone who consents to something cannot complain afterwards that he has suffered a wrong. Someone who chooses freely to be a boxer cannot then complain if they are sometimes the recipient of hard blows. The *volenti* principle formulates the meaning of consent. It seems however that 'consent' does not always preclude unlawfulness.[26] Even if the person indeed had a true desire to be killed and eaten, the other person should never have acted upon this wish. No one should intentionally take the life of another, even if they request it. The *volenti* principle does not override the duty to respect the life of another person. This immediately leads to the second aspect we have encountered: the right to life is not transferable. In this respect this right differs from many rights. I do not have free disposal of my life, which is Beccaria's view. Something similar is the case with slavery. A contract consciously and freely entered into whereby I transfer complete control of my life to another cannot be legally, let alone morally valid. According to Kant, such a contract is internally inconsistent: the person who consents to a contract in order to become a slave ceases to be a legal subject and therefore the contract is invalid.[27]

Most cases in which the pursuit of a 'good death' clashes with the right to life are more familiar than the cannibal case. They usually concern people who, explicitly or otherwise, have made it known that they prefer death to life when they find themselves in certain difficult circumstances, such as suffering from ALS, a deadly muscular condition in which the sufferer becomes completely

---

[25] The ultimate decision on this case by the German Constitutional Court can be found at BVerfG 2 BvR 578/07, www.bverfg.de/entscheidungen/rk20081007_2bvr057807.html.
[26] Remember the similar case of Wackenheim, discussed in Chapter 4.
[27] Immanuel Kant, *Metaphysik der Sitten*, AA VI, 330.

imprisoned in their paralysed body, or from being in an irreversible coma or from Alzheimer's disease. Many persons are convinced that in such circumstances they would no longer wish to continue to live. At the same time, they are frequently no longer able to bring an end to their own lives if these conditions have reached an advanced stage. The question then is whether it is permissible to accede to their appeal for help to die.

Various legal systems give different answers to this difficult question, but one thing is clear: it is not self-evident that the person whose life is at stake can simply dispose of it. The right to life is a right over which the living themselves or others acting in their name do not have complete command. This has been apparent in a number of internationally known cases. In 1990, the United States Supreme Court had to adjudicate on the question of whether Nancy Cruzan could be allowed to die. Following a car accident, Cruzan had been in a vegetative condition for seven years. Her parents believed that their daughter would have wanted to die. The Court found that there was insufficient evidence that this was indeed her wish, in other words, what she would have wanted done. The interest of the state in preserving and protecting life was therefore decisive, even when that might not be in the interest of the person whose life was in question. It seems that the objective interest of the state with regard to life can – in cases such as Cruzan's – prevails over the subjective interest of a living person, which implies that the right to life in fact becomes a duty to live.[28]

What could such an objective interest be? In the first place it lies, says Griffin, in safeguarding the societal respect that is due to human life in general.[29] Secondly, it consists in the value of life itself, independent of the person who is living that life and the value it has for others. In particular this second aspect seems to contradict the value of self-determination. It was precisely on that ground that Diane Pretty, in another well-known case, appealed to the Director of Public Prosecutions in the United Kingdom for reassurance that her husband would not be prosecuted for assisting her in the future, at her express request, to commit suicide, a criminal act under the law. Affected by motor neuron disease, Pretty wanted to be able to die with dignity once her disease had progressed to the point that she was suffering unbearably. Pretty's request was rejected, which she regarded as an infringement of her right to life, as laid down in Article 2 of the European Convention. As we have seen, however, this Convention does not provide a right to a dignified death, only a right to life that is protected by the law and that no one may intentionally be robbed of. Assisted suicide does not fall within the exceptions provided in the second clause of this Article. On this basis, the Court decided, back in 2002, that the right to die (with the assistance of others) cannot be inferred

---

[28] I follow here the interpretation of this case by Ronald Dworkin, 'Do We Have a Right to Die?', in *Freedom's Law: The Moral Reading of the American Constitution* (Oxford: Oxford University Press, 1996), 130–46.

[29] James Griffin, *On Human Rights* (Oxford: Oxford University Press, 2008), 219.

from the right to life.[30] According to this judgement, the right to life should not be equated with or be seen as derived from the right to self-determination.

The question whether there is a right to die has led to many discussions and to different answers in different legal systems even if they all endorse the same right to life. In some countries, such as the Netherlands, legislation is more accepting with regard to assisted suicide and it does approach euthanasia indeed from the point of view of self-determination. In 2002, the Dutch legislator passed an Act concerning the 'Termination of Life on Request and Assisted Suicide', on the basis of which euthanasia and assisted suicide remain criminal offences, but medical doctors who offer such help will not be prosecuted if they have strictly followed a number of formally laid out regulations of both care and caution. Once assistance has been given and the patient has died, the doctor involved must, by way of the municipal coroner, report his assistance to a so-called regional euthanasia review committee, which will examine whether the case has been handled in accordance with the regulations and (thus) with all due care. The most important criteria that must be fulfilled (apart from consulting a second doctor) concern the doctor's conviction that the request for assistance with dying is made of the patient's free will, and that it has been well considered and is concrete and clearly expressed, and that the situation of the patient is one of unbearable suffering without any prospect of relief. If all these criteria are met, then the doctor finds himself, so it is legally construed, facing conflicting duties. On the one hand, it is the duty of a doctor to respect and preserve life, but on the other he is (also) obliged to relieve unbearable and hopeless suffering. If he has given the most weight to this latter duty, then the penalties laid down in the Dutch penal code do not apply to him. Under these criminal provisions, those who 'terminate the life of another person at that other person's express and earnest request' and those who 'intentionally assist in the suicide of a person or provides him with the means thereto' remain criminally accountable.[31]

With this law, the Dutch legislator aimed at striking a fair legal balance between the will of those who no longer want to live because of their unbearable, hopeless suffering and the respect for the right to life. Obviously, whether the right balance has been struck has been contested. Some might suggest that Dutch law is in violation of Article 2 of the European Convention which states that 'no one shall be deprived of his life intentionally'.[32] Others, mainly from abroad, have sometimes suggested that the old and sick in the Netherlands are put under pressure to no longer be a burden to their family and to society. Still

---

[30] Case 2364/02, *Pretty v. The United Kingdom* [2002] ECHR. In a more recent case, the Court seems to have moved in the direction of understanding 'assisted suicide' cases under the right to respect for private life (Article 8 of the Convention). See Case 31322/07, *Haas v. Switzerland* [2011] ECHR.

[31] Articles 293, 294 Dutch Criminal Code.

[32] Obviously, very much depends on what 'intention' means. If pain relief is the doctor's intention and death the foreseeable side-effect, this would be a fine example of the well-known doctrine of double-effect.

others see problems in quite another direction. The law demands that any request for assistance should be well-considered, and the result of unbearable suffering. But which persons can make such a request? Only those in physical pain and distress? Or perhaps those who suffer not physically, but from serious mental problems without any hope of relief, and those old persons who consider their lives completed as well? Does the law provide an answer in such cases? *Should* it offer an answer?

In other countries, such as the United Kingdom, no such general rules for euthanasia and assisted suicide are (yet) in place. But here too, cases have to be decided, sometimes quite tragic ones, such as this relatively unknown one which became before a UK judge in 2012.[33] The case concerned a thirty-two-year-old British woman, who was traumatized during her childhood and suffered from severe anorexia nervosa and other chronic health problems for many years. An appeal was made to the Court of Protection when it became known that she had refused to eat and was receiving palliative care to allow her to die in a local hospital. The Court was asked to review the case. Should this woman simply be allowed to die, as seemed to be her clear wish? Or should her life be protected – which in her case would involve an invasive life-sustaining treatment – as would seem to follow from Article 2 of the European Convention and as interpreted by this Court as containing the presumption that all steps will be taken to preserve it, unless the circumstances are exceptional?

In order to resolve this dilemma, the Court basically had to answer two questions. The first question concerned self-determination: did the woman have the mental capacity to make decisions, to which she is in principle entitled, for herself including about what she will and will not eat. Based on what appears to be a conscientious consideration of the case, the Court ruled that the woman did not– at that time – have the required mental capacity, nor at an earlier moment in time in which she had made a so-called 'advance decision' concerning such a life-saving treatment. After so answering this first question, the second question arose: what solution, letting her die or making her live, should be considered in the woman's best interest? Was it, given her very difficult and complicated medical condition, in her best interests to die, or should she be 'given' the possibility to regain her independence, even if the chances for recovery were limited and the costs of medical treatment high? This literally meant that the Court had to decide between death and life. In its quite moving concluding motivation, the Court acknowledged that the competing factors in favour of either outcome were 'almost exactly in equilibrium'. The balance would, nonetheless, 'unmistakably' tip in the direction of life-preserving treatment, because the right to life is the most fundamental right human beings have: 'we only live once – we are born once and we die once – and the difference between life and death is the biggest difference we know.'

---

[33] *A Local Authority v. E* [2012] EWHC 1939 (COP), www.bailii.org/ew/cases/EWHC/COP/2012/1639.html.

'from two evils, then, doing injustice and suffering injustice, in my opinion the first is the greater, the second the lesser'.[22] But according to these same spokespersons, this does not apply in the debate on torture, because at issue there is not a particular person deciding either to commit or to undergo torture. The scenario is one in which a large group of persons is in a threatening situation and then someone in authority has to decide for them whether or not to take immediate action. A decision has to be made. One would then from a person in an authoritative position expect to take responsibility for the well-being of society as a whole, which may mean that he has to dirty his hands.[23] It is simply not true that the moral considerations that have validity for an individual who is only responsible for himself are the same for those with a responsibility for the society or the state. In the ticking bomb scenario, a politician cannot be bound by an absolute prohibition as is found in the CAT, so it is argued. If the stakes are extremely high and information is the most important 'weapon' to prevent a threat from materializing, then torture must at least be excusable. Only a mere theorist would still maintain that the prohibition on torture is categorical.

Reasons to Uphold the Categorical Character of This Prohibition

It might seem that we have reached the end of the discussion with the utilitarian 'winning' the argument. This would imply that the drafters of the Universal Declaration and the states that agreed with the (wording of the) Convention Against Torture either made a moral mistake with the categorical prohibition of torture or were naïve in their hopes for a world in which torture would no longer occur. With the rise of terrorism since the start of the third millennium, an absolute ban on torture can no longer be upheld, and an absolute respect for some central human rights is a luxury that 'we' can no longer permit ourselves.

This, however, is too facile. The architects of the Universal Declaration were certainly not naïve. In 1948, the barbarous acts of the Nazis were still fresh in their memory. In the run-up to the acceptance of CAT, there was enough public awareness of the cruelty of torture carried out for example under Apartheid in South Africa, where it ended the lives of Steve Biko and many others. In other words, the proponents of a categorical ban on torture knew what they aimed to achieve. The arguments in favour of outlawing torture were and still are quite strong. First, the accusation of them supporting an 'abstract and unworldly' position could easily be reversed, especially regarding ticking-bomb scenarios from which the utilitarian approach and that of the lesser of the two evils derive their plausibility. It is relatively easy to think of ticking

---

[22] Plato, *Gorgias*, 509c.
[23] See Michael Walzer, 'Political Action. The Problem of Dirty Hands', in *Torture: A Collection*, ed. Sanford Levinson (New York: Oxford University Press, 2004), 61–75.

bombs in theory – or for a film or television. Think of the successful television series 24.[24] It revolved around threatening situations which had to be resolved within 24 hours. Its protagonist Jack Bauer – with whom the viewer could identify, because of a clever split-screen technique which gave the viewer an overview over all the action including that of the villains – managed to remove the deadly threat often by resorting to torture, which always seemed effective and thus 'justified'. In real life, such omniscience does not occur. One very rarely – if ever – finds in history situations which fulfil the conditions for such a scenario: a terrorist bomb threatens a relatively large part of the population; the person (or persons) who has the information to avoid the catastrophe has been caught; there is no other way to obtain the needed information; there is a reasonable chance that torture will be effective and the person or persons who is or are tortured has indeed sufficient control over of the situation, such that they can stop the threat by providing information. Even if there are real ticking bombs, it seems that these rarely – if ever – fit the scenario in which torture seems morally justified.[25]

Secondly, the utilitarian calculus based on the advantages and the disadvantages of the limited use of 'torture' in specific emergency situations is not unambiguously positive. A philosophically untrained person who considers this dilemma would be inclined to look solely at the situation as such and what should be done now. Such an approach is called act-utilitarianism: the calculus of pain and pleasure is made on the basis of a particular situation and a single action, that of putting pressure on a single individual and rescuing the endangered population. Generally, however, act-utilitarianism is not considered a very plausible interpretation of utilitarianism. A more adequate manner to make the calculus is the rule-utilitarian approach, which holds that the benefits and the downsides of an act must be calculated as the instance of a certain rule ('in certain circumstances act x has to be done by person y') and against the background of the institutions necessary for the existence of that rule.[26] It then

---

[24] This American TV series, produced by Fox network, ran between the end of 2001 and 2010. The series portrayed torture as rather trivial and effective so that at a certain moment the US military asked them to stop suggesting the violation of the law (which prohibits the use of torture) as being legitimate in order to secure the country. The unethical and illegal behaviour depicted in '24' had an adverse effect on the training and performance of real American soldiers. See Jane Mayer, 'Whatever it takes: The politics of the man behind "24"', New Yorker, 19 February 2007, www.newyorker.com/magazine/2007/02/19/whatever-it-takes.

[25] A large debate exists on the question whether 'torture' can be effective. We saw that threatening to torture Gäfgen was effective (though it did not save his victim). A similar US case from 1984, Leon v Wainwright, in which a captured kidnapper was tortured in order to reveal the location of the victim who was being held captive by another kidnapper, is discussed in Michael Kramer, Torture and Moral Integrity: A Philosophical Inquiry (Oxford: Oxford University Press, 2014), 60–1. The conclusion of this book is that torture is and should be categorically prohibited, but that not torturing a suspect might in some circumstances not be 'morally optimal'. On the basis of extensive historic research, it has also been argued that torture does not work; see D. Rejali, Torture and Democracy (New Jersey: Princeton University Press, 2007).

[26] I take this distinction from John Rawls, 'Two Concepts of Rules', The Philosophical Review (1955) 64: 3–32.

turns out that things are more complicated. The costs of torturing an individual consist not only of the pain done to the 'victim', with the benefits being for society. Bentham realized this. There will be societal costs, such as when mistakes are made as to which individual should be tortured in order to retrieve the needed information. It can hardly be presumed that a perfect procedure exists to detect the culpable person who has the valuable information. Costs also consist in institutionalizing 'torture'. Contrary to what is perhaps assumed, interrogation with violence is a specialized business. Only with training can as much pressure as possible be brought to bear, while using as few means as possible, as proportionality requires. Moreover, information on (effective methods of) torture must be collected. There must be places where the torture takes place. Personnel are needed, ranging from medical observers to cleaners and guards. Finally, torture demands authorization and oversight, in order to be confined within the narrow boundaries of the emergency situation. But this means that through the legislative and the judiciary, society as a whole somehow gets involved in the practice of 'enhanced interrogation', and then as the saying goes, 'whoever touches pitch shall be defiled'. It is of course possible that a state chooses to have its torture done in secret, but then it not only obviously violates the right not to be tortured but also abandons the spirit of the Universal Declaration altogether. In short, the utilitarian argument in favour of a limited use of interrogational torture and its rejection of the categorical prohibition is perhaps less strong that originally thought.

Thirdly, even under carefully designed institutional circumstances, there is no guarantee that 'enhanced interrogation' will prove successful. Empirically, it is clear that statements made under extreme pressure are often highly unreliable. Many well-known examples exist of miscarriages of justice as the result of coerced 'confessions'. In real life, averting terrorist threats usually requires the collection of small bits and pieces of information from various sources. These parts should then be fitted together carefully like a jigsaw puzzle to perceive a coherent whole. In real situations of war or public unrest, torture is seldom used on a small scale and targeted on specific 'culpable' individuals picked out for their knowledge. Usually torture takes place after a dragnet operation, whereby a great number of more or less suspicious individuals are rounded up and roughly interrogated. This was the case for instance in the Algerian War of Independence in the 1950s. The memoires of the then head of the French Intelligence, Aussaresses, do not demonstrate the correctness of the ticking bomb argument, but show us a dragnet operation in action in which 30 to 40 per cent of all Algerian men were tortured during that war. When information is in short supply and the situation is or seems threatening, torture is likely to occur.[27]

---

[27] See Jean Maria Arrigo, 'A Utilitarian Argument against Torture Interrogation of Terrorists', *Science and Engineering Ethics* (2004) 10: 543–72.

How difficult it is to keep torture limited, that is, within the boundaries of exceptional emergencies, is also apparent when we look at the state of Israel. During the first Intifada in the late 1980s, the Landau Commission, set up by the Israeli government, established guidelines for the use of coercion ('moderate measures of physical pressure') by the Israeli security services. The result was widespread physical violence against those arrested in the Occupied Territories. This attempt to regulate a form of authorized violence clearly failed, and in a famous case in 1999, the Israeli Supreme Court ruled these guidelines illegal as being in conflict with the right not to be subjected to torture.[28] To be more precise, the Court ruled that these coercive interrogational methods were illegal because the necessity defence could not be invoked *ex ante*, but only, if at all, *ex post*.[29] In other words, torture should be categorically prohibited, although the Court would not rule out that someone would claim 'necessity' when criminally prosecuted for torturing someone and that this claim would be accepted. But it also ruled that *ex ante* general directives governing and authorizing the use of physical means during interrogations could not be based on defences to criminal liability such as necessity.

So, there are utilitarian arguments for upholding the prohibition of torture. The costs of 'permitting' 'enhanced interrogation' or 'moderate pressure' are far greater than would appear at first sight; the slippery slope argument indeed applies. A different kind of argument can be found in an interesting observation of the Israeli Supreme Court in the case mentioned. It stated that upholding the rule of law and fundamental rights such as the prohibition on torture are essential to the democratic form of government of Israel. Allowing or tolerating torture would have an important symbolic function. This leads us back to the deontological reason for the categorical prohibition. Torture, so it is argued, is the prime example of the violation of human integrity and dignity. A society which openly or secretively allows the use of torture, implicitly acknowledges that human dignity is not its core value. Thus, making 'torture' legally or morally possible has a deleterious effect on the self-understanding of a society. By upholding the categorical prohibition on torture, on the other hand, a society publicly subscribes to the symbolism of human dignity.[30] This also seems to have been the understanding of the drafters of the Universal Declaration. The prohibition of 'torture' marks a society that takes human rights seriously.

Finally, one could ask why the prohibition on torture has such symbolic significance, more even than the prohibition on killing, which is not categorical. Someone might, again, argue that if the greater evil of a violation of the

---

[28] *Public Committee Against Torture in Israel v Israel*, 38 I.L.M. 1471 (1999), www .stoptorture.org.il//eng/images/uploaded/publications/18.pdf.

[29] Accepting that there have been cases in which physical coercion in interrogations had saved Israeli lives, www.stoptorture.org.il//eng/images/uploaded/publications/18.pdf, para. 1.

[30] Oren Gross, 'The Prohibition of Torture and the Limits of the Law', in *Torture: A Collection*, ed. Sanford Levinson (New York: Oxford University Press, 2004), 234.

right to life is permitted in some cases (see Chapter 6), why not the lesser evil of torture where the victim stays at least alive? Perhaps the answer is that it is not certain whether torture really is the lesser evil. Psychological research has shown its pernicious effect not only on those who undergo it but also on the perpetrators, however much justification they may invoke (and need). Who would claim that the life of a torturer is a good or flourishing life? While executioners who carry out a death sentence are generally not admired, those who do the 'enhanced interrogation' are generally despised, often even by the society in whose name they act. Obviously, the fact remains that being tortured is pre-eminently damaging for the victims. According to a recent analysis, this may have to do with the phenomenology of the 'evil' of torture. During torture the victim is in a perverse fashion set up against himself. He is forced to violate his own dignity and to betray himself.[31] That perhaps is the reason why this prohibition has such a high status and allows of no exceptions. 'Do not torture' is indeed the prime example of a categorical imperative, even if this prohibition is not based solely on deontological considerations. The Universal Declaration therefore rightly attaches great importance to the right not to be subjected to torture.

[31] See David Sussman, 'What's Wrong with Torture', *Philosophy and Public Affairs* (2005) 33: 1–33.

8

No One Shall Be Unfairly Punished

Few themes are so emphatically bound up with human rights as criminal law and punishment. This is surely due to the fact that the inequality of power between the state and the citizen is rarely greater than at the time when they are prosecuted and punished by the state. Also, the sanctions that can be imposed on the citizen are extremely drastic. Therefore, it is of the utmost importance that individuals are sufficiently protected against the state whenever it intends to take criminal measures against them. One of the oldest rights, which is often regarded as a precursor to human rights – as seen in Chapter 3 – is habeas corpus. This means, roughly, that when someone is arrested on suspicion of a criminal act, they must be brought before a judge without delay and informed of what they are accused of. It is not surprising then, that the Universal Declaration pays considerable attention to these kinds of situation. Thus, on the basis of Article 9, no person shall be arrested or detained arbitrarily.[1] In both cases there must be legal grounds. Further, on grounds of Article 6, every person, including suspects and criminals, have the right to be acknowledged as a person and to be treated in a respectful manner. Article 7 stipulates that everyone is equal before the law and can claim the same protection of the law as everyone else, including – as stated in Article 8 – the right to a remedy once a right has been violated. This all means that no person should ever be regarded as a kind of object against whom disciplinary or quarantine measures can be taken. Whenever criminal proceedings are initiated against a particular person, they have the right, on the basis of Article 10, to a fair and public treatment of their case, by an independent and impartial judicial body. Even though the concept of the rule of law is never mentioned in the Universal Declaration, it clearly lies implied in these provisions.

Still, it is important to note that criminal punishment as such is not a violation of human rights. The Universal Declaration does not dispute the state's right to punish, as long as the following conditions are met: punishment is the outcome of a fair trial; every person is considered innocent until criminally convicted by a court; no person shall be punished for an act that

---

[1] This Article also prohibits arbitrary exile; the themes of emigration and immigration will be further explored in Chapter 12.

was not considered by national or international law to be punishable at the time it was committed. This last condition is well-known under its Latin formulation: *nulla poena sine lege* (no punishment without law, or a legal basis) and is formulated in Art 11.[2] From a philosophical perspective, at least three major questions arise now that punishment as such is not a violation of human rights. The first question is that of the justification of criminal punishment: what is the basis of the authority of the state to punish? Next to the issue of authority is the question of the aim or the purpose of public punishment: what 'good' does it serve? The final question concerns the limits of the authority of the state to punish as a result of the *nulla poena* principle: why is the use of open norms in criminal law prohibited, and how should this principle be interpreted in politically disputed cases? Can punishment be justified if, strictly speaking, it has no basis in positive law?

The Right of the State to Punish

Concerning the right of the state to impose criminal punishment, the primary question is that of the justification of that right: why is it the state that can impose punitive sanctions on a citizen? Why is the state justified in imposing penalties on certain citizens? Or, to put the same question slightly differently, under what conditions is the state entitled to punish certain individual citizens? The further question would be: if the state has the authority to do this, what kinds of punishment may it impose and to what degree? In this regard, we have already seen (in Chapter 6) that the state may not deprive its citizens of their lives, since capital punishment is prohibited. A next question would be the following: if it is indeed the right of states to apply punitive sanctions, is this an exclusive right? In the present-day world there are international criminal bodies, such as the International Criminal Court based in The Hague, that have the authority to punish criminals too. From where do these international courts acquire this authority? Relevant as this last question may be, this chapter will leave that complicated issue relatively untouched, although at the end of this chapter some cases before the European Court of Human Rights will be considered in which international law places a role. In Chapter 2 we noted the complexity of the issue of authority and legitimacy of the International Military Tribunal at Nuremberg.[3] Indeed, the criminal code developed on the basis of an agreement between the Allied powers, the Charter of London, was contested by the accused in Nuremberg. Within the context of contemporary international criminal law, such questions have not disappeared, and

---

[2] This principle is also known as the legality principle and forms part of many legal codes, including the European Convention on Human Rights (Article 7).

[3] A similar discussion arose with regard to the criminal trial against Eichmann in the early 1960s in Jerusalem, see Thomas Mertens, 'Memory, Politics and Law – The Eichmann Trial: Hannah Arendt's view on the Jerusalem Court's Competence', *German Law Journal* (2005) 6(2): 407–24.

require detailed explanation.[4] This, however, exceeds the confines of this chapter.

To start with the issue of the legitimacy of the state to punish: why does it exist, and is it justifiable? In contemporary societies it has become almost self-evident that only the state can apply public criminal sanctions. This is the result of a historical process in which the modern state gradually gained a monopoly of power, on which, in line with Weber's definition of law mentioned in Chapter 1, the justice system is based. This is often viewed as a positive thing. There are still societies, it is true, that lack a strong central authority and where punishment is left to the victim, or the victim's family or tribe. This is a system in which punishment is, so to speak, decentralized. The main disadvantage of such a system of private punishment of criminality is that the person who is harmed and members of their family take upon themselves the role of judge and executioner in their own case. They determine for themselves that a crime or a wrong has taken place, what the crime is and the punishment that is deserved. When the same party is simultaneously victim, prosecutor, judge and executor of punishment, the outcome is unlikely to meet normal standards of fairness or objectivity. A system of private punishment can hardly be distinguished from revenge, which may easily provoke counter-revenge, with the very real risk that the violence will not stop. Humans are rarely impartial when damage, wrong or injury is done to them or to their family. While they generally take very seriously anything bad happening to them, they can easily trivialize any wrong or harm they do to others. Leaving crime and punishment to individual persons resembles the situation in the state of nature, a concept that has been introduced already. According to Locke, in the state of nature, every person has the right to punish crimes, but that is precisely the reason that the state of nature cannot be maintained. For 'men are partial to themselves, so that passion and revenge are very apt to carry them too far ... in their own cases; and their negligence and lack of concern will make them remiss in other men's cases'.[5]

The authority to punish must therefore be transferred to a central body, the state in Locke's terms. The right to punish must lie with the state, which is established, as Locke has it, by means of a social contract: all individuals have, as it were, combined their natural right to punish violations of natural law and transferred it to the state so that this right can be used effectively and impartially. The claim on a monopoly of criminal justice by the state on the basis of such a fictitious agreement between citizens does not mean, of course, that private justice will definitely no longer be pursued. The state's monopoly of 'punishment' exists due to the general belief that it exercises that authority in a legitimate manner. Where such conviction is present only to an insufficient

---

[4] A stimulating discussion here is David Luban, 'Fairness to Rightness. Jurisdiction, Legality and the Legitimacy of International Criminal law', in *The Philosophy of International Law*, ed. Samantha Besson and John Tasioulas (Oxford: Oxford University Press, 2010), 569–88.

[5] John Locke, *Two Treatises of Government*, 2.125.

degree, the risk of (a return to) private justice lurks. This can occur, for instance, when certain actions are seen as criminal in a particular culture, but do not occur in a society's official criminal code. One can think of cases of honour killings. A number of years ago a shooting took place in a school in the small village of Veghel in the Netherlands. A youth, urged by his father, attacked his sister's boyfriend because he had taken her on holiday to Turkey, contrary to the rules accepted in the culture of the family. Taking an adult young woman on a holiday, however, is not considered a criminal act according to the Dutch criminal code. For the father, who was prosecuted, the family's honour was at stake. During the trial the defence lawyer presented what is known as the 'cultural defence' as a mitigating factor, but this was rejected by the courts.[6] Private punishment is strictly prohibited. The risk of private justice also looms when criminal punishment for certain crimes, such as murder or child abuse, is considered too lenient by a part of the population.

Since the state has this claim to a monopoly of violence and prohibits private punishment, it also decides what is considered criminal and what is not, stipulates the kinds and degrees of punishment and executes these punishments. This requires public laws with which the community as a whole is supposed to consent. These laws must – in Rousseau's words – be decided by the general will and the criminal sentence in an individual case must be decided – as Montesquieu says – by a judge who is so to speak blindfolded and merely speaks the law, as its voice.[7] This seems to fit the Universal Declaration's image of criminal law as a system of laws that meets the requirement of a centralized punitive authority and of a public criminal code on which punitive measures are based. One could perhaps wonder why such punitive measures should be based on codified laws. Why not leave it to the centralized punitive body to decide in individual cases who should be punished, on what grounds and with what sentence? Why should the state be bound by criminal laws? The idea that these laws should be codified is a very old one. Perhaps the oldest codification is that of King Hammurabi of Babylon, in the eighteenth century BCE. Already there one finds the rather obvious argument in favour of the codification of criminal law. If the problem inherent in private punishing is arbitrariness and partiality, why would that problem be solved solely by centralizing punitive authority? A state could equally well be arbitrary and partial. A recent example is Nazi Germany, where criminal law was turned into an instrument of arbitrariness and terror by means, among other things, of the suspension of the prohibition on analogous interpretation.[8] This prohibition protects a suspected citizen

---

[6] Hoge Raad (Supreme Court of the Netherlands), 17 September 2002, ECLI:NL:PHR:2002:AE6118.

[7] Jean Jacques Rousseau, *The Social Contract or Principles of Political Right*, 1.6; Charles de Montesquieu, *The Spirit of the Laws*, Book 11, ch. 6: 'the national judges are no more than the mouth that pronounces the words of the law, mere passive beings, incapable of moderating either its force or rigour.'

[8] See, for the original legal documents Martin Hirsch, Diemut Majer and Jürgen Meinck, *Recht, Verwaltung und Justiz im Nationalsozialismus* (Baden-Baden: Nomos, 1997), 432–9. The suspension of the prohibition of analogous interpretation was widely discussed and enthusiastically supported

against being prosecuted for some supposedly criminal act on the basis of its analogy with an act which is criminalized. Suspending the analogy ban meant that it became possible to apply a piece of criminal legislation to a situation which was unlegislated merely because of its analogy to a situation envisioned by that legislation. If such arbitrariness were possible in the case of a centralized right to prosecute and punish, persons in the state of nature would never agree to transfer their individual authority to the state. To paraphrase Locke again: why would men be so foolish as to give themselves over to lions in order to escape the danger presented by pole-cats or foxes?[9]

The transition from private to public punitive authority is thus a positive improvement only if the state exercises its authority (and its power) on the basis of generally accepted laws because of legal certainty, which is an extremely important value. What calls for punishment, and what does not, must be fixed in advance in clear legal terms. That which is not codified as being criminal cannot be punished. This need for prior and clear codification can also be explained in another manner. When some act is not declared in advance to be criminal, one cannot, strictly speaking, be punished for such an act. This follows from the concept of punishment itself. To be punished means that a sanction is imposed on you for the transgression of a rule that was known to you. Punishment is different from, for example, the taming of an animal by means of positive and negative stimuli. Punishment presupposes rules and predictability. Indeed, a state can cause distress and pain to an individual because of an act they committed, but such distress or pain can only be understood as a punitive sanction if this individual could know that the act constituted a violation of a criminal law. This is the basic idea behind the principle of *nulla poena sine lege*: one cannot be punished for an act that one did not know or could not know was criminal. This prior knowledge forms part of the concept of punishment. Indeed, an animal, properly speaking, cannot be punished. Punishment presupposes not only an act which is criminally prohibited, but also the knowledge that this act was contrary to the law. Anglo-Saxon criminal law demands for conviction not only a reprehensible *actus reus* (guilty act) but also *mens rea* (guilty mind). For this reason, a person who clearly commits a criminal act in a state of mental disturbance cannot be punished but should instead be mentally treated.

We have now answered the first question. There are indeed good reasons to locate the authority to punish in the state and to allow it to make use of this authority only on the basis of general rules that are made public in advance. A further requirement is that it must be possible to comply with these public rules. It would be unjust to be punished for the violation of rules that one cannot possibly obey. Imagine a criminal statute that prohibited breathing or

---

by Nazi criminal law scholars, see, for example, Herlinde Pauer-Studer and Julian Fink, eds., *Rechtfertigungen des Unrechts: Das Rechtsdenken im Nationalsozialismus* (Frankfurt am Main: Suhrkamp, 2014), 91–3, 114.

[9] John Locke, *Two Treatises of Government*, 2.93.

thinking. No one could comply. Therefore, the saying *ultra posse, nemo obligatur*. No one can be held to the impossible, and positive law should take into account 'the salient characteristics of human nature'.[10] But to what can citizens be held? What basic rules and main objectives should be included in a proper criminal code? This is the second question that needs answering. Here too, the answer initially seems quite obvious: the state has the authority to punish in order to protect what deserves protecting, and this according to Locke is every human's right to life, liberty and property. Criminal law is a means to protect these fundamental interests by taking legal action as soon as these are violated. Criminal law has the aim of preventing behaviour which is contrary to these interests. Plausible as this may sound, this answer is nonetheless only partially correct, as will become apparent.

Prevention Is the Aim of Punishment

At first sight, conceiving of prevention as the aim of criminal law makes a lot of sense. It is attractive not to see punishment as a goal in itself but as a means of making society as a whole better off. It is not difficult to recognize utilitarianism as the main idea behind prevention as this aim. We remember that utilitarianism makes the moral quality of an action, including that of the state when it punishes, dependent on whether it improves the overall welfare of society. Punishment in the form of 'pain' applied to the criminal by means of a sentence in principle cannot be justified, since it reduces the overall welfare of society. One can only do such a thing when the 'pain' is compensated by the 'pleasure' it brings to society. This 'pleasure' for society can take two forms: an improvement of the behaviour of the criminal in the future, and deterrence of those who might contemplate criminal behaviour.

This is the advantage of the state of law over the state of nature. Whereas punishment in the state of nature is neither possible in a fair and unbiased manner nor can it benefit society, now, in the state of law, it proves to have beneficial effects. Punishment indeed serves the future welfare of society, either by improving the criminal, or by having a deterring effect. Clearly, then, herein lies the limitation of the right of the state to punish: punishment is only justified if it is useful for future society.[11] If not, punishment makes no sense. According to the eighteenth-century scholar Beccaria, the practical side of punishment, that is, the sentence, must be guided by this trade-off between pain and pleasure as well. In Chapter 6 we saw Beccaria advocating abolition of the death penalty and other forms of extreme physical punishment, even though it was considered normal in his time – to use the words of the French philosopher Foucault – to

---

[10] This is the reason why Hart accepts, despite his positivist approach to law, the so-called minimum content of natural law; see Herbert Lionel Adolphus Hart, *The Concept of Law* (Oxford: Oxford University Press, 1994), 193.

[11] See, for example, Ted Honderich, *Punishment: The Supposed Justifications* (London: Pluto Press, 2006), ch. 4.

execute the punishment on the body.[12] Beccaria used a utilitarian argument against these forms of punishment: cruel physical punishment makes a deep impression on the human mind, but has no lasting effect and therefore has very little deterrent effect. For a lasting deterrent effect on the potential criminal, it is necessary that the disadvantages of punishment are perceived by society to be much greater than the momentary advantages gained from crime. Therefore, a long period of incarceration is more appropriate than brief physical punishment. According to Beccaria, it is not the intensity of the pain that has the greatest effect on the human mind, but its continuance. Weak but repeated impressions are more effective than violent but momentary impulses.[13] The prospect of severe and cruel punishments can even be counterproductive: criminals who know they run the risk of say capital punishment have nothing to lose and will resort to extreme acts in order to prevent being caught. Furthermore, a system of cruel punishment has deleterious effects on society as a whole. People will lose their moral sensitivity and become blunted by it. Finally, a system of physical punishment is difficult to reconcile with the principle of proportionality. According to this principle, every punishment must stand in a proportionate relation to the crime committed. There must be a fair balance between the unjustified advantage enjoyed by the criminal as a result of their crime and the punishment as the price they must pay for it. With cruel punishments it is hardy possible to differentiate between more severe and less severe crimes. Beccaria also points out – and this is now a widely accepted view – that the best way to prevent criminal activities is to make sure that the chance of criminals being caught is high. The likelihood of being caught has greater deterrent effect than harsh punishment.

The utilitarian approach to punishment with its emphasis on prevention and proportionality led in the nineteenth century to the development of a modern system of punishment, in which the prison sentence plays a central role. Bentham made an important contribution with his idea of the panopticon, a prison of particular architecture in which the guards have a view of every inmate at all times. This idea has resulted in the so-called dome prisons, where inmates are disciplined simply through their constant visibility. Here too, the aim is to increase the well-being of society by disciplining criminals. Punishment takes place not because a crime has been committed, but so that no crime will take place in the future.[14]

---

[12] This is the main thesis of Michel Foucault in *Discipline and Punishment: The Birth of the Prison* (New York: Random House, 1978). It starts with a description of the gruesome torture the convicted Damiens has to undergo as his penalty which is then contrasted with the daily schedule of the inmates of a prison just some time later.

[13] Cesare B. di Beccaria, *An Essay on Crimes and Punishments: By the Marquis Beccaria of Milan, with a Commentary by M. de Voltaire. A New Edition Corrected* (Albany: W.C. Little & Co., 1872), http://oll.libertyfund.org/titles/beccaria-an-essay-on-crimes-and-punishments.

[14] This idea is already formulated by Seneca and attributed to Plato (Seneca, *De Ira*, 1.19): 'no wise man punishes anyone because he has sinned, but that he may sin no more.' In short and in Latin: *punitur, ne peccetur.*

This all seems quite reasonable, but this view has an important downside as well. If punishment is only legitimate if some advantage can be obtained, either special or general prevention, the question arises whether punishment must be stopped if none of these advantages can be achieved. This is especially relevant with regard to the aim of special prevention. Putting criminals in jail seldom seems to have a beneficial effect on them. Prisons are often considered colleges for criminality. At least some inmates will leave prison as hardened prisoners rather than as rehabilitated citizens. It is thus doubtful that a cost-benefit analysis of a prison system will lead to a positive outcome. What about deterrence or general prevention? When we look at the category of criminals who have committed their crimes in very rare circumstances, such as situations of war, should they be punished at all? Imagine that it is foreseeable that nobody in the future will find themselves in such rare circumstances: should such criminals not be prosecuted even though they may indeed have committed atrocious crimes because of the absence of 'pleasure' for society?

These considerations have led to several reactions. Some argue that it is better not to punish at all. These so-called abolitionists dispute the state's right to punish and want to look at criminals and criminality not in isolation, but in the context of society. Criminality is the result of injustice in society. Since the nineteenth century, thinkers inspired in particular by Marxist views have been convinced that social structures in capitalist society, especially the right to private ownership of the means of production, are wrong and have led to severe poverty and social exclusion. This is the cause of criminality. It would make no sense to react to this with severe criminal punishment, because this would address only the symptoms and not the underlying causes.[15] Some others, however, have come to a completely different conclusion. They have no problem with the fact that punishment often has no beneficial effect, because the aim of punishment is not prevention, but retribution. Those scholars argue – and here we find the main alternative justification of punishment – that the aim lies in righting a wrong. Punishment is justified as a matter of retribution: *punitur, quia peccatum est.*

Retribution Is the Aim of Punishment

In order to better understand this idea of retribution, it is useful to take a small step back. It has been said (for example in Chapter 6) that one finds at present two main schools of ethical thinking. Actions are morally evaluated either by looking at the positive or negative consequences of these actions, and such moral evaluation is forward-looking. The alternative is morally evaluating actions by looking at the motivation and the intention of the agent, and then the evaluation is backward-looking. Utilitarianism is clearly recognizable in

---

[15] A critical approach to crime and punishment is Alan Norrie, *Crime, Reason and History: A Critical Introduction to Criminal Law* (Cambridge: Cambridge University Press, 1993).

the idea of punishment as a means to prevent crime and to make society safe. The deontological approach starts with moral duty and concentrates on the intrinsic quality of an action. Kant's ethics, as discussed in Chapter 4, is a prime example of this approach. The question here is whether a punitive action as such, and irrespective of its consequences, is justified. Punishment cannot be justified merely as a means to an end, but it must be justified in and of itself. Otherwise the person who is punished is treated as a mere means and not as an end in itself. At first sight this may seem a remarkable view in the context of criminal law, but the following two examples can help to clarify the idea.

Suppose that some horrible crime is committed, and that only many years later is the criminal is caught. They committed the crime under exceptional personal circumstances. In view of their advanced age and their radically changed personal life it seems impossible that they would ever be in a position to commit such a crime again. In the intervening years they have behaved as a model citizen. Special prevention is not needed. General prevention is not served either because of the exceptional nature of the crime. Punishing this criminal would not have any beneficial effect. Would punishment therefore not be justified? Many would argue that the fact that they committed the crime is sufficient reason to punish them: they deserve punishment because of the crime. This example is not completely fictitious. Imagine a former Nazi concentration camp guard who committed hideous crimes but led a decent life after the war ended. Should he be prosecuted?[16] Many would argue that he deserves to be punished.

The following example is the opposite. A hideous crime has been committed and emotions in society are running so high that it may lead to civil unrest. The police are thus under great pressure to find the criminal or criminals but are unsuccessful so far. Would it be justified, given such circumstances, to arrest a person who might have committed the crime but is in fact innocent?[17] Justification could not be found in special prevention or rehabilitation because the person is innocent, but the arrest, prosecution and punishment would certainly have a calming, beneficial effect on society: the risk of civil unrest disappears and others in society would be discouraged from committing similar crimes. Is it permitted to let general interest override the right of an innocent person not to be punished? It would seem that the utilitarian approach does not, in principle, oppose punishing an innocent person in such exceptional circumstances. Of course, if this happened on a regular basis, the deterrent effect of criminal law in general would be endangered.

---

[16] Think of the well-known case of John Demjanjuk who was accused of being a Nazi criminal (then known as Ivan the Terrible) and was brought to trial in Israel in the 1990s.

[17] Here one might think of the Birmingham Six, arrested and convicted of bomb attacks in that city on behalf of the Irish Republican Army (IRA) in 1975, despite evidence that they were innocent. See also Herbert L. A. Hart, *Punishment and Responsibility: Essays in the Philosophy of Law* (Oxford: Oxford University Press, 2008), ch. 1: 'Prolegomenon to the Principles of Punishment'.

But this is not the case when occasionally someone innocent is sacrificed for the greater good. A deontological approach would reject this, because it holds that punishment is justified if and only if it is deserved.

A criminal conviction is not prohibited by the Universal Declaration, as has been said. Yet Article 9 opposes arbitrary detention and Article 11 condemns conviction without a fair and public trial. It seems therefore that the Universal Declaration subscribes to the deontological view: punishment must always be deserved, and in order to be convicted an accused must be found guilty of a crime, and not because it may have some individual or collective beneficial effect. Punishment by the state is thus endorsed by the Universal Declaration, but it has clear limits: the presumption of innocence, meaning that an accused can only be punished if proven guilty, and the principle of proportionality, meaning that the sentence should be proportionate to the crime and the degree of guilt. These requirements determine who can be punished and to what extent. If guilt is the determining factor in handing out punishment, then only criminals who have made a conscious choice to commit a crime can be punished. If someone commits a crime in a moment of diminished responsibility and does not, strictly speaking, bear full guilt, he must be mentally treated, but not punished.[18] Because the utilitarian approach does not require a strict connection between punishment and guilt, it does not preclude the punishment of some accused person despite diminished responsibility, because doing so may still have a deterrent effect on others. General welfare is the main goal of the utilitarian approach, not making sure that no innocent person is punished. If punishment, however, is determined by retribution, then the crucial question for punishment is whether the accused freely chose to commit the crime. Only if he did, is full punishment 'deserved'.

At this point a critical note is needed. Retributivism, at least historically, has put so much emphasis on guilt and deserts that it easily assumes responsibility, whenever there is a crime. It thus tends to overlook the social circumstances that may have led to crime. Modern criminological research indicates that claiming 'where there is crime, there is also guilt' is oversimplifying reality. Kant, perhaps the most classic protagonist of this approach, may well be a case in point because of his rigidity. Chapter 4 emphasizes that according to Kant, persons have to treat themselves and others as an end in themselves and not merely as a means. Here lies Kant's problem with justifying punishment on the basis of prevention or deterrence: a convicted criminal is then merely seen as a means in order to advance social happiness. We saw that persons are, according to Kant, beings with a free will. This needs to be presupposed because they are obligated by the categorical imperative. Therefore, his presumption is also that all criminals have chosen to commit their crimes and must face retribution. Kant acknowledges that a person is not responsible

---

[18] An excellent discussion of this can be found in Mark Tebbit, *Philosophy of Law: An Introduction* (London: Routledge, 2005). Chapters 12 and 14 are on guilty minds and on insanity.

for the 'attributes' he has been given as a natural being, such as skin colour, height, intelligence, character and social class, but he does not seem to acknowledge weakness of the will or diminished responsibilities due to extra-ordinary circumstances. Through no cause in the world, Kant writes, can a person cease to be a freely acting being.[19] In other words, Kant presupposes that a person's free will enable them to choose how to use their natural attributes, either in a morally good or in a morally bad manner. Therein lies the difference between humans and other animals. That is why a person can be punished (or praised), while animals cannot.

Kant therefore calls the criminal law a moral imperative: wherever there is a crime, punishment must follow categorically. The rigidity of this becomes apparent where Kant writes that even if the citizens of a state decide to dissolve their political unity, before doing so they must execute the last murderer that remains in prison. Every murderer deserves death, and unless these citizens obeyed this obligation, blood guilt would be clinging to them.[20] There is little room for mitigating circumstances or clemency in Kant's retributivist theory of criminal law. This seems overly harsh. Yet, there is also something to be said in favour of this rigidity. If we made punishment dependent on considerations of prevention and deterrence, as advocated by utilitarianism, we would have to be able to predict the future. But that is extremely difficult. How can one predict the deterrent effect of a particular punishment or the possibility of rehabilitating a particular criminal? And since criminals and their crimes are different, should sentencing be different as well, in accordance with their personalities and particular circumstances? Is equal treatment and equality before the law, as required by Article 7 of the Universal Declaration, guaranteed in a utilitarian theory according to which estimations of future effects of punitive measures must be taken into account? Therefore, it is perhaps best to follow Kant's position despite its rigidity, albeit not in his defence of capital punishment, and defend that applying criminal law should depend only on the principle of guilt.

For Kant the idea of retribution as the aim of punishment is intrinsically connected with the principle that similar cases ought to be treated similarly. In his view equality must not merely be understood in a formal sense, namely that lesser crimes deserve lesser punishment and that more serious crimes should be more severely punished. For Kant, equality of crime and punishment should be taken quite literally. Therefore, murder can only be punished by death, for there is no similarity between life, however wretched it may be, and death.[21] Kant admits that strict equality is not always possible, so that we do not need to follow him here altogether. Taking equality literally would lead to an eye for an eye and a tooth for a tooth, which might bring us back to private revenge instead of public punishment. We can adhere to a mere formal understanding

[19] Immanuel Kant, *Die Religion innerhalb der Grenzen der blossen Vernunft*, AA VI, 41.
[20] Immanuel Kant, *Metaphysik der Sitten*, AA VI, 333.   [21] Ibid., AA VI, 333.

of equality in the sense of proportionality. The law-giver must determine not only what counts as a criminal act, but also give guidelines as to how mild or severe criminal sentences should be.

Two major questions with regard to punishment have now been answered: what is the basis of the exclusive authority of the state to punish, and what is the aim or the goal of punishment. The answer to the first question was not difficult to find: it is reasonable to suppose that citizens would agree to provide the state with this right. To the second question two very different answers were given: prevention or deterrence and retribution. Is it possible to bring these answers together into one theory despite the difference between the utilitarian and retributivist approaches? In recent literature an effort has been made to do precisely this and thus to escape the tension between the two answers. The starting point of this effort is that the questions with regard to punishment must be formulated somewhat differently. At first the question should be raised as to what is the general justifying aim of criminal law. This question should be separated from the question of who should be punished and to what extent. If these are the three main questions, it is clear that the two approaches of prevention and retribution can be integrated. It would be nonsensical to answer the question of 'the aim' of criminal law as an institution – the criminal code, the courts, the judiciary and the judicial offices, the prison system and so on – with 'retribution'. The general justifying aim of criminal law is protecting essential human interests and establishing incentives in order to discourage potential criminals from certain courses of action by penalizing them. Here only the utilitarian answer fits. But prevention does not provide us with an answer as to who must be criminally punished and to what degree. The question of the fair application of criminal law is not answered by prevention, but by retribution and desert. Thus, as regards the question of how to distribute (to whom and to what degree), retribution gives the right answer. Only those who are guilty of committing criminal acts can be punished, and only to the degree of their guilt or culpability. To make this distribution dependent on considerations of prevention and deterrence would sever the link between crime and punishment and neglect the importance of the principle of equality before the law and that of the presumption of innocence.

This synthesis of elements of prevention and retribution is known as the unified theory on punishment.[22] It combines the two theories by giving each its proper place: prevention (and deterrence) as the general justifying aim of criminal law and retribution as the criterion of applying criminal law. It is in the interest of society to prevent criminality, but in order to answer the question of how to apply punishment, we need the principles of guilt and proportionality as derived from the concept of retribution. These principles should be regarded as categorically valid. Everybody should be punished

---

[22] Most prominently the unified theory is developed in Hart, *Punishment and Responsibility*, ch. 1: 'Prolegomenon to the Principles of Punishment'.

proportionally, and no one can be convicted unless he is criminally guilty on the basis of a pre-existing criminal law. This is the so-called legality principle, formulated in the Universal Declaration as Article 11, clause 2: 'No one shall be held guilty of any penal offence on account of any act or omission which did not constitute a penal offence, under national or international law, at the time when it was committed.'[23] Obviously, this is a very important principle. It deserves some further attention as it is not always entirely clear what it entails precisely, especially with regard to complex criminal cases.

The *Nulla Poena* Principle Is Contested

So far, we have found that every person has the right not to be punished arbitrarily, which means without a proper legal basis. This is the essence of the Universal Declaration, Article 11, clause 2. But it is not always clear what this might mean in practice. Is it always a violation of someone's human right if they are criminally punished for an act they committed when there was not a positive law explicitly prohibiting what they did? How strictly should the principle of criminal guilt be taken? In theory there is a clear moral basis for limiting the power of the state to punish on the grounds of the *nulla poena* principle. In practice, however, criminal cases occur in which a prosecutor holds that criminal guilt exists because of the violation of a criminal rule, while the defence claims that the rule did not exist. In Chapter 2 we have already encountered this problem in connection with the International Criminal Tribunal against Nazi leaders in Nuremberg in 1946. These leaders challenged the legality of the rules under which they were prosecuted because they were established after their acts. The Nuremberg Court rejected this challenge and convicted these leaders (but not all of them) nonetheless. In later cases the same problem arose; now two cases will be discussed briefly in order to show the importance of the *nulla poena* principle and the importance of legal theory.

The first case has become known as the Berlin wall shootings case. This case would never have occurred without the political developments that led to the reunification of Germany in 1990 that ended the division between West Germany and East Germany (DDR). This reunification was one of the consequences of the end of the Cold War after the collapse of the communist regimes in Eastern Europe and in the Soviet Union. Almost until that very moment, the border between the two Germanies was closely guarded, mainly to prevent DDR citizens from fleeing to West Germany. This strict border control was later regarded as one of the many political crimes of the DDR regime. After reunification the question arose as to what should be done with those individuals who had initiated and upheld this border regime. The question became particularly urgent with regard to those soldiers and border

---

[23] UN General Assembly, Universal Declaration of Human Rights, 10 November 1948, Resolution 217A, www.un.org/en/universal-declaration-human-rights.

guards who while protecting this internal German border had caused many deaths. It is estimated that around eight hundred persons died while trying to cross this border. Should those border guards and their superiors be prosecuted, despite the fact that protecting the border had a legal basis in the law of the DDR and that unauthorized crossing of the border was criminal? To put it differently: could legal action be initiated against these border guards and their political superiors who had killed those who tried to flee? Such a case could not easily be made. Obviously, there was a criminal statute in the DDR prohibiting the killing of another person, but this law was not deemed applicable to border guards when they could not stop persons from committing the crime of crossing the border in any other manner than to shoot them. In such a case, there was, according to DDR law, a justification for shooting even if this led to the death of the person. The crime of unauthorized fleeing from the DDR had to be prevented at all costs, such was the DDR law.

The legal situation can thus be summarized relatively simple.[24] During the DDR regime it was a crime to leave the DDR unauthorized on the basis of Article 213 of its criminal code. The border guards had the task of preventing illegal border crossings. Physical barriers in the form of barbed wire and minefields were put in place. Anyone who managed to cross these physical barriers could be stopped by force, possibly and as a last resort by using firearms. This was laid down in clause 27(2) of the State Border Act: 'the use of firearms is justified to prevent the imminent commission or continuation of an offence [*Straftat*] which appears in the circumstances to constitute a serious crime [*Verbrechen*].' Can one afterwards prosecute a person for such use of firearms? It would seem not: it did not constitute a criminal act at the time. The *nulla poena* principle would appear to constitute an insurmountable barrier to prosecuting and convicting those wall shooters. No one can be punished for an act which was not criminal at the time it took place. This principle rules out criminalizing acts retroactively. It was also part of the German Reunification Treaty: in the reunited Germany, criminal acts committed in the DDR would be prosecuted on the basis of the criminal code in force at that time, as demanded by the *nulla poena* principle, Article 11, Universal Declaration and the (West) German Constitution, which states in its Article 103 (2): 'an act shall not be punishable unless it has been so defined by law before it was committed.' Whether the shooting of potential escapees constituted a criminal act is a matter of the law at the time. Those border guards were, so it appears, upholding the law, not committing crimes.

Despite all this, the border guards and their superiors were prosecuted and convicted for those killings. They objected and maintained during the many

---

[24] As regard the legal situation, including the relevant criminal rules, I rely on the European Court of Human Rights, Case 34044/96, 35532/97, 44801/98, *Streletz Kessler and Krenz v Germany* [2001] ECHR. For an excellent interpretation on the matter see Robert Alexy, *Mauerschützen: Zum Verhältnis von Recht, Moral und Strafbarkeit* (Hamburg: Vandenhoeck & Ruprecht, 1993).

trials and lengthy procedures that their conviction was a violation of that principle and thus a violation of their human right not to be criminalized retroactively. This objection was put aside by all the courts involved, up to and including the highest court, the German Federal Constitutional Court and also by the European Court of Human Rights. At first instance this objection was put aside on the basis of an argument developed by Radbruch, whom we encountered in Chapter 2. The judge at first instance ruled that the State Border Act in question, which should have provided a justification for these acts, was 'intolerably' in violation of justice and had therefore lost its legal validity. The appeal of the accused that they had a legal justification for their lethal acts, carried no legal weight according to this court. They were thus convicted. One could perhaps say that in this first judgement, justice overruled positive law, including the *nulla poena* principle. None of the higher courts in these cases adopted such an outspoken natural law perspective. The higher courts rather attempted to find a basis for upholding these convictions in rules of positive law to the same effect, namely that Article 27 of the State Border Act provided no justification. When the claim of a violation of the *nulla poena* principle was finally rejected by the German Federal Constitutional Court, those former guards and their superiors turned to the European Court of Human Rights, arguing that their conviction constituted a violation of Article 7 of the European Convention: 'No one shall be held guilty of any criminal offence on account of any act or omission which did not constitute a criminal offence under national or international law at the time when it was committed. ... '.[25] However, the wall shooters did not win their case in Strasbourg either and their conviction was upheld.

Looking back at the long trajectory which in the end made the conviction irrevocable, one finds a whole list of arguments to justify this conviction despite the *nulla poena* principle. All these arguments consist in downplaying the importance of the State Border Act's Article 27. First, as we saw, it was argued that this provision intolerably violated the requirements of justice. Higher courts argued that Article 27 may indeed have been part of positive law in the DDR, but not the shooting instructions that were based on that Article. These were so indiscriminate and so extreme that they could not justify those killings. These instructions quite literally stated that those attempting to flee the DDR must be 'annihilated'. It was further argued that the *nulla poena* principle is typical of the rule of law, but that the DDR did not respect the rule of law. It did not recognize the separation of state powers nor did it subordinate the state to the law, so that the principle of legality was not fully recognized. The demands of the *nulla poena* principle cannot be separated, it was also argued, from other human rights, such as the

---

[25] Council of Europe, ETS 5, European Convention for the Protection of Human Rights and Fundamental Freedoms, as amended by Protocols Nos. 11 and 14, 4 November 1950, www.refworld.org/docid/3ae6b3b04.html.

right to leave one's country. No justification for killings could be accepted if this amounted to 'annihilating' human beings who solely tried to cross a border unarmed.

As said, all the higher German courts upheld the first court's conviction, confirming that there had not been a justification and that justice is more important than Article 27 and the subsequent instructions. The *nulla poena* principle should be understood against the background of the illegitimate regime of the DDR and therefore cannot be taken as absolute. This was also the European Court's position. It argued that there was no violation of the *nulla poena*, because the (former) DDR legal order was internally contradictory. On the one hand it contained lower legislation such as the State Border Act and these instructions, but on the other hand it contained constitutional principles in which the right to life was fully acknowledged. The border guards and their superiors should have been aware of this contradiction and should have given priority to the legal duties arising from that higher legislation, rather than to duties resulting from these lower rules. They could and should have known that those killings at the border constituted a violation of those fleeing citizens' right to life.

Of course, the case is legally closed once Strasbourg has spoken, but morally speaking there is still room for reflection. Is it true that the *nulla poena* principle is not violated because all these courts say so? One could argue that punishing these wall shooters was a politically motivated manner of dealing with an abject regime from the past. How strong is the argument that the constitutionally entrenched human right to life and the (very restricted) right to leave one's country, both part of the DDR Constitution, should have carried more weight for simple young border guards than Article 27 of the State Border Act and the instructions, so that complying with the latter norms could afterwards reasonably be construed as a violation of these higher norms and thus as already criminal at that time? Obviously, those guards were not and would not have been prosecuted in the DDR, because they had upheld the law and supported the state. Really, no violation of the *nulla poena* principle? Cynically, one might perhaps even argue that it had been sensible for the DDR to keep its borders closed. Once a DDR citizen succeeded in crossing the border, he or she was immediately granted citizenship by West Germany, even though there is no human right to acquire citizenship of another country, as we shall see in Chapter 12. Article 14 of the Universal Declaration entitles humans to ask for asylum in other states, but it imposes no duty on those states to give asylum-seekers residency or citizenship. Today, many desperate asylum-seekers try to cross the border into the European Union or into the United States and they are not welcomed enthusiastically.

With regard to these border guards, but not with regard to their superiors, *mens rea* is also an issue. These young soldiers were educated in the DDR and probably indoctrinated with its values. They would have known what these shootings resulted in the loss of lives, but probably considered their acts to be justified in the name of the DDR. Would they have been aware of the criminal character of their acts? Prosecuting their political superiors would then seem more appropriate, but then another question arises: is criminal law the appropriate tool to deal with political criminality? Other former communist states were much more reluctant to initiate criminal proceedings against former members of the communist regimes, and perhaps wisely so. It seems impossible to maintain that wherever one finds criminal guilt, punishment ought to follow, as Kant asserted. Sometimes, guilt is so great and so widespread throughout society that criminal law is either powerless or counterproductive.[26] Think of South Africa after the Apartheid regime: large-scale criminal proceedings for the many atrocities committed during Apartheid might have led to civil war. Resorting to other mechanisms, such as establishing a commission for truth and reconciliation, was judged to be a better way forward for society than criminal justice.

A second example of the difficulty of the *nulla poena* principle concerns events that took place even longer ago. It concerns the case of Vassili Kononov, convicted for war crimes he committed in Latvia more than fifty years ago when the legal case was tried. This conviction was also upheld by the European Court of Human Rights as not in violation of Article 7 of the European Convention.[27] What was the case about? In 1944, a Latvian citizen, Kononov, serving as a soldier in the Soviet Red Army, led a group of partisans in a military operation against a village in the area not far from where he grew up. These villagers were suspected of collaborating with the German occupiers. This military operation resulted in nine deaths among the villagers, including a pregnant woman. In 1998 – not long after Latvia had regained its independence – Kononov was accused, prosecuted and convicted for war crimes. Upon appeal, the conviction was upheld by the Latvian courts. Kononov finally turned to the European Court, arguing that his conviction constituted a violation of his human right not to be criminally prosecuted retroactively. In Strasbourg, Kononov was initially vindicated, but at second instance, before the Grand Chamber, his conviction was upheld. No violation of Article 7 was found.

Apparently, the Court was deeply divided about this case and especially on how to understand the law of war as it applied at that time. Were Kononov's acts in 1944 unambiguously criminally prohibited? Obviously, the humanitarian law of war prohibited certain acts as war crimes, but this law was valid between states and did not yet constitute with absolute certainty individual criminal responsibility. Such individual responsibility was established only a short time later by the Charter of London, established as the criminal code

---

[26] Reflecting on cases of widespread criminality during the Nazi regime, Karl Jaspers distinguishes between criminal, political, moral and metaphysical guilt, in *Die Schuldfrage: Von der politischen Haftung Deutschlands* (Zürich: Lambert Schneider, 1946).

[27] Here I rely, as far as the facts and the law are concerned, on Case 36376/04, *Kononov v Latvia* [2010] ECHR.

for the International Criminal Tribunal at Nuremberg. This Charter was established not only after the horrible events in Latvia had taken place, but it was also explicitly designed to prosecute only those persons who had committed war crimes in the service of the Axis powers.

According to Article 1 of that Charter, the International Military Tribunal was established 'for the just and prompt trial and punishment of the major war criminals of the European Axis'.[28] The Charter does not envision the prosecution of war crimes by members of the Allied forces, such as those committed by Kononov and his men who were fighting against the Germans. The European Court, however, brushed this problem aside and stated, rather casually in my view, that individual criminal responsibility already existed at the time. According to the Court, the London Charter did not establish individual criminal responsibility, but merely declared what the legal situation was at the time. In other words, the London Charter's prohibition on war crimes was not applied retroactively (*ex post facto*) to Kononov, because that prohibition was already valid in 1944.

The fact that the Court found no breach of Article 7 does not mean that one has to agree. What happened in this small village in Latvia was horrible, but was it criminal at that time? Kononov fought in the Red Army; the London Charter was not intended to initiate the prosecution of war crimes committed by the Allied forces, such as the bombing of open cities or the mass rape of the women of Berlin. If there were serious doubts with regard to the law valid at the time,[29] should one then not stick to the maxim *in dubio pro reo* (in case of doubt decide in favour of the accused)? Even if one accepts the principle that punishment should follow whenever there is criminal guilt, should guilt not be beyond reasonable doubt? According to Kononov, supported by the Russian Federation, his conviction was a case of applying a criminal law *ex post facto*. Whether the *nulla poena* principle is violated or not depends thus on how the law is read. Should the humanitarian law of war be read extensively, as the European Court seems to do, or narrowly, with Kononov? Valid in 1944 or not?

Both in the Berlin wall shootings case and in the Kononov case the Grand Chamber of the European Court seems to have been inspired by natural law. It considers the ill-treatment and killing of nine villagers by Kononov and his men as 'flagrantly unlawful'. Even on the 'most cursory reflection' they could have been aware of this.[30] The criminality of Kononov's acts may not have been clear on the basis of positive legal norms, but they were evidently

---

[28] United Nations, Charter of the United Nations, 24 October 1945, 1 UNTS XVI, www.un.org /en/sections/un-charter/chapter-i/index.html.

[29] Even within the Grand Chamber itself. In his dissenting opinion, Costa, the then President of the Court, writes: 'we consider that the acts in issue could not be classified as war crimes in 1944 in the absence of a sufficiently clear and precise legal basis'. See Case 36376/04, *Kononov v Latvia* [2010] ECHR; dissenting opinion of Judge Costa joined by judges Kalaydjieva and Poalelungi, para. 19.

[30] *Kononov v Latvia* (36376/04), Grand Chamber decision, 17 May 2010, para. 238.

criminal. If this is indeed what the Chamber held, then it implicitly invoked the distinction, already mentioned in Chapter 2, between *malum prohibitum* and *malum in se*. Kononov's conviction was based not so much on what was criminally prohibited (*prohibitum*) by law, but on his acts' inherently evil nature (*in se*). Punishment should follow whenever there is guilt.

9

Everyone Has the Right to Their Own Space

So far, a number of rights have been discussed that are concerned with the protection of the physical integrity of persons: the rights not to be killed, tortured or arbitrarily arrested and punished. A human being however is more than a creature concerned with their physical integrity. After the Articles that protect this integrity, the Universal Declaration enumerates a mixed series of other rights. At first sight they may give a rather random impression, as if these rights have emerged at some time in history and now had to be given a place within the new document. This impression is unjustified, since it is perfectly plausible to bring these rights under a single heading, namely as the right to have something as one's own. This chapter will discuss what I call 'the right to one's own space'. The next chapter will then be dedicated to the right to one's own property.

The Need for Space

To make clear what is meant by space, one should consult some of the classical authors, such as Aristotle. In one of his texts dealing with politics and the state one finds his well-known definition of a human being as a political animal.[1] What is meant by this is that a person can only be truly human if they are a member of a political community. Someone who does not belong to such a community is either a beast or a god. Of course, Aristotle, who also worked as a zoologist,[2] knew very well that in the animal world one also finds creatures such as bees and ants that live within communities. But, as already noted in Chapter 5, humans distinguish themselves from such creatures by the gift of speech. Social animals communicate with one another by means of voice, by which they can express what is pleasant and painful, but only humans are capable of communicating beyond that level and expressing themselves on what is useful or useless and also on what is just and unjust. Therefore, every

---

[1] Aristotle, *Politics*, 1253a.
[2] See, for example, Armand Marie Leroi, *The Lagoon. How Aristotle Invented Science* (London: Bloomsbury, 2014).

political community must offer its members the space to communicate on these issues with each other. At least this is what Aristotle suggests.

Several centuries later we find in Kant a similar, but somewhat more elaborated idea. Kant defines the human being as a creature in which two 'axes' are brought together. Humans are characterized by 'unsocial sociability'.[3] Everyone wants to socialize with others, but this disposition is accompanied by a certain resistance and by the inclination to disrupt this social union and to remove oneself from the company of others. Accordingly, human beings feel the need to share their thoughts with others, but at the same time they want to keep things to themselves. This ambivalent tendency to simultaneously socialize and isolate is, according to Kant, a good thing. Only because of this natural dual tendency is progress both on the personal and on the social level possible. They who allow themselves to be constantly led by others will not become autonomous beings. But a person who clings only to isolation shuts themselves off from the opportunity to learn from others and to contribute to society. Something similar is true for science: scientific progress is only possible because sometimes stubborn individuals abandon the well-trodden paths and blaze their own trail; but a scientific community would not be possible if there were only such headstrong individuals. It needs cooperation and sharing as well.

According to Aristotle and Kant, therefore, human nature requires space in which human beings can socialize and communicate with each other and space in which they can be on their own. It would be contrary to how humans are constituted if the state tried to drastically limit the space for humans to come together. Therefore, the existence of such space should have the status of a human right. History gives us quite a few obvious examples of societies that tried to abolish or drastically limit such societal space. According to Hannah Arendt, the totalitarian regimes of the twentieth century were a case in point. By using terror, they tried to limit and to channel the spontaneous communication between individuals and to replace it by an 'iron band' that would bind them so tightly together that their plurality would vanish into one person of gigantic dimensions.[4] Totalitarianism is an attack on human nature by its attempt to abolish that space. Some individuals in such totalitarian societies – the Sacharovs, the Grossmans, the Niemöllers, the Havels and many others – have nonetheless managed to lead a dignified human life, but for the construction of a decent society such heroic individuals cannot be regarded as the norm. It is better that a decent society acknowledges such a human right to space.

There are various manners in which such space can be realized, but in this chapter we will briefly discuss 'space' in three important domains of human

---

[3] Immanuel Kant, *Idee zu einer allgemeinen Geschichte in weltbürgerlicher Absicht*, AA VIII, 20.
[4] Hannah Arendt, *The Origins of Totalitarianism. New Edition with Added Prefaces* (New York: Harcourt Brace Jovanovich, 1973), 312–13.

life: private life, public debate and religion. Obviously, these domains are very large and therefore only a few aspects will be considered here. In later chapters, aspects of the first two domains will be elaborated further. With regard to private life the rights to property (Chapter 10) and to family and culture (Chapter 13) are important. The right to democracy (Chapter 11) is linked to public debate as its essential precondition. The importance of the right to have space for one's religious convictions for the development of the idea of human rights as such has already been mentioned in Chapter 3.

The Right to Privacy

If there indeed exists such a human right to one's space, then it must certainly include the right to organize one's own life, and not to have one's life interfered with by others or by the state. Article 12 of the Universal Declaration states that everyone must be protected by law against 'arbitrary interference in his personal affairs, family, home or correspondence', and against any 'attacks upon his honour or reputation'. While such arbitrary interference is impermissible, the state does have the authority to legally regulate on these issues, such as to decide on what counts as family or as correspondence. But when the law regulates on these matters, it should respect the legitimate interest that everyone has with regard to one's 'own space'. The question then is where to draw the line between legitimate regulatory measures on the one hand and respect for each human's private space on the other. Obviously, to mention just an example, no arbitrary interference in someone's family life is permitted, but that does not mean that no action can be taken in cases of domestic violence. Is there a criterion by means of which the domain of private space can be separated from what can be regulated because of public interest?

The utilitarian philosopher John Stuart Mill tried to give a clear answer as to where to draw this line. The state should abide by the so-called harm principle, which Mill hoped would be a quite straightforward and simple principle. Only if actions of an individual person harm or threaten to harm another individual or other individuals, may the state act to prevent or to sanction such actions. In his famous 1859 *On Liberty* Mill writes that 'the sole end for which mankind are warranted, individually or collectively, in interfering with the liberty of action of any of their number, is self-protection. That the only purpose for which power can be rightfully exercised over any member of a civilized community, against his will, is to prevent harm to others. Over himself, over his own body and mind, the individual is sovereign.'[5] From this it follows that the state has no right to interfere in one's privacy as long as one is not harming or offending others.

---

[5] John Stuart Mill, *On Liberty, Utilitarianism, and Other Essays*, ed. Mark Philip and Frederick Rosen (Oxford: Oxford University Press, 2015), 12–13.

As a utilitarian, Mill does not ground this harm principle on the human right to space. He holds that this principle is the best way to improve the overall welfare of society. This welfare is, he thinks, best served by granting liberty to individuals. Only if the law allows individuals as large a space as possible with regard to their personal affairs, their living conditions and their communication with others and the like, are they able to lead a human, satisfactory life. This will then increase the welfare of society as a whole. Therefore, it is important to separate the private and the public spheres. The state with its laws may regulate the public sphere and intervene only when the interaction of individuals threatens to lead to harm. Despite Mill's insistence on maximizing welfare, his emphasis on individual liberty fits well with the importance the Universal Declaration attributes to each individual's freedom. Mill even seems to subscribe fully to Article 4 of the French Declaration of Human Rights: liberty consists in the freedom to do everything which injures no one else.

Of course, the problem is not solved by formulating a 'simple' and 'straightforward' principle such as the harm principle, as Mill apparently hoped.[6] What constitutes 'harm to others'? Is it possible to ever attribute harm exclusively either to others or to oneself? Is it indeed possible to separate harm to oneself from harm to others? Can the act of an individual person harm the invisible fabric of society, or should a harmful act always harm specific individuals within society? Sometimes it is argued that Mill's conception of harm is too restricted, because harm does not necessarily have to be individual harm. Therefore it is argued that state regulation must go beyond merely preventing harm to specific individuals. Society consists of more than mere individuals and their individual attempts to maximize their prosperity. It also consists of norms and values that tie these individuals together and these values cannot be reduced to the individual's pursuit of happiness. Individual acts can damage the cohesion of society, even if no specific individual is harmed. Suppose that influential persons within society express themselves in an insulting way about a minority group without targeting any specific individual. Or suppose that persons in the privacy of their own homes do things that are not really harmful to others but are regarded by these others as offensive. Should that lead to the intervention of a public body in private space or not? The first example mentioned concerns the freedom of speech and whether there are limits to the freedom of speech. The second example concerns the manner in which persons organize their private and intimate lives. If individuals choose a lifestyle that differs radically from what the majority of population including their neighbours regard as 'normal', should this be accepted or is public interference permitted? When seeking an answer to these questions it turns out to make little difference whether we use the vocabulary of human rights or that of the harm principle.

---

[6] The most extensive inquiry into the harm principle probably still is Joel Feinberg, *The Moral Limits of Criminal Law*, 4 vols (Oxford: Oxford University Press, 1984–90).

Let us look a bit closer at one of these contested issues. In many societies today it goes almost without saying that sexual orientation is a matter of individual preference and free choice. This is in line with Article 12 of the Universal Declaration which prohibits 'arbitrary interference' in personal matters. But for a long time, the right to live according to one's sexual orientation was not recognized and it was unthinkable that – as has since happened in quite a number of legal systems – marriage would be open to couples of the same sex: Chapter 13 goes deeper into this. Only in the 1950s, probably under the growing influence of the harm principle and the importance given to human autonomy (as recognized in the Universal Declaration) did sexual morality, for example with regard to homosexuality, become more liberal. In the United Kingdom the Wolfenden report, named after the chairman of the responsible parliamentary committee, was very influential. Before the legal reforms initiated by this committee, homosexuality was regarded as a crime that deserved penal sanction. The committee's report recommended decriminalization of homosexuality on the basis of the harm principle. As long as mutual consent was guaranteed, there was no reason for interference by the state, even if a majority of the population considered homosexual behaviour as immoral. Immorality as such is no ground for state interference. In line with Mill, the committee argued that without individual harm, personal freedom and the right to a private space should be given priority. It is not the task of the state to educate its citizens to be virtuous persons, because what is considered virtuous is contested in a liberal society, as is the case with moral values in general.[7]

The Netherlands has seen a similar development since the 1960s. Its legislation of 1911 included 'crimes against morality', such as adultery, homosexuality, the use of contraceptives and pornography. The law was supposed to combat immorality and to stimulate a virtuous lifestyle. Only later did human rights and the harm principle become important and in combination with what is now called the sexual revolution, the Netherlands too liberalized its legislation. Without harm individual liberty should prevail, according to a parliamentary committee. The state should in principle not interfere in its citizen's private lives. Gradually, it was accepted that individual rights mattered more than moral views on what is appropriate and what is not. The prohibitions on brothels and on pornography were repealed. Unfortunately, the implementation of this liberal approach did not solve all problems. Prostitution may no longer be criminalized and the production and consumption of pornography no longer prohibited, but society does not consider, and perhaps rightly so, prostitution an ordinary profession: unemployed women cannot be compelled by the state to accept jobs in this field of

---

[7] This report was widely discussed; the most important texts are by Patrick Devlin, 'Morals and the Criminal Law' and Herbert Lionel Adolphus Hart, 'Immorality and Treason', both to be found in Ronald Dworkin, *The Philosophy of Law* (Oxford: Oxford University Press, 1977), 66–82, 83–8.

work when there are vacancies, even if they then would no longer be in need of social benefits. The free availability of pornography (on the internet) today is not necessarily an enrichment of society. Nor did the decriminalization of prostitution bring to an end the exploitation and trafficking of (mainly) women.

In the terminology of the two freedoms, the right to private space can indeed be understood as a form of 'negative freedom', namely the right to be free from interference by the state. That same right can however also be regarded from the perspective of positive freedom. Some would perhaps say that the right to have one's private life organized according to one's own views contributes to autonomy. Others might perhaps argue that the freedom to consume pornography or to visit prostitutes does not contribute to leading an autonomous life and that freedom should be the means to lead a life of human dignity. As long as the right to private space is used in very different ways by different persons, there will be a discussion on what is morally reprehensible and what is not, and on whether the state should put restrictions on how to make use of the right to private space. Where the boundaries lie between what belongs to the private sphere and what to the public space will remain contested. Those in favour of the harm principle will be challenged by those who emphasize the importance for society of shared moral values. This debate on the boundaries between the private and the public spheres is equally important when discussing the right to participate in public debate.

The Freedom of Expression

Private space gives individuals the opportunity to organize their lives autonomously. Freedom of expression gives them the opportunity to contribute to the formation and organization of their communal life by expressing their viewpoints. Aristotle said that humans have speech in order to establish what is useful and what is not, and what is justified and what is not. This freedom to communicate is formulated in Article 19 of the Universal Declaration, granting every human being the right to hold an opinion 'without interference' and 'to seek, receive and impart information and ideas through any media and regardless of frontiers'. One gets the impression that this is a very comprehensive right, but is it unlimited? Sometimes it seems that everyone, especially on the internet, now claims the right to say and write whatever they like. But Article 12, just discussed, mentions a limit to the freedom of expression, namely that every person has the right to be protected against 'attacks upon [their] honour and reputation'. Obviously, freedom of expression is a very important right and it is also part of the European Convention on Human Rights and of the International Covenant on Civil and Political Rights. But here too, limits are explicitly mentioned and they include not only harm to reputation, but also concerns of national security, public safety and health and even morals.

Should it come as a surprise that this important right is immediately constrained by such broadly formulated limitations? Is public debate not of such importance to a democratic society that there should be no limit on what can be said and published? Isn't freedom of expression the guarantee for every person to be able to contribute to the formation and the organization of society? The Universal Declaration subscribes to the importance of such a free debate. Contrary to totalitarian and dictatorial regimes where this free-dom is absent, democratic societies subscribe to it in theory, but in practice they often wish to exercise oversight over what is being said and published. The emotions when this happens – think, for example, of the controversy sur-rounding the Danish cartoons depicting the prophet Mohammed in a negative manner – frequently run high and there seems to be little consensus on how to understand the freedom of expression and its limits.

Perhaps it is helpful here to reflect on what a right in general is. Its structure has already been used in earlier chapters and will be further explored in Part IV. In contrast to 'the law' as the totality of all valid legal standards within a particular territory and period of time, a subjective 'right' is a concept that is relational in the sense that the person who has a right is authorized to put someone else under an obligation.[8] Now it is rarely the case that complete authorization lies with the holder of a particular right – in this case freedom of expression – and the corresponding duty completely on the bearer of the duty – all others. This is perhaps only the case with regard to the right not to be tortured where the duty not to torture is valid irrespective of what the holder of that right has done. This is due to the categorical nature of this right, but even this is not, as we have seen, uncontested.[9] But with regard to perhaps all other subjective rights it is simply not the case that the right holder has complete authorization and the duty bearer mere obligations. Think of the right to participate in elections: everyone who has that right has at the same time the duty to comply with the procedural rules with regard to the actual voting. Or think of the right to life: right-holders are obliged to respect the right to life of others. Otherwise they might forfeit their own life (in a criminal system that accepts the death penalty). Something similar can be argued with regard to the freedom of expression. As a human right it is shared by all human beings. But this sharing implies procedures and rules to enable everyone to have their say. No one can express their viewpoint if all others do the same thing at the same time. Even parliament, in which members of parliament have a more extended freedom of expression than ordinary citizens, has procedural rules as to who can speak at what moment and for how long. Without rules to coordinate limited speaking time, one would end up with a parliament of fowls.

---

[8]   I here follow Kant's definition of a right, as the authorization to put another under an obligation and to use coercion against someone who infringes upon that right. See, for example, Immanuel Kant, *Metaphysik der Sitten*, AA VI, 230–1.

[9]   Jeremy Waldron, 'What Are Moral Absolutes Like?', *The Harvard Review of Philosophy* (2012) 18: 4–30.

There is another important element that needs mentioning here, namely that freedom of expression is one right among many. We have seen that the Universal Declaration consists of a collection of individual rights, and this presupposes that each of these rights should be considered in relation to the other rights. If freedom of religion is acknowledged – as is the case – it is the duty of the holder of the right to freedom of expression to ensure that this right is compatible with that other right. Therefore, it is better, as Rawls rightly suggests,[10] that the principle of equal freedom for all does not apply to isolated rights, but to all fundamental rights taken together, so to speak as a package. Equality means that the totality of rights of the one is compatible with the totality of rights of all others. Individual rights must thus be considered in relation to other rights and to other right-bearers.

Again, it is not at all exceptional that fundamental rights and liberties are limited. Consider the following example. On the basis of Article 13 of the Universal Declaration everyone has the right to free movement within the borders of their state. So, on a fine spring day I can make a tour on my racing bike, but making use of this right does not mean that during my bike ride I can ignore traffic rules. My freedom to cycle must be compatible with the freedom of others to make use of the roads as well and with the interests of society as a whole. The state has the right to ban certain parts of the public road system to cyclists, for instance motorways. For the protection of important officials it might be necessary to limit the freedom of movement of ordinary citizens by excluding them from certain areas. Such limitations only constitute a violation of the human right to freedom of movement if one wrongly holds that having rights contradicts having duties. No one would reasonably argue with the idea that a limit can be placed on the right to freedom of movement. Because some course of action is a right for everyone, it is indeed necessary to have a system that in principle allows everyone to perform such actions.

The fact that freedom of expression is a right of all implies a degree of respect for other people's opinions. Generally speaking, there are two justifications for the right to freedom of expression, and both imply such respect. The first of these is instrumental, considering that no single person really knows the way society can be best organized. Therefore, it is necessary that numerous opinions on this subject are expressed, on the basis of which the best or most convincing can then be selected. This argument is also often heard in academic circles: free competition of ideas is needed, in order that in the final analysis the best idea may emerge. Just as in academia, society has no benefit from censorship. It rather needs a certain openness to what every person has to impart. The second justification for freedom of expression starts with the idea that humans are autonomous beings and on this basis each of them always has the

---

[10] John Rawls, 'The Basic Liberties and Their Priority', in *Political Liberalism* (Cambridge, MA: Harvard University Press, 1993), 289–370.

right to make their opinions or views public. Respect for somebody else's view is necessary, namely for their autonomous status.[11]

The right to freedom of expression is not limited only by the reasons inherent in this specific right, but also, as Rawls says, because of other rights. We have already seen that no one can claim freedom of expression for the mere purpose of slandering someone else's reputation or good name. It is most certainly not easy to decide beforehand when the exercise of freedom of expression constitutes mere defamation or a valid contribution to public debate. Still, the mere fact that the right to have one's reputation protected exists along with the right of free expression in the Universal Declaration means that the possibility exists of a clash between these two rights. Many legal systems have rules in place, in both private and criminal law, to protect individuals from defamation or intrusions into their privacy. Freedom of expression can also be limited because of the general interests of society. A well-known example is that no one can claim freedom of expression when shouting 'fire' in a crowded cinema, thereby causing mayhem, when no fire is anywhere to be seen.[12] On the basis of Mill's harm principle the freedom of expression cannot be acknowledged when it would lead to a situation of a 'clear and present danger'. The international human rights covenants acknowledge public safety, order, health and rights and freedoms of others as possible justifications for limiting this right. Freedom of expression may not be used to evoke hate or to incite violence. Nor is it permitted to violate duties of professional confidentiality, of, for example, lawyers or medical doctors, by appealing to freedom of expression.

The European Convention mentions 'moral decency' as a limiting ground. Certain well-known and scarcely contested limitations on freedom of expression fall in this category. Many states have criminalized racist expressions, expressions of Nazi sympathies, or anti-Semitism and the denial of the Holocaust. Generally, such prohibitions are not regarded as violations of the freedom of expression. Whereas statements defending the view that the sun circles the earth, or that Father Christmas truly exists, might be regarded as false, but rather innocent beliefs, this is not the case when someone for instance denies the Holocaust. Such expressions are not merely insulting to the victims and their descendants but are also in conflict with moral decency, or – perhaps put better – with the fundamental values of the Universal Declaration.

In conclusion, freedom of expression can only be exercised when consistent with similar rights of others and with fundamental values of society. There is little reason to give this particular right a paramount status, higher than, for example, the right to privacy, religion or property. This is not to downplay the

---

[11] Ronald Dworkin, 'Why Must Speech Be Free?' in *Freedom's Law: The Moral Reading of the Constitution* (Oxford: Oxford University Press, 1996), 195–213.

[12] For a careful analysis of the case law in the US see Rawls, 'The Basic Liberties and Their Priority', 340–56. See also Jeremy Waldron, *The Harm in Hate Speech* (Cambridge, MA: Harvard University Press, 2012).

importance of the right to freedom of expression. In a pluralist society it is important that many different opinions and ideas can be voiced. When certain media concerns have attained a dominant position within society it may be the case that particular views are frequently heard whereas others remain unnoticed. Organizations such as Freedom House draw attention to the multiple ways in which freedom of expression can be endangered.[13] It is detrimental not only to freedom of expression but also to democracy when, for instance, elections are decided by who has the most money to spend on an election campaign.

Right to Freedom of Religion

So far we have discussed the 'right to space' as the right to private life and the right to express oneself and to contribute to public debate. But it also includes the right to adopt a certain attitude or view to life in general. This right is found in Article 18 of the Universal Declaration, on the basis of which 'everyone has the right to freedom of thought, conscience and religion'. It includes, among other things, the right to practise, alone or with others, one's religion or belief, both in private and in public. It prohibits coercion in religious matters, although, obviously, parents may raise their children in accordance with their own convictions. This right is not without limitations. The European Convention on Human Rights and the International Covenant on Civil and Political Rights mention that these limits must be based in law, be necessary in a democratic society and concern – similarly to freedom of expression – public safety and order, health and morals.

Freedom of religion – and certainly freedom of conscience – goes back a long way. For a long time, it was held that even if political authority and religious authority were not the same, they were at least closely connected to each other. In the particularly influential Epistle to the Romans, St Paul, regarded by some as the real founder of Christianity, stated that everyone must obey the governing authorities to which they are subject, for there is no authority except that which God has established.[14] In the modern era, however, the spheres of politics and religion are separate; the idea of the state as being neutral in religious matters, and the right of individuals to choose their own religion or not to have any religious belief have emerged as the result of a long historical development, which was mentioned in Chapter 3. Under the influence of the reformist ideas of Luther and Calvin in the sixteenth and seventeenth centuries, controversies emerged in Europe as to the true version of Christianity. These religious controversies brought about the devastating religious wars of early modernity, most notably the Thirty Years War. Political

---

[13] See Freedom House, 2018, https://freedomhouse.org/.

[14] Romans, 13:1. This position, with an important proviso, is still defended by Kant. He writes (*Metaphysik der Sitten*, AA VI, 371): 'Obey the authority that has power over you (in whatever does not conflict with inner morality).'

leaders, mainly kings, saw it as their duty to defend what they regarded as the true version of Christianity and to impose it on their subjects. Yet, because of the horrors of these wars, those political leaders decided in the 1648 Peace of Westphalia, primarily for pragmatic reasons, to give up their hegemonic ambitions and to accept that each leader would decide on the form of Christianity within their own territory (*cuius regio, eius religio*). Only later was a minimal religious freedom accepted, meaning no more than the mere right to have one's own religious convictions (but not to express them).[15] Over time, however, this minimal right gradually developed into freedom of religion and then led to the neutrality of the state with regard to the religious convictions (and differences) among its subjects. This position was adopted in Article 10 of the French Declaration of the Rights of Man and Citizen. With the separation between church and state and the right of all humans to choose and to practise their religion, the principle of toleration became institutionalized. Even in a state with a clear religious majority, minorities have the right to practise their own religions or to reject any religion and to criticize religious views, as some atheists do.

The legal acknowledgement in principle of religious freedom does not determine how much space shall be given to religious convictions and practices or to churches. At present, states within Europe, for example, have institutionalized very different regimes with regard to the relation between church and state. Some of them have opted for quite secular regimes whereas others have not. Think for instance of the United Kingdom, where the head of state is also the head of the Church of England. The human right to freedom of religion does not dictate what regime should be adopted. There are also limitations as to what can be called a religion. It is certainly not the case that anyone can just establish a church with some friends or business colleagues. Not every claim to 'religion' or 'church' can be recognized. A number of years ago, a brothel in the Amsterdam red light district advertised itself as a 'religious community' with quite unusual rites. It was however clear that this 'community' had made a religious claim because of the tax advantages attached to having the status of a church. In court this 'church's' claim was rejected. Sometimes, however, it is more complicated to determine whether a particular community is a church or not. Think of the Church of Scientology, which is tolerated by some states but is contested in others, for instance in Germany. Is it indeed a church, or a rather abusive society? Another complex issue is what can be claimed as a religious practice or requirement. On the one hand, every human being has the right to practise their belief. On the other hand, no human right comes without responsibilities. Therefore, there must be limits to religious practices. When certain religious

---

[15] Ben Vermeulen, 'The Freedom of Religion in Article 9 of the European Convention on Human Rights: Historical Roots and Today's Dilemmas', in *Freedom of Religion*, ed. Bram van de Beek, Eddy van der Borght and Ben Vermeulen (Leiden: Brill, 2010), 9–30.

groups hold to the idea that children may not be vaccinated against particular illnesses ('the Lord gives, and the Lord takes away'), or that their children should not be subjected to compulsory public education, then such beliefs are not automatically accepted.[16] Some religious demands can in no way be met. When a particular religion prescribes human sacrifice, and certain persons with an eye to their future spiritual well-being put themselves voluntarily forward for this end, this demand is still unacceptable.

Conflict between 'Spaces'

It is indeed very important to have the space to shape one's private life, to be able to voice one's opinions about society and to have one's own philosophy of life as a whole. However, that does not mean that these various aspects of the right to space always fit smoothly together. It happens quite often that the organization of one kind of space is difficult to reconcile with that of another kind. As a first example: the right to freedom of religion includes the right of parents to bring up their children according to their religious convictions. But that right also includes everyone's right to alter their religious belief or philosophy of life, and in those areas outsiders shall not exercise any pressure. These aspects of the same right may lead to conflicts, when the right of parents to educate their children religiously clashes with the right of adolescent children to change or reject that religion. In Chapter 13 we will discuss another related clash: on the grounds of the parents' right to bring up their children in accordance with their own beliefs, they might claim that the public space for their school-going children must be free of religious symbols. Should the school or the state accommodate this?

A second example concerns the tension between freedom of speech and freedom of religion. On the basis of the former it should be permitted to make derogatory comments about religion in general and specific religions in particular, as long as these comments do not incite hatred or violence. Criticism of religion is simply part of the discussion on how to organize society in the best possible manner. Problems arise when criticism of religion can easily be interpreted as criticism of those for whom religion – on the grounds of freedom of religion and their right to private space – is essential. Not only is their freedom of religion then at stake but also the protection of their reputation, for example according to Article 10 of the European Convention on Human Rights. Where does the exercise of one right stop in order not to violate the exercise of another right? Does the right to freedom of speech include the right to insult? A similar clash occurs when on the grounds of religious freedom, homophobic opinions are voiced that run counter to the right to private space,

---

[16] Here one finds a clear health concern. For an excellent discussion of this issue, see Roland Pierik, 'Mandatory Vaccination. An Unqualified Defence', *Journal of Applied Philosophy* (2018) 35: 381–98.

such as one's own sexual orientation. All freedoms have their boundaries, but how to decide when these boundaries can be drawn in different ways? Who makes the final decision as to where they lie in a particular case? Not everything that presents itself as a religion can be accepted as such. After all, a brothel is not a church. But what to do when, on the grounds of freedom of speech, influential public persons denounce a particular religion such as Islam as a mere political ideology? Where to draw the line between a religion and an ideology? Do not all religions have views on what society should look like? Precisely on the grounds of freedom of religion and the separation of church and state, the state must be neutral and cannot claim to be able to decide what religion is or is not. That was the lesson learned from the wars of the sixteenth and seventeenth centuries: the claims of truth of conflicting religions should be put in parenthesis in order for an orderly living together of persons with different views to be possible.

10

Everyone Has the Right to Property

The right to property will now be considered as the last of the so-called negative rights. This is obviously an important right. After all, human dignity presumes not only that a person has control of their life and their physical integrity, that they cannot be subjected to criminal procedures without a proper reason and that their physical and mental space cannot be arbitrarily invaded, but also that their property, 'the mine and thine', is respected. Humans must be able to have what is theirs, to support themselves, and for that they need property. Article 17 of the Universal Declaration stipulates that everyone has the right to own property alone as well as in association with others. It also declares that no one shall be arbitrarily deprived of their property.

It was obvious that the Universal Declaration would include a provision for the right to property, since it was the successor to the eighteenth-century declarations of human rights, in which this right played an important role as well as in the revolutions of that period. This right featured prominently in the French Declaration, where property is considered 'an inviolable and sacred right'. No one should be deprived of their property unless 'public necessity, legally determined, shall clearly demand it' and if the owner is 'previously and equitably indemnified'.[1] The need to include the right to property was also evident in the light of more recent events. Not only during World War II, but also in the period leading up to it, large groups of people had been mercilessly deprived of their property. The best-known example of such expropriation – or more accurately, state robbery – concerned the Jewish population. Before the war some, mainly rich, Jews could leave Germany by, as it were, 'buying' their right to emigrate,[2] which resulted in them arriving totally destitute in the surrounding countries, which were, moreover, mostly very reluctant to let

---

[1] Declaration of the Rights of Man and Citizen, Paris, 26 August 1789, www.conseil-constitutionnel.fr/sites/default/files/as/root/bank_mm/anglais/cst2.pdf.

[2] The method of doing this accurately was the result of the (legal) work of many but especially Adolf Eichmann, who was considered an expert, especially in Vienna after Austria's unification with Nazi Germany. See David Cesarani, *Eichmann: His Life and Crimes* (London: Vintage, 2004).

them in.[3] Later the property of the less well-to-do Jewish population, both within Germany and in the occupied countries, was completely confiscated. According to some historians, the Nazis were able to maintain German morale and continue the war economically only because of the robbery on such a large scale in the occupied lands.[4] It was only towards the end of the war that the German population suffered from poor living conditions. Nazi Germany was certainly not alone in disrespecting property rights. Similar stories can be told of the territories occupied by the Japanese, not to mention the confiscations in the Soviet Union which led to horrendous famines in Ukraine, nowadays called the Holodomor.

In response to these flagrant violations of the right to property it was necessary to reconfirm this right. Nonetheless, the victims of these involuntary property transfers, or their descendants, encountered many difficulties when they claimed their property back after the war. Especially, restitution claims with regard to art objects led to protracted procedures. For instance, the prominent Nazi Field Marshal Hermann Göring was a fanatical art collector and had managed to lay his hands on many important works of art during the war. After the war these works, many of which had fallen into the possession of the various states in which these objects had been stored, and had then found their way into national museums, were reclaimed by their owners or the owner's heirs. This often led to long and complicated judicial procedures. In a quite recent case, it was decided that a Madrid museum would be allowed to keep a Pissarro painting, despite the fact that it originally belonged to a German Jewish family and had been taken from them by the Nazis.[5]

The Right to Property in Human Rights Conventions

For other reasons, however, it was not so obvious that the right to property would be included in the Universal Declaration. The manner in which and the degree to which (private) property is regulated by the law determines to a large extent the shape of society. A capitalist regime that allows a great deal of space for private property and for market transactions is very different from a communist regime in which the collective means of production are in the hands of the state and private property plays only a limited role. Both 'regimes' were represented in the United Nations and in the commission which was to

---

[3] A moving account on this can be found in the biography of the wife of the famous philosopher and Kant scholar, Cassirer. Toni Cassirer, *Mein Leben mit Ernst Cassirer* (Hamburg: Felix Meiner, 1981).

[4] See, for example, Götz Aly, *Hitlers Volksstaat* (Frankfurt am Main: Fischer, 2005). Translated as *Hitler's Beneficiaries: Plunder, Racial War and the Nazi Welfare State*, trans. Jefferson Chase (New York: Holt, 2008).

[5] Raphael Minder, 'Court Rules Spanish Museum Can Keep a Painting Seen as Nazi Loot', *New York Times*, 1 May 2019, www.nytimes.com/2019/05/01/arts/design/court-rules-spanish-museum-can-keep-a-painting-seen-as-nazi-loot.html. See also the 1988 Washington Principles on Nazi-Confiscated Art (www.lootedartcommission.com/Washington-principles).

draft the Universal Declaration. Given its universal character, it was not meant to choose between these two regimes. Therefore, Article 17 declares that everyone has the right to property 'alone as well as in association with others'.[6] Thus, Article 131 of the Constitution of the Soviet Union – then in force – did not contradict this provision, even though it emphasized collective ownership and the duty of every citizen 'to safeguard and strengthen public, socialist property as the sacred and inviolable foundation of the Soviet system'.[7]

It is therefore little wonder that it was difficult to 'translate' Article 17 into the human rights conventions. The International Covenant on Civil and Political Rights does not contain any allusion to the right to property, nor does it figure in its socio-economic counterpart, the International Covenant on Economic, Social and Cultural Rights. Article 15 of that convention, however, adopts for every person the protection of their scientific, literary and artistic production. However, this is not an application of Article 17 but of Article 27, second clause. The European Convention on Human Rights, drawn up shortly after the Universal Declaration, does not contain the right to property either. This right was only added years later to that Convention, as its first protocol. Its careful and complicated formulation is telling:

> Every natural or legal person is entitled to the peaceful enjoyment of his possessions. No one shall be deprived of his possessions except in the public interest and subject to the conditions provided for by law and by the general principles of international law. The preceding provisions shall not, however, in any way impair the right of a State to enforce such laws as it deems necessary to control the use of property in accordance with the general interest or to secure the payment of taxes or other contributions or penalties.[8]

On the basis of this protocol a couple of rules with regard to property have been developed, such as that property has to be respected and that the state must in principle refrain from interfering in the property of any natural and legal person. Infringement of the right to property by means of confiscation or regulation is possible only in the general interest, on the basis of statutory provisions and justificatory grounds. Furthermore, case law has made it clear that 'property' must be understood broadly.[9]

---

[6] UN General Assembly, Universal Declaration of Human Rights, 10 November 1948, Resolution 217A, www.un.org/en/universal-declaration-human-rights.

[7] This is from the *1936 Constitution of the USSR*, trans. Robert Beard (Lewisburg: Bucknell University, 1996), www.departments.bucknell.edu/russian/const/36cons04.html.

[8] Council of Europe, European Convention for the Protection of Human Rights and Fundamental Freedoms, as amended by Protocols Nos. 11 and 14, 4 November 1950, ETS 5, www.refworld.org /docid/3ae6b3b04.html.

[9] Property not only consists of physical goods, but also includes, for example, shares (Case 15375/ 89, *Gasus Dosier- und Fordertechnik GmbH v The Netherlands* [1995] ECHR) and intellectual property, as we will see later in this chapter.

Since the right to property is so important and so extensive, it is simply not possible to discuss it here completely. This chapter will discuss only a few themes that are particularly relevant for legal philosophy. It will move away, especially in the beginning, from positive law. The first part of this chapter considers important modern and present-day philosophical positions regarding property. Next, attention will be given to the place of property in our present society and try to answer the question as to how far that right may reach. Can anything and everything become someone's property? Finally, we will have a brief look at intellectual property.

A Brief History of the Modern Concept of Property

Perhaps it seems odd when considering property to go back to Adam and Eve, but the book of Genesis contains two elements that crop up regularly in ideas on property. These two elements even reflect the two axes of the human being. The first element is the idea that God made man in his own image after his likeness in order to rule over the earth and everything in it. On the basis of this, it is often argued that the earth and everything on it is the common property of mankind as a whole. As a consequence of the fact that the earth – to use a modern concept – is a *commons*, private property needs to be justified. The second element is that God exiled Adam and Eve from paradise after they had eaten from the Tree of Knowledge of Good and Evil. Thenceforth, they had to earn their bread by the sweat of their brows. This means making an individual effort, that is labouring, in order to make a living. Since the fall, the earth that has been given to humankind as common property is no longer so generous that everyone, without effort, can enjoy its fruits. There is scarcity, says the Bible, and we must work. It is only a slight exaggeration to say that the discussion about the right to property is the ongoing demonstration of the tension between common property on the one hand and private property as the result of everyone's individual effort, by means of work and acquisition, on the other.

In the Middle Ages Thomas Aquinas took common property as the starting point.[10] No one may keep for himself that which belongs to another. Because God created the earth, He is the ultimate owner. However, one may, according to Aquinas, distinguish between the 'nature' of the earth and its 'use'. Even though it is the nature of the earth to be God's property, humankind can make use of it for their own ends. In the context of that usage the institution of private property is readily defensible. According to Aquinas, humans care much better for those things that they consider their own than for things that are common to all or to the many, 'since each one would shirk the labour and leave to another that which concerns the community'. For reason of order and peace it is also better that humans have individual care for external

---

[10]   Here I rely on Thomas Aquinas, *Summa Theologica*, Secunda Secundae, Questio 66.

matters: human affairs will then be conducted in a more orderly fashion and quarrels will arise when such a division of things is absent.

However, if an individual person then makes use of property as their own, they must not act as if what they own is exclusively theirs. They must consider things from the perspective of the commons. Following the apostle Paul, Aquinas holds that the rich should be generous and succour those in need. According to this view, the poor do not even need to wait for the generosity of the rich when they are in dire need. Some would argue that theft is wrong in all circumstances, but this is not true according to Aquinas. In cases of need the human institution of private property has to give way to the natural law of the commons. The original rule that everything is given to humankind as a whole trumps the private law rules according to which a division of things has taken place, because 'whatever certain people have in superabundance is due, by natural law, to the purpose of succouring the poor'. For Aquinas there is no such thing, as the French Declaration has it, as a 'holy and inviolable' right to private property. According to Aquinas, natural law does not prescribe a particular manner in which private property must be instituted. God has given the earth to humankind to fulfil their needs and therefore any human system of dividing private goods loses its validity in the case of obvious and extreme necessity. Consequently, private property is, in his view, not a human right. Aquinas's view accords much better with Article 25 of the Universal Declaration, which states that everyone has the right to a standard of living adequate for the health and well-being of themselves and their family.

This balance between commons and private property has clearly shifted when we consider the influential view of John Locke in his *Second Treatise on Government*, published a few centuries later.[11] At first sight it may seem as if little has changed, since biblical sources are for Locke too of paramount importance: God has given the earth to the whole of mankind in common. But while Aquinas accepted the institution of private property only as a means to manage efficiently this common property for the benefit of all, private property becomes crucial for Locke. Even though he confirms that in the end humankind itself belongs to God (as is noted in Chapter 6 with regard to human life), he nonetheless accepts a strong institution of private property and considers individual labour as its origin. Since humans are the owner of the investment of their labour, they are also the owners of its fruits. In other words, Locke considers private labour as the origin of private property. Humans add value to nature by their labour and to this added value no other person can make any claim than the labourer, even though the earth is originally given to all. For Locke, therefore, the second element taken from Genesis becomes crucial: When God gave the world to all mankind, He also commanded them to labour.

---

[11] Here I rely on John Locke, *Two Treatises of Government*, 2.5.

Now the following rejoinder is obvious. If someone acquires private property as the result of labour, do they not then remove something from the common store in order to do that? By so doing the common store seems to be reduced to the disadvantage of all others. Locke rebuts this contention with a whole series of arguments. First, he states that God gave humankind the earth in common with the intention that it should be cultivated, not that it should lie unused. Thus, the earth is not for 'the quarrelsome and contentious', but for the 'industrious and rational', who develop it through their labour. In this way, the 'original' common property is presented as a sort of situation prior to private property, not as something that can be invoked in the case of necessity. Second, Locke introduces a proviso. If someone picks something up from the common store and starts cultivating say a piece of land thereby taking possession of it, they must leave sufficient land ('enough and as good') for others: 'for he that leaves as much as another can make use of, does as good as take nothing at all.' The transformation of parts of what was originally held in common into private property is thus not, according to Locke, to the disadvantage of anyone, as long as no one takes more for themselves than they can use. Nothing was made by God for humans to spoil or destroy.

Locke's third argument is the decisive step in the justification of private property: the enormous increase in value as a result of labour. If we were to compare the value of what God gave to mankind in common and the value that is created by the private labour of human beings, then the relation would be closer to one to a hundred (or even a thousand) than to one to ten. So even though Locke subscribes to the common ownership of the earth, he downplays its importance. The commons have little value or significance compared to what the labour of (industrious) human beings adds to it. Look at America, Locke writes, where 'a king of a large and fruitful territory there feeds, lodges and is clad worse than a day-labourer in England'.

Here a follow-up rejoinder comes up: how is it possible that – on the basis of this theory – some men turn out to be 'day-labourers' and others find themselves able to take into service these labourers? After all, the proviso stipulates that no one may own more than is needed for their own use and that it is not permitted to let things decay. On this basis there seems to be little room for large differences in private property. Locke replies as follows. The limits on private ownership on the grounds of one's own use and the prohibition of decay are raised at the moment when the surplus products acquired through someone's industrious labour could be exchanged for things 'that fancy or agreement hath put the value on' – such as gold, silver and diamonds. The invention of these special 'things' and later of money in which value can be stored meant that persons could preserve their surplus value without the risk of decay. One could then of course object: if economic value is stored by some, is there still 'enough and as good' for others? It is easy to understand that enough remains for others as long as private ownership is limited to what an individual person can accumulate for the use of themselves and their family. But this is perhaps no longer the case after the invention of money and other precious goods enabled the few to acquire property on a large scale. According to Locke, however, the proviso is still met after the invention of money when accumulating capital becomes possible, since it remains true that the origin of economic value does not lie in that which God gave to all human beings in common, but in human labour. If some industrious persons cultivate certain parts of the earth as common property of humankind and thereby become wealthy, it is still the case that the overall value has increased and that this will in the end be beneficial for all.

One notices here the development of a whole new concept of property. In Aquinas's thought, common property still played a central role, but this is no longer the case with Locke. He attributes the status of natural law not to common property but to private property. Of the two elements found in Genesis, priority is given now to God's command to (individually) cultivate the earth. The emphasis is not on the earth as divine creation, but on the (human) right to private property as the result of one's labour. The introduction of money removes any quantitative limitation on private property; the inequality between persons with private property and those with little or no property at all finds a basis in natural law.

It would obviously go too far to call Locke the sole inventor of capitalism, but nowhere else at that time can one find such an influential defence of private property. According to Locke the right to private property can be found in the state of nature and it is built on the tacit consent of all because of the enormous increase of economic value. Therefore private property can only be regulated but not abolished in the political state. For Locke, the creation of private property comes prior to the establishment of the political order; its raison d'être merely securing, protecting and regulating claims of private property. While Aquinas holds that the rules of private property are merely a matter of positive law, these rules now acquire the status of natural law. Locke is not alone in the view that the 'preservation of their property is the chief end of men uniting into commonwealths and putting themselves under government'.[12] Although Kant – more than a century later – rejects labour as the basis for private property (and instead insists on the right of first acquisition[13]), he too holds that law concerning private property is prior to the state and that it is not the task of the state to redistribute property in order to make its citizens more economically equal.[14]

It is not surprising that in the nineteenth century Marx regarded the right to property as the pivotal human right. He labelled it as egoistic, as a right to care only about oneself, and he rejected it as a legitimation for capitalism. Since

---

[12] Locke, *Two Treatises of Government*, 2.9.

[13] Immanuel Kant, *Metaphysik der Sitten*, AA VI, 269: in order to be able to cultivate land, one already needs rightful possession.

[14] Ibid., AA VI, 314–15. Those with private property are regarded by Kant as active citizens. They have the right to vote, whereas passive citizens are a mere part of the state and do not.

1989, when communism as a form of government disappeared, Marx's view on property has been out of sight. He is seen principally as the advocate of a communist utopia, or rather dystopia, in which private property would be completely abolished. But this seems unjustified, as Marx's writings point at the problems arising from an excessive and exclusive emphasis on private property, such as the poverty and disenfranchisement of the working class. Anyone who wants to read about the societal conditions Marx condemned should for instance read Dickens' *Oliver Twist*. It is true that economic language dominates Marx's later works, but especially his earlier work dissects carefully the workings of society based on capital.[15] Marx agrees with Locke (and others) that labour is the ultimate source of all economic value, but he resists a legal system which allows for the societal means of production to be in the hands of only a few individuals. He rejects the idea that such an accumulation of property can be justified by a theory, such as that of Locke.

As a critic of religion, Marx does not use biblical language to analyse capitalism. Religion is for Marx primarily the opium of the (ordinary) people, through which they can console themselves over their dire living conditions. Nevertheless, one can chart Marx's intentions with the help of the two elements from Genesis. In a sense, he attempts to reintroduce the idea that the earth is given to humankind in common and he seems to agree with Aquinas that private property is a mere human institution that should serve humanity as a whole that owns the earth as a commons. Therefore, private ownership should play only a limited role and the collective means of production such as land, natural resources, factories, machines etc. should never be privately owned. According to Marx, social means of production should be owned by the state as the representative of the community. Aquinas would probably not go so far, but he would agree that society needs to set limits to the accumulation of private property.

According to Locke and Kant, private property is a natural, innate right. Given this status the quantity of property a person owns is irrelevant. Property can be accumulated and it is the state's task to protect existing property relationships as these develop 'naturally'. As long as this view is accepted, Marx would argue that the equal right to property for everyone is a mere smoke-screen for social inequality; this right works in fact in favour of the social class of property owners and to the disadvantage of those without property. For Marx it was no coincidence that in his description of the natural state Locke speaks of 'the turfs my servant has cut'. Locke takes for granted the distinction between labourers and masters who have servants cut turf and become its owners. He also mentions 'the inland vacant places of America' – despite nomadic peoples living there – where the population would be so much better off once private ownership of land had been introduced. Even if value is constituted by labour, one need not reach Locke's conclusion that 'men have

---

[15] See, for example, John Lancaster, 'Marx at 193', *London Review of Books*, 5 April 2012, 7–10.

(thus) agreed to a disproportionate and unequal possession of the earth'. This is at best a naive tale that does not take into account the role of violence, robbery and theft in the emergence of private property. At worst, it is an ideological legitimation for the existing relationships of exploitation, whereby abstract equality before the law obscures the material inequality in real life.

According to Marx, human rights as they emerged in the course of the French and American Revolutions were a mere means to uphold or promote existing material inequalities and to confirm the power of the capitalist class. These human rights were therefore nothing other than the confirmation of those 'egoistic' rights of the upper class. It would seem that later developments with regard to human rights have reduced the importance of the right to property. Property, as Article 17 has it, can be owned 'alone as well as in association with others'. Socio-economic rights have been introduced in Article 25 in order to secure for every human being 'a standard of living adequate for the health and well-being of himself and of his family'. Maybe Marx was correct in his analysis then – albeit not in his solution of the problem – and his analysis may still be valid today. Remember that in Locke's view 'the invention of money' is crucially important for the accumulation of economic value. Today, the whole of social life even more perhaps than ever before seems to revolve around the acquisition and accumulation of capital with the serious risk that economic value will overshadow and endanger all other values. Indeed, in Marx's view the bourgeoisie 'has left remaining no other nexus between man and man than naked self-interest, than callous cash payment'.[16] Capitalism is a revolutionary force that destroys all traditional ties and creates a world after its own image. Observing our present world one can hardly disagree with this. Our world is dominated by money. Is there anything that is not for sale?[17]

A Brief History of the Contemporary Concept of Property

Let us move on to our own times. Important developments have happened with regard to the right to property. Due to the influence of Marx the significance, or at least the presence, of socio-economic rights has increased. Still, the basic positions just outlined are easily discernible in today's discussion. Think of the most important work in legal philosophy of the twentieth century, Rawls's *Theory of Justice* published in 1971. This book revives the theory of the social contract as developed by Locke, Kant and others. Under the

---

[16] Karl Marx and Friedrich Engels, *Manifesto of the Communist Party*, trans. Samuel Moore (Moscow: Progress Publishers, 1969), ch. 1, www.marxists.org/archive/marx/works/1848/communist-manifesto/.

[17] Even today, many criticize this dominance of money. See, for example, Michael Sandel, *What Money Can't Buy: The Moral Limits of Markets* (New York: Farrar, Strauss & Giroux Inc., 2012). Debra Satz, *Why Some Things Should Not Be for Sale: The Moral Limits of Markets* (Oxford: Oxford University Press, 2010).

influence of utilitarianism and Marxism, this theory had been neglected, but is now brought to a new, more abstract level. Rawls's main idea is that the principles of justice for the basic structure of society must indeed be based on consent of the members of that society. In order to prevent them from adopting all kinds of biased and selfish principles, these members – or the representatives of various social positions – must be placed in a position of impartiality when they debate different possible principles for society.

It is important according to Rawls that individuals who decide on the basic structure of society indeed do not adopt principles that would only support their own interests. Only behind a veil of ignorance with regard to their own position within society, will they be able to agree on principles that are fair to all and for all. This agreement in which the situation of the social contract is easily recognizable does not, in Rawls's view, lead to the utilitarianism of Bentham and Mill. The representatives will not choose for a society that has the maximization of utility as its fundamental principle. This principle would be rejected because it does not consider 'how this sum of satisfaction is distributed among individuals'.[18] The principle of maximizing utility allows that the greater advantage for the larger group of individuals compensates for the disadvantages of the smaller group. For instance, a violation of the right to physical integrity of a few terrorists could be made good by the greater safety of many. A utilitarian society could possibly even be compatible with institutions such as serfdom and with violations of other human rights. The representatives in the 'original position' will according to Rawls also not consent to this principle because they would prefer to live in a society in which their rights as individuals are respected. They will also reject Marx's principle of justice: 'from each according to his abilities, to each according to his needs'.[19] According to Rawls, such a principle of justice is unrealistically utopian, because it presupposes that every human being is willing to contribute to society to the best of their ability, and also that no one will claim or receive more than is really needed.[20] According to Marx, the situation of scarcity will eventually disappear and this will end the situation in which a society faces competing interests. This is the complete opposite of the egotistical image of humans that Marx attributed to the view of eighteenth-century human rights declarations, but Rawls is not convinced that this is possible or even desirable.

At the heart of the problem of justice lies distribution: distribution of rights, distribution of benefits and burdens. In Rawls's view, this problem should be resolved by adopting two principles of justice: first, fundamental rights should be distributed equally: each person should have the most extensive total system of basic liberties compatible with a similar system of liberty for all; second,

---

[18] John Rawls, *A Theory of Justice. Revised Edition* (Oxford: Oxford University Press, 1999), 23.

[19] Karl Marx, *Critique of the Gotha Programme* (Moscow: Progress Publishers, 1970), Pt 1, www .marxists.org/archive/marx/works/1875/gotha/.

[20] John Rawls, *Justice as Fairness: A Restatement* (Cambridge: Harvard University Press, 2001), 4, 157, 177.

socio-economic inequalities should be arranged in such a manner that they are expected to be to everyone's advantage; nor should these socio-economic inequalities hinder equal access for everyone to societal positions and public offices.[21] Rawls's position can be seen as an attempt to conflate the two elements of Genesis, or, put differently, to harmonize the positions of Locke and Marx. One can also recognize in the first principle the list of 'negative rights', such as the right to physical integrity and the right to space, discussed earlier in this book. The right to property is also part of the first principle. According to Rawls, this right is a necessary condition for a person's autonomy and respect for oneself and for others. However, Rawls differs from Locke, because the right to property is not considered 'inviolable' and does not necessarily include the right to private property in natural resources and the means of production: 'they should be socially owned'.[22] This should come as no surprise because of the second principle, which allows for economic inequalities only when they are also beneficial for all, especially for those least off in society. This is the so-called 'difference principle': socio-economic differences are permitted only with an eye to the least advantaged in society. Think of the following simple choice. Imagine a society with two classes, the highly educated and those with a low level of education, and three possibilities qua division of income: (1) the members of both classes earn the same income, say €25,000 per year; (2) the highly educated earn a good income and the poorly educated a relatively small income, say €70,000 against €10,000; (3) the highly educated earn less than in the second possibility and those with a poor education earn significantly more, say €50,000 against €20,000. If one follows the difference principle, the third possibility should be preferred, even though the combined income is larger in the second possibility.

This is obviously a poor example, because it does not take into account how economic output is influenced by these income differences. But this is why Rawls allows for differences: they are economically efficient. Making all humans equal qua income or capital is economically inefficient. Remember Aquinas's argument in favour of private property: humans tend to care better for things they consider their own. Therefore, Rawls wants to combine the element of economic incentives with the idea of society as a system of social cooperation. Therefore, impartial representatives in the 'original position' would consent to the principle that everyone, and not just the well-educated or the rich, should benefit from that co-operation. Therefore, they would consent to some mechanism whereby socio-economic inequalities can be moderated, like a progressive taxation system. In a society based on 'his' two principles the right to property cannot be absolute. Rawls is a secular thinker and the biblical idea that God gave the earth to humankind in common forms no part of his theory. Nevertheless, the idea of the commons and the axis of the human being as a social creature is clearly present. Rawls agrees with Locke

[21] Rawls, *A Theory of Justice*, 53, 220.   [22] Rawls, *Justice as Fairness*, 114.

that private property must be respected, but he also agrees with Marx that society is a matter of cooperation from which every citizen must profit.

Rawls rejects the unconditional character of the private right to property, but he also rejects Marx's view that liberty rights have the mere ideological function of disguising underlying unequal socio-economic relationships. As a liberal, Rawls even prioritizes the first principle of justice over the second. Liberty rights can only be curtailed for liberty's sake, not for the sake of an increase in economic well-being. For example, it is justified, according to Rawls, to sometimes limit freedom of speech out of respect for other liberties, such as being free from slander. The same is true for other liberty rights. The freedom of association, as in Article 20 of the Universal Declaration, can be limited if it is used to set up a criminal organization. Liberty rights should be protected, in Rawls's view, by giving them constitutional status. But this is not needed for the difference principle. Its aim to keep socio-economic differences in check must be realized by ordinary legislation. Since the right to property is not absolute, property can be regulated without this leading to a violation of the classical liberty rights.

In an effort to synthesize the emphasis on liberty in the thinking of the seventeenth and eighteenth centuries with that on equality in the nineteenth century, Rawls seems to follow the position adopted by the Universal Declaration in which social rights are included and the right to property is not identified with private ownership. Nonetheless, this position has not remained uncontested. It has been argued that Rawls's emphasis on equality leads to pressure on liberty. That is at any rate the contention of the so-called libertarians. It would seem that Rawls's plea for the difference principle and for redistribution is quite understandable if one takes a quick glance at a Forbes 400 or at statistics of the (global) distribution of capital, assets and income.[23] The differences in incomes and assets within states and between states are probably greater now than ever before in human history.[24] According to libertarianism, however, differences in wealth and income are not as such indicative of injustice. As far as justice is concerned, the only relevant question is whether income and wealth are acquired with or without theft, fraud or violence. According to libertarians, there is no general pattern for 'just' socio-economic relationships within in society (such as economic equality, the 'difference principle' or the principle of maximizing utility).[25] The concept of justice is only applicable to transactions between individuals: they can either

[23] A recent influential and well-known publication in this regard is Thomas Piketty, *Capital in the Twenty-First Century*, trans. Arthur Goldhammer (Cambridge, MA: Belknap Press, 2017).

[24] Whether this is indeed true depends on empirical research and on what standards for measuring poverty and wealth are used. Piketty's findings are contested, for example, in Stephen Pinker, *Enlightenment Now: The Case for Reason, Science, Humanism and Progress* (New York: Viking Press, 2018), ch. 9.

[25] The most famous libertarian author introduces as an example the basketball player Wilt Chamberlain who became wealthy because so many people wanted to pay in order to see him play. Is it unjust that he earns more than his fans? No, because these fans are willing to pay their

be based on mutual consent and then they are just, or they are based on deception or force and then they are unjust. Therefore, any form of distribution in the name of equality, as advocated by Marx, or of the difference principle, as proposed by Rawls, must be rejected.

A utilitarian argument for redistribution of wealth may initially also seem strong but it can easily be refuted. Suppose that 500,000 persons in the United Kingdom live in relative poverty and that a transfer of a billion pounds from for instance the royal family would give each person 2,000 pounds. For persons on a low income that is a substantial amount that would increase their well-being considerably, while conversely such a 'donation' would scarcely be noticed by this very wealthy family. Thus, such a transfer seems justified from a utilitarian perspective, but this is not the case. Utilitarians would argue, first, against such a transfer because it would endanger any incentive for the poor to work themselves out of their position and it would, secondly, damage the stability of property and the trust required for example when making investments. Perhaps in the short term social welfare would increase, but in the long term such transfers could be counterproductive, certainly if they were to take place frequently. Libertarianism would object to redistribution on a totally different ground. Such transfers violate the liberty of persons to do with their property whatever they like. Any compulsory transfer from the rich to the poor is a violation of the right to property. The rich could of course be encouraged on moral grounds to assist the poor, but they should do so from the goodness of their hearts, not because of the force of the law. Regulating and facilitating private property by means of setting up decent rules of private law and enforcing contracts is a task of the state, but it is not the state's task to redistribute property. Libertarians agree with Locke that private property must be considered an individual, inviolable natural right; the thought that the earth is the common property of all mankind is not considered important or relevant.

Since liberty rights have an almost absolute status according to libertarianism, the only legitimate state must be a minimal state: its sole task is to protect these rights and to leave as much as possible to the market. Modern states have now unfortunately adopted tasks that go well beyond this: they enforce road safety by making seat belts compulsory and they ban smoking in order to enhance public health. Many libertarians would regard these measures as unjustified restrictions of liberty. They oppose, as we have seen, taxation of the rich to help the poor. They are in favour of free individuals coming together in the market place and engaging in voluntary transactions. This explains why some individuals, such as Bill Gates or Wilt Chamberlain, arch-libertarian Nozick's famous example, are wealthy and other less so. Is that unjust? Not as

---

entrance tickets and Chamberlain is willing to play for them. Their transaction is consensual. See Robert Nozick, *Anarchy, State and Utopia* (New York: Basic Books, 1974), 160–1.

long as transactions are based on consent. Any distribution of income, however equal or unequal, is fair as long as this distribution is based on voluntary transactions between individuals.

According to libertarianism there is no fixed and just pattern of dividing income and wealth. Every attempt to bring about a certain socio-economic distribution involves coercion by the state and is therefore unjustified. All obstacles to the free market, such as the minimum wage, should be removed. It is not the state's task to regulate the economy. Margaret Thatcher, the former prime minister of the United Kingdom, gave voice to this view in the following manner: 'There is no such thing as society. There are individual men and women and there are families.'[26] In Chapter 12 we will come back to libertarianism where the moral significance of state borders is discussed.

Limits on the Right to Property

With the discussion between Rawls and libertarianism the historical development of the concept of property has come to a provisional conclusion. It seems that in today's world the view on property as private property and as an inviolable right dominates, and that the view on man as a social being who has to share the world with all others does not play a major role. Many people, including scholars and politicians, are convinced that ultimately the free market is the best mechanism to create prosperity for all. Is this true? Let us look at a few critical comments.[27] First, with regard to the wealth of the Wilt Chamberlains and Cristiano Ronaldos of this world, it is true that the enormous wealth of football players and movie stars is the result of voluntary transactions between them and their fans. A football player sells his great talent by playing in huge stadiums and on TV so that his audience can enjoy a good match. Many come to see the movie star in yet another blockbuster. They surely are the owner of their talents, because who else could lay claim to these? The case is, however, more complex than a simple series of transactions between star and admirer. The match in which this great football player participates, or the movie in which the star features, are part of an enormous infrastructure in which other players, clubs, film production companies and advertisers play important roles. This infrastructure and the economic situation at a particular moment in time determine how much the talent of this or that star is worth. Their economic value is surely not only the result of individual talent, but also of these circumstances and thus of luck. Nozick focuses on individual transactions but leaves these circumstances out of the picture. Think now of a similar situation in which transactions take place: between a (male or female) prostitute and their client. According to libertarians, there is nothing wrong with such a transaction as long as it is based on

---

[26] Douglas Keay, Interview with Margaret Thatcher, *Woman's Own*, 23 September 1987, 8–10.
[27] I am helped here by Sandel, *What Money Can't Buy*.

consent. But here too, the economic value of the talent that is on offer depends very much on the environment: the infrastructure in which sex work takes place, demand and supply, just as in the case of a football player or a movie star. But in this second case, it is perhaps less difficult to imagine that both parties do not always have the same bargaining position and that consent might become tainted by dependencies. Given such inequalities the question arises whether the state should or should not step in to protect the weaker party to the transaction.

A second and related problem is the fact that most legal systems block a number of transactions, even though they do not contradict the logic of libertarianism according to which demand and supply should be able to meet on the market. The crucial point is whether or not persons have the full right to self-determination, already discussed in Chapter 6, and whether the well-known principle *volenti non fit iniuria* is always valid. Most legal systems prohibit the sale of body parts, like kidneys, criminalize assisted suicide and block the hiring out of bodily functions, as in commercial surrogate mother-hood. Yet, these transactions need not contradict consent: there is a great demand for kidney donors and most persons can live perfectly well with one kidney only; many old persons would like to receive help with dying when they feel that their life is complete. Why would any state prohibit the selling of one's 'spare' kidney or prohibit assisted suicide? If football players, movie stars and prostitutes are allowed to make money with their bodies, why should someone not be allowed to sell one kidney or assist another person with dying? Suppose that someone does sell his kidney in order to pay for the university education of his eldest daughter, why should he then subsequently not be permitted to sell his second kidney for his second daughter's higher education, even if this would kill him? If someone is the owner of one kidney, he is certainly the owner of the other kidney as well, even though he will not survive the loss of this second kidney.[28] If I own my life, why can I not decide to ask someone else to support my wish to die? Why prohibit someone offering himself for con-sumption on the internet and someone else accepting this offer, as in the cannibal case?

One would expect that libertarians would accept the possibility of tainted consent and completely unreasonable agreements, and that public measures must be undertaken to ensure that all transactions are voluntary and consen-sual. But they would still defend that individuals may in principle do with their bodies and live as they please, despite the fact that most legal systems do not subscribe to the libertarian logic. Certain transactions are prohibited, such as the sale and purchase of kidneys, as mentioned, or the case of consensual slavery, because it is considered doubtful that such transactions could ever be fully consensual and that such transactions do not belong to the market. One

---

[28] I am inspired here by (and take this example from) Michael Sandel, *Justice: What's the Right Thing to Do?* (London: Allen Lane, 2009), 72–4.

could of course argue that this is paternalism and that such restrictions are simply morally wrong and impose unjustified limits on the right of property. One could also defend that these prohibitions reflect deeply held moral convictions with regard to the limits of consent and of what can be considered 'property'. Libertarianism takes for granted that members in society should be considered formally equal but that does not solve the problem of material inequality that underlies many transactions. Nor does it acknowledge that most presently existing property relations reflect an inequality within societies and between societies that is often the result of historic injustices such as violence, robbery and theft. Libertarianism is only a convincing view on the right to property if the bargaining positions on the market are much more equal than is now the case. Creating more equal bargaining positions would require an extension of the duties of the state beyond those of a mere minimal state.

The fact that certain transactions are legally banned in many places despite possible true consent, indicates another problem with libertarianism. According to Locke 'the invention of money' was a crucial element in the development of mankind. Money makes the accumulation of wealth possible without violating the criterion of proviso and decay. It is therefore not merely a neutral instrument that facilitates exchange and accumulation. Money has the tendency to reach out to all domains of human existence. That was at least in Marx's mind when he called money 'the universal pander' and quoted Shakespeare's *Timon of Athens* when describing money as the 'common whore of mankind, that put'st odds among the rout of nations'.[29] Similarly disapproving is Kant's rejection of a notorious saying attributed to an English parliamentarian, namely 'that every man has his price, for which he sells himself'.[30] Kant insists, as we have seen in Chapter 4, on the fundamental difference between price and dignity, and thus on the limits of the market.

It could thus very well be that the transactions ruled out by many legal systems point beyond tainted consent at the existence of important social values other than money, markets and private property. Walzer and others defend that 'money' and 'supply and demand' should have no place in certain social 'spheres', as Walzer calls them. For instance, human life itself and human body parts should never be valued by the laws of demand and supply, even if occasionally someone would like to sell part of their body (the donation of a kidney to a family member is then an entirely different matter) or sincerely wants to become someone else's slave.[31] That is not compatible with human

---

[29] Quoted in the important chapter 'Money and Commodities', in Michael Walzer, *Spheres of Justice. A Defence of Pluralism & Equality* (Oxford: Blackwell, 1983), 95–6.

[30] Immanuel Kant, *Die Religion innerhalb der Grenzen der blossen Vernunft*, AA VI, 38.

[31] A transaction by which someone by 'his own consent' makes himself a slave is impossible (even) according to Locke, *Two Treatises of Government*, 2.23: 'Nobody can give more power than he has himself; and he that cannot take away his own life, cannot give another power over it.'

dignity. So too should the sphere of political power and influence be free from the market. It is not permitted for either individuals or groups in society to sell their votes to the highest bidder at elections, not even when certain of the enfranchised would be happy to make some money with their votes. In Rawls's view the right to vote is so crucial in a just society that a voting system must be set up in such a manner that every vote cast has the same weight. Therefore, he argues that 'big money' should play no major role in elections.[32] Public functions should also be exempt from the law of the market. On the basis of the principle of equal opportunity they must go to those most competent and qualified or to those who have been freely elected for such a post. The value attributed to marriage, rightly or wrongly (see Chapter 13), should not obey the logic of libertarianism. Most existing legal systems do not allow polygamy and prohibit a marriage between more than two partners, irrespective of whether the would-be participants would consent in such an arrangement. The value of honouring extraordinary achievements or the value of friendship should not be for sale either. These 'goods' simply do not belong to the free market, so that at a certain moment our fictional football player or movie star may have to admit they have few real friends, just as our fictional prostitute knows quite well that their transactions have nothing to do with love.

It is correct to acknowledge the importance of the right to private property, but this right should not be overemphasized, as libertarianism does. Other rights and freedoms are also important and they may involve limitations on the right to property. Certain transactions run the risk of not being truly consensual, given unequal bargaining positions, and certain other transactions should be protected from the market. One does not need the theological argument that God gave the earth to mankind in common, in order to acknowledge that libertarianism as an anthropology leaves too little space for the human being as a social being.

Intellectual Property

It would seem, however, that libertarianism is correct with its emphasis on private property with regard to one specific type of property, namely intellectual property. It receives special attention in the second clause of Article 27 of the Universal Declaration: 'Everyone has the right to the protection of the moral and material interests resulting from any scientific, literary or artistic production of which he is the author.' This provision is made within the context of everyone's right to take part in the cultural life of their community (in the first clause), but it could also be read independently, as a human right to intellectual property concerning the 'productions' of which one is the 'author'.

---

[32] John Rawls *Political Liberalism* (Cambridge, MA: Harvard University Press, 1993), 328 argues that it is needed 'to keep political parties independent of large concentrations of private economic and social power'.

From a legal perspective, many areas could be brought under this right, such as patent law and copyright. The idea behind this right would then be as follows: the person who has invented something, becomes thereby the owner of that 'thing'. They should be rewarded if others want to make use of this 'thing' and they may control the dissemination of this invention.

We saw that everyone, according to Locke, has the right to remove something from the common store and add value to this 'something' by means of labour, thereby making it their property. But this is conditional upon respecting the proviso that nothing may decay and that there must be enough left for others. Well, this proviso, it could be argued, is certainly not applicable to cases of intellectual property. Nothing is taken from the common store because something new has been brought into existence. Therefore, the inventors of these new 'productions' have surely not taken anything from others or deprived others of something. They should therefore be entitled to the revenues of these inventions. In other words, the wealth of people such as Bill Gates and Mark Zuckerberg springs from their inventiveness and creativity. They do not build on already existing practices, as in the case of football players or movie stars. Their wealth cannot possibly be the result of a violation of the property of others. Since nothing is taken from the commons, there is no reason whatsoever that others should be compensated. In brief, the argument that private property is an absolute right is certainly valid in the case of intellectual property. Those who invent something that did not exist before have the exclusive authority over the use of that 'something' and can sell it to others on the market if they want to. After all, that is what ownership means: the exclusion of others from the use of one's property. That is the case with houses, bicycles and furniture, and most certainly with something that did not exist before – productions or ideas. These lead to a special category of property, intellectual property.

Let us focus on this argument, for example with regard to the intellectual property of the pharmaceutical industry in connection with newly developed medications or drugs. In this case there appears to be not only a libertarian but also a utilitarian justification for the property right of those new drugs. The development of any new drug or treatment for which there is great need demands enormous investment in research and development and this can only be recovered if the result, in the form of the new medicine, is protected against intellectual pirating, for example against illegal copying. Due to globalization, such pharmaceutical firms have become multinational businesses and pirating can take place anywhere. Therefore, important international rules have been put in place to protect such intellectual property. A significant part of these rules is to be found in the so-called TRIPS Convention (Trade-Related Aspects of Intellectual Property Rights), agreed in 1994 in the framework of the World Trade Organization.[33] This convention obliges the

---

[33] On the importance of such institutional agreements, see Thomas Pogge, *Politics as Usual: What lies behind the pro-poor rhetoric* (Cambridge: Polity Press, 2011), 20–1.

signatory states to grant a twenty-year patent to pharmaceutical inventions such as medication and vaccines. In this way the pharmaceutical industry can recover its investments and make a profit by selling the new drugs and vaccines on the market. Other companies cannot simply analyse and copy those new products and then bring them on the market at a much lower price.

Such a system obviously can have detrimental effects, for instance when not all of those who could benefit greatly from this new drug have access to it due to the high price. Nozick would consider this an unfortunate turn of events, but he would deny that those who need but cannot buy this new medication are treated unjustly. After all, by developing it, the pharmaceutical industry brought something new into existence to which no one is entitled. It made use of various resources, techniques and ideas that, in principle, were also available to others. By developing this drug, the firm has acquired the exclusive right to the result of this new combination of resources, techniques and ideas. And, again, nothing has been removed from the common store. No one was ever entitled to this new product, and therefore it is obviously the property of the developer. In the same way, Picasso became the owner of what he painted. Who makes something new, is in a certain sense like God who 'in the beginning' created the earth *ex nihilo*.

Is this argument convincing? Can an exclusive private right be accepted for intellectual property? It would seem not. Pogge has come up with some powerful counter-arguments. One could ask, first, whether the private property right of the pharmaceutical manufacturer is really so strong that it outweighs other considerations, such as the value of the lives of a great many persons who are mortally in danger without access to this drug. Compare it with the following situation. A number of persons are trapped in a burning house and the fire brigade needs water to fight the fire in order to save them. The only water available in the vicinity is a lake close by that belongs to the owner of the estate. Can the owner insist on their exclusive right to property, or is this a case of 'necessity breaks the law'?[34] In line with such reasoning, the South African government argued in 1997 that in cases of extreme necessity, the state could decide on the manufacture of what are known as generic medications. What was the situation? The spread of the HIV virus had reached epidemic proportions and antiretroviral medications were available on the market only for a price determined by the pharmaceutical industry on the basis of its right to intellectual property. This price was far too high for the vast majority of those infected. When the state decided to produce this medicine itself so that it could be sold for much lower prices, the pharmaceutical industry brought a legal case against the state for dereliction of its duty to protect intellectual property. Ultimately the court case was dropped by the

---

[34] Thomas Aquinas (*Summa Theologica*, Secunda Secundae, Questio 66, Article 7) would argue that in such a case, natural law trumps human law: 'If the need be so manifest and urgent, that the present need must be remedied by whatever means be at hand . . . then it is lawful for a man to succour his own need by means of another's property, by taking it either openly or secretly.'

plaintiff, partly due to the pressure of public opinion that blamed the industry for considering profit more important than saving human lives.[35]

A second counterargument by Pogge runs as follows:[36] suppose that in some distant past a clever woman made the useful invention of the wheelbarrow. With that knowledge she could copy her invention and sell the extra wheelbarrows to those who could afford to pay her price. But would this woman have the right to claim that the 'idea' of the wheelbarrow is hers and that no one else can make a wheelbarrow at their own initiative, even though the knowledge concerning wheelbarrows is now available? Or take other examples, such as the invention of a new dance or a new recipe.[37] Can the inventor exclude others from making similar bodily movements or cooking the same meal?

These arguments show that the libertarian view on an absolute private right to intellectual property seems untenable. It would easily come into conflict with other rights, such as the right to life, but also the freedom to disseminate scientific findings. If those findings are published in journals that are owned by big publishing houses and these publishers decide to make these publications accessible to others only at a high price, then research is hampered. In universities one finds today much support for 'open access' of research. Publications should be accessible to all. This is indeed a return to the idea of the commons. Intellectual property must be protected just like any other type of property, but it should not be understood as an absolute or sacred right.

There is every reason, as Rawls suggested, to understand the right to intellectual property as part of a set of liberty rights. It needs protection, because the utilitarian argument that the development of new medications demands large investments is correct. Such investments will only be made if there is sufficient certainty that these will be paid back, with a profit. But that is something entirely different from considering private property as a natural right. Indeed, in this context, Bentham is correct that natural rights are claims on the basis of which some individuals prioritize their private interests over those of the community as a whole. The human right to property must therefore be understood in conjunction with other fundamental rights and common welfare.

At present there are quite a few scholars – possibly Lessig is the best-known of them – who hold that the current intellectual property law no longer fulfils the purpose for which it was intended, namely providing security to inventors and authors without stifling creativity.[38] Now the right to property has become

[35] David Barnard, 'In the High Court of South Africa, Case No. 4138/98: The Global Politics of Access to Low-Cost AIDS Drugs in Poor Countries', *Kennedy Institute of Ethics Journal* (2002) 12: 159–74.

[36] Aidan Hollis and Thomas Pogge, *The Health Impact Fund. Making New Medicines Accessible for All* (Incentives for Global Health, 2008), 64–5. See www.healthimpactfund.org.

[37] Thomas Pogge, 'Pharmaceutical Innovation: Must We Exclude the Poor?', in *World Poverty and Human Rights* (Cambridge: Polity Press, 2002).

[38] Lawrence Lessig, *The Future of Ideas: The Fate of the Commons in a Connected World* (New York: Vintage, 2002).

so rigid, it is argued, that is a threat to creativity. Under the banner of the commons a plea for a return to the idea of common property is made, especially with regard to the world of ideas and creativity. Although the internet is increasingly dominated by big players, several noteworthy initiatives in the spirit of the commons, such as Wikipedia, still exist that depend on volunteers both for input on its pages and financial support.

Finally, many now acknowledge that Locke's idea of the value of what nature gives to mankind as almost negligible, in comparison with the value produced by human labour, is wrong. The living environment in which mankind finds itself is not a rather worthless store from which everyone can take as they please and in which everyone can dump anything they want to get rid of. It must be regarded as a common good or common heritage that needs to be governed in a proper manner if mankind wants to survive. Many argue that we have entered a threatening new geographical era, called the Anthropocene.[39] This closes the circle of this chapter. Two elements have been taken from Genesis: God has ordained that the earth and everything on it is the common property of mankind, and humans must earn their living by the sweat of their brow. It seems that the first element, under the influence of Locke and others, has become increasingly forgotten. Now, however, the boundaries of an exclusive emphasis on private property have been reached. Whether this will lead us back to Thomas Aquinas, who argued that private property is only a means to manage that common property in a decent manner, is yet to be seen. But his view is not so bad: humanity is permitted to possess external things, but not as if they are completely their own. These things are to be regarded in the light of the common interest, so that humankind 'is ready to communicate them to others in their need'.[40]

---

[39] See, for example, Jedediah Purdy, *After Nature: A Politics for the Anthropocene* (Cambridge: Cambridge University Press, 2015).
[40] Thomas Aquinas, *Summa Theologica*, Secunda Secundae, Questio 66, Article 2.

Part III
Positive Freedom

11

Everyone Has the Right to Take Part in the Government of Their Country

After discussing the rights that concern humans primarily as individuals in Part II, Part III discusses humans as societal beings and begins with the right of every person 'to take part in the government of his country, directly or through freely chosen representatives'. This is laid down in Article 21 of the Universal Declaration, which then goes on to state that 'the will of the people shall be the basis of the authority of government; this will shall be expressed in periodic and genuine elections which shall be by universal and equal suffrage and shall be held by secret vote or by equivalent free voting procedures'. That same Article 21 also states, although this seems something quite different, that everyone shall have 'equal access to public service in his country'. Although the Article clearly refers to the principle of democracy by mentioning concepts such as elections and representation, the concept of democracy itself is absent from the Universal Declaration. Only at its very end, in Article 29, is 'a democratic society' mentioned as the basis for limiting the exercise of individual rights and freedoms. While today the concept of democracy enjoys perhaps greater popularity than ever, and while according to some classic authors the right to contribute to the laws of one's state is the main characteristic of a free citizen, there is strictly speaking no human right to democracy. According to the Universal Declaration there is merely the right to participate in government. This chapter will show that there are a number of good reasons for the Universal Declaration to be cautious with using the concept of 'democracy'. Democracy is a contested concept that has at least two fairly distinct understandings.

In the historic context of the Universal Declaration it is really understandable that the word 'democracy', classically 'defined' by Winston Churchill as the worst form of government, except for all those other forms that have been tried from time to time, is avoided. In the interbellum period before World War II, democracy did not have a good name. It was regarded as a weak system of government, with the Weimar Republic perhaps the prime example. During the war this proved to be a false impression, since two of the three prevailing powers, the UK and the US, were functioning democracies. In 1948, however, there was no agreement as to what democracy meant or that it was the best form of government. Some prominent states of the time called themselves people's democracies, and the text of the Universal Declaration left open the possibility that the people could choose between what is now considered a democracy or communism as long as regular elections or popular consultations were held. Moreover, the General Assembly of the United Nations consisted of only around sixty states. A large part of the world's population was still colonized and not represented in that Assembly. Article 21 was certainly not intended as an invitation to insurgency or a call for self-determination of those oppressed peoples.

In later human rights conventions too, the concept of democracy is scarcely mentioned. The European Convention on Human Rights does not formulate a human right to democracy and only mentions 'a democratic society' in connection with the grounds for limiting the 'right to one's own space', as discussed in Chapter 9. These limits must be necessary 'in a democratic society'. In this way the value of democracy is implicitly acknowledged, while it prevents at the same time complaints being made to the European Court on violations of the 'democracy' right by one of the member states of the Council of Europe. This was a wise decision, because what 'democracy' truly is, is much contested. Does democracy require proportional representation, or is first past the post also democratic? Is a high electoral threshold for entering parliament democratic or not? Unsurprisingly, Article 25 of the International Covenant on Civil and Political Rights repeats almost verbatim the formulation in the Universal Declaration. In the context of that time – the political process of decolonization – it is evident that the right to self-determination of all peoples occupies a very prominent place in that covenant. It constitutes its first Article, as well as being the first Article of the Covenant on Economic, Social and Cultural Rights. By virtue of that right all peoples have the right to freely determine their political status and to pursue their economic, social and cultural development. Because these covenants were concluded between the then-existing states which were supposed to represent their peoples, self-determination here meant political sovereignty and territorial integrity as a collective right and not as a human right or as encouraging internal democracy within these states, let alone as an argument which minority groups could use to secede. Democracy was and is up to now a contested concept.

A Brief History of Democracy

The history of 'democracy' begins in Athens in the fifth century BCE, more precisely with the funerary oration held by the statesman Pericles, as recorded by the historian Thucydides. Pericles gave this speech on the occasion of the ceremonial burial of a number of Athenian soldiers who had died in the war against Sparta, now usually called the Peloponnesian War. In the speech Pericles contrasted war-like Sparta with democratic Athens, with its virtues of tolerance, openness, free trade and above all self-rule. Our constitution is called democratic because power does not lie in the hands of the few, but in those of all the people, so says Thucydides's account.[1] The dead soldiers had fought for a good and noble cause and Athens is an example to the rest of Hellas. These words of Pericles have become famous: they were intended to be used as a motto for the rejected European Constitutional Treaty of 2005 (which has since then been replaced by the Treaty of Lisbon without a motto).

Nevertheless, there is every reason to be cautious about this paean to 'democratic' Athens. In his history of the Peloponnesian War, Thucydides makes it clear that the strife between the two great Greek city states was for power, and that democratic but imperialistic Athens was prepared to do almost anything to gain the upper hand. For instance, our historian recounts an episode in which Athens captures the island of Melos in a ruthless fashion. The claim of the islanders to neutrality was simply ignored by an appeal to power. According to the Athenians it was just 'right' that the strong do what they can and the weak suffer what they must.[2] The liberty of Athens over which Pericles waxed lyrical, is apparently not valid for weak states. Moreover, the statement that Athens was ruled by all of the people must be taken with a pinch of salt. In fact, the power lays with a minority of native Athenians, because the majority of the inhabitants of Athens were not considered citizens: slaves, women and Greeks not born in Athens, but merely living and working there (Aristotle was one of them) had no say. There was no democracy in the sense of universal suffrage and free and secret voting.

In the (legal) philosophy of that time, democracy did not always have a good name, Plato being one of its main critics. One of his objections against democracy is that it considers all preferences of individual citizens equal. This is forcefully rejected. Just as not all desires are equal – some are noble and others are not – no more are all preferences equal. Because this is nonetheless believed, writes Plato, persons in a democracy become overly sensitive to anything that tends towards authority and servitude. That irritates them and is perceived as a violation of equality. Therefore, a democratic man refuses to recognize any law, written or unwritten.[3] Why should anyone have a better understanding of how to rule a city? Because in a democracy all viewpoints are of equal value, there is only one sort of power – the power of numbers. But since democracy is at the same time characterized by this aversion to authority, democracy tends to degenerate into anarchy, which is then by necessity followed by the worst form of government, namely tyranny, when some leader promises to make an end to this democratic chaos. For Plato, democracy is a bad form of government that will be torn apart by rivalries and thereby paves the way for a coup d'état by a single individual.

---

[1] For the whole funeral oration, see Thucydides, *Peloponnesian War*, Book 2, 34–66.

[2] Thucydides, *Peloponnesian War*, Book 5, 84–116. An extensive and interesting analysis of this so-called Melian Dialogue is given in Michael Walzer, *Just and Unjust Wars: A Moral Argument with Historical Illustrations* (New York: Basic Books, 2000), 4–13.

[3] Plato, *Republic*, 563d–564b.

While Plato's disparagement of democracy is based on his philosophy of forms or ideas – the state must be based on the idea of justice, not on what happens to be the viewpoint of the majority – Aristotle rejects simple democracy on the grounds of empirical research. Only an examination of the existing forms of government can establish which of them is best. For such an examination, one needs a classification and according to Aristotle such classification should be based on two criteria: the first concerns who wields the power of government: a single individual, a group of individuals or all individuals; the second looks at the purpose for which power is exercised: for the benefit of those in power, or for the general interest. On the basis of these criteria Aristotle distinguishes between six forms of government, of which the first three are considered 'true' forms of government (monarchy, aristocracy and 'constitution') and the other three 'perverted' (tyranny, oligarchy and democracy).[4] Thus in Aristotle's view democracy is a bad form of government whereby the common people, the 'many', exercise the power of government for their own benefit and not for the general interest. According to many classical authors a true form of government will, over time, inevitably deteriorate into a bad form of government because they hold on to a cyclical conception of time. This degeneration can be postponed or perhaps even prevented only by adopting a hybrid form of government in which elements of monarchy, aristocracy and 'constitution' are combined. Such a hybrid form was advocated by, among others, Cicero,[5] who tried (in vain) to prevent the demise of the Roman Republic and the emergence of the imperial form of government. For a long time, this mixed form of government was regarded as ideal, including during the Middle Ages, although monarchy gained more prestige than the classical authors would have felt desirable. A simple democratic principle was certainly not seen as the ideal.[6]

Wildly exaggerating and ignoring any historical subtlety, one could say that it is only since early modern times that democracy has been presented as an ideal form of government, and this coincides with the emergence of the social contract doctrine. We have already come across this theory as the historic cradle of human rights, so it is not surprising that some authors see human rights and democracy as inextricably linked: they appear to spring from the same source.[7] This, however, is not self-evident, but depends very much on how we understand democracy. The suggestion here is that two main authors play a key role. The first is Locke, who during the political strife between

---

[4] Aristotle, *Politics*, 1279b.

[5] Cicero, *De Re Publica*, Book 3. Cicero defends the Roman Republic's mixed constitution of the royal element (consuls), the aristocratic element (the senate) and the democratic element (the people).

[6] See, for example, Thomas Aquinas, *De Regno (on Kingship)*.

[7] See, for example, Jürgen Habermas, *Between Facts and Norms: Contributions to a discourse theory of law and democracy* (Cambridge, MA: MIT Press, 1996), ch. 3; Jürgen Habermas, 'On the internal relation between the rule of law and democracy', in *The Inclusion of the Other: Studies in Political Theory* (Cambridge: Polity Press, 1998), 253–64.

monarch and parliament in the seventeenth century made a clear choice of legitimate power being with parliament. His famous *Two Treatises of Government* (1690) form the justification of this choice. In the first treatise Locke demolishes the claim of the divine right of kings to rule and in the second treatise he argues that political power ultimately stems from the consent of the citizens. Therefore, political power should be exercised by themselves and for their benefit. In a certain sense, Locke anticipates the later definition of democracy given by the American President Lincoln – also in a funeral oration[8] – as government of the people, by the people, for the people. That is not surprising because Locke's philosophy was an important source of inspiration for those who fought in the American War of Independence. This is also clear when reading the American Declaration of Independence.

According to Locke, the power of the state is ultimately derived from its citizens who have 'agreed' by means of a social contract that their natural rights – to physical integrity, freedom and property – are to be ensured by a state. The form of such government consists of a legislature and an executive power including judicial power as a reflection of the two natural powers of those citizens.[9] Originally, humans had the natural power to make laws for the preservation of themselves and others and the power to punish crimes committed against the law of nature. Thus, consent is the basis for the legitimacy of the state and for its three powers, when the second natural power was divided over two instances, the power to adjudicate crimes and the power to execute sanctions. Obviously, this transfer by means of a social contract requires limits on the state because centralizing political powers brings the risk of the abuse of power. Therefore, these limitations of governmental powers need to be institutionalized. The newly established state shall not act in conflict with the original interests of individual human beings. Whenever the state does act in a manner which is inconsistent with the aim for which it has been created, it loses its legitimacy. According to Locke, citizens would then have the right to revolt against the government; they have not completely relinquished their original rights because of the social contract. The state has, as it were, only a mandated authority, and when it does not keep to the mandate, it loses that authority. That was then supposed to be the case when the king of England usurped political power at the end of the seventeenth century and when the English government suppressed the rights of the American colonists at the end of the eighteenth century. According to this first reading, the essence of democracy is that the state governs by the grace of its citizens' consent and that it respects their substantial rights.

The second key author is Locke's eighteenth-century counterpart, Jean Jacques Rousseau, who was an important source of inspiration for the French Revolution. Although Rousseau subscribed to the idea of the state

---

[8] The Gettysburg Address (1863).   [9] John Locke, *Two Treatises of Government*, 2.128.

being based on the social contract, he did not agree with Locke's interpretation of that contract. According to Rousseau, Locke's model could first of all not explain the stability of the state. If the social contract was established with the explicit proviso that it would lose its legitimacy if the original rights were not respected, it would not be possible for a stable state to arise. The question would be asked immediately as to who decides in the case of a disagreement about whether or not the state abides by the contract. If every individual had the authority to do so, then the laws of the state would not have much force. And that would mean that the natural condition of individuals living next to each other without any superior power would in fact continue. Anyone could withdraw from the contract, if they felt that their rights were not respected. Thus, Locke's theory does not really explain the transition from the state of nature to the political state. The continued validity of natural rights threatens the political order. Secondly, according to Rousseau it becomes insufficiently clear from Locke's account that the social contract cannot be a contract between citizens on the one hand and the state on the other, but solely a contract between individuals with the aim of establishing a post-state-of-nature entity. Democracy in Rousseau's view means that political power is derived from the people as the result of a complete and unconditional transfer of the original rights of the people to the state. These natural rights are completely transformed into civil rights. Therefore, citizens in the political state cannot claim any proviso on the grounds of their natural rights, but they can only appeal to their rights as determined by the general will of the state. The social contract establishes this general will, the *volonté générale*, and this will is focused on the general interest and not on the private interests of the many individuals or groups within the state. This is what Rousseau calls *volonté de tous*.[10]

Rousseau knew well that in this relationship between the general interest and particular interests some persons would be prepared to present their private interests as the general interest. The question then is: how to ensure that the general will is formed? It is essential for a democracy that the will of the people, the *volonté générale*, prevails and not those particular interests. This is possible, says Rousseau, by adopting a particular procedure which guarantees that the general will prevails and that prevents any particular interest from gaining the upper hand in society. This procedure consists in rejecting or prohibiting any faction within society and any form of political representation. The implication of rejecting representation is that any true democracy is a direct democracy and that democracy is only possible on a limited scale, namely that of the city state. Only on such a scale can self-interested minorities and majorities be prevented from ignoring the interests of the people. Rousseau thus subscribes to a historically long-held view that democracy on a large scale is not possible.

---

[10] Jean Jacques Rousseau, *The Social Contract or Principles of Political Right*, 1.6.

From this very brief overview a few lessons can be learned. From the classical mistrust of democracy, we learn that democracy is not only a system of government, but that it is also – in Plato's words – connected with a particular type of human being: a person who is primarily focused on his own interests and inclined to reject authority because of equality. Within the early modern embracing of democracy one finds two main strands of democracy as either a form of government in which the substantial interests of the citizens must be ensured, or as a form of government in which a particular procedure produces a superior will of the state. Locke and Rousseau represent these two strands. The former stresses the need to harmonize the will of the state with individual rights and tends towards a constitutionally understood form of democracy. The latter stresses the need to establish a will of the state that cannot be thwarted by particular interests. Therefore, democracy is basically a procedure, which is ultimately some kind of majority rule – whether or not on the basis of direct or indirect elections. That (indirect) democracy was possible on a larger scale than a city state was convincingly demonstrated by the American constitutional experiment at the end of the eighteenth century.

Two Concepts of Democracy

It is impossible to give an overview of the contemporary literature on democracy, but even so, it is possible to recognize the general lines of Locke and Rousseau. There is still a clear distinction between the concept of democracy, which with Rousseau emphasizes the procedure by which the will of the state is formed, and another concept that, like Locke, focuses on the substantial rights of citizens. There is something to be said for both interpretations. At first sight, the procedural or formal concept of democracy is perhaps the most common one, for what is democracy but a procedure to come to a decision based on the preference of the majority? Accordingly, democracy is then just a form of government in which ultimately the will of the majority – and thereby the will of the people – decides on what is to be done. If democracy is indeed primarily a procedure, it must be neutral with respect to substance – political viewpoints and ideologies that present themselves and are in competition to gain a majority. This would imply that democracy itself is not a specific political ideal, but a neutral method by which various political groups compete with each other to gain the upper hand.

Still, this is not completely correct. Democracy distinguishes itself from autocracy, says legal positivist Kelsen, precisely because of such a neutral and relativistic attitude with regard to competing political viewpoints and ideologies. According to Kelsen, who wrote in the 1920s on the nature and value of democracy,[11] democracy indeed implies relativism and therewith distances

---

[11] Hans Kelsen, *Vom Wesen und Wert der Demokratie* (1929), translated as *The Value and Essence of Democracy*, trans. Brian Graf, ed. Nadia Urbinati, Carlo Invernizzi Accetti (Lanham: Rowman Littlefield, 2013).

itself from autocratic regimes. Roughly, his argument is as follows. Anyone who, like Plato or believers in natural law, asserts that an absolute true political viewpoint is possible and that a fully just society can be established, can never be a democrat. For falsehood, even if it is believed by a majority, must always give way to the truth. Therefore, the political system should not be left to the majority, but to those who have access to this truth, and in Plato's opinion those were the philosophers. They must rule according to correct ideas and need not concern themselves with majorities. According to Kelsen, all political theories concerning the state are either autocratic and based on the idea of truth, or democratic and accept that there is no such thing as political truth. Only a democrat is prepared to accept that the truth is always relative and that one's own convictions can be wrong. Democracy thus presupposes the willingness to accept the view of others as a valid legal rule when such a view is democratically supported by the majority. Democracy and value relativism are linked: one must be willing to grant every political viewpoint equal value and accept that the legal rules within the state reflect the majority view.

Recently, Robert Dworkin has called this the majority interpretation of democracy.[12] Democracy as 'government by the people' must imply that the political process leads to a result that is supported by the majority of citizens. In other words, democracy enacts legislation and forms aims for government that have the consent of that majority. This approach is indeed neutral qua substance: whether a particular rule is democratically valid is not determined by its substance or content, qua legislation or aim, but by the procedure through which this rule is created. In a democracy the preferences of the citizens must be expressed and then the majority decides. This is according to Dworkin a 'statistical' conception of collective action. This may need some further clarification. Democracy is, as said, government by the people, but of course the people as such does not exist. The 'people' consist of a collection of individuals who on the basis of certain criteria, such as citizenship, are regarded as part of a particular political entity. If the people are to govern themselves then a way must be found to allow these constituent individuals to make a decision. According to the majoritarian reading, political decisions must reflect the preferences of the majority of all those individuals who have the right to participate in the decision-making process. From a statistical point of view, the influence of each individual is equal and the majority is just a matter of counting. For a democracy not the substance, or the outcome, of legislation or governmental aim matters, but whether the decision reflects the preferences of the majority.

Although this interpretation of democracy may seem plausible, one must ask, says Dworkin, whether it is really correct or desirable. Majority opinions are transient and can easily be manipulated. Sometimes this interpretation of

---

[12] Ronald Dworkin, 'Introduction: The Moral Reading and the Majoritarian Premise', in *The Moral Reading of the American Constitution* (Oxford: Oxford University Press, 1995), 1–37.

democracy is challenged by the argument that Hitler came to power in 1933 in a 'democratic' manner. This *argumentum ad Hitlerum,* however, lacks an adequate understanding of the complex historical circumstances that ended the Weimar Republic.[13] This republic was already on its last legs by the end of the 1920s, and a civil war between the Nazis and the Communists raged in its streets. When at the beginning of 1933 President von Hindenburg appointed the leader of the then biggest political party – the NSDAP (National Socialist German Workers' Party) – as chancellor, Hitler became head of a minority cabinet that was not supported by a majority in parliament, but rested on the constitutional authority of the president. Immediately and very skilfully Hitler extended his powers. However, his party still failed to win an absolute majority in parliament during the last free general elections, although Hitler's government had declared a state of emergency enabling him to restrict several civil liberties, including the freedom of the press. After this election, Hitler abolished parliamentary democracy by letting, or better coercing, parliament pass what is known as the Enabling Act. This piece of legislation enabled the government to enact legislation without the approval of parliament. The Enabling Act by which parliament set itself aside, did gain parliamentary approval because Hitler had imprisoned a number of members of parliament, despite their parliamentary immunity, and by sending armed forces of the NSDAP into the Reichstag, the German Parliament, to supervise the voting and intimidate the parliamentarians of the opposition. This parliamentary vote that Hitler won was certainly not free and it is in fact surprising that so many members of parliament, notably from the SPD, had the courage to vote against the act.

But we do not need Hitler to see the shortcomings of the majoritarian view on democracy. We would be better considering Kelsen's contemporary legal philosopher, Radbruch, who also defended democracy's relativism.[14] According to Radbruch – whom we encountered in Chapter 2 – democracy indeed implies the rejection of absolute values, such as those found in the natural law tradition and in authors such as Plato. It can never be scientifically proven, says Radbruch, that one (political) value is better than another. Only facts can be established objectively, not values. It is impossible to decide on the basis of scientific truth which value should be embodied in law. Therefore, the law can only be established on the basis of the value that has gained most political support. That is what democracy requires. If truth cannot be decisive for law, no other criterion exists than the will of the majority. This, however, does not imply, according to Radbruch, that democratic majorities can decide whatever they like. Because political competition between viewpoints and values cannot be decided objectively, it cannot be brought to an end by

---

[13] An excellent and succinct overview of the dismantling of the Weimar Republic is provided in David Dyzenhaus, *Legality and Legitimacy: Carl Schmitt, Hans Kelsen and Hermann Heller in Weimar* (Oxford: Oxford University Press, 1999), ch. 1.

[14] Gustav Radbruch, 'Der Relativismus in der Rechtsphilosophie', in *Gesamtausgabe*, ed. Arthur Kaufmann, vol. 3 (Heidelberg: Müller, 1990), 107–14.

a majority decision. A majority decides only on what the (legal) rule will be, not on the truth. Therefore, a rule based on a majority decision must always remain open for discussion and contestation. Democracy's relativism implies not only that decisions are made on the basis of majorities, but also that certain fundamental rights are accepted on the basis of which every citizen is entitled to express their views on the present legislation and government aims. In other words, democracy does not mean that the (present) majority is sacrosanct or that criticism of a democratic majority should be impossible. Therefore, every democracy must provide for the opportunity of the present minority to become the future majority, and this implies regular free elections. To prevent the present majority from usurping political power, it must respect the rule of law and the separation of governmental powers. A democratic majority may not simply do whatever it takes to remain in power. Democracy's relativism implies respect for different political viewpoints and for those who hold these views. In Radbruch's view, democracy demands even a form of 'socialism', since citizens can only live in dignity and develop their own values if some minimal standard of living is provided. Also, good citizenship is not possible without a decent educational system.

According to Radbruch, quite some content or substance is derived from the normative relativism of democracy: fundamental rights, rule of law, separation of powers and citizens' mutual respect. The procedural or formal view of democracy as 'merely' a decision-making process must include the possibility for a change of majorities. Even if 'formal' democracy is initially defined by 'procedure' only and not by substance, material or substantial elements unavoidably come to play a role. In this manner we approach the other concept of democracy that focuses on substance and outcome. Our best guide here is perhaps Dworkin, mentioned earlier. Against the majoritarian and procedural concept of democracy he posits its constitutional reading. In most existing democracies it is not the case, he holds, that the majority view is always decisive. Nowadays, many democratic states have constitutions in which not only the democratic procedures and the functions of the state are laid down, but in which also individual rights are enshrined in a way that protects them against majority decisions after a simple decision procedure. While it is true that democracy means in principle that all viewpoints have equal standing and that ultimately the people are the source of political authority, this does not mean that rather arbitrary and temporary majorities can always make decisions concerning controversial and important issues. Constitutional democracies acknowledge that majorities will not always take sufficient account of crucial interests of individuals and groups. In order to prevent a 'dictatorship of the majority', constitutions have safety valves built in. One of these safety valves has already been mentioned, namely the inclusion and protection of fundamental rights that no ordinary majority can abrogate. Another such safety valve is the possibility of adopting a federal state structure so that legislative authority is spread over different public bodies such as member states. Or to spread legislative power over more than one parliamentary chamber, such as a lower and an upper house, or a congress and a senate. These chambers can then check each other's legislation and make sure that legislation is not based on insufficiently considered grounds or on temporary emotions.

If such 'safety valves' are indeed part of the concept of democracy, then democracy is not identical to the immediate will of the majority of the people. Democracy is then not merely a simple procedure, but it includes substantial values. Accordingly, the legitimacy of a certain piece of legislation does not lie only in the question of whether it is based on a majority decision according to the prescribed procedure, but also in whether these values are respected. This is the material or substantive definition of democracy. In a democracy so understood, collective decisions are taken by political institutions in such a way that the citizens of the polity are treated as free and equal partners. Respecting and safeguarding this status of equality of citizens even becomes the essence of democracy, according to Dworkin's proposed constitutional interpretation of democracy. Its central notion is not majority but equality. While the statistical reading sees a democratic decision as the result of the sum of individual preferences, the constitutional reading conceives of such a decision as that of a collective agent, as that of society as a whole. Dworkin asks us to compare it with an orchestra which is only able to play a Brahms symphony well when each individual musician understands themselves to be part of a community, and pays attention to the conductor and to the other musicians. In order to play they must act as an orchestra. This requires a collective action and not merely the summation of individual actions. The constitutional view on democracy is that of citizens acting as a people, as a community.[15]

Dworkin's substantial interpretation contains not only elements found in Radbruch's account, but also elements that go back to Locke and Rousseau. One could say that Dworkin asserts with Locke that the 'original' rights in the state of nature are not completely abolished when entering the political state by means of a 'social contract'. This would be implied by the statistical view of democracy, according to which majorities decide on what rights individual citizens have. Dworkin strongly advocates a system of constitutional review on the basis of which the judiciary, generally a constitutional court, is authorized to decide whether positive legislation respects to a sufficient degree individual rights enshrined in the constitution. But Dworkin also seems to side with Rousseau, in so far as he conceives of a democratic decision as taken by a community, by the *volonté générale*, and not by the *volonté de tous*.

Nice as this synthesis may sound, the question is whether such merging of the two conceptions of democracy, of Locke and Rousseau, is possible. There are a number of serious objections against Dworkin's conception of democracy. First, look at the comparison he makes with a symphony orchestra. This

---

[15] Dworkin, 'Introduction', 20.

is interesting and appealing, but does it make sense? Let us imagine that all the musicians do indeed have a common aim: they all want to play a Brahms symphony in the best possible manner and thus act as a community. But less idealistic readings of their efforts are also possible: since they do not want to lose their jobs as musicians in this orchestra, they have to play together in at least a decent manner. Is a democratic society like an orchestra? Do citizens, like those musicians, have a common aim, or is democracy a mere conglomerate of citizens with very different individual and collective aims that may easily compete with each other? Kelsen would argue that the 'community' of the state is characterized not by homogeneity but by the heterogeneity of different interest groups.[16] Could the emphasis on the communal will not be detrimental to minorities who do not like to sing along with the majority hymn? Too much emphasis on the *volonté générale* could easily lead to a neglect of the *volonté* – perhaps not of *de tous*, but certainly of some, of *de quelques*. A classic reproach made to Rousseau's account of democracy is that its emphasis on unity is too strong. If society consists of radically different interests and political viewpoints, as Kelsen plausibly thinks, would then the simple, statistical counting of votes not be the only way to come to a fair decision?

The second objection would be the following: suppose individual rights are enshrined in the constitution, why should it be the task of the judiciary to adjudicate whether pieces of democratic legislation are compatible with these rights, as Dworkin defends? Are judges better equipped for this task than the legislative body? Is review by unelected judges not an undemocratic provision rather than a democratic safety valve, given that all sovereignty only resides in the nation, as the French Declaration of the Rights of Man and Citizen says? Many modern constitutional democracies have incorporated forms of judicial review, but does this mean that Rousseau's idea of a *volonté générale* ultimately formed by a majority vote is obsolete? Plus, why must certain rights of a minority be protected against the will of the majority? The general interest should certainly carry more weight than individual interests, as utilitarians argue. Admittedly, human rights put certain individual interests (such as life or freedom of expression) beyond the reach of ordinary regulation by the state. They are supposed to form a bulwark against the omnipotence of the state. But these rights need to be interpreted, and should these limits not be determined by the legislator? Is the judiciary's wisdom superior to that of the legislator?[17] According to Kelsen, democracy implies relativism with regard to values. Should such relativism then not also apply to the reach of individual rights? These rights are vigorously defended by Locke and Dworkin. But, after all, they too can make no claim to represent the final 'truth'.

---

[16] Kelsen, *The Value and Essence of Democracy*, ch. 2.

[17] The best-known criticism of judicial review is Jeremy Waldron, *Law and Disagreement* (Oxford: Oxford University Press, 1999), especially Pt III.

A third problem with Dworkin's constitutional reading of democracy concerns the characterization of a democratic society as community. According to this reading all citizens of a polity must be treated with equal status and equal concern,[18] but who are 'all citizens'? In other words: what are the boundaries of the polity? Dworkin seems to remain silent on the question of who belongs and who does not. From his point of view this is not problematic, as his considerations, fair enough, usually take existing constitutional democracies, often the United States, as a point of departure. Here the borders are fairly well defined. Since the Civil War in the nineteenth century this state has had *one nation under God* as its constitutional nucleus. In a similar vein, France declared itself to be one and indivisible in the first Article of its 1793 Constitution. However, the question remains whether democracy is only possible within a nation state with well-defined and protected borders. Is it possible for political configurations larger than nation states to be governed in a democratic manner? Suppose that this was not possible, then projects such as the democratization of the organization of the United Nations or making the European Union more democratic would be in vain. Therefore, the question of whether democracy has a particular 'habitat' is an urgent one. Is democracy a form of government within the city states, as some classical authors believed, or within national polities in which a clearly delineated *demos* can be found, as some modern authors held? What about democracy beyond the state?

Democracy beyond the Nation State?

According to both the Greeks and Rousseau, democracy must be direct and non-representative and is thus only possible for a polity in which citizens could know each other personally. Today it is regarded as almost self-evident that democracy – whether it is understood in either its formal or its material meaning – is possible in the nation state in which representation is inevitable. In such a state, citizens cannot know each other personally, but they are often connected by the bonds of language, religion and a shared history. In this way, these citizens form a community, nowadays famously called an *imagined community*.[19] The question is whether democracy as a mode of government can even transcend the nation state and be applied to political configurations that are larger than the nation state? Is democracy possible on a continental or even on a global scale? Opinions are divided: some are sceptical, while others are decidedly positive. It is not easy to give a definitive answer to where the political or geographical limits of democracy lie. Perhaps it is therefore instructive to examine a concrete case and look at the arguments about

[18] Dworkin, 'Introduction', 10.
[19] Benedict Anderson, *Imagined Communities: Reflections on the Origin and Spread of Nationalism* (London: Verso, 1983).

democracy that have emerged in the context of European integration. For this we need to look back into recent European history.

What was known as the Constitutional Treaty – or its official name: the Treaty Establishing a Constitution for Europe – was in 2005 rejected in referenda by the electorates of France and the Netherlands for a variety of reasons, among them the lack of transparency and democracy in the European Union. After this rejection, the (still) urgent need to reform the institutions within the process of European integration was met by the Treaty of Lisbon, in which the (earlier) Treaty on European Union and the Treaty on the Functioning of the European Union were integrated. However legally complex the Lisbon Treaty may have become, one word had to be avoided when drafting its text, namely 'constitution'. This concept was supposed to be only applicable to political unities like the state, but not to an intergovernmental body such as the European Union. Only a people can constitute itself as a state and since there is no European people (only European peoples exist), there can be no European state, but merely structures of intergovernmental integration.

Within the debates surrounding the referenda on the European Constitution, 'democracy' played an important role. Large parts of the European population, as testified by the French and Dutch majorities, held that there could be no such thing as a constitution of Europe. It was not the first time that the issue of the democratic component of Europe (or the lack thereof) had emerged in discussions. Earlier, in the context of the Treaty of Maastricht, in 1992, the question of whether this important treaty was compatible with the constitutional demands of democracy within the member states was put to various national constitutional judiciaries and also to the electorates in a few member states. And this led to interesting views concerning the scope of democracy.

Here, the background needs to be explained. The Treaty of Rome, establishing in 1957 the European Economic Community, initiated a process of European integration which over the years both widened, as more European states joined this process of integration, and deepened, as more competences were attributed to its administrative centre in Brussels. The idea was that the co-operation and the integration of the European peoples 'in an ever closer union' would prevent their states from relapsing into periods of inter-state war.[20] In order to achieve this, it was necessary to erect various European institutions such as the European Council (consisting of the heads of the participating governments), the European Commission (as an executive body) and the European Court of Justice.[21] Initially, this European project

---

[20] These words – notorious according to some and famous according to others – form part of the Preamble of the 1957 Treaty of Rome. European Union, Treaty Establishing the European Community (Consolidated Version), Rome Treaty, 25 March 1957, www.refworld.org/docid/3ae6b39c0.html.

[21] The European Parliament was (gradually) established later. Since 1962, some form of a European Parliament existed, but it only acquired serious powers such as budgetary powers after 1975.

proved to be very successful, especially in the field of economic integration because all kinds of trade and tariff barriers were removed. Originally starting out as a kind of (limited) customs union, 'Europe' developed into an internal market defined by four freedoms: of goods, capital, services and labour. In order for the Treaty and other agreements to be interpreted in a uniform manner across the member states, the European Court of Justice, located in Luxemburg, had to play an important role. Through a number of important rulings, such as the landmark *Van Gend & Loos* decision,[22] the European Court of Justice became an important motor behind European integration. Gradually, the question arose: if indeed 'Europe' takes such important legal decisions with far-reaching political implications, does it have sufficient democratic legitimacy? It is difficult to call it democratic when unelected bodies such as the European Commission and the European Court of Justice are as important, if not more important, for the gradual development of a European legal order than the constituent member states in the European Council, which represent only the governments. From a democratic viewpoint there seemed to be two possibilities: either there should be – on the European level – a truly elected legislative power, say a Parliament, or the European project should remain intergovernmental, guided and guarded by the European member states as the masters of the treaties.

The question of democratic legitimacy became urgent in 1992 with the signing of the Treaty of Maastricht. At that time, a new treaty was deemed to be necessary because the European political context had changed completely. The European Community had become much larger after integrating many new member states, mainly from Central and Eastern Europe, which became possible after the end of the Cold War. These developments also made the question of German reunification urgent. Against the background of these developments the Maastricht Treaty decided on a reform of the European institutions and on an extension of the economic community with a monetary union. These changes were drastic and questions were raised as to the democratic legitimation of these changes. For the first time perhaps 'Euroscepticism' emerged outside the United Kingdom. The fear was that the noble dream of European integration would lead to the nightmare of an undemocratic European super-state. Was the transfer of sovereignty to a body with doubtful democratic credentials ever permissible, certainly now with the possible creation of a monetary union? Were these reforms democratic enough so that the national legislation needed in many states for the ratification of this new treaty

---

[22] Case 26/62, *NV Algemene Transport- en Expeditie Onderneming van Gend & Loos v Netherlands Inland Revenue Administration* [1963] ECR 1; [1963] CMLR 88. In this 1963 case, the European Court decided that European law would have so-called 'direct effect', which roughly means that it can be directly applied by the national courts of the participating states. It also stated that the European Community 'constitutes a new legal order of international law for the benefit of which the states have limited their sovereign rights, albeit within limited fields'. See for an extensive and superb analysis Joseph Weiler, 'The Transformation of Europe', in *The Constitution of Europe* (Cambridge: Cambridge University Press, 1999), 10–101.

could be approved by the parliaments of the member states? Would it be democratic if national legislative bodies accepted the transfer of crucial elements of state sovereignty to a possibly undemocratic Europe?

This issue was discussed extensively in many European member states and their parliaments and, sometimes, courts. The decisions of the German Federal Constitutional Court, the Bundesverfassungsgericht, were especially important in discussing in-depth the issue of the so-called democratic deficit of Europe. The immediate occasion for this judgement, the so-called *Brunner* judgement or Maastricht decision,[23] was a formal complaint made by several German citizens, Brunner being one of them, that the ratification act in the meantime approved by the German parliament constituted a violation of the German constitution and of their constitutional rights. To be specific, these citizens argued that the Maastricht Treaty violated the following constitutional provisions: 'the Federal republic of Germany is a democratic and social federal state'; 'all state authority is derived from the people' and members of the German parliament shall not be 'bound by orders or instructions'.[24] The complainants argued that the Treaty of Maastricht would institutionalize a form of state power that is not derived from the (German) people and that German parliamentarians would be bound by legal regulations and decisions on the European level.

It is not difficult to understand why these complaints were taken so seriously. The provisions in the German Basic Law on democracy, on the federal structure of Germany's state and on the independence of its parliamentarians must be understood against the background of the traumatic dismantling of the Weimar Republic in 1933. The German post-war Constitution was meant to be a bulwark against undemocratic regimes. It is also understandable that the German Federal Constitutional Court rejected the complaints and ruled that the Treaty of Maastricht was not incompatible with the German Constitution. The German government had already concluded this Treaty with other governments, the German parliament had already given its approval to the Treaty and Germany had always been politically committed to the project of European integration. Still, the decision of the German Federal Constitutional Court contains a number of noteworthy and important observations on democracy and on the European integration. In its ruling, the Court clearly stated that the democratic legitimation of 'Europe' could only come from its member states and that it did not have its own source of democratic legitimacy. The Court thus did not accept the existence of a European democracy beyond the democratic nation state. The only source of European legitimacy would be the democratic consent of the member states with the establishment of the European Union by means of ratifying the Maastricht Treaty. The European Union is thus bound by that consent and should not be

---

[23] German Constitutional Court, *Brunner v European Union Treaty*, 12 October 1993, BVerfG 89/155.

[24] Arts 20, 38 GG (Germany).

allowed to develop itself legally or politically beyond the confines of that treaty. According to the German Court, the European Union is nothing more (and nothing less) than a body of international law that has no more authority than what it receives from its member states. The European Union is not a political or legal entity in and of itself, because it lacks a number of pre-juridical societal conditions such as a free discussion among social forces, interest groups and parties within society from which a unified political will can be constructed. Such a public sphere exists (only) in nation states but does not exist in Europe according to the Court. Its underlying idea seems to be that Europe as such cannot be, or at least is not yet, a democracy because there is no European people. And without demos, a nation, no democracy. Qua democratic legitimacy, the European Union fully depends on its member states, because only they can express a (general) will of its own. This volonté reflects, to a certain extent, the unity and the homogeneity – socially, politically and spiritually – of the (national) people. The Treaty of Maastricht can thus not be regarded as the foundation of a European state but it must be considered simply as the basis of a federation of European states that depends qua authority completely on these 'masters' of the treaty. The European Union does not have the competence to determine autonomously what its competences are. This is the decision of the member states, its parliaments and its judiciaries. Only these member states have full democratic legitimacy.

This court's decision and its implications for the meaning of democracy on a European scale were widely discussed.[25] Some welcomed the decision with approval.[26] Democracy is indeed possible only at the national level. Political configurations beyond this level can only be the result of an international agreement. If an international body such as the European Union wants to exercise authority with direct effect, then this is never a sovereign authority, because sovereignty only lies with the European nation states. Since there is no European demos, the European Union is faced with a democratic deficit which cannot be overcome. The basis of democracy is – as Rousseau had already stated – a more or less homogenous will of the people. This democratic deficit of the European Union cannot be overcome by establishing a European Parliament with legislative powers equal to those of national parliaments. Parliament is an expression of democracy, but it is not sufficient to create a democracy. Democracy presupposes an already existing unity among a people, so that those who govern can be perceived as equal by those who are governed.[27] For similar reasons, the concept of a 'constitution' should not

---

[25] For an extensive overview of the reception of the Court's ruling on which I rely here: Joseph Weiler, 'Does Europe need a constitution? Demos, Telos and the German Maastricht Decision', *European Law Journal* (1995) 1: 219–58.

[26] An important voice in this regard was Dieter Grimm, 'Does Europe need a Constitution?', *European Law Journal* (1995) 1: 282–302.

[27] According to Carl Schmitt, democracy is the identity between governed and governing. Carl Schmitt, *The Crisis of Parliamentary Democracy*, trans. Ellen Kennedy (Cambridge, MA: MIT Press, 1985), 14.

be applied to the European Union. A constitution is much more than the set of most fundamental norms (written or unwritten) within a state. It signifies that an independent political body is constituted by the people as a state. Just like democracy, a constitution presupposes a 'demos' that has constituted itself as a state. A constitution is, to use Rousseau's language, an original contract. Without a people, no constitution. For this reason, so it is argued, the preamble to the Treaty of Rome correctly refers to the 'ever closer union' of European peoples instead of to a European people. There is no such thing as a European people.

Others, however, were disappointed by the rather conservative interpretation of 'democracy' and 'constitution' in the ruling of the German constitutional court.[28] The view that democracy can work only within a nation state with an independent popular will ignores a number of important issues. First, under the present economic circumstances of globalization in which multinational corporations are active, the room for manoeuvre, that is for independent economic decision-making on, say, taxation, labour law, environmental regulation and employment is rather limited, especially for smaller states. Some of these multinationals are economically bigger than the gross national product of those small states. These states are either compelled to develop at least a decent relationship with these major economic players or they have to co-operate among themselves. As regards the democratic process, one has to bear in mind Rousseau's fear that the particular interests (*volonté de tous*) would interrupt the formation of a genuine common will (*volonté generale*). The economic influence of these economic powerhouses, along with that of wealthy individuals and powerful media companies, is a case in point, unless these states form a counterweight by creating entities such as the European Union. Therefore, it is proper that the democratic formation of a political will should also take place on a level beyond that of the nation state. Within the context of the European Union, the peoples of Europe will be better equipped, so this argument goes, to make their own political decisions independently of these economic forces.

What is, secondly, also ignored in the supposedly conservative reading of democracy is the level to which many nation states no longer are 'nations' in the sense of being homogeneous. Due to migration and (the recognition of) multiculturalism the idea that the state should or could reflect the true will of a uniform people has become increasingly unrealistic. The underlying assumption of the German court is untenable: the nation state itself, the people, is a conglomeration of various groups, interests and individuals. According to Kelsen, this has always been the case. Since such a heterogeneous political

---

[28] An important voice in this regard was Jürgen Habermas, 'Remark on Dieter Grimm's Does Europe Need a Constitution?', *European Law Journal* (1995) 1: 303–7. See also Jürgen Habermas, 'The European Nation-State: On the Past and Future of Sovereignty and Citizenship', in *The Inclusion of the Other: Studies in Political Theory* (Cambridge: Polity Press, 2005), 105–28.

unity did and does manage to govern itself in a democratic manner, why would this not be possible for an indeed heterogeneous unit such as the European Union? Could it not develop its own democratic mode of governance, without ignoring spheres of autonomy of its member states?

With this last element, the idea of nationhood and its link to democracy, we approach the theme of the next chapter: everyone has the right to nationality. Therefore, we must here be brief as regards the German court's view that a European people does not exist. It is undoubtedly true that not many citizens in Europe would identify themselves as 'European'; most would call themselves German, or French, or Polish. But this does not mean so much. In earlier days, Germans did not exist, but Bavarians and Prussians. From the fact that something does not exist now, it does not follow that it cannot exist in the future. If the argument is that democratic legitimacy requires a relatively homogeneous people, we will see in the next chapter that, historically, no homogeneous people stands at the origin of any state. It is rather the state which lies at the basis of a more or less homogeneous population: 'from peasants to Frenchmen', as we will see. Indeed, at the start of the French Revolution in 1789, the revolutionaries made an appeal to the nation as the source of 'national' sovereignty, but empirically this nation had still to be formed. Perhaps the European nations are much stronger today, as certain events such as Brexit seem to suggest, but why could in principle a process of 'nation formation' at a European level not take place? Such a European 'nation' would then probably not exist on the basis of a common culture, religion or language, but it could perhaps find its basis in shared values, such as dignity, the rule of law and a particular way of understanding the relation between church and state. There are in fact quite a few examples of relatively well-functioning democracies, such as Switzerland, Canada and the United States, that are not based on some form of homogeneity but on the loyalty of culturally different groups of citizens.

To resume, it seems that the German court in its Maastricht judgement adopted a rather cautious, conservative view of democracy, namely that of a form of government that belongs to the nation state. This may give rise to associations with a not-so-pleasant recent past, in which authoritarian leaders claimed to represent the will of the people. In that past, parliaments may have played a role, but merely as the body in which the unity of the people was supposed to manifest itself. In the opposing view, such as that of Kelsen,[29] parliament is the space in which groups with opposing interests and values meet each other face to face and have to reach some sort of compromise. In that view, the people as such does not exist, but is merely the 'name' for the collection of those interest groups and these different views on society. This picture would fit the European Union in which indeed many different nations, states and interests meet. If that is the case, then the authority of the European

---

[29] Kelsen, *The Value and Essence of Democracy*, ch. 2.

Union need not necessarily be in competition with that of the member states. Why would Europe and its constituent member states find themselves in a zero-sum game? Historically, it even seems that the project of European integration has rescued those nation states.[30] Could something similar not be possible in the future, in an increasingly global world with very few really powerful states? What the European Union gains in competences need not necessarily be at the cost of the member states. It is already now the case that one can simultaneously be a citizen of one's nation state and of the Europe Union and exercise one's democratic rights on both levels.

In the history of European integration one finds, as has been argued by Weiler, one of its finest commentators, two rival concepts of Europe: on the one hand Europe as a sort of proto-state and on the other Europe as a community of states. The German court clearly rejected the first concept, which may indeed be both unrealistic and unattractive, but this leaves open the possibility of the European Union as a community of member states. Well into the twenty-first century, one can imagine Europe as a democratic polity in which its citizens are defined both by their national and by their European identity. In fact, the introduction of European citizenship was one of the elements of the Treaty of Maastricht. The Union belongs to its citizens who do not have, nor need to have the same nationality. Precisely because they are all citizens of the Union, they have the right to participate in its government, just as required by Article 21 of the Universal Declaration on Human Rights.

The question whether democracy is possible beyond the level of the nation states has obviously not been answered by this rather brief excursion into democracy in Europe. But it has at least shown that 'democracy' can be understood in different ways. Rather than having a fixed meaning, it is open to various interpretations. With hindsight, it therefore seems wise that the Universal Declaration was reluctant with the use of the concept and did not outright proclaim a right to democracy.

---

[30] This is the view of at least the early stages of the European integration in Alan Milward, *The European Rescue of the Nation-State* (London: Routledge, 2000).

12

Everyone Has the Right to 'Nationality'

In Chapter 11 we saw that Article 21 of the Universal Declaration considers the will of the people to be the basis of the authority of government. That chapter was primarily concerned with the history of the current concept of democracy and also with the question of whether democracy is possible at a level beyond that of a people and the nation state. The question whether 'the will of the people' could refer to the whole population of the world, to mankind as such, was not examined. That was not necessary. It is clear that the Universal Declaration does not contemplate world government. That is hardly surprising: the Declaration was initiated by states within the context of the newly established United Nations and these states clearly, as is evident from the Charter of United Nations, had no intention whatsoever of subjecting their authority to some world government.

The Universal Declaration and the Existence of States

It is clear that, just like the Charter, the Universal Declaration presupposes the existence of states. That follows from Article 13, which lays down that everyone has the right to move freely within their own state and the right to leave their country and to return to it. Banishing certain citizens to particular towns or regions within their own state with an explicit prohibition against leaving the area, a practice that was used by the Soviet Union against dissidents, is in principle prohibited. Yet, this provision does not deny the possibility of the (incidental) closure of access to or exit from certain areas, for example for medical reasons, for the security of important state officials, or because these areas are reserved for military installations or manoeuvres. Nowadays there are also areas that are out of bounds to specific individuals on the authority of mayors or city councils, as when football hooligans are not allowed to enter the centre of a town. This is clearly not in conflict with the Declaration's prohibition on confining citizens to certain areas. The International Covenant on Civil and Political Rights repeats in its Article 12 almost verbatim the Declaration, but it wisely adds that there can be laws limiting freedom of movement if these are needed for national security, public order, public health and morals. Acknowledging the need for limits to the use of fundamental rights is not unusual, as seen before. In a general sense these rights obviously find their limits when they are incompatible with equal rights of other human beings.

The existence of states is also presupposed by Article 14, which proclaims the right of every human being to seek and to enjoy asylum from persecution in another country. That presupposes a plurality of countries: the political world envisioned by the Universal Declaration is not a cosmopolitan state but a multitude of autonomous political entities that live in peace side by side. The rights stipulated in Arts 13 and 14 confirm this. Although every human being has the right to leave their own country and seek asylum elsewhere, there is no corresponding duty to be found in the Declaration which obliges states to allow entrance to non-citizens to their territory or to grant them asylum. Later – in 1951 – the Convention Relating to the Status of Refugees – often called the Refugee Convention – laid down the specific categories of human beings to whom states would have such an obligation. These are refugees who report at the border of another state due to a real fear of persecution on grounds of race, religion, nationality, membership of a particular social group, or political conviction. In brief, only true political refugees can claim admittance to another state; there is no entitlement of entrance for all who seek entry to another state. Thus, the Universal Declaration does not proclaim a right of all human beings to freely travel around the globe and to be admitted to whatever country they want to enter. In the course of this chapter we will consider whether there are good grounds for this position.

The third clear indication that the Universal Declaration presupposes a plurality of states and not a world state is Article 15, which prescribes that every human being has the right to nationality and that no one may be arbitrarily deprived of their nationality. It is not surprising that, immediately after the World War II, this right was included. It had a certain urgency, because that war and the crimes committed during that war made it clear that human rights did not count for much if one was not a national of a particular state. Especially those minorities who also lacked citizenship, suffered greatly. The disintegration of the Russian Empire, the Habsburg Dual Monarchy and the Ottoman Empire and the establishment of new states at the end of World War I led to a great number of stateless persons, primarily minorities finding themselves on the wrong side of a border, that is within the borders of one of the newly established states, without full citizenship. Statelessness was also the fate of the Jews who were robbed of their citizenship under Nazi rule, both within Germany and in the occupied territories. The lack of nationality turned out to be identical to the lack of any right. The lesson to be learned was that anyone who is not a citizen of a (nation) state is in peril: without civil rights, human rights seem to have little significance.

Reflecting on these historical events led Hannah Arendt to the provocative and now famous statement that there really is only one human right – the right to have rights. She quotes with approval Edmund Burke, the conservative eighteenth-century commentator, who wrote that it is much wiser for everyone to rely on national rights than on 'the inalienable rights of man'. The loss of national rights entails the loss of human rights. The world, writes Arendt, finds 'nothing sacred in the abstract nakedness of being human'. The concept of human rights based solely on belonging to the 'human family' has little or no value for individuals who have lost all attributes but being human. Finding oneself in a situation in which one is merely 'human' is dangerous, as is clear from the experiences of 'survivors of the extermination camps, the inmates of concentration camps and internment camps'.[1] Today too, many human beings find themselves in situations where they are merely human. One might think here of illegal immigrants who have no legal status in the country where they find themselves; they are often not or no longer recognized as citizens of the countries from which they have fled. Their state is one of statelessness and often of homelessness as well. They have scarcely any rights and are dependent on the goodwill of the states in which they are staying, or of some of the citizens of those states.

If it is indeed the case that human rights are only relevant for those who are members of a political community in which their voice is heard, then Arendt is correct: the most important right is the right to have rights or 'the right to belong to some kind of organised community'.[2] Therefore Article 15 is of crucial importance: the right to nationality and the protection against being arbitrarily deprived of it, could perhaps, following Arendt, be considered more important than the right to life, because life needs protection which is or ought to be provided by the state. Often the right to nationality is 'acquired' at birth when a child's name is entered into the civil register. Being a national of a particular state is not a natural phenomenon, but requires an administrative action based on positive law. Article 15 stipulates that every human being is entitled to such an administrative act of a community – often the state in which they are born.

The important phenomenon of nationality and the nation state will be considered further in this chapter. We shall also look at free movement according to the Universal Declaration: human beings have the right to move freely within their own state, but this freedom of movement is restricted to one's own state or to the community of states in which free movement is allowed, as in the case of the European Union. Would it not be morally better if every human being had the right to move freely throughout the world, even if this were to limit the significance of state borders and reduce the importance of nationality and citizenship? Of course, these are major issues; only a few facets can be touched upon here.

---

[1] Hannah Arendt, *The Origins of Totalitarianism: New Edition with Added Prefaces* (New York: Harcourt Brace Jovanovich, Publishers, 1973), 299–300.
[2] Ibid., 296.

A Brief History of 'Nationality'

In order to understand the significance of nationality, the nation state and the concomitant idea of nationalism, it is important to return to one of the predecessors of the Universal Declaration. The 1789 French Declaration of the Rights of Man and Citizen was formulated at the beginning of the French Revolution and its principle of liberty, equality and fraternity was regarded as something of universal value. Yet, the French Declaration was still merely a statement in which the rights of the French were announced, both in their capacities as human beings and as citizens. It was not a universal declaration for all human beings. Therefore, it is not so important now to look precisely at which rights were then announced, but to look carefully at the important definition of political authority given in its Article 3. This declares that the principle of all sovereignty lies with the nation ('Le principe de toute Souveraineté réside essentiellement dans la Nation')[3] and that no institution or individual may exercise any authority that is not derived from the nation. Herewith the notion of the sovereignty of the nation replaces and puts to an end the notion of monarchical sovereignty. The French Declaration of 'human' rights was issued by the Third Estate, which had previously severed itself from the Estates-General (representing the three estates of clergy, nobility and bourgeoisie), which was summoned for meetings earlier by the king. This 'Third Estate' had then declared itself to represent the whole of the nation and called itself the *Assemblée Nationale*, the National Assembly. That was indeed what the French Revolution brought about – the replacement of monarchical sovereignty by national or popular sovereignty.[4]

But what exactly is the nation, and what is a nation state? Initially, this question seems easy to answer – the French nation, that is the French, is the source of that state's power. But this is much easier said than understood. The matter is complicated: who belongs to the nation and what constitutes the people? Some argue that the 'people' or the 'nation' which was invoked by the Third Estate and then by the French revolutionaries, did not in a sense exist at the time. Suppose one were to take a common language as the criterion for the French 'people' or for human beings to belong to the French 'nation', then linguists tell us that there was little linguistic homogeneity on France's territory at the end of the eighteenth century. People spoke Breton, Flemish, Aquitaine and many other languages and dialects. Therefore, if language is the criterion for a nation on which the central authority of the state can be built, then there was no 'nation'. It should be added that the 'French' state, as European states in general in those days, were not yet very centralized. On France's territory, there existed not only linguistic heterogeneity, but also a great deal of *de jure* or *de*

---

[3] Declaration des Droits de l'Homme et du Citoyen, Paris, 26 August 1789, https://fr .wikisource.org/wiki/Déclaration_des_Droits_de_l'Homme_et_du_Citoyen.

[4] See, for example, William Doyle, *The French Revolution: A Very Short Introduction* (Oxford: Oxford University Press, 2001).

facto regional autonomy, as was the case elsewhere. In a sense, then, the French Revolution continued a process of unification and homogenization that had already started under the French kings and lasted well into the twentieth century.[5] The nation or the people referred to by the French revolutionaries should thus not be seen as a historical reality, but more as an invented or 'imagined community'.[6] This non-existent community was subsequently brought into reality by these revolutionaries and by their revolutionary state through taxation, compulsory language education and conscription, and sometimes through wars against certain 'French' regions which insisted on their autonomy. What was true of this process within France also applied, *mutatis mutandis,* to most of the rest of Europe in the following years. The unification of Germany, to mention just one example, only took place in the late nineteenth century. At the end of the eighteenth century one finds a lot of dissatisfaction with monarchical sovereignty and calls for republican reform or even revolution were loud but not always successful. Nonetheless, the idea that the nation or the people should form the basis of the political unity and authority proved to be powerful and appealing, despite the historical reality of much linguistic and cultural diversity in many then existing states.

The popularity of the idea that the law should be the expression of the will of the nation was due to the influence of Enlightenment writers such as Rousseau and Kant.[7] From the early nineteenth century up to today one finds many national or nationalistic political movements that aim to establish a constitution based on the 'nation'. The process of decolonization in the second half of the twentieth century was played out in terms of national liberation. The violent disintegration of the former Yugoslavia towards the end of the twentieth century must be explained in part by the power of nationalism and the call for (separate) nation states. Some of the present multi-national states, such as Belgium, Canada, Spain and the UK or perhaps even the European Union (if is perceived as a proto-state), have come under pressure from secessionist or even separatist movements. The idea of the sovereignty of the nation is still one of the most powerful concepts of our times, even if it is not always clear what constitutes a nation.

Nationalism must thus be understood as the effort to establish a nation state.[8] As a political principle, nationalism holds that national units and political units should be congruent. It further holds that every nation, or people, has the right to their own political state and that every state should be based solely on a particular nation. When this political principle is violated – which often

---

[5] Eugen Weber, *Peasants into Frenchmen, The Modernisation of Rural France 1870–1914* (Stanford: Stanford University Press, 1972).

[6] Benedict Anderson, *Imagined Communities. Reflections on the Origin and Spread of Nationalism* (London: Verso, 1983).

[7] See, for example, Kant, *Metaphysik der Sitten*, AA VI, 313: 'The legislative authority can belong only to the united will of the people.'

[8] There is a vast amount of literature on nationalism. My reading of this phenomenon is strongly influenced by Ernest Gellner, *Nations and Nationalism*, 2nd ed. (Oxford: Blackwell, 2006).

happened and still happens – it gives rise to nationalist sentiments in order to set political things 'right'. A violation of this principle can take multiple forms: the state boundaries may include most members of the nation, but not all (think of ethnic Russians who used to live on the territories of the former Soviet Union but ended up living outside the present Russian federation); or a nation and its people may form part of several states yet have no state of their own (as is the case with the Kurds); or various nations or peoples live within one state (as in the former Yugoslavia or in the present Belgium); and finally colonial rule, where a nation is ruled by outsiders, by persons who do not belong to that nation (as in the case of the Tibetans, who are ruled by ethnic Chinese). All these are violations of the principle of the nation state which holds, formulated slightly differently, that political authority is only legitimate when it is based on or derived from the nation. Many commentators assert that democracy is intimately linked with the nation state, because the concept of 'democracy' means that power lies with the demos, the people. In Chapter 11 we have seen that some argue that democracy is only possible within a nation state and that supranational political units, such as the European Union, can per definition not be democratic. The European Union is composed of several nations and it therefore lacks its own 'demos'.[9] Others, however, would defend that the two concepts of nation and democracy should be kept separate. In the procedural understanding of democracy the manner in which collective decisions are to be reached is emphasized, but not the unit, or the collectivity, for which decisions need to be taken. Some would even say that everyone who can be affected by a particular collective decision should be democratically involved in the decision-making process.[10] Sometimes democratic decisions can be taken at the level of the nation state, but sometimes they must be taken on a broader level. But it remains the case that 'nationalism' is a powerful principle which holds that the world should be organized politically in a particular manner, namely divided into a plurality of territorially separated national states which are to a large extent ethnically homogeneous. The Universal Declaration does not oppose this view, for it argues in favour of every human being's right to nationality and that must mean the right of every human being to be a member of a (nation) state.

Now that we have seen the theory behind the nation state, it is important to pay attention to its historical reality. It is remarkable that the principle of nationalism is very powerful, but that it rarely matches that reality. It is notoriously difficult to give a comprehensive definition of a nation or a people. Therefore, it is also difficult to say with some precision or objectivity whether and when the boundaries of state and nation are congruent or not. The political reorganization of Europe after World War I in the Treaty of Versailles was based on this principle, but

---

[9]   See Chapter 11. As mentioned, excellent is: Joseph Weiler, 'Does Europe need a constitution? Demos, Telos and the German Maastricht Decision', *European Law Journal* (1995) 1: 219–58.

[10]   This is called the all-affected principle, see, for example, Michael Zürn, 'Democratic governance beyond the nation-state', *European Journal of International Relations* (2000) 6: 183–221.

applying it gave rise to numerous problems with regard to minorities who found themselves in the 'wrong' state. An attempt was made to find a solution for the unclear situation by international provisions for minorities and by minority rights. Arendt's statement that there is only one human right, namely the right to have rights or the right to belong, was born out of this ambiguous state of affairs. The Universal Declaration also tried to find a solution for this difficulty not by acknowledging collective minority rights, but by granting rights to every individual, in this case by proclaiming the right to nationality as a human right.

But is it possible to solve the practical problems inherent in the principle of the nation state either by establishing minority rights or by proclaiming the human right to nationality? That depends on how serious these problems are. Some argue that problems of establishing fixed criteria for the existence of a 'nation' or a 'people' cannot be solved. Imagine, for the sake of simplicity, the following two criteria, either separately or in combination, for a nation: a common language and a common religion. But then one faces the sheer number of existing languages and religions. This earth certainly does not have the space for a viable political state for each and every language and religion. The number of potential 'peoples' or 'nations' is far greater than the number of possible nation states. It is therefore unavoidable that the claims of only some nations are met, while others are rejected, with the consequence that national, ethnic or religious minorities persist. Some of these minorities will feel that their national identity is not sufficiently recognized, on either the national or the international level. Does the Universal Declaration, with its right to a nationality, solve this problem? Probably not, because no one has the right to choose one's national citizenship. With merely the right to seek and enjoy asylum in other countries but no corresponding duty on states, the danger of statelessness remains; Arendt's emphasis on the right to have rights therefore remains relevant.

It has become clear that the state and the nation are two different things. From a sociological viewpoint the state is nothing more than an institution that holds a monopoly on legitimate force within a particular territory. In contrast to previous political configurations – such as feudalism in the Middle Ages – modern states are indeed characterized by the exercise of centralized power and the use of force by its citizens is, apart from cases such as self-defence, prohibited. Whether a state is able to maintain this monopoly of (legitimate) force determines the difference between weak and strong states. Not all states can acquire or uphold such a monopoly, due to, for instance, the existence of criminal groups or national minorities. Generally, however, states do their utmost to maintain a position of superior power. They can do so by coercion – for example by forbidding the use of the language of minorities or by stripping regional authorities of their powers – or by force directed at criminal groups or separatist movements. In the nineteenth century Nietzsche characterized the state as the new idol and as 'the coldest of all cold monsters. Coldly lieth it also; and this lie creepeth from its mouth: "I, the state, am the people".'[11]

The fact that the nation gained importance in modernity has a sociological explanation in the changes during the transition from the earlier agricultural communities to modern industrial societies. According to Gellner and other scholars, both the state and the nation are modern phenomena that find their origin in this transition. The argument is as follows. While an agricultural society is small and local, an industrial society or one that is in the process of industrialization demands a more homogenous population. An industrial society assumes a complex process of the division of labour and it therefore requires mobility. Participants in that labour process must be able to work with one another, and thus to understand one another in order to produce goods for the market. This demands standardization, both in production and consumption. In a modern society the members of the population can no longer be culturally divided but must become (to a large extent) homogenous – and that is the moment that the nation and the state come together. The task of creating such cultural homogeneity is one that the state has taken upon itself by setting up a single language as a national guideline and by introducing compulsory (primary) education in that language. The example here would be the French state. After the French Revolution, it established not only the supremacy of Paris as the centre of political power, but also that of the French language. The process of doing so, and thereby marginalizing regional autonomy and regional languages, was legitimated by an appeal to the nation. Remember again the French Declaration of the Rights of Man and Citizen's Article 3: the principle of sovereignty resides in the nation and no one and no other body can exert authority unless it emanates from the nation. Therefore, it could be said (and it was famously confirmed by General de Gaulle in 1960)[12] that the French nation owes its existence to the French state. It was not the nation that invented the state, but the state that invented the nation, despite the claim of nationalist thinkers that the roots of the nation can be traced back to the (ancient) history of a people. Bearing in mind the changes that took place in modernity, 'nationalism' is not – although it sounds odd – the result of the actions of nations, but nations are the result of nationalism, namely the need of modern society for a certain cultural homogeneity. Nationalism is a typically modern phenomenon that has led to the disappearance of a great number of so-called low cultures in favour of a privileged national 'high' culture.[13]

As the eighteenth century was once regarded as the century of the Enlightenment, with the first declaration of human rights, the nineteenth century and the first half of the twentieth century are known as the age of

---

[11] Friedrich Nietzsche, *Thus spoke Zarathustra*, ed. Robert Pippin, trans. Adrian Del Caro (Cambridge: Cambridge University Press, 2006), 34.

[12] 'There is a France only thanks to the state', quoted in Sudhir Hazareesingh, 'Haughty Dirigistes', *London Review of Books*, 23 May 2019, 25.

[13] Gellner, *Nations and Nationalism*, ch. 4.

nationalism, which led to the creation of nation states. Nationalism has various forms: in addition to the French revolutionary form, other forms of nationalism developed within the territory of the former Habsburg Empire. Hungary for example saw many efforts to establish its own national 'high' culture on the basis of which political autonomy could be called for. In the politically fragmented Italy and Germany one finds attempts to constitute unified states on the basis of an already existing 'high' culture. In the German case, it was sometimes said that the (German) 'nation' already existed and was just waiting for its own state. Finally there is the nationalism of the diaspora, the efforts of kindred minorities dispersed over various states to establish their own national homelands, especially when the position of these minorities in these states – as a result of their nationalisms – was becoming rather untenable. A prime example here is Zionism. The original call for a Jewish homeland came from Theodor Herzl in *Der Judenstaat* published in 1896, which ultimately led to the foundation of the state of Israel after World War II.

The Universal Declaration can be read as a reaction to extreme forms of nationalism as one of the prime causes of two world wars, indeed set in motion by nation states that claimed regional supremacy and national superiority for themselves. The Universal Declaration was not the only answer to these excesses. The carefully steered process of European integration, which started out in 1952 as the European Coal and Steel Community between a mere six states, is another. Nationalism has certainly not disappeared and it is still a mighty force. The post-World War II process of decolonization was characterized as 'national' liberation, led by national liberation movements. As already pointed out, the first Article of both human rights conventions after the Universal Declaration is a confirmation of the nation state in the form of the right of all peoples to self-determination. Within the present European Union, various national movements within member states strive for greater autonomy and less European oversight. Despite the economic advantages that are inextricably linked to the European Union, 'Brussels' is often resented due to its supposed lack of respect for national sovereignty. The call for greater unification of Europe is repudiated by voices that point out the great significance of the nation state.

Considering all this, it seems prudent that the Universal Declaration proclaimed everyone's right to nationality, and not a right for everyone to be recognized as a citizen of the world. After all, the political world consisted then and now of nation states and there is little reason to believe that they have had their day or that there is on the horizon a world state of which everyone could be a world citizen. Still, it can be asked whether this choice for a 'right to nationality', prudent as it may be, is morally preferable as well. On the grounds of Arts 13 and 15, human beings have the right to citizenship of their national state and the right to move freely within their own state, but this is only a limited freedom of movement and depending on the size of the territory of their states some persons seem to have more 'freedom' than others. Is limiting freedom of movement to one's state morally preferable? Would it not have been morally better if the Universal Declaration had proclaimed the right for all humans to move freely throughout the whole world?[14]

Universal Freedom of Movement?

The Universal Declaration, as we saw, does not foresee a world government and formulates the right to free movement within one's own state only. It also formulates a right for everyone to return to their own state after having been elsewhere and the right not to be deprived of one's nationality. But at the same time no one has any claim based on human rights to be admitted to another state. Whoever reports at the border of another state can only make a request to be admitted, but that other state has no duty to grant this request and allow entrance. The interaction between me, as a foreign national, and the immigration official who has to decide whether to admit me or not, is not a matter of human rights, but of international law. This can easily be seen from a quick glance at some passports: according to my Dutch passport (which is, interestingly, not my property but that of the Dutch state) it is the highest national authority that requests the authorities of another 'friendly power' to allow the bearer of this passport 'to pass freely without let or hindrance'. In other words, my permission to enter another state depends on the goodwill of that state, not on my (human) right. Obviously, when I ask for permission to enter another state, human rights, such as the right to life and the right not to be tortured, still are in place. The state to which the request is made has to respect these rights, but it is not obligated to grant that request on the basis of human rights. The Universal Declaration does not proclaim a right to move freely across the globe. States are sovereign with regard to deciding whom they allow or refuse entrance. A state's refusal to allow entrance to a particular person does not constitute a violation of that person's human rights, unless the person is a political refugee according to the Geneva Refugee Convention, in which case allowing entrance is obligatory. With respect to issues concerning migration the position of states is very strong and that of individual human beings relatively weak, depending on the state whose citizenship they have. Is the position of states too strong? In other words, would it not have been much better if the Universal Declaration had adopted a broader alternative for Article 15, on the basis of which every human being would have the right to move freely throughout the world?[15]

---

[14] Here one could even add the thought, sometimes defended by philosophers, that the earth was given in common to all humans (see also Chapter 10). To mention just one example: Immanuel Kant (*Metaphysik der Sitten*, AA VI, 250–1) speaks of the 'innate possession [of land] in common' and the 'original community of land'.

[15] This right could perhaps have been formulated along the lines introduced by Kant as the cosmopolitan right, that is, the right to visit. This is the right to present oneself to another society in order to establish friendly relations. Kant explains that originally no one has more

Some scholars and lay people indeed argue that the present restrictive migration rules are unfair and should be repealed; they advocate open borders and the right of all individuals to settle where they want.[16] This position can be defended on the basis of a variety of good moral reasons. First: is there a valid ground for the legal and moral right of a state and its citizens to deny entrance to citizens of another state? Why would those foreign non-citizens not have an equal right to attempt to build a decent life 'here' as citizens? Many humans are born in a state in which their economic prospects are so bad that it may put their lives and that of their children in danger. Why should a state have the obligation to grant entrance to political refugees on the basis of the Refugee Convention, but not to economic refugees, whose needs are often equally pressing? Why should the rule be that national borders are closed unless there are good reasons to allow individual human beings to enter? Should the rule not be the reverse: state borders are in principle open unless there are good reasons to keep out certain individuals (such as those belonging to criminal gangs or those who carry contagious diseases)? Instead of having to give a justification for opening the state borders for particular individuals, the situation should be such that states need to justify whenever they want to close their borders. The right of every individual human being to decide where he wants to reside should take precedence over the right of collective entities such as states to decide who to let in and who not. Should something like the freedom of movement of persons, accepted today (at least in part) as a reality within the European Union, not be introduced for the world as a whole?

In addition to the argument based on the right of individual human beings, there are at least two other reasons to advocate open borders: the first argument is that of the free market. According to many scholars, economic prosperity is best served by having markets be as free as possible. This, one would expect, would then also apply to the labour market. Prosperity increases when those who seek employment and those who have jobs on offer have few hindrances to meet each other on the market. When certain employers are on the lookout for certain employees, or when certain employees want to offer their services to these employers, the meeting of demand and supply should not be hindered by obstacles in the form of state borders. From this economic point of view, free movement of persons is preferable to the present situation with closed state borders. The supply of cheap labour would lead to a reduction of the price of goods and thus an increase in prosperity from which more persons would profit than is now the case. Moreover, free movement of persons is compatible with the right to property, which entails the right to do with my property whatever I want, including hiring cheap labour from

---

right to be on a particular place of the earth than anyone else. See Immanuel Kant, *Zum ewigen Frieden. Ein philosophischer Entwurf,* AA VIII, 357–8.

[16] A classic article in this regard is Joseph Carens, 'Aliens and Citizens: The Case for Open Borders', *The Review of Politics* (1987) 49: 251–73.

abroad. No one should be hindered in the use of his capital by state borders. The position of libertarianism, discussed in Chapter 10, can easily be detected in this economic argument for open borders.

The final argument for open borders is based on global justice. We have seen that the Universal Declaration presents us with a vision of a just world in which all human beings are free from fear and want and in which their rights are respected. The argument here is that the right to a limited freedom of movement only is an obstacle to an equitable distribution of wealth on a global scale. This limited freedom of movement means that wealthy countries can stop poor job hunters at their borders in order to protect their own prosperity and to give opportunities for employment only to their own people. Why would egoistic behaviour, the argument continues, that is generally considered morally reprehensible, suddenly become morally acceptable on the collective scale, on the level of the state? By keeping prosperity or natural resources for one's own collective self and by excluding outsiders, notably economic refugees or those fleeing situations of extreme need, one becomes partly responsible for the terrible practices of exploitation and human trafficking when those desperate persons attempt to cross the borders illegally. Even if they succeed, they often end up living in those new societies without a proper legal status. If they do not succeed in crossing the border, they may either pay with their lives or end up living in overcrowded and unsafe refugee camps. These are the consequences of the principle of closed borders. By removing the right of states to keep their border closed, the world as a whole would become a more just place.

This moral argument for more open borders is often supported by religious authorities. An example would be an older encyclical, *Pacem in Terris* of 1963.[17] In this document, Pope John XXIII declares that everyone should have the right to migrate to another country, when there are reasons of justice for doing so. It is also argued that a person is never merely a citizen of a particular state, but also a member of the human family and citizen of the common, global community of mankind. In the Bible it is written that you must not 'mistreat the stranger residing in your land. You shall love him as yourself; for you were strangers in the land of Egypt'.[18] The idea that the territory of a state is the 'property' of its citizens is also in conflict with the idea of Thomas Aquinas discussed in Chapter 10, namely the original common property of the earth. Therefore, it is considered unjust for states to have an admittance policy that benefits only those who are already 'in'.

Despite these forceful arguments it is not difficult to come up with counterarguments that underpin the choice for relatively closed borders as made in the Universal Declaration. Imagine that one proposes to a random layperson the idea of open borders; they would probably retort immediately that this would

---

[17] The document can be found here: Pope John XXIII, *Pacem in Terris*, 1963, www .papalencyclicals.net/john23/j23pacem.htm.
[18] Lev. 19:33.

lead to chaotic situations. At this moment wealth and poverty, security and insecurity are very unequally divided over the population of this world. Opening the borders would probably result in a great wave of migration of poor and endangered people to the richer and safer parts of the world in the search for a better future. Would this be a good thing for all? Some may perhaps remember Malthus who, in the eighteenth century, warned of an uncontrolled increase in population which would lead to dangerous situations. The supporters of relatively open borders may attempt to mitigate the fear of mass migration. On the one hand they could agree that the prospect of a country being overwhelmed is a reason not to open the borders completely, but they could, on the other hand, stress that a considerable increase in immigrants does not necessarily destabilize society, as long as the opening of borders does not mean that all newcomers would receive access to all services of the receiving state. Remember that an important argument for open borders comes from the libertarian idea of free markets, and within this idea there is not much room for a nanny state. Those who on the basis of open borders have access to another state still have to support themselves and cannot make any claim to housing, social services or work.

It is unlikely that this argument will fully lay to rest the concern about open borders. It would rather give rise to another complicated issue. If indeed ordinary state services are made inaccessible to newcomers, the arguments for open borders given by those in favour of free markets and by those in favour of justice and charity diverge. According to the first argument, open borders merely mean that immigrants are granted access to the territory of a state and to its labour market. The second argument, however, stresses that immigrants are persons who are in need of help and support, and this is not what will happen by merely opening the borders. A free labour market dominated by the law of supply and demand and by the availability of cheap labour will result in exploitation and a drastic fall in wages for all. A human right to move freely throughout the world and the abolition of states' pre- rogative to control its population need not lead to more justice but can result in a race to the bottom. State functions that are considered normal nowadays such as the protection of social rights might become endangered.

Perhaps it is therefore better to abandon the libertarian idea of free markets when dealing with the issue of migration and to seek help in Rawls's theory of justice, which was already mentioned several times. In Chapter 10, we saw that Rawls advocates two principles for a just society: the principle of freedom on the grounds of which everyone must have as large a system of fundamental freedoms as is possible, and the difference principle on the grounds of which socio-economic inequalities are acceptable only if they ultimately benefit the least well-off in society. On the basis of the latter principle, differences in income and wealth are acceptable, but they have an upper limit: social prosper- ity must in the end also be to the benefit of the least privileged in society. The state has the obligation to guard this limit and it can do so by means of a system of redistribution, for instance by (progressive) taxation and inheritance law. From Rawls's point of view, there is not much room for 'open borders'. Unregulated migration will probably mean that the state is no longer able to fulfil its responsibility for redistribution. The cohesion and stability of society as a whole would come under pressure through the disruptive effects of large numbers of migrants. Because it is, according to Rawls, a natural duty to build and support just institutions, a general right to migration cannot be recognized. This natural duty argues against the opening of state borders.

Rawls at the same time holds that there is another natural duty, namely to help others when they are in need or in jeopardy, if this help can be provided without excessive risk or loss to oneself.[19] Therefore, if desperate migrants show up at the borders, they cannot simply be turned away. Perhaps the borders should not be opened up completely, but at least help should be provided, and perhaps they should be open to larger groups than citizens of friendly states and political refugees only. This is perhaps a respectable position between fully closed and fully open borders, but then the question arises as to what a just criterion to regulate entry of those who want to migrate would consist of. Establishing such a criterion is certainly no simple task. Trebilcock provides us with various possibilities, but from the viewpoint of justice and the natural duty to help, all these possibilities seem somewhat arbitrary.[20] One could opt for a quota system and hopeful immigrants would then be allowed in on the principle of 'first come, first served', but would it be fair to grant the still scarce immigration places to the ones who happen to apply first for the quota? Would it not be fairer to decide who gets those places by lot? Against both proposals, quota and lot, can be brought in that the places are not allotted to those who might need them most. A very different possibility would be to sell the available places on the open market or grant them to those who would be of the most use to the host state. In both cases the state of origin of these migrants is then disadvantaged because it would lose either its wealthier or more skilled citizens. In short, it is not a simple matter to develop an equitable regulation for 'more open' borders.

One could say that the problems mentioned so far are merely pragmatic in nature. In the literature one also finds a more principled objection to open borders. It is not based on the fear that the state would be rapidly overwhelmed, but on a reflection of what a nation state is. We have seen that the idea of the nation state is very powerful; clearly open borders would undermine the cohesion of such a state. Nation states are willing to open their borders when potential immigrants belong to the same 'nation' or when they are refugees with whom the citizens of the nation state feels a sufficient degree of affinity. In their immigration policy such states are apparently guided not

---

[19] John Rawls, *A Theory of Justice: Revised Edition* (Oxford: Oxford University Press, 1999), 99.

[20] Michael Trebilcock, 'The Case for a Liberal Immigration Policy', in *Justice in Immigration*, ed. Warren Schwartz (Cambridge, Cambridge University Press, 1995), 219–46.

only by the principle that only political refugees must be admitted, but also by national, cultural or ethnic affinity.

This attitude of prioritizing some foreigners over others could be dismissed as unjust prioritizing of one's own cultural identity that must remain free of foreign contamination. But such an accusation is probably too simple. Indeed, the identity of a nation state is not static, and sometimes indefensible racist motives play a role in the question of who is and who is not admitted. This does not alter the fact that our political world does not consist of mere unencumbered individuals with their rights – as liberal philosophies would have us erroneously believe – but of socially embedded human beings. Neglecting the axis of sociability is to misunderstand legal and political reality.

The most prominent present-day representative of the perspective of the nation state as a 'community' is Walzer. According to him, the introduction of the human right to universal freedom of movement, in his words 'the tearing down of the walls of the state', would not lead to 'a world without walls', but to the establishment of 'thousands petty fortresses' behind which groups of powerful human beings would entrench themselves.[21] This phenomenon can already be observed in many places of the world where the rich live in gated communities. One could object to Walzer's view by arguing that he deals only with facts and neglects moral imperatives. The fact that people in a borderless world would probably retreat into defensive forts does not enable us to deduce anything about the moral desirability of a human right to universal freedom of movement. This counterargument, however, is again too simple. Human beings often seek surroundings that are familiar to them not only to protect their interests and those of their group, but because these surroundings are familiar so that they can trust one another. According to Walzer, nation states should not be understood as voluntary associations to selfishly protect individual interests, but as being analogous with families, neighbourhoods and clubs. Such groups do not primarily revolve around private interests, but around a shared general interest. Members of such groups are committed to each other and to the general interest they share because they derive their identity from such groups and believe that the other members do so as well. Nation states can only exist on the basis of mutual trust even if they are merely 'imagined communities'. That does not mean that mutual trust is quantitatively similar in every nation state, nor that trust would be impossible in supranational constellations. It does however mean that radically opening a state's border could endanger the trust as it exists among its members. The idea of open borders gives rise therefore not only to practical but also moral problems.

In conclusion: did the Universal Declaration strike a good balance between the interests of individuals and those of states? It limits, in Article 13, the freedom of movement to one's own borders and it limits, in Article 14, the

---

[21] Michael Walzer, *Spheres of Justice: A Defence of Pluralism & Equality* (Oxford: Blackwell, 1983), 39.

right to asylum to those who are politically persecuted. Given the dire circumstances in which a large proportion of the world's population finds itself (this will be further discussed in Chapter 14), it would seem that the right of an individual human being to seek refuge elsewhere carries too little weight, and the collective rights of states too much. Given this balance, states have little inclination to consider the needs of those who are not their own citizens. The fact that the Universal Declaration does not sufficiently help human beings in this world to deal with their problems should not be understood as a plea for restricting the importance of nationality in favour of everyone's right to universal freedom of movement. However, the borders of states are often and increasingly guarded too closely, even if one recognizes that state borders do have moral significance.

13

Everyone Has the Right to Belong

Part III of this book focuses on the human right to have access to societies. Obviously access to societies, small and large, is important because human beings are societal beings. Every one of us is part of a particular society, and societies or communities come in many shapes and sizes. In the previous chapters, two of the rights involved have been considered – the right to take part in the government of one's country (Chapter 11) and the right to belong to a nation (Chapter 12). Membership of state and nation is to a certain extent a rather deliberate matter. Taking part in one's government often means at least the active use of one's voting rights. Being part of a particular nation often involves an active identification with other members of that nation. Human beings, however, form part of societies at a much more immediate and less deliberate level. Everyone is born out of other human beings and is thereby part of a particular family and in a similar way one is born into and raised within a particular cultural and linguistic community. No one has much influence on these matters; they are a given. Being born to a family and belonging to a particular culture are part of the human condition.

A Universal Declaration of Human Rights would not be worthy of its name and aspirations if there were to be no recognition of or space given to such 'societies'. Of course, there are many more groups that help people order and give meaning to their lives, and in Article 20 the Universal Declaration asserts a general human right to assembly. This chapter, however, will concentrate on family and culture, since both are important and constitutive to the identity of each and every person. The Universal Declaration recognizes this by proclaiming both the right to be part of a family and the right to live within a particular culture. The access to these 'goods' must be facilitated so that family life and cultural identity have the chance to develop. Yet at the same time, the human right to family life and cultural identity cannot be to the detriment of other human rights. Human beings can legitimately claim respect for how they form their identity, but such respect has its limits. The rights to family and culture are not the only human rights. Furthermore, it is important to note that the rights under consideration here are not merely negative, namely as being shielded from state interference. They are also positive claims to protection and to provisions. Precisely because family and culture are both important and wide-ranging, in what follows only a few aspects of these rights will be discussed.

Marriage and Family

Let us begin by looking at what the Universal Declaration says about family and marriage. With respect to the latter, Article 16 prescribes in the first clause that both men and women of full age have the right to marry and to start a family without any limitation based on racial, national or religious considerations. Today this might seem self-evident, but in the historical context in which the Universal Declaration was framed this formulation was very significant. It could be seen as a reaction to the 1935 Nuremberg race laws by which German Jews were first robbed of their citizenship and then prohibited from marrying Germans – or indeed from having any sexual relations with them – in order to 'preserve German blood and German honour'.[1] Still, the equal approach chosen in Article 16, and confirmed in the second clause, which provides that the free and full mutual consent of spouses is a requirement for marriage, was not well received by all United Nations member states. In particular, Saudi Arabia refused to support the Universal Declaration because of this provision. Such an approach to marriage would be in conflict with Islam, in which there are many arranged marriages (as there are in a number of other religions). Moreover, Islam, like many other religions such as Catholicism (at least for a very long time), has little sympathy for giving men and women from different religions the right to intermarry.

The controversy of our days is less that of interreligious marriage or of equality between man and woman than whether the institution of marriage should only be accessible for two persons of different sex. On a literal reading, Article 16 does not exclude same-sex marriage. It merely states that men and women of full age have the right to marry and start a family, and not that men may marry only women and women only men. However, opening the possibility of same-sex marriage was certainly not intended by the drafters of the Universal Declaration or by the states which supported it. Clause 3 of the same Article 16 points to the family as being the natural unit of society. At that time such a unit was certainly considered to consist of a man, a woman and children. We saw in Chapter 9 that the process of decriminalization of homosexuality only began long after the Universal Declaration. Even today there are still a considerable number of countries in which homosexuality is a criminal offence; and in some so-called liberal states, certain religious groups oppose the societal acceptance and legal recognition of homosexuality as an ordinary sexual preference.

---

[1] For an excellent, authoritative collection of legal documents, including the Nuremberg laws, see Martin Hirsch, Diemut Majer and Jürgen Meinck, *Recht, Verwaltung und Justiz im Nationalsozialismus* (Baden-Baden: Bund Verlag, 1997).

The Netherlands was the first country, in 2001, to enable men to marry men and women to marry women, by changing its marital law. The law now simply states that a marriage can take place between two people of different sex or the same sex. This opening up of marriage to same-sex couples was not achieved without fierce opposition. In many countries around the world same-sex marriage is not legally recognized. At the moment, no consensus exists on the status of the right to marry someone of the same sex as a human right, although the number of states recognizing same-sex marriage is growing. At first sight, this lack of consensus may to a certain extent be astonishing, because denying homosexual couples the right to marry seems to contradict many provisions of the Universal Declaration that explicitly prohibit discrimination on the basis of sex. Consider for instance Article 2, which stresses that everyone is entitled to all the rights and freedoms of the Declaration without any distinction, including that of sex, and Article 7 which emphasizes that all are to be equal before the law. Despite these provisions, marriage was, and still is, regarded by many as an institution for the union between a man and a woman.

From a historical perspective, however, it is not surprising that same-sex marriage is controversial. If there is one statute within positive law that seems to be grounded in higher or natural law, it would be traditional marriage between man and woman. As we saw earlier (for instance in Chapter 1), the approach of natural law is to stress the necessary connection between positive law and higher standards of morality or religion. Or, to put it differently, law as it is should not deviate from law as it ought to be. What the law ought to be can then be derived from the nature of the law, revealed either via the objective 'nature' of mankind or via higher religious norms. Regarding the character of marital law, one then turns – as in Aristotle or in Roman law – to the supposedly natural relationship that exists between man and woman. Only these two are able to conceive and start a family from which later a political society can emerge. The objective or 'true' nature of the law on marriage is thus derived from these physical characteristics and from the fact that every human being is born out of a union of a man and a woman. As far as religious norms are concerned, it is argued that marriage is instituted by God, specifically for the bond between man and woman that is characterized by a unique affective, yet hierarchical relationship which enables mankind to procreate.

Often these natural law arguments are supplemented by historical arguments: marriage between a man and a woman is a centuries-old institution that should not just be set aside and opened up to couples of the same sex. Moreover, why open up marriage to same-sex couples, when a good legal alternative for them to regulate their affective relationship exists? In many countries, same-sex couples can have their partnership officially registered. This often leads to a legal situation in which these homosexual partners have the same rights and duties to each other as marital partners within a (heterosexual) marriage. Since civil partnership exists – so it is argued – there is no need to make marriage available for couples of the same sex.

These arguments (based on natural law, history and the availability of an alternative) were often not strong enough to refute claims that marriage should be opened for same-sex couples. Those in favour of the idea of opening marriage argued that this would be an important milestone in the recognition of homosexuality and would symbolize equality between persons with different sexual preferences. Still, it should be remembered that the emancipation of homosexuality and its social acceptance was and still is not an easy process, even if it was rapid in some countries. This process only started in the 1960s,[2] with the decriminalization of homosexuality and – in less than forty years – led to the legal recognition of same-sex marriage in a few countries. It seems likely that the emphasis on the equal rights of individuals as proclaimed by the Universal Declaration contributed to this rapid process.

It is indeed important to emphasize the speed with which this development took place. In a 1986 decision of the US Supreme Court, sodomy was still described as an unspeakable crime of greater evil than rape. For this reason, a criminal conviction for sodomy – in this case in the state of Georgia – was not considered in violation of the basic liberties as enumerated in the American Constitution.[3] Noteworthy are the dismissive qualifications used by the Court to describe this crime. They can easily be traced back to the classic writings in legal philosophy such as Blackstone's classic commentary of English law. Both the medieval Thomas Aquinas and the Enlightenment scholar Kant condemned homosexuality in very strong terms as an unnatural vice.[4] Despite this history, one finds in the United States (and elsewhere) a fairly rapid change of opinion. In 2003, the same court reached a very different conclusion, namely that such behaviour, if taking place between consenting adults, was protected against state interference as part of the constitutional right of personal freedom.[5] In other words, what was considered unnatural or even against nature and thus deserving of criminal punishment in 1986 was, a short time later, recognized as a matter in which the state should not interfere. In this shift, the arguments based on interpretations of nature, history and God's will made way for ones that were based on consent, privacy and the prohibition of discrimination. It indeed seems odd that the very same act that is not punishable between adults of different sexes would be punishable between adults of the same sex.

---

[2] Important in this process was - as already mentioned in Chapter 9 - the UK Wolfenden report from 1957, which recommended the decriminalization of homosexuality and prostitution, with important contributions by Patrick Devlin who criticized the findings of the report ('Morals and the Criminal Law') and Herbert L. A. Hart who defended its liberal position ('Immorality and Treason'). Both classic texts can be found in Ronald Dworkin, *The Philosophy of Law* (Oxford: Oxford University Press, 1977).

[3] I rely here on Martha Nussbaum's chapter on 'Sodomy Laws: Disgust and Intrusion', in *From Disgust to Humanity: Sexual Orientation & Constitutional Law* (Oxford: Oxford University Press, 2010), 54–93.

[4] See, for example, Immanuel Kant, *Metaphysik der Sitten*, AA VI, 277–8.

[5] *Laurence v. Texas*, 539 US 558 (2003).

The significance of this 2003 US Supreme Court ruling is in no way diminished by the fact that the anti-homosexual regulations in place in some US states had not been applied for quite some time and that such acts rarely led to prosecution. The very existence of these regulations symbolized that homosexuals were second-class citizens, with all its negative impact on their position within society. To be clear, this 2003 judgement concerned only homosexual acts and had nothing to do with legalizing same-sex marriage. In 2003, same-sex marriage was recognized in only a few of the states in the United States and it met very strong resistance. But only a few years later, the US Supreme Court had to rule on the constitutionality of same-sex marriage and then it ruled that states were constitutionally required to include same-sex couples in their definition of marriage.[6]

The upshot of this is that the moral condemnation of certain sexual acts by a part of the population – even if it is a large one – is not sufficient ground to legally prohibit these acts. The state does not have the authority to impose a particular moral view on sexuality on its citizens, but it does have to protect their liberties. Moreover, it must ensure that its citizens are not subjected to discrimination, but are treated equally, even if this may mean opening up an age-old institution such as marriage to same-sex couples. The argument based on equal treatment, as said before, has certainly gained force by the increased emphasis on the human right to equality. Obviously, more factors have contributed to this development, most notably the sexual revolution of the 1960s, which included among other elements the introduction of the contraceptive pill and the increased availability of pornographic material. In the United States and elsewhere this availability was defended by a number of arguments as well, but individual freedom, now that of expression and privacy, played a crucial role. Despite initial contestation – even before the US Supreme Court, in a case on which the movie *The People vs. Larry Flynt* was based[7] – the views on sexuality of many people changed and it is safe to say that the view that sexuality can be expressed only within marriage in a morally responsible manner, as claimed, for example, by Thomas Aquinas and Kant, is no longer dominant.

The text of the Universal Declaration certainly did not include the promise of a full 'emancipation' for homosexuals, but its emphasis on rights and equality certainly contributed to their emancipation. The same text however does give us quite some clues on how it understands marriage and its relation to family: marriage is regarded as the basis of the family; the family is seen as 'the natural and fundamental group unit of society and is entitled to protection by society and the State'.[8] Article 23 of the International Covenant on Civil and Political Rights (ICCPR) speaks of the family in exactly the same words. As

---

[6] *Obergefell v. Hodges*, 576 US _ (2015).   [7] *Hustler Magazine Inc. v Falwell*, 485 US 46 (1988).
[8] Universal Declaration of Human Rights, Article 16, clause 3.

a result, everyone has the (human) right to family life (which turned out to be of great importance in the domain of the right to family reunion and in the domain of asylum) and the right to be free of arbitrary interference in family life (in connection with Article 12 of the Universal Declaration). Article 25 of the Universal Declaration again emphasizes the importance of a family. According to its first clause, everyone has the right to a standard of living that is sufficient not only for themselves but also for their family. It is clear, unsurprisingly in those days, that the Universal Declaration presupposes the traditional breadwinner family model, in which the father works to support his family. In the case of unemployment, he has the right to social security for himself and his family. The impression that it is the man who is meant in the first clause is confirmed in the second, according to which 'mother and child' have the right to special care and assistance. Finally, on the family, Article 26 states that the upbringing of children and their education is a matter of responsibility and choice of the parents.

On the matter of the family and its children, the Universal Declaration has a clear view. Raising children and educating them are primarily the responsibility of the parents and not – to give just one alternative – the state. In the *Republic*, Plato argued in favour of an alternative, at least for part of the population; according to Plato, a just society requires that children be removed from their parents' care and raised by the state, for it is the state that can make the best use – that is, free of emotional bias – of children's various talents.[9] In modern times, one finds a similar idea in *Brave New World*, the 1932 dystopian novel by Aldous Huxley. An example of what the drafters of the Universal Declaration might have had in mind is the manner in which the Nazi regime tried to indoctrinate the German youth by means of a variety of state-led organizations, such as the Hitler Youth.

Just as important is the Universal Declaration's emphasis on the family as the 'natural' unit of society. This suggests that the state as an artificial unit must as a matter of principle respect family life and should interfere in the family only if it has good reasons to do so. Such an approach to the family is not unproblematic. A first problem is that the concepts of 'nature' and 'natural' are contentious. We have learned from cultural anthropology that family relationships are very diverse and vary from polygamy to monogamy and from the extended family to the nuclear family. There is no consensus as to what is the best way to raise children; children are nowadays born both within marriage and out of wedlock, and raised in families of very diverse composition. Maybe there are good reasons to give preference with the Universal Declaration to the nuclear family, but this cannot be based on nature. Moreover, an argument based on nature is in general not very convincing. From time immemorial nature has been used as a justification for the subordinate position of women in relation to men, certainly within marriage. Today, many children are born as

---

[9] Plato, *Republic*, 457–66.

a result of in vitro fertilization. If 'natural' in this context means without artificial, scientific-medical intervention, then the families in which these children grow up certainly cannot be considered natural. Besides, 'natural' cannot always mean good: earthquakes, infections and pandemics are part of nature. We are sensible enough to try to limit the impact of such natural phenomena by building homes in a particular way and through vaccination programmes and other medical interventions.

A second problem with portraying the (nuclear) family as natural is that its position and that of parents and children within the family are not natural at all. They are to a large extent shaped by the legal system. In many legal systems – including the Netherlands until 1956 – married women were not regarded as legally competent persons: they could not upon their own initiative open a bank account or make a legally binding contract. They also did not need to do these things, because important matters had to be dealt with by the 'head' of the family. Women were expected to care for the household and to raise the children, rather than to work outside the home. Tax law is important here as well. If tax law observes the breadwinner principle, it is often financially quite disadvantageous for a family when the woman has a paid job. When the legal and financial possibilities to end a non-functioning marriage are scarce – such as a divorce with mutual agreement and an alimony arrangement – then a family can become a prison rather than a 'natural unit'. In short, there is very little that is natural about the family. Its position is determined by the legal rules and institutions of the society in which it operates.

Considering the family as a 'natural unit' has further important implications, namely that the family as a natural unit is perceived as having a very different foundation than the public realm. This is a third problem. Since the public realm is supposedly based on an artificial, social contract aiming to bring an end to the state of nature (see Chapter 3), it remains the domain in which conflicting interests have to be solved, ideally on the basis of the agreed rules of justice. In contrast, by portraying the family as a natural unit, the suggestion is that the family is a harmonious unity in which the interests of its members are fairly represented by its head. The life of the family is supposedly beyond justice.[10] It is not in need of being controlled by justice, because it is held together by mutual love and altruism. If this is indeed the Universal Declaration's picture of the family, it reflects views long held in the history of (legal) philosophy. To give just two examples, love (and therefore not justice) is, according to Hegel, the determining principle of the family and, as such, he characterizes family life as 'immediate substantiality of mind'.[11] Despite his very detailed account of justice, Rawls hardly pays attention to the family. Sometimes Rawls even presents the participants in the original position – in

---

[10] Martha Nussbaum, 'Justice for Women!', *New York Review of Books*, 8 October 1992, www.nybooks.com/articles/1992/10/08/justice-for-women/.

[11] Georg Wilhelm Friedrich Hegel, *Philosophy of Right*, trans. Thomas Malcolm Knox (Oxford: Oxford University Press, 1952), 110–11.

which the principles of justice must be chosen – as heads of families, thereby suggesting that the family precedes the conflicts of interests in society which justice has to solve.

If the image of the family as a natural unit of love is correct, then we should regard the human right to marry and start a family primarily as a negative right that protects the spouses and the family from external interference. The choice of a marriage partner must be free; the choice of education for children must rest with their parents and family life must not be infringed. With regard to the natural love of the spouses and the mutual commitment of family members, public neutrality would be the only appropriate attitude. Sadly, however, it is well known that families are not islands of serenity, love and harmony in a societal ocean of discord. We have seen that the form of family life within society is largely the result of positive law. As such, the family is not the 'natural' unit that precedes society. Historically, many societies regarded the man as superior to the woman and that too has had a great influence on how families are formed. Within marriage and families, decisions were made on the division of benefits and burdens, with the latter often unequally resting on the shoulders of women, with detrimental consequences for their position within society. Most importantly, it is widely known that behind closed family doors, terrible forms of domestic violence occur, both against partners and against children. Everyone has, on the basis of the Universal Declaration, the right to physical integrity and the right to be free of slavery or degrading treatment. These rights are frequently violated within the life of the family. Portraying the family as a 'natural unit' should not function as a denial of violence among family members. The Universal Declaration emphasizes marriage and family life as forms of society deserving of human rights protection, but this does not mean that the state has only negative duties in relation to the family. It should actively ensure that fundamental interests of family members are respected. For these reasons, Article 16's formulation of the family as a 'natural group unit' seems not particularly well-chosen.

The Right to One's Own Culture

Although marriage and family are often considered to be natural phenomena, they are in fact societal institutions, and like all other institutions they should not infringe human rights. A similar observation can be made with respect to culture. Culture is often regarded as natural, but even if it were, it needs to respect individual rights. Article 27 of the Universal Declaration recognizes the right of everyone to freely participate in the cultural life of their community, but this must not be at the expense of the (other) rights of the individual. Individuals cannot be imprisoned in their culture, important as it may be. 'Cultural rights' are called, in Article 22 of the Universal Declaration, 'indispensable' for the 'dignity and free development' of everyone's personality. The Universal Declaration does not specify the kinds of communities within which persons may develop their cultural identity. In principle this community could be the nation state, but Article 27 of the International Covenant on Civil and Political Rights makes it unambiguously clear that the right to participate in one's own culture applies primarily to ethnic, religious and linguistic minorities in states in which another culture is dominant.

Cultural rights are thus connected with the important theme of minority rights. As a consequence of colonization, migration and globalization, almost all states in the modern world have various cultural groups within their borders. There is no longer any state that is a culturally homogeneous nation state, but even so – as we saw in Chapter 12 – the nation state is still regarded as the basis for democracy. This has led to heated discussions on multiculturalism in both the popular media and academic literature. These discussions mainly revolve around the question of what space a cultural majority should offer to cultural minorities and or to what space these minorities are entitled. On the one hand we find, in the Universal Declaration, Article 21, clause 3, which determines the will of (the majority of) the people as the basis for government. On the other hand it demands space for the cultural rights of minorities and thus a balance has to be found between the claims of the democratic majority and the rights of minorities.

This balance must certainly lie between the two extreme positions implicitly condemned by the Universal Declaration. The first extreme is assimilation and homogenization, in which minorities are required to fully adapt to the demands of the majority, not only legally but also culturally and morally. At the other extreme, segregation or apartheid, majorities and minorities live in the same state, next to but completely separate from each other. Both extremes are viewed as equally undesirable and morally objectionable, but unsurprisingly – immediately after World War II – the Declaration explicitly rejects the first extreme. In 1948, many abhorred the efforts of certain states, like Nazi Germany, to homogenize their populations by assimilating or eliminating minorities. The Universal Declaration supports a certain level of multiculturalism, without endorsing the other extreme of segregation. The concept of minorities does not appear at all in the Universal Declaration and that is remarkable.

Obviously, the phenomenon of cultural and religious minorities was not new; an acceptable means of accommodating minorities has been sought in Europe at least since the Reformation and the Treaty of Westphalia. Very often – as in the League of Nations – the choice was made to merely tolerate minorities, so that states were obliged to respect their minorities but not owed them positive assistance towards equality.[12] The Permanent Court of International Justice – established by the League of Nations and the forerunner

---

[12] The problematic nature of this construction of minority rights in and after the Versailles Treaty comes out vividly and movingly in Philippe Sands, *East West Street: On the Origins of Genocide and Crimes against Humanity* (London: Knopf Publishing Group, 2016).

of the International Court of Justice – developed case law in respect of the claims, justified or not, of minorities to retain their cultural and religious identities. One of its best-known cases is the condemnation of Albania in 1935, when it sought to close private schools of the Greek minority. The Court held that members of a minority must be treated equally to other citizens of the state, and that a minority should have the right to retain its ethnic and national characteristics.[13] International agreements for the protection of minorities and the supervision of these agreements by the Permanent Court unfortunately could not ensure that minorities received the protection they needed and deserved. During the 1930s, states such as Germany and Italy with expansionist aims used the excuse of the infringement of the rights of 'their' minorities across their borders, in other states, to justify why they threatened and later attacked those states.

In the wake of World War II, the Universal Declaration took another direction. It did not recognize cultural minorities, which would anyway have been at odds with a declaration of human rights, but it recognized the right of each human being to their cultural identity. The aim was to ensure the existence of cultural minorities by granting cultural rights to individuals and thereby to ensure a peaceful coexistence between cultural majorities and minorities. It can be doubted that this strategy has been a success. Since 1948, the question of minorities has regularly led to conflict, perhaps the most distressing recent European example being the disintegration of multi-ethnic Yugoslavia and the accompanying conflict and violence.

In theory, it seems sensible that the Universal Declaration rejected the two undesirable extreme positions, but it is not at all clear in practice what the recognition of individual cultural rights entails or what can be demanded on the basis of cultural rights. Does the individual right to freely participate in the cultural life of one's community include the right to one's own language in both public and private? According to the Permanent Court in the Albania case it does, but the question is whether the same decision should be taken in other contexts as well. It is not difficult to imagine that in certain situations the recognition of the right of a minority to, for example, education in their own language, hinders the ability of its members to integrate and participate independently in the wider community, so that the danger of de facto segregation looms. In other contexts, the right to education in one's own language might perhaps prevent assimilation. Something similar could be said with regard to clothing rules, such as the headscarf. Obeying cultural rules here might mean that members of minorities become locked up in their own culture, but it is also quite possible that recognition of the right to wear a headscarf encourages the integration of minorities on their own terms. Again and again, the need of ensuring the unity of a society whilst guaranteeing the rights of the variety of cultural groups within society requires decision-

---

[13] *Advisory Opinion on Minority Schools in Albania* (1935), PCIJ Reps. Ser. A/B, No. 64.

makers to attempt to find the right balance. The Universal Declaration gives no answer to how such a balance is to be achieved. It only rejects the two extremes: with regard to cultural minorities, both assimilation and segregation must be avoided.

As there is no clear-cut recipe for dealing with this problem, practical wisdom is required. Perhaps such wisdom can be gained from concrete cases. To round off this discussion, let us look at two cases. The first – fictional[14] – case examines the sort of respect that minorities deserve. The second – a real case – does the opposite. First, let us imagine a sports hall that was once built for indoor football but has since been used for other sports as well. After intensive use over the years, the hall is somewhat dilapidated and in need of renovation, and that requires new investment. To this end, money donated by all the users of the hall is used and a matching subsidy granted by the local council completes the budget. Indoor football is still the most popular sport and there are more players of this sport than players of all the other sports put together. Here we have a 'multicultural' sports hall, but the indoor footballers are in the (absolute) majority.

How should the collected money be invested? Obviously, the requirements of the various users of the hall are not identical. Would it be advisable to leave the decision on how to spend the money to a simple majority on the grounds of the procedural conception of democracy mentioned in Chapter 11? Bearing in mind the interests of all the persons who use the hall for other sports, this does not seem fair. A sporting minority has the right to preserve its sporting identity. In the final decision on how to invest the funding, the wishes of the indoor footballers should indeed weigh heavily, but not so heavily that they outweigh the interests of other sports and users. These users already use the hall and have contributed to the renovation fund. The common interest in facilities for all sports should weigh more heavily than the majority interest of still more or better facilities for indoor football. In short, it seems only fair to take the interests of the sporting minorities into consideration.

One of the problems with the procedural conception of democracy is that it is not really able to take into account the weight that sporting minorities, but also cultural minorities, give to their specific interests in any final decision. This is particularly the case when the majority can only guess how important a particular decision is – such as rules allowing or prohibiting certain clothing – that does not really affect them but has consequences only for a minority. Precisely when a certain decision affects mainly or exclusively a minority and puts a burden on them, members of that minority may feel that they have not had a fair share in the decision process and have thus not been treated equally. This is certainly the case when certain groups in society are regularly placed in a minority position by the decisions of the majority. Plato, as we have seen, was

---

[14] I am inspired here by David Miller, *Political Philosophy: A Very Short Introduction* (Oxford: Oxford University Press, 2003), esp. ch. 7 on feminism and multiculturalism.

no advocate of democracy, precisely because it unjustly assumes that all preferences and desires have the same value and that conflicting desires can be decided on the basis of the numbers involved. According to Plato, it is important that only the right desires form the basis of the laws. This objection to democracy is clearly 'elitist' in character and this objection that only numbers matter has to be rephrased in the context of 'cultural rights'. Since a democratic decision-making process runs the risk of permanently overlooking the perspective of a cultural minority and the weight they attach to certain facilities, coerced assimilation becomes a danger. This extreme position of assimilation might even stem from the well-intentioned majority's fear of segregation, the other extreme. This risk can be reduced by ensuring that cultural minorities are well-represented in the bodies that make important decisions, perhaps with more voting rights than could be justified on the basis of quantitative considerations alone in order to protect their cultural identity. Justice might very well require that in the meeting that decides on the renovation of the sports hall the sporting minorities are over-represented.

Of course, human rights alone might already function as a protection mechanism for minorities. The interest protected by a human right is, after all, already in principle outside the scope of a simple majority decision, by entrenching those rights as basic rights in the constitution. But is it enough? Another mechanism to protect cultural minorities is to give them the authority to regulate certain areas of their lives. This was the position taken by the Permanent Court of International Justice in 1935. Here, the Greek minority was only able to retain its identity when it could decide the language used in their schools. Obviously, such a decision entails the danger of segregation, but this is perhaps sometimes inevitable in order to avoid assimilation. The task set by the Universal Declaration is to find a reasonable balance between the claims of the majority and those of the minority. It cannot be expected that all the users of the renovated sports hall will play indoor football or give in to the wishes of those playing football: there must be room for sporting minorities as well.

The example of the sports hall illustrates the danger of the tyranny of the majority. On the basis of the human right to participate in one's culture the majority is not allowed to enforce their will to the detriment of the identity of the minorities. What does this imply for the public space within a multicultural society? Must such a space – because of this right – be completely free of symbols of cultural and religious (or sporting) majorities? In other words, should the public sphere be neutral? Let us look briefly at an important case that came before the European Court of Human Rights in 2011.[15] In accordance with certain Italian legal regulations, crucifixes hang in every classroom in Italy. Mrs Lautsi objected to these classroom crucifixes because she did not want her children to be confronted with the symbols of any particular religious

---

[15] Case 30814/06, *Lautsi v Italy* [2011] ECHR.

group. She started a case against the Italian state based on the First Protocol of the European Convention, which provides parents with the right to ensure that their children have an upbringing and education in accordance with their own religious and philosophical beliefs. A similar viewpoint can be found in Article 26, clause 3, of the Universal Declaration. At first instance, the European Court decided in Mrs Lautsi's favour. The Court held that the display of a symbol that could reasonably be associated with Catholicism – the religion of the majority in Italy – did indeed violate the pluralism of a democratic society and the state's duty of ideological and religious neutrality; even more strongly, the Court stated that the state's duty of neutrality and impartiality is irreconcilable with any judgement on the part of the state regarding the correctness of religious convictions. In other words, precisely because of everyone's human right to culture the state should be extremely reticent regarding religious symbols, certainly when this represents the majority's view.

This decision led to a storm of protest. On the basis of a very specific case, the Court seemed to have made a far-reaching conclusion with regard to the relationship between state and religion. Its judgement that the state should be entirely neutral seemed irreconcilable with the variety of ways in which the states that are the signatories to the European Convention shape the relation between state on the one hand and religion and church on the other.[16] Just to give a few examples, France upholds a strict separation (*laicité*), while in the United Kingdom the monarch is not only head of state but also head of the Anglican Church; Denmark has Lutheranism as the state religion, and the royal family in the Netherlands has strong ties with the Protestant Church. All of these constitutional provisions, whether explicit or not, would suddenly become illegitimate because of this bold decision of the European Court. During the case, the Italian state had similarly argued before the Court that its connection with Catholicism was so close that a prohibition on the public use of crucifixes would amount to an encroachment on its national identity. Moreover, Italy – less convincingly – had argued that the crucifix had become a general symbol. It need not necessarily be associated with Catholicism, it argued, but had acquired a general meaning of compassion.

To the relief of many and the disappointment of others, the Grand Chamber of the European Court reversed the decision of the Chamber on appeal. According to the European Court's final decision, a state has the authority to decide by which symbols it is represented, even if those are the symbols of a religious majority. This falls within its 'margin of appreciation'. The Court added the important proviso that the state is not free to indoctrinate school-children by means of these symbols because that would indeed be a violation of religious freedom and of a multiform society in which parents can raise their children in accordance with their religious and philosophical convictions. The

---

[16] See, for example, Joseph Weiler, 'Freedom of Religion and Freedom from Religion: the European Model', *Maine Law Review* (2013) 65: 760–8.

display of a religious symbol in itself, however, does not have any decisive influence on the way pupils form their own (religious) judgements.

According to most commentators, the Court has in this way found the right balance between the right of the majority to decide about the arrangement of the public space and the human right of members of minorities to their own cultural life. It cannot be inferred from the human right to culture – especially with regard to the protection of cultural minorities – that this amounts to a right to live in a society in which the public space is ideologically neutral. Moreover, one could add, it would be an illusion to believe that such a fully culturally neutral space is possible anyway. After all, as this chapter started out: every person is born from other persons and grows up in communities with their own histories and characteristics. The idea of a neutral public space – for example the French neutrality – could itself be considered an 'ideological' standpoint. A society is more than just a collection of individuals who freely give form to their lives and pick their ideological loyalties purely on the basis of choice. All humans are born into and raised by communities that already have a particular communal identity. A multicultural state consists of a plurality of such communities, each with their own cultural and religious characteristics. According to the Universal Declaration, the state must respect such plurality and refrain from indoctrination, but it is neither necessary nor possible in the name of sterile neutrality to pretend that the relation between majority and minority does not exist. The fact that there are crucifixes in Italian classrooms does not automatically imply – as Mrs Lautsi claimed – that the Italian state is assimilationist, in contravention of cultural rights. Her right to bring up her children in accordance with her own convictions is in no way limited by this fact. At the same time, her children learn that they are part of a society with a particular history and culture. In this way, the extreme of segregation is avoided.

It seems to be a bridge too far if, on the basis of recognition of cultural human rights in Article 22, minorities may demand of majorities that public spaces should become entirely free of any form of symbolism. Rather, because there is no human rights magical formula that enables legislators and courts to always find a reasonable balance between the two extremes, each time and in each case, such a balance has to be sought anew. As in the Italian case, societies must find an equilibrium between the claims of the majority and respect for minorities.

14

Everyone Has the Right to a Decent Standard of Living

Article 28 of the Universal Declaration states that 'Everyone is entitled to a social and international order in which the rights and freedoms set forth in this Declaration can be fully realised.' Earlier in the Declaration, Article 25 had announced everyone's 'right to a standard of living adequate for the health and well-being of himself and of his family'. What is 'adequate' here? According to the Declaration, it means a lot: not only food, clothing, shelter and medical care, but also social services and support in cases of unemployment, illness, invalidity, old age, or in case of 'other lack of livelihood in circumstances beyond his control'. Article 23 announces everyone's right to work with a just and favourable remuneration so everyone can provide for themselves and their family.

With these Articles, we clearly find ourselves within the part of the Universal Declaration which deals with social and economic issues. But interestingly, the Declaration adds to these rights, the so-called human rights of the second generation, a new right, namely the right to a social and international order which ensures that these rights are met. This is remarkable, but was it wise to emphasize a right to an international order which provides a decent living standard for all humans, while the world was – and still is – a place with gross material inequalities, between obscene wealth and degrading poverty? Perhaps it would have been prudent not to announce what is perhaps not attainable. For this reason, some scholars, politicians and laypersons are unhappy with the formulation of these 'rights' and their inclusion in the Declaration. Others, however, would stress that a human being's dignity is not only violated by denying them the right to a fair trial or by the use of torture. A large part of the world population has to live in deplorable conditions on a very small income, and that too is a violation of their dignity, the more so because poverty is not the result of some natural, inevitable catastrophe. A few others live in extreme wealth and do not seem to care much about the Declaration's promise of a world in which everyone is entitled to a decent standard of living. The lack of fulfilment of this promise has given rise to an important debate under the heading of 'global justice'. This debate is the subject of this chapter.[1]

---

[1] My views in this chapter are influenced by Thomas Pogge, 'The international Significance of Human Rights', *The Journal of Ethics* (2000) 4: 45–69.

Perhaps a good starting point is the view, still held by many, that the most extreme forms of poverty, so-called famines, have little to do with the international order, but are the result of natural disasters like droughts, as in the Horn of Africa, or earthquakes, as in Haiti. Such situations would then also have little to do with human rights.[2] If such disasters occur, wealthy individuals and rich societies are called upon to contribute to the alleviation of the suffering, perhaps not so much because justice or human rights so require, but because of beneficence or considerations of common humanity. A closer look at such situations, however, shows that the problem of global poverty, even of the calamities mentioned, has structural causes and should be understood against the background of the prevailing economic, political and legal global structures. In order to address the problem of poverty at least two proposals are made: more intensive international co-operation to stimulate development projects, and a change of the current way in which trade relations are organized so that the very poor could benefit from a more just international order. If the global poor have insufficient access to the markets of the rich and if it is relatively easy for the rich to dump their surplus goods and waste at a bargain price on the doorstep of the poor, they will never be able to build decent economies or to reach a decent standard of living.

There seems to be room for both more intensive development projects and better, more equitable trade relations. Fighting world poverty does not necessarily require more wealth on a global scale. A fairer distribution of the current wealth would seem sufficient. Some states, such as the Gulf states and in the wealthy north, as well as some individuals – for example, those listed on Forbes 400 – are extraordinarily rich. The present gap between the global rich and the global poor is surely not in line with the promise of the Universal Declaration's Preamble, namely a world in which all human beings 'shall be free of fear and want'. If living within dire poverty is indeed an attack on someone's dignity and the solution lies in providing every human being with a decent standard of living, how can such a situation be achieved?

The Interpersonal Approach

If (extreme) poverty is a violation of human rights and human dignity, the question arises as to who can be accountable for this violation. Who should solve this problem? The most obvious answer would perhaps be the states that are responsible for the present international economic order. States are responsible for concluding trade agreements and for granting or denying access to markets. The responsibility for achieving a decent living standard for all humans in this world falls on them. Many states, however, do not

---

[2] This view can clearly be contested. Famines are said to be more the result of distribution than of lack of food. See the classical study by Amartya Sen, *Poverty and Famines: An Essay on Entitlement and Deprivation* (Oxford: Oxford University Press, 1981).

consider themselves – rightly or not – wealthy enough to provide everyone in this world with such a standard of living. Generally, states consider themselves responsible for the well-being of their own citizens. Moreover, there is a collective action problem: even if the wealthy states considered themselves responsible for addressing the problem of world poverty, they would face the problem of which state does what? According to what criterion could a decision on burden-sharing be made? Imagine that states refuse to do any-thing at all, or at least fail to do enough collectively – is that the end of the story? Or does the duty to ensure compliance with social and economic rights then fall on ordinary human beings?

The contemporary philosopher Peter Singer thinks that this is the case. In an epoch-making article from 1972, entitled 'Affluence, Famine and Morality',[3] he almost singlehandedly started the discussion on world poverty. His argu-ment runs as follows: if the problem of world poverty is not dealt with at an institutional level by states, then ordinary persons ought to deal with it on what I would call here the 'interactional level'. This approach focuses on what ordinary people can and ought to do on the interpersonal level, neglecting or bypassing the state as an intermediary. What matters here is determining what the right thing to do for individuals is. In daily life, a large number of moral rules are already in place that govern our behaviour towards others, such as the prohibitions on lying and stealing and the duty to comply with one's obliga-tions, in short: do no harm to others. These moral rules also tell us how to act when others are in need. The main rule is that one should help where one can. This would mean that the victims of famines or earthquakes as well as those who are the victim of structural poverty must be helped. Because the focus here is on moral rules between individuals, institutional arrangements such as states and international rules are not taken into account. Perhaps they will appear at a 'later' moment, if it becomes apparent that states or aid organizations are much better equipped to provide help than individuals. But only if that is the case, the question arises as to what human beings owe each other in terms of institutions. Initially, Singer focuses on what obligations human beings have towards each other regarding socio-economic human rights and the problem of world poverty. The question thus is: do wealthy humans have an obligation to give material help to the poor of this world?

Perhaps some might argue that rich persons in one part of the world have no obligation to poor persons in another part of the world. It is often asserted that the moral duty to help others in need only applies to the dear and near, and not to the unknown. However, this is not the view in the famous biblical parable of the Good Samaritan.[4] In this story someone lies badly wounded in a ditch after being robbed; a priest and a Levite pass by, but they do not feel the need or the duty to help this person; only a later passer-by, a Samaritan, a relative outsider, responds positively to the call of duty and provides the needed assistance to the

---

[3] Originally published in *Philosophy and Public Affairs* (1972) 1: 229–43.   [4] Luke 10, 25–37.

victim. According to the Biblical story we should follow the example of the Samaritan. It is morally wrong not to help someone in need if one is able to do so. Singer endorses the biblical answer: suffering and death as a result of a shortage of food, shelter and medical care are wrong. These 'basic goods' are the most important conditions for leading a decent life. According to Singer, if it lies within our power to remove such wrongs, then we should do so.

Obviously, the general statement that help should be given does not answer the more concrete question as to how much and how often assistance must be given, let alone to whom in particular. Most persons would agree that one should help someone if one can: someone is about to miss a train and I point out to the conductor that this person is running for it. Such help does not 'cost' me anything. What, however, should I do if real costs are involved? Singer differs perhaps from most people with his answer to this question. He holds that help should be given even when the cost is quite high. When I am confronted with the poverty and misery of others then I must support those persons up to the moment that the basic level of my own well-being becomes threatened. The fact that my prosperity diminishes because of my help is not a valid reason not to help. According to Singer, this follows from two premises: avoidable hardship, suffering and poverty of persons are wrong, and all persons in this world are of equal worth. Singer agrees with the Universal Declaration that all human beings are entitled to a decent standard of living, as formulated in Article 25. The obligations persons have vis-à-vis each other on grounds of their common humanity and their equal status are far-reaching and much more costly and demanding than most people would assume. Only when a decent standard of living is achieved for every person would the obligation to give material support to the poor no longer exist. Because of equality, the obligation to help rests on all and the distinction between those dear and near who 'deserve' our help and those unknown to us who do not, is not valid according to Singer.

Singer uses a clear example that has become famous. Suppose I am on the way to an important meeting and I pass a pond in which I see a child struggling and about to drown. Here it is obvious what I should do: I must help, even if this would lead to a soaked suit and a missed appointment. It would be morally wrong to value my suit and meeting more than a child whose life I could save. According to Singer, this situation is analogous to the situation of any rich person in this world towards the global poor, particularly those in Third World countries. If suffering due to lack of food, shelter and safety is a wrong and preventable, then the situation of the drowning child is not qualitatively different from the circumstances of say a Bengali woman suffering during the famine that plagued Bangladesh at the time of Singer's writing. Something must be done in order to rescue the drowning child and assistance must be given to save human beings from poverty. The lesson from this example is that the psychological barrier that I feel whenever an appeal is made to me to relieve the poverty and suffering of persons far away may indeed be bigger than when an appeal is made by someone I know or with whom I am physically connected. But morally speaking, psychological or physical distance has no significance.[5] My relation to the child at the point of drowning is in essence not different from my relation to the unknown Bengali woman.

Singer's argumentation seems plausible. Like the Universal Declaration, he emphasizes the equal worth of each individual on this globe. Therefore, everyone has a moral obligation to provide help if possible. Nonetheless, many people remain sceptical and unconvinced by Singer's analogy. In situations close to home where children can be saved, rescue efforts are generally made, but there is generally much less enthusiasm for supporting the unknown poor in faraway regions of this world. Unger, a supporter of Singer's position, reports that many people find it easy to throw away a written request or to delete an email asking for a donation coming from Oxfam or UNICEF.[6] Most people react differently to an appeal made on behalf of malnourished and sick children who live far away than to a child who is about to drown close by in a pond. Saving that child is perceived as a clear moral duty, whereas to make a donation for a good cause it is merely seen as act of beneficence: good to do, but not morally wrong not to do. A generous person will donate, but a less generous person not. According to Singer, this difference in attitude can very well be explained psychologically, but it is morally untenable. Psychologically, it feels 'natural' to do one's duty in situations in which the distance is small between those in need of help and those able to give help.[7] Indeed without geographical or ethnic proximity to unknown people in need, there is little willingness to provide help. Many will say: why should I care for these strangers? Will the funds be efficiently used? Isn't it their own fault that they live in such dire circumstances? Why should I behave as a Good Samaritan; let someone else do something.

While Singer acknowledges these considerations based on physical and psychological proximity, he nonetheless rejects the moral relevance of distance. The principle that one ought to help another person if this can be done at a relatively low cost to oneself is valid, irrespective of what people generally think. Suppose again that I walk by a pond and see a drowning child; suppose that other persons are present as well, and see the problem but don't act. Does this mean that I ought not to do anything as well? Of course not! The fact that others do not do their moral duty, does not free me from my duty. Aid organizations are aware of these psychological mechanisms and they try to break through these barriers by giving a face to the people in need, so that it becomes less easy to brush moral duty aside. Singer does not oppose the use of

---

[5] This provocative statement has aroused lots of discussion. See, for example, Deen K. Chatterjee, *The Ethics of Assistance and the Distant Needy* (Cambridge: Cambridge University Press, 2004).

[6] Peter Unger, *Living High and Letting Die. Our Illusion of Innocence* (New York: Oxford University Press, 1996).

[7] Singer points out that this is certainly not always the case. Many people do indeed not feel the need to help beggars sleeping rough on the street of their own city centres.

such strategies because they may help to improve the fate of the global poor. Still, such a personalization is merely a tool to overcome the motivational barrier. It remains the case that everyone has a moral duty to provide aid and to contribute to the goal set by the Universal Declaration: ensuring that every human being has a decent standard of living.

Singer insists that there is a strong obligation to help solving the problem of world poverty. But then another objection against his approach arises: whereas it is possible to save the drowning child, this is not the case with world poverty. I have a duty to save the child because it is possible, whereas it is not possible to solve the problem of world poverty. This objection does not hold water either, according to Singer, even if one cannot know for sure that it is possible to establish a world in which every person is free from 'want'. It is true that a significant difference exists between the situation of the child in the pond and that of world poverty, and that this lies in the magnitude of the latter problem. It may indeed not be possible to provide all starving persons with sufficient food, all sick persons with adequate medical care or all persons without shelter with decent housing. The magnitude of the problem may indeed have a psychological impact: my financial contribution is insignificant; it is merely a drop in the ocean. But, Singer holds, the moral duty to provide aid when needed and possible remains valid, since at least a part of the problem can be tackled and for the persons who benefit from my assistance, it may mean the difference between life and death.

The goals set out in Arts 25 and 28 lead, according to Singer, to everyone's moral obligation to give material support to all those in need wherever they are if one can. The two objections mentioned – the lack of a physical or personal link with the 'victim', and the magnitude of the problem – have only a pragmatic, psychological or logistical significance, but lack moral traction. Still, he recognizes these objections as a problem. Arguing that these objections are not relevant to the moral obligation one has, is not enough to solve the motivational problem. It is one thing to have a strong argument that the duty to assist exists, but it is quite another thing to motivate the global rich to comply with this duty. Things may be true in (moral) theory but might not work in (everyday) practice.[8] Thus the question arises: how to bring practice closer to theory? If most persons would 'feel' the duty to rescue a drowning child, how to tackle the problem that they do not 'feel' a similar duty in the case of world poverty despite the (theoretical) similarity between the two situations? Without solving this problem the realization of an international order in which everyone has 'a standard of living that is high enough for the health and well-being of himself and his family' would be very difficult. In Singer's view 'justice' demands of all of us that we be impartially concerned with the

---

[8] An allusion to the title of a famous article, published by Kant in 1793. *Über den Gemeinspruch: Das mag in der Theorie richtig sein, taugt aber nicht für die Praxis*, AA VIII, 273–313.

suffering of everyone else. It would be a moral failure to think that the obligation to assist those in need increases or decreases with distance, geographically and emotionally. Nevertheless, this is in practice what many believe: suppose that there are two children in the pond, and one is our own child. Obviously one would see it as one's duty to save one's own child first. It is 'natural', so the argument continues, that the duty to provide aid is stronger when it concerns persons with whom we have special ties, via family, language and nation.[9] If there are so many in need, choices have to be made.

Singer attempts to challenge this 'natural view' in various ways in order to bring practice closed to moral theory. Of course, I am entitled to save my own child first, but not when this entails the deliberate killing of the other child. I am also entitled to rescue my kinsmen from a calamity first, but not if this would involve stealing from others so that they would end up in extreme poverty. The problem of magnitude is indeed a serious problem. The duty to provide every person with a decent standard of living might lead to the problem of 'over-demandingness': asking too much. Even if it is correct in moral theory that rich persons have a duty to save the life of an unknown child in Haiti or in Pakistan, even at a considerable cost, the moral obligation would become in practice excessively demanding and could lead to inertia instead. There are simply too many such children in need. Singer acknowledges this, and in an effort to bring practice closer to moral theory, he introduces a distinction between a more extreme and a more moderate variety of the obligation of material aid.

Originally Singer argued that the moral duty to assistance did not stop until the moment in which one would have to sacrifice something of moral significance comparable to the situation one tries to solve. In other words, the duty to help and support those who are in need and live in extreme poverty, would end only when the person who is helping is on the brink of sinking to the level of material well-being of the person in need of help. This would mean that one would be morally required to give up every possible luxury in order to help others in need. These are Singer's words: 'If it is in our power to prevent something bad from happening, without thereby sacrificing anything of comparable moral significance, we ought, morally, to do it.'[10] Giving up that much would indeed be too demanding. Because in practice not many people would be prepared to go this far, even if such a sacrifice were to be asked in the name of moral duty, it is best, according to Singer, to 'soften' the claim of moral duty and to replace its strict version by a more moderate version: one should prevent bad things, such as hunger and lack of shelter, from happening unless in order to do so one would have to sacrifice something morally significant.[11] The difference between these two versions is important. The 'extreme' or

---

[9] This is a view that goes back to at least Cicero, *De Officiis*, 1: 53. See also Martha Nussbaum, 'Duties of Justice, Duties of Material Aid: Cicero's Problematic Legacy', *The Journal of Political Philosophy* (2000) 8: 176–206.

[10] Singer, 'Affluence, Famine and Morality', 231.   [11] Ibid., 241.

strong version demands that the rich support others in need until the point at which they and their family reach the same level of well-being, or poverty, whereas the 'moderate' version 'merely' demands that they sacrifice only that which has no real moral significance – truly luxurious goods like five-star holidays or luxury clothing while the old clothes are still good enough. In order to make sure that every human being has a decent enough standard of living, moral duty requires from those who are well off to give up their superfluous luxuries, but not the things considered morally significant, such as investing in their children's future or supporting cultural institutions. The moderate version accommodates moral practice and allows more space for the ways in which the well-off of the world organize their lives. Thus, to give another example, while having a second (holiday) home does not seem to have moral significance (many persons do not even have a 'first' home), living in a comfortable house in which one's family feel happy and secure is morally acceptable.

This moderate version indeed seems less demanding, but is it enough? It surely asks less in terms of sacrifices. The duty to help others to attain a decent standard of living does not reduce all persons to roughly the same level of material well-being. There are, however, serious problems with this moderate version, as Singer acknowledges. First of all: what does 'morally significant' mean? Why should my duty to help be less stringent when I am confronted with a person who is unable to live a decent life, because it is for me 'morally significant' to attend a Wagner opera? Should the duty to help persons in dire need not carry more moral weight than attending an opera? If every human being has a human right to a decent standard of living, why make concessions? Thus, the criterion that nothing of moral significance needs to be sacrificed for one's moral duty to help is not very clear and does not bring us very far. Therefore the strong version seems morally preferable: if every human being has the right to a standard of living that meets basic needs, then those who can help should do so until the situation is reached in which everyone's basic needs are met. If this leads to a motivational problem in the sense that many are not prepared to do their duty, this lack of motivation should be addressed rather than 'moderating' the moral duty itself.

A second problem with Singer's approach is of an entirely different character. It resides in the presumption that an analogy exists between the child in the pond and the situation in which the global poor find themselves. Are these situations truly analogous? Certainly, the child ought to be saved in a situation of emergency – and it can be done by me. Certainly, the Universal Declaration states that every human being is entitled to a decent life, but this problem of world poverty is complex, has a long historical background, and cannot simply be solved by me. The first situation clearly asks for a simple 'interpersonal' approach, but the absence of a decent standard of living for many in this world has institutional causes and would require institutional solutions. The child who is saved presumably goes back to its parents and to the safety of a normal family life. But there is no simple solution or default position for those who have no adequate standard of living; giving money alone is certainly not enough. And even if it were, money would have to be collected, transferred to where it is needed and then distributed. That alone demands an infrastructure. Focusing on infrastructure and institutions might have an additional advantage because – or so its defenders claim – it can solve the problem of motivation. Solving the problem of world poverty might require the introduction of a special tax regime, which would solve the problem that helping the poor in the interpersonal approach depends on the beneficence of individuals to contribute. It is remarkable that Singer in the first instance – in his famous article – seems to underestimate the institutional side of the problem.[12]

The third problem is connected with the second. Singer's approach to the problem of world poverty emphasises the duty of those well-off to support the less well-off, but the problem of who is responsible for the present unequal socio-economic situation is not addressed. The rich are not somehow responsible or accountable for world poverty, so that the duty to assist the poor is the result from their acts. Singer's starting position is the simple utilitarian viewpoint that well-being ought to be maximized and suffering minimized. The well-being of the rich certainly increases with all the luxuries they can afford, but this increase pales in comparison with the increase of well-being which would result from a transfer of their wealth to the poor. Obviously, utilitarianism presupposes, as we saw in Chapter 10, some kind of moral solidarity between human beings: each person counts as one. Sadly enough, in the real world such feelings of solidarity and sympathy have only limited motivational power.[13] Perhaps then, the duty of the rich to contribute to a decent standard of living for all would fare much better if it was not based on beneficence but on something else. If it could be shown that rich persons and wealthy states are causally linked with the poverty of those less well-off, then the stronger moral principle that harm should be compensated and injustices rectified would become applicable. This principle is indeed much stronger than solidarity and sympathy. When an appeal to solve world poverty can be made on the basis of the harm principle, discussed in Chapter 9, instead of utilitarian sympathy, a solution to the problem seems much more likely.

Thus, we have to introduce another approach, which revolves around institutions and accountability. This approach seems promising because it not only helps with regard to institutional problems such as world poverty, but also with regard to natural disasters. After a natural disaster there is obviously an appeal for aid, but how large the disaster will turn out to be and how much aid is

---

[12] In his later work, Singer adopts a much broader perspective. See Peter Singer, *One World. The Ethics of Globalisation* (New Haven: Yale University Press, 2002) (revised version published as *One World Now*, 2016); Peter Singer, *The Most Good You Can Do: How Effective Altruism is Changing Ideas on Living Ethically* (New Haven: Yale University Press, 2015).

[13] This is for Rawls one of the reasons to reject utilitarianism as the basis for a theory of justice. See John Rawls, *A Theory of Justice* (Oxford: Oxford University Press, 1999), para. 30.

needed, is to a large extent dependent on where the disaster occurred and what institutions were in place prior to the disaster. A 'natural' disaster is rarely if ever only natural. Compare the earthquake in 2010 in Haiti with that in Chile a few years earlier. The force of the earthquakes was about the same, but the impact in Haiti was much greater than in Chile, because the former country is much poorer and had not made provisions for such a disaster. Or consider the floods in New Orleans in 2005. The disaster was caused not merely by Hurricane Katrina but also by a lack of maintenance on the old dykes that should have protected the city. The institutional approach focuses on the institutions that may have caused the problem of world poverty and 'natural' disasters in the first place, and institutional changes that can solve the problem.

The Institutional Approach

Today, the promise of the Universal Declaration of a world without want as a result of the human right of a decent standard of living has certainly not been fulfilled. The reason for this is not so much that people in general did not sufficiently heed their moral duty to give material support as Singer requires, but that economic, legal and political structures uphold a world which generates extreme wealth as well as extreme poverty. It is a well-known statement by the Nobel Prize-winning economist Amartya Sen, that there has never been a great famine in a country with a well-functioning democracy, with periodic elections and active opposition parties and where freedom of speech and relatively free media are safeguarded.[14] This teaches us two things, namely that the global political world is not made up of well-functioning democracies, and that political structures matter. The institutional approach therefore departs from the idea that world poverty is the result of a particular international order, namely the economic, political and legal structure of the present-day world. This structure not only determines the effects of natural disasters, as in the Haiti/Chile comparison, but also provides an explanation of why many millions of people live in terrible conditions. That means that the issue of who is accountable or responsible for the present global structure and its resulting world poverty must be addressed. Such a structure is not a natural phenomenon but is man-made. The real question is not how to motivate the rich to provide the poor with a decent standard of living, but how the child ended up in the pond or why the Bengali woman, Singer's contemporary example, lives in such a dire situation. While the utilitarian morality 'only' urges us to increase general well-being, the institutional approach wants us to concentrate on who is accountable for world poverty.

Sure, the institutional approach as such does not imply that the socio-economic human rights as mentioned in Article 25 will automatically be better guaranteed. It is after all quite possible that those who live in extreme poverty

---

[14] Jean Drèze and Amartya Sen, *Hunger and Public Action* (Oxford: Oxford University Press, 1989).

ultimately bear the (institutional) responsibility for their situation; if that is the case, then there is no responsibility on others to support them. Someone who chooses to be poor is not entitled to the support of others. According to the libertarian view that we encountered in Chapter 10, persons are in principle responsible for their own lives, so that the social position in which they live is the result of their own choices. Libertarianism fits well with the so-called American dream: from rags to riches; with hard work anyone can be successful. Obviously that story cannot be right. While it is perhaps true that every individual under certain favourable conditions has the chance to escape poverty, it is not true that all of them will be successful in doing so. Only a few will succeed. Generally speaking, people, like the Bengali woman, are born into particular situations from which it is very difficult or almost impossible to escape. Take life expectancy as an example. It makes an enormous difference where a person is born. Various reports, such as the United Nations Development Programme or World Health Statistics, show that the average life expectancy of persons living in prosperous states such as the United Kingdom is much higher than in poor countries such as the Democratic Republic of the Congo.[15] The difference in the level of education, health care and safety between the two countries is enormous.

These facts make the presupposition of libertarianism that everyone is ultimately able to move from rags to riches quite implausible. The situation in which individuals find themselves is to a large extent not of their own doing but follows from the way in which the world is organized economically, legally and politically. It is not plausible, according to the institutional approach, that those who lack a decent standard of living are personally responsible for the situation in which they live, nor is it only the result of the rich refusing to do their moral duty. The situation of the poor is not the result of interactions between individuals, as the interpersonal approach argues, but of the ways in which the world is organized, institutionally and structurally. In short, the cause lies with the 'basic structure' – a concept introduced by Rawls – of the world with its economic, political and legal rules. This structure is not natural nor God-given, but the outcome of legal and political decisions made by politicians and lawyers, often on behalf of the states that they represent. According to Thomas Pogge, one of the main spokespersons for the institutional approach, millions of persons live in extreme poverty and find their socio-economic human rights unfulfilled because of a particular global basic structure which is to a large degree determined by the rich countries for whom this structure is highly beneficial.

If Pogge and others are able to show that this is indeed the case, they would be in a much better position than Singer to argue in favour of the duty to fulfil socio-economic rights. While Singer only appeals to utilitarianism and to

---

[15] See, for example, United Nations, 'United Nations Development Programme', www.undp.org /content/undp/en/home.html.

feelings of solidarity and sympathy, Pogge and others invoke the harm principle which is widely recognized as a valid moral principle. It is a classical demand of justice to do no harm to others and to compensate the ones who are being harmed by us. If it could be made plausible that the global basic structure indeed harms large parts of the population of this world, it is clear that this basic structure needs to be changed so that the global poor are no longer harmed. Upholding a basic global structure which harms the poor while a better alternative is available, is a violation of justice. The basis for the obligation to fulfil Arts 25 and 28 does therefore not lie with solidarity, sympathy or beneficence but with justice.

Earlier, in Chapter 10, we saw a simple example of the workings of such a global basic structure: intellectual property law, as used by the pharmaceutical industry in the case of newly developed medication. Such a legal regime has advantages and disadvantages: persons living in great poverty have no or only very limited purchasing power, and thus often lack access to the 'medical care' to which they are entitled according to the Universal Declaration.[16] The way in which the protection of intellectual property is regulated is an example of the basic structure. At this moment it works to the disadvantage of the poor and to the advantage of the rich as their medical needs (and money) are an important incentive to the pharmaceutical industry. This industry has a much more limited interest in developing medications that would primarily benefit the poor because of their lack of financial resources. Therefore, Pogge argues in favour of another (legal) structure that can better serve both the medical needs of the poor and the financial interests of the pharmaceutical industry. Such a structure could be developed by initiatives such as the Health Impact Fund.[17] But the present structure, if it remains in place, constitutes a wrong to the poor who are deprived of the necessary health care. It would be a violation of moral duty not to change an unjust structure. Analogously, it would be a wrong not to take precautionary measures in order to prevent children from falling into a pond.

The citizens of prosperous countries rarely see, according to Pogge, their relationship to the poor peoples of developing countries in terms of human rights and rarely acknowledge the need for redistribution. But they do regard those people as the beneficiaries of aid or support. The idea is that poor people need help and that the rich are prepared to give aid from the goodness of their hearts, but it is not common to understand that those who are prosperous are in one way or another benefiting from and thus accountable for the poverty of

---

[16] The 1966 International Covenant on Economic, Social and Cultural Rights proclaims in Article 12 'the right of everyone to the enjoyment of the *highest* attainable standard of physical and mental health' (emphasis added). UN General Assembly, International Covenant on Economic, Social and Cultural Rights, 16 December 1966, Treaty Series, vol. 993, p. 3, www.refworld.org /docid/3ae6b36c0.html.

[17] 'Health Impact Fund', Wikipedia, accessed 5 April 2019, https://en.wikipedia.org/wiki/ Health_Impact_Fund.

others. Yet, the rich and the poor, along with the states to which they belong, with multinational businesses and the amalgam of bilateral and international treaties and agreements, form part of an international basic structure that systematically puts some individuals and states at an advantage and other individuals and states at a disadvantage. Think of a simple example: the support given by western politicians and governments to certain dictatorial or authoritarian regimes in order to gain access to resources at low costs. The same politicians and the citizens of those states even refer to universal human rights without acknowledging their contribution to a global basic structure in which socio-economic human rights remain unfulfilled and without seeking to develop an alternative structure in which these rights would be met.

In Singer's view it is quite irrelevant whether poverty is the result of natural disasters, wrong political choices, a global basic structure or a combination of these. The obligation to give material aid does not depend on the causes of poverty. Causality is in a sense irrelevant: human suffering is wrong; whenever I can alleviate that suffering without sacrificing anything morally significant, I ought to do so. According to the institutional approach, this approach leaves the moral obligation to help or to redesign the global basic structure unfounded. Anyone who rejects Singer's utilitarian viewpoint can simply shrug off the duty and remain indifferent to the misery of others. Indifference to others and brushing aside the responsibility for the violation of the socio-economic human rights is no longer possible when a causal connection exists between the wealth of the few and the poverty of the many.

Is it clear that such a causal link exists? Many hold that national or domestic factors are responsible for the differences in the wealth of nations, not the global structure. Prosperity or poverty in a particular state and the concomitant distribution of wealth would be the result of the choices being made in the state in question. Electing or re-electing honest or corrupt politicians obviously has consequences for how a state does economically. Pogge rejects this 'explanatory nationalism': the causes for the problem of world poverty cannot be found in the national basic structures of certain states, because the choices within one state are to a large extent determined by the international basic structure of the world as a whole. Therefore the obligation on prosperous states and wealthy individuals to provide assistance is not so much a positive duty to help those in need, but a much stronger negative duty not to impose on them an unjust basic structure. Their duty is, again, not based on sympathy or beneficence, but on justice. If the present global basic structure harms the poor while this can be prevented by changing that structure, it is a duty to do this, and that rests on everyone, in particular on the most powerful states.

Is it true that the international basic structure is causally connected with the problem of world poverty? There are good reasons to think this is the case. First, there is a historical link between developed, generally rich, states and under-developed, generally poor, states due to their common past as either colonizer or colonized. The socio-economic starting position of certain states is much more favourable than that of others. The prosperity of some and the poverty of others has historical roots. It is true that the present citizens of the former colonial powers are not guilty of their ancestors' colonialism, but in so far as they still benefit from the past, they are obliged to make certain reparations.

Rich and poor states are, secondly, bound together by a network of international treaties and agreements such as the Agreement on Trade-Related Aspects on Intellectual Property, mentioned earlier. Undeniably, this network benefits the prosperous states more than the poorer states. A simple example: a rich state can either exploit its own natural resources or buy those raw materials from elsewhere and then make an economic profit on them. A poor state, however, is often technically unable to exploit its own resources or unable to sell those resources at a sufficiently high price. The present global (economic, political and juridical) basic structure determines that the person or persons who have the monopoly of (political) power within a particular state – in other words: those who have 'effective control' – are authorized to sell in the name of the state the country's natural resources or to borrow money in its name. This stimulates power-grabbing. Thus, if a dictator (they would obviously call themselves president) comes to power in a certain poor state, they may not have domestic legitimacy since they have not been elected, but they have international legality to act on behalf of the state. When such a head of state sells natural resources or grants concessions to exploit those resources, the purchaser, often an international cooperation, becomes the legal owner of the resources. The same head of state can also borrow money internationally, which then becomes the debt of the state. Pogge calls these international rules privileges: the international resource privilege and the international borrowing privilege.[18] Such heads of state do not sell or borrow in the interest of the population of 'their' state. Rather, it is more likely that a part of the money is used to uphold a repressive regime and that the rest of the money is put in their own pockets, or safely stored in Swiss bank accounts. If Plato had to rewrite chapter VIII of his *Republic*, he would probably add 'kleptocracy' to the list on unjust regimes. Such regimes, led by thieves like Suharto and Mobutu, the former 'presidents' of respectively Indonesia and Zaire (now called Democratic Republic of the Congo), exist not because the people of these states were simply mistaken when electing leaders, but because the international basic structure forms an incentive for such crooked individuals to seize power.

We have now seen that solving the problem of world poverty would require changing the international basic structure, for example, by making the international standing of a particular regime (to do transactions in the name of the state) dependent on its internal domestic legitimacy. Why do such changes not take place? This is the third problem, and the answer is relatively simple: the

---

[18] Thomas Pogge, 'Moral Universalism and Global Economic Justice', in *World Poverty and Human Rights* (Cambridge: Polity, 2002), 91–117.

existing basic structure works to the advantage of the prosperous states and their citizens (and their companies). Therefore they have no incentive to change the current structure. The political leaders of most poor states have little interest either in changing the rules of the global game, because they personally benefit from it. They are also unable to change these rules, because of insufficient bargaining power. Negotiations on changing certain global rules in the context of say the World Trade Organization are complicated, and this puts the less powerful or less well-informed states at a disadvantage.

For all these structural reasons, it is surely impossible to solve the problem of world poverty and the scant implementation of social human rights by insisting on solidarity and sympathy. The poor must not be 'aided', but the unjust international basic structure that harms millions of persons must be replaced by a more just one. What matters is not the positive obligation to help, but the negative duty not to do harm. The institutional approach has serious advantages: the tendency to blame the poor themselves ('they are lazy and corrupt'; 'all they do is make war') is certainly wrong, however much it serves the complacency of the rich; the tendency to regard poverty as a matter of fate is also wrong. In today's world everything is connected with everything, but things can be changed by addressing the important role of global institutions; the tendency to focus on the interaction between individual persons only is also wrong because it ignores the importance of global rules. If world poverty is caused by an existing global basic structure that privileges the few and harms the many, it is a duty to develop alternative structures and institutions.

At the same time, the institutional approach faces serious problems as well. It is not at all easy to give an exact assessment of the harm done by the global structure in a particular case. Imagine a state with a large number of poor persons and the issue is: what role do domestic decisions play in the present situation and what role does the international global structure play? If harm has to be rectified, one needs to know who is accountable for what. Sometimes there may be good reasons for certain global rules, even if they are advantageous to some and harmful to others. The agricultural policy of the European Union is perhaps a good example. The saying goes that a cow in the European Union 'receives' more 'aid' than a child in a developing country. Due to the European farming subsidies and import restrictions it is very difficult for African farmers to gain access to the European market. An alternative structure would be to open up the European market for agricultural products from around the world. Do the European Union member states have valid reasons for protecting their agricultural market? Is safeguarding the ability of European farmers to make a living on its lands, and preventing Europe becoming completely dependent on food production elsewhere, a good enough reason to uphold this agricultural policy? It seems that the institutional approach goes too far in the direction of 'explanatory internationalism' and ignores domestic factors and legitimate national interests.

The problem of motivation is not only a problem for Singer, but also for the institutional approach. World poverty and the lack of fulfilment of socio-economic rights cannot be solved by solidarity and sympathy, but can it really be solved by justice and the harm principle? This may, again, be true in theory, but not in practice. We already know that it is extremely difficult to determine who owes what to whom in complex situations, such as cases of fraud in which many individuals and companies are involved, or in large-scale criminal activities with all sorts of intermediaries who may or may not be aware, or half aware, of the criminal nature of what they are doing as individual actors.

In an abstract, theoretical sense, it could be argued that every citizen of wealthy and powerful states has an influence on the drafting and upholding of international rules that are detrimental to the poor and that they have the duty to help to change these rules. But how much real influence do ordinary citizens of prosperous countries have? They could vote for political changes on the international level, but in practice they will have little understanding of the complexity of these rules and must leave concrete decisions to the specialists who as the representatives of their states defend the interests of their citizens. Since ordinary citizens have very limited influence on organizations such as the World Trade Organization or the World Bank, they will perceive as negligible their contribution to the possible harm done by these institutions. Therefore the institutional approach's call for a duty to compensate the harm done by the global basic structure will often fall on deaf ears. In the context of a global basic structure, the connection between what an ordinary citizen does and the problem of world poverty is so indirect that the problem of motivation re-emerges. Both the interpersonal and the institutional approach face the same problem. It may be possible to solve it in theory, but not in practice.

Global Justice

This chapter began with the human right to live in an international order in which the rights and freedoms of the Universal Declaration are realized, including the right to a decent standard of living. The present-day world certainly does not provide this. It seems that in recent decades the inequality in the world has increased enormously, with large numbers of people living beneath the poverty line and some individuals, like Jeff Bezos and Bill Gates, being extremely wealthy, as shown in, for example, the World Inequality Report 2018.[19] Many children in this world die not because of falling into a pond, but because of avoidable illnesses and a lack of access to healthy food.

That is why a change in the present global structure is needed. But that is not easy. Abolishing the two privileges mentioned, the international borrowing

[19] 'World Inequality Report 2018', World Inequality Lab, accessed 15 May 2019, https://wir2018 .wid.world/.

privilege and the international resources privilege, would require the establishment of a truly cosmopolitan regime of governance. It is not likely that states would agree to such a system of governance in the short term, and it would be very difficult to determine its precise rules. In comparison, the interpersonal approach defended by Singer has the beauty and attractiveness of simplicity. The duty to help others to acquire a decent standard of living is based on the simple principles that suffering is bad and helping others if possible is good. In order to establish the duty to assist there is no need for causal links between suffering and international institutions.

It now turns out that the human rights in the Universal Declaration have more far-reaching consequences than its drafters may have realized. If the Declaration demands the realization of all the rights included, it has formulated a goal that can only be realized in the long run, since human rights are not merely meant as domestic basic rights, but have international, perhaps global relevancy. If a violent calamity occurs in one state or between two states, it is thus a matter of concern for all human beings. Should therefore the international community have the obligation to come to the rescue of the victims of those violent calamities? Think of a repressive regime with no regard for human rights at all; it deliberately violates its citizens' rights and freedoms, as if it wages a war on its own population. Should the international community take steps to stop the violence? What does Article 28 of the Universal Declaration imply in those circumstances? An obligation to intervene, if necessary militarily? This question will be discussed in the next chapter.

15

Everyone Has the Right to International Legal Protection

In the Chapter 14 we saw that every human is, on the basis of Article 28 of the Universal Declaration, entitled to a particular social and international order, namely an order in which the rights and freedoms of the Declaration can be fully realized. This means that within the range of all possible orders the one in which human rights can be realized must be established. Article 28 reiterates what the Preamble had already stated, namely that human beings irrespective of their belonging to different states, are 'all members of the human family'. Even though the Universal Declaration primarily considers the rights of individuals in relation to their own state, states have certain obligations to citizens of other states, as Chapter 12 explained. In line with Article 14 of the Universal Declaration, states must grant them asylum if they are politically persecuted; on the basis of Article 22 states have the duty to co-operate internationally to realize the economic, social and cultural rights of their citizens.

The importance of Article 28 lies in its reiteration of the cosmopolitan ideas of the Preamble. Since there is an individual human right to a particular international order, states have duties to citizens of other states that go far beyond granting them asylum occasionally and bringing about economic co-operation. States have to establish a structure that realizes or at least promotes human rights globally. We also found that the Universal Declaration does not advocate or anticipate a world state. Considering that the task of drawing up the Universal Declaration was given by the Organization of the United Nations, the drafters must have had an organization like the United Nations in mind when they came up with Article 28. After all, this organization wants to renew the belief in human rights, according to the Preamble of its Charter. In short, the United Nations and its member states have to look after human rights throughout the whole world.

Does this mean that Article 28 gives states – either individually or collectively – the right, or perhaps even the obligation, to act when human rights in another state are violated on a large scale? In other words, do human beings in one state have the right to have their human rights protected by other states when those human rights are violated by their own state, even if this might mean, in the last instance, military force? Surely, military intervention is not justified when a human right is violated within a certain state sporadically, nor when it concerns non-urgent human rights.[1] According to quite a few scholars,[2] it follows unambiguously from the Universal Declaration that states ought to ensure not only respect for human rights in their own lands, but also to intervene in other states if serious large scale violations of human rights take place there, in particular violations of the urgent rights to life (especially when these violations amount to genocide) and the right to be free of slavery. States have what in modern parlance is known as the *responsibility to protect*, a commitment adopted by all members of the United Nations in 2005.[3] In such crisis situations, outsider states should in the first instance try to protect human rights by means of diplomatic and economic pressure, but in the end military force cannot be ruled out in order to save an endangered population. In such a case, intervention is allowed on humanitarian grounds.

It could also be argued that this cannot be correct. The Preamble of the Universal Declaration states that human rights must form the basis for a world ruled by freedom, justice *and* peace. How can human rights as a means to establish peace also be used to justify military engagements? This objection can easily be set aside, because the Universal Declaration envisions such a peaceful and free world only in a utopian future. As long as we live in a non-ideal world the possibility of a justified war in order to stop gross violations of human rights cannot be ruled out. When a state or an alliance of states intervenes militarily in another state to stop human rights violations, it acts, so to speak, in the name of the international community which has not yet been sufficiently institutionalized. It acts as if authorized by Article 28. Still, true as that may perhaps be, it nevertheless remains paradoxical that a war may be waged on humanitarian grounds, for is war not antithetical to humanity and in contradiction to human rights?

Unsurprisingly therefore, the so-called humanitarian intervention is highly controversial. This chapter deals with this issue in three stages. Because a humanitarian intervention is often seen as a justified war, I will first examine the classical doctrine of the just war. After that, the Charter of the United Nations concerning war and peace will be considered. It will appear that human rights are surely not the only value of the Charter. It strongly emphasizes the respect that states owe to each other's sovereignty. The value of state sovereignty is not mentioned in the Universal Declaration, but it is not completely absent. Remember that Article 21, clause 3 speaks of 'the will of the people' as the only basis for 'the authority of the government' (as was discussed in chapter 11). Moreover, the right to political self-determination

---

[1] I follow here John Rawls's view in *The Law of Peoples: with the Idea of Public Reason Revisited* (Cambridge, MA: Harvard University Press, 2001), 45–69.

[2] See, for example, Fernando Tesón, *Humanitarian Intervention: An Inquiry into Law and Morality* (New York: Transnational Publishers, 1988).

[3] See for example Anne Orford, *International Authority and the Responsibility to Protect* (Cambridge: Cambridge University Press, 2011).

has a prominent place in the covenants based on the Universal Declaration. Common Article 1, clause 1 of both the International Covenant on Civil and Political Rights and the International Covenant on Economic, Social and Cultural Rights state that all peoples have the right of self-determination. On the basis of this right peoples decide their own political status and freely pursue their own economic, social and cultural development. Finally, philosophical arguments both in favour and against military intervention will be presented. It will become apparent that these arguments centre on what the right balance should be between the values of collective self-determination and individual human rights.

The Doctrine of the Just War

Over the centuries, questions about whether war can ever be justified and what actions within the context of war would be permissible have been discussed at length. This is not surprising, given the frequency with which war was (and is) waged and the devastation and the cruelty it brought (and brings) along.[4] It is possible to distinguish, roughly, three main positions with regard to war and peace. One of these positions is the just war doctrine, or the just war tradition. For many, this doctrine is an attractive middle ground between the two other positions; it has therefore acquired prominence when thinking about war and peace today. The two other positions, pacifism and realism, are often regarded as unattractive. Pacifism takes as a starting point the prohibition on killing, which is certainly valid in the context of a conflict between states. It repudiates war on moral grounds: killing is wrong, and even more than in the context of inter-personal conflicts the danger of escalation of interstate violence is very great. Often, but certainly not always or exclusively, pacifists are inspired by the teachings of Jesus in the New Testament: 'he who lives by the sword, shall die by the sword'; 'And unto him that smiteth thee on the one cheek, offer also the other'.[5] The costs of war are also pointed out: war comes at a high price, and rather than solving a political problem, it often leads to more wars. According to Erasmus, hardly any peace is so unjust that it is not preferable to a war, however just that might be.[6] In the view of Martin Luther King it is morally obligatory to constantly search for non-violent means when challenging the injustice and violence of certain societal relationships.[7]

Not many find such an attitude of complete non-violence morally convincing or acceptable. Sometimes violence must be resorted to, certainly in the

---

[4] One of Kant's arguments against war is the following: 'war is bad in that it makes more evil people than it takes away', in Immanuel Kant, *Zum ewigen Frieden. Ein philosophischer Entwurf*, AA VIII, 365.

[5] Matt. 26: 52; Luke 6: 29.

[6] Desiderius Erasmus, *Complaint of Peace*, in *Collected Works of Erasmus, Vol. 27*, ed. Anthony Herbert Tigar Levi (Toronto: University of Toronto Press), 310–11.

[7] Martin Luther King, 'Letter from Birmingham Jail', for example in Aileen Kavanagh and John Oberdiek, eds, *Arguing about Law* (London: Routledge, 2009), 254–62.

case of defending others, according to St Augustine, and it would be wrong to lump together all forms of violence in war, Thomas Aquinas adds. Self-defence is not an unjustified form of violence.[8] According to these authors, pacifism fails because it refuses to make morally relevant distinctions. It does make a difference whether violence is used in self-defence or for aggressive purposes. Defending yourself against an unjustified attack is often even regarded as a natural right, the right of self-preservation. Military force can take the form of terror and genocide, or it can be aimed at the removal of an unjust (military) opponent. Therefore, it seems necessary to distinguish morally between different kinds of (military) violence.

The same kind of objection is often raised against realism, the third position. The only difference is that pacifism condemns (military) violence, whereas realism accepts military violence as an unavoidable part of human life. It is a mere fact of life that violence plays a significant role in the development of human societies and that it is more or less beyond human control. According to realism it makes little sense to ask whether the use of force is justified or to set moral standards for the resort to violence or its methods. The inherent tendency to escalation means that violence will break through these limits anyway. A classic example of realism stems from the classical world: the invasion and the sacking of the island of Melos by the Athenians. Whereas the Melians defended themselves by appealing to the right to remain neutral vis-à-vis the Peloponnesian war between Athens and Sparta, the Athenians simply stated that everyone is compelled by the law of nature to dominate everyone else if one can.[9] One should have no illusions: war is a world of its own in which ultimately only self-interest counts and the necessity of ensuring one's victory; war is beyond moral judgement and therefore the saying goes: when the weapons speak, the law remains silent.[10] In interstate relations the only thing that matters is the national interest – the *raison d'état*.

Many believe that realism is wrong. It is simply not true that moral considerations with regard to the start of war and the methods of warfare are irrelevant. Even realist politicians, however cynical they may be, will argue that the wars they intend to initiate are justified and their military means proportionate and just. It is even true that moral arguments have a significant influence on whether a particular war can be begun and on how it should be waged. Think of the Vietnam War in the twentieth century; many historians are now in agreement that the United States lost that war on the home front: the people of the United States could not be convinced of the moral necessity of the continuation of that war and were shocked when the news broke about

---

[8] See for example texts by Augustine and Thomas Aquinas, reprinted in David Kinsella and Craig L. Carr, eds, *The Morality of War: A Reader* (London: Rienner Publisher, 2007), 59–69.

[9] Thucydides, *The Talks at Melos*, as reprinted in Kinsella and Carr, *The Morality of War*, 18, 20.

[10] This saying is by Cicero (*Pro Milone*, 4.11). For Cicero, this meant that the human laws were silent during war, but not the divine laws.

atrocities committed by their own troops.[11] This ideological conflict over this war was carried out in the vocabulary of the tradition of the just war: was this a just war and was it waged by justifiable means?

The tradition of the just war is an attractive alternative to both pacifism and realism. In contrast to realism it maintains that wars are not beyond moral judgement, and in contrast to pacifism it holds that while wars in general are morally reprehensible, this is not so in all cases. Sometimes war is simply a necessary evil to prevent a greater evil, and then it is justified. In war not all means and methods of violence are permissible, as realism claims, but not everything is prohibited as pacifism holds. The just war tradition states that war must be waged in accordance with certain moral criteria, both with regard to its beginning and to its conduct – *ius ad bellum* and *ius in bello*.

Under the heading of *ius ad bellum*, one finds the moral criteria that must be met for war to be started justifiably.[12] These criteria are the following: just cause, proper authority, right intention, final resort, reasonable chance of success and proportionality. The criterion of 'just cause' is perhaps the most important element of *ius ad bellum*. After all, war is a morally ambiguous undertaking and thus only in the most urgent of causes should there be a resort to arms. In the tradition of just war thinking, various causes have been given most prominently war as a response to military aggression, that is, as a response to a violation of the right to national self-determination; in this case war is an act of self-defence. Internationally, the waging of a war of aggression is a crime against peace. As noted in Chapter 2, it was considered an international crime in the Charter of London and during the Nuremberg Trials. This chapter thus needs to discuss the question of whether the violation of human rights in a state constitutes a just cause for other states to intervene. According to the criterion of proper authority the decision on war should be made by the highest authority within the state. It is not always easy to determine who the holder of this highest authority is. Since the rise of the modern nation state it would seem that it lies with the national state, but this has not really restricted the occurrence of war. States saw the resort to war as their prerogative. Since World War I and then World War II attempts have been made to establish an international legal order, which would hold ultimate authority. According to the Charter of the United Nations, military means can only be used legitimately in two ways: on the authority of the Security Council and in self-defence. The Charter does not mention the protection of human rights as a just cause. The other criteria mentioned in the tradition are also important: a war can only be initiated with the right intention, namely the righting of a wrong and not for example the desire to acquire foreign territory or to punish a neighbouring state. The criterion of final resort determines that

---

[11] Michael Walzer's epoch-making book *Just and Unjust Wars: A Moral Argument with Historical Illustrations* (New York: Basic Books, 2000) was a reaction to that particular war and it subsequently led to a revival of just war theory.

[12] A thorough examination of these criteria can for example be found in Helen Frowe, *The Ethics of War and Peace: An Introduction* (London: Routledge, 2016).

war should only be an 'ultimate resort'; all other means to resolve a dispute should have been tried before resorting to war. Finally, it is only permitted to initiate a war if there is a reasonable chance of success. Otherwise it would make no sense to start a war. Taking these criteria together, the just war tradition emphasizes that the costs of waging war must be proportionate to the wrong that war aims to address.

Ius in bello, the law during war, concerns the conduct of war, and its general aim is to limit military violence as much as possible. This counts for every war, and thus a war of 'humanitarian intervention' must also be conducted in accordance with the (humanitarian) law of war, which consists of three criteria. The criterion of usefulness or utility states that military violence may be used only if it serves a military purpose; the use of random violence, just for the 'fun' of it or to terrorize a civilian population is prohibited. The second criterion of proportionality adds to this that no more military means shall be employed than is strictly necessary to achieve a military purpose. Bombarding a whole city to destroy an arms factory within that city is disproportionate. The criteria of utility and proportionality are limitations on military force of a utilitarian character. The (third) criterion of discrimination is of a different nature. It states that combatants should be distinguished from non-combatants and that the war effort can only be legitimately directed against combatants. The immunity of civilians must be respected, even if an assault on those civilians would serve a purpose from a military point of view. This is a deontological restriction on the use of military violence. It is not always simple to know how to apply these restrictions. When is military force useful and proportionate? Who belongs to the category of non-combatants? Probably not those civilians who work in the arms factory, but what about civilians who supply the military with food and drink? Also, from the military standpoint, it is often not possible to leave civilians and civilian targets completely untouched. Sometimes what is called *collateral damage* is unavoidable: the damage to civilians and civilian targets is then the price to be paid for a 'just' war, as long as this damage is not directly intended.[13]

To summarize, these *ius ad bellum* and *ius in bello* criteria paint a picture of a just war as one into which one of the parties enters for a justifiable reason, and which is conducted with respect for the limits on warfare by at least one of the two parties. According to the traditional understanding of the just war the criteria of *ius ad bellum* and those of *ius in bello* are ultimately independent of each other.[14] A war can thus be started in violation of *ius ad bellum* but still be conducted in accord with *ius in bello,* and vice versa. There are very good reasons for the distinction: usually the warring parties are not in agreement about the justice of the war. Making the rights and obligations of warring

---

[13] This is also called the doctrine of double-effect, probably formulated for the first time in a very clear fashion by Thomas Aquinas, *Summa Theologica*, Secunda Secundae, Questio 64, Article 7.

[14] This is highly contested by the so-called revisionist interpretation of the just war thinking; see Jeff McMahan, *Killing in War* (Oxford: Oxford University Press, 2009).

armies dependent on the *ius ad bellum* would be very risky: it would raise the likelihood of the escalation of the conflict. Today the rules of *ius in bello* are laid down primarily in the Geneva Conventions, while the Charter of the United Nations constitutes for the present day the *ius ad bellum* rules.

The International Framework of the UN Charter

At the centre of present international law stands the Charter. It contains both a strict prohibition on waging war – as a consequence of the duty of states to respect self-determination of peoples – and respect for human rights. As regards the first aspect, Article 2, clause 4 states: 'All Members shall refrain in their international relations from the threat or use of force against the territorial integrity or political independence of any state, or in any other manner inconsistent with the Purposes of the United Nations.'[15] To this, Article 2 clause 7 adds: 'Nothing contained in the present Charter shall authorise the United Nations to intervene in matters which are essentially within the domestic jurisdiction of any state'. We have already seen that this Charter came into force after World War II as a result of a treaty between states to establish a peaceful order among them and to rein in war as much as possible. This aim was understandable after the experiences of World War II, but it can obviously only be achieved if states not only solemnly acknowledge each other's right to self-determination but also establish a mechanism to ensure that this mutual respect can be enforced. This ensuring mechanism is provided in Chapter VII of the Charter, on measures dealing with threats to peace, breaches of peace and acts of aggression. Article 39 determines who is ultimately responsible for peace: 'The Security Council shall determine the existence of any threat to the peace, breach of the peace, or act of aggression and shall make recommendations, or decide what measures shall be taken in accordance with Articles 41 and 42, to maintain or restore international peace and security'. Article 41 concerns non-violent measures that can be undertaken against a state or states that in the Security Council's opinion threaten the peace. On the basis of Article 42 – when the measures of Article 41 are considered insufficient – the Security Council can 'take such action by air, sea, or land forces as may be necessary to maintain or restore international peace and security. Such action may include demonstrations, blockades, and other operations by air, sea, or land forces of Members of the United Nations'.

Article 42 had been left dormant as a consequence of the Cold War – the Security Council could not reach an agreement with regard to peace and breaches of the peace – and was used for the first time in the history of the UN after the annexation of Kuwait by Iraq in 1991. Based on this Article, the

---

[15] United Nations, Charter of the United Nations, 24 October 1945, 1 UNTS XVI, www.un.org /en/sections/un-charter/chapter-i/index.html.

Security Council passed some resolutions which made the restoration of the territorial integrity and political sovereignty of Kuwait by military means possible. Legally speaking, the rule of the Charter is thus a prohibition of war and the protection of states against the military aggression of other states. There are only two exceptions to this rule: military measures based on authorization by the Security Council on the basis of Article 42, as in the case of Kuwait, and self-defence based on Article 51 of the Charter, because states have 'the inherent right of individual or collective self-defence if an armed attack occurs'. This provision forms part of the Charter's Chapter VII and applies to those cases in which the Security Council is unable to react quickly enough to a breach of the peace. States who are faced with aggression do not have to wait for the Council's approval to act when they are attacked.

Humanitarian intervention is not part of the Charter, although – as is apparent in the Preamble to the Charter – the promotion of human rights is one of the purposes of the United Nations. This is also clear from Article 1, clause 3: the purpose of the UN is 'promoting and encouraging respect for human rights and for fundamental freedoms for all without distinction as to race, sex, language, or religion'. Human rights thus play a role in the Charter, but the use of military means can only be authorized by the Security Council when international peace and security are threatened, not for the protection of human rights. Even so, the formulation of the prohibition on the use of force leaves room for interpretation. Recall that Article 2, clause 4 emphasizes non-intervention, to which clause 7 adds that 'Nothing contained in the present Charter shall authorise the United Nations to intervene in matters which are essentially within the domestic jurisdiction of any state'. But what is meant by 'matters which are essentially within the domestic jurisdiction of any state'? Because the Charter and the human rights conventions are explicitly committed to promote human rights and because everyone is entitled according to Article 28 of the Universal Declaration to an international order in which the rights and freedoms of the Declaration can be fully realized, it would seem that whether or not to respect human rights is not a matter which resides within the jurisdiction of any states. States have to respect human rights; as members of the United Nations they have committed themselves to promote 'universal respect for, and observance of, human rights and fundamental freedoms for all without distinction as to race, sex, language or religion' and to take joint and separate action for the achievement of this purpose (Charter, Articles 55, 56).

Moreover, within international law the interesting concept of *obligationes erga omnes* has emerged. In 1970, the International Court of Justice ruled that states had obligations to the international community as a whole: these are obligations that are concerned with those matters in which all states have an interest. They arise from the fact that matters such as aggression and genocide are forbidden under international law. In the Court's opinion one of these obligations is respect for the fundamental rights and freedoms of mankind. All states have the duty to respect the core of human rights and it is irrelevant whether or not they have signed and ratified conventions to that effect. Neither can a state deviate from this core of human rights by means of a convention or a reservation.[16] One could say that this is the implicit acknowledgement by the Court of the existence of some 'natural law' principles. *Obligations erga omnes* are not the result of positive law created by international conventions. This would mean that a state violates its obligations to other states, when it violates human rights internally, within its own borders. This would suggest that nothing stands in the way of one state interfering in another state if it violates human rights internally.

It would be an overly hasty conclusion to hold that states therefore have a right to interfere militarily in another state on grounds of humanitarian concerns. Interfering is a much broader concept than military intervention. Such an intervention without authorization of the Security Council would be a violation of the prohibition on the use of force. The only legally available option for humanitarian intervention would be for the Security Council to consider gross and flagrant violations of human rights within a particular state as threats to international peace and security and then to authorize the use of force (in the framework of Articles 39 and 42). But this route sets the threshold very high. The Security Council is a highly politicized organ, and because it is politically divided, it often cannot come to an agreement. Is a unilateral or multilateral humanitarian intervention legally possible, without such authorization? In such a case one would have to define humanitarian intervention as the threat or the use of force by one or more states against another state, with the single aim of stopping large-scale violations of fundamental human rights without authorization of the Security Council, and obviously also without permission of the state under attack. The sole justification would then lie in the simple consideration that 'necessity knows no law'. This would then be similar to ordinary criminal law: an attack on another person's body is permissible in case of a necessary defence of one's own person or that of another against an immediate unlawful attack. In other words, although an attack on another person or state is prohibited in normal circumstances, this prohibition is not valid in order to prevent serious, lethal 'criminal' acts on others.

Is this enough to give humanitarian intervention some legitimacy? Some would say yes, but others would raise serious objections. Giving states a moral justification for military intervention may easily lead to a situation in which states abuse this justification and begin an intervention without a serious emergency situation. For who is to decide on an emergency? This risk is perhaps not so high within the domestic sphere. If someone kills another person and claims to have acted in self-defence or in the defence of another, they can and probably will be held accountable in a court of law. Because there is no such court on the international level, states can 'easily' abuse military

---

[16] *Case concerning Barcelona Traction, Light and Power Co. (Belgium v Spain)*, ICJ Reports 1 1970.

force for their own national interests and claim an emergency. It was and still is the purpose of the Charter to outlaw war by denying states the right to go to war. If states would have the right to defend human rights wherever they are violated on a large scale, it would seem that the right to war re-emerges. Therefore it is perhaps safe to conclude that humanitarian intervention should not be considered as a legitimate ground for the use of military force within international law.

Philosophical Arguments

We have seen that the international legal situation is complicated and the hope is that philosophical arguments may bring some solution. Unfortunately, this is not the case and that should not come as a surprise. It is clear that two values play a role in the debate, that of respect for a political community and its collective self-determination on the one hand and that of individual human rights on the other. These values cannot easily be harmonized. In the eighteenth and nineteenth centuries, influential philosophical voices held that the first value should have priority. Aggression against a state is never permissible except in self-defence, and thus not for humanitarian concerns. If war is permitted solely in self-defence, states have an unconditional duty to respect each other's political sovereignty and territorial integrity. Allowing an exception to this prohibition would open Pandora's box and introduce a situation in which states could unilaterally decide whether and when they would respect the 'political sovereignty and territorial integrity' of another state. This would amount to an international state of nature among states in which war might break out at any moment.

According to Mill, humanitarian intervention is almost always wrong: if a state treats its citizens wrongly and violates their human rights, other states have the right to condemn this, but they may not intervene. Mill considers self-determination paramount, since political freedom cannot be imposed from without. If citizens live under an evil regime, they have to liberate themselves. Just as an individual cannot be forced to live a virtuous life – Mill opposes state paternalism – people cannot be forced by external force to establish a free form of government. When individuals choose to harm themselves, this is ultimately up to them; others, including state authorities, may advise them against so acting, but they may not stop them from harming themselves. Coercion is only permitted when there is harm or the threat of harm to others. This is also true internationally: self-determination means that people have the right to realize their freedom by their own efforts.[17]

Earlier, in the eighteenth century, Kant adopted a similar position. According to his famous essay *Toward Perpetual Peace*, states can only

---

[17] John Stuart Mill, 'A Few Words on Non-Intervention', in for example Kinsella and Carr, eds, *The Morality of War*, 191–5.

establish a lasting situation of peace on the basis of unconditionally accepting the principle of non-intervention. Kant formulated, in one of the so-called preliminary articles to a perpetual peace, the following 'categorical' imperative: 'no state shall forcibly interfere in the constitution and government of another state'.[18] In Kant's view, a state is not a 'thing' about which outsiders have any say; it is a community of persons who have to determine their political fate by themselves. If a state is internally badly constituted and 'great evils' take place, then this is surely regrettable. Outsiders are permitted to express their views, but they are not entitled to intervene militarily. Like Mill, Kant makes the analogy with ordinary citizens: if they harm (solely) themselves, they set a bad example to others, but they may not be punished. They become punishable only by harming the rights of others. Whoever acknowledges even the most minimal right of intervention, introduces, according to Kant, the right to war, and this must be prevented at all costs.

For both Mill and Kant, the value of political self-determination is of paramount political importance. Ultimately, all citizens in the world will benefit from this principle, because it alone makes 'perpetual peace' possible. In our days, many commentators find their arguments no longer convincing. Both Mill and Kant use the analogy between individual citizens and individual states, arguing that both can only be free by their own efforts. However, the situation in which an individual harms himself without harming others is evidently not analogous to the situation in which the leadership or government of a state harms a part of its citizenry, without violating other states. Such a political situation is not one of self-harm. Legally, a state may be considered an individual entity, but in reality it is composed of many individuals that are part of social groups. If a state violates human rights, it is one group, most likely the one in power, against another group. Such a situation cannot be compared with for example a drunk, who is not a virtuous person but does not harm others. Such drunkards harm themselves, but a state that violates human rights harms human beings who often lack the power to defend themselves. Do outsiders then not have the right to come to their rescue? It would be a sign of cynicism to hold that it is a matter of self-determination when a state violates the human rights of a part of its population.

Many scholars today do not regard the right to self-determination of a state as an absolute right or as the highest value. Morally speaking, self-determination cannot mean that the political leadership of a state has a mandate to do whatever it wants. Self-determination can only mean that the government of a state derives its authority from some kind of a will of the people. The collective right to self-determination of a state is ultimately nothing else but the expression of the collective will of the citizens of that state. This is not far from what Article 22 of the Universal Declaration requires: everyone has the right to take part in the government of their country

---

[18] Immanuel Kant, *Zum ewigen Frieden: Ein philosophischer Entwurf*, AA VIII 346.

(discussed in Chapter 11). Therefore, collective self-determination depends on the possibility of the citizens of the state to exercise their individual rights and freedoms. On the basis of such a reasoning it is now argued, in opposition to Mill and Kant, that the right of self-determination for states is a conditional right.[19] Their right to political sovereignty and territorial integrity is dependent on whether citizens in a particular state are able to organize their own political, economic and cultural life. If this is the correct line of argument, then the priority given by the Charter to state sovereignty must be reversed and human rights must be given more importance. With this, the possibility of a military intervention in order to defend human rights in another state is back on the table. This could in principle be a just war.

For some in the debate, such as Walzer, who we met in Chapter 12, a complete reversal of priority goes much too far. His famous *Just and Unjust Wars* does not endorse a categorical prohibition on intervention, like Mill and Kant, but neither does it defend that sovereignty can simple be set aside because human rights are violated. Mutual respect of states for their political sovereignty and territorial integrity should remain the default position. Only in three extraordinary circumstances, deviating from the principle of self-determination for states is permissible. First, there is the exceptional situation in which a state consists of more than one political community and one of them seeks to secede. Next is a situation during a civil war where one of the sides receives support from outside; then a third party may, perhaps, intervene in support of the other party. Finally, Walzer would find intervention permissible when a state violates fundamental human rights, such as the right to life, on such a large scale that 'the conscience of mankind' is shocked. The last situation especially constitutes an emergency, and then the principle applies that whoever can help must do so: people need to be rescued. Therefore, it does not really matter for Walzer whether a humanitarian intervention is unilateral, multilateral or takes place under the banner of the Security Council of the United Nations.[20]

Walzer holds that both values, political self-determination and respect for human rights, are important and that in principle, respect for self-determination of peoples carries heavier weight. Peoples and their communities with their political, cultural and economic differences are represented at the international level by states and that diversity should be respected. Whether a particular form of government or a particular regime fits the political community over which it rules – in other words, whether a government is legitimate – cannot be decided by outsiders, but only by insiders: that is the heart of self-determination. Only the most exceptional circumstances can refute the presumption that there is a fit

---

[19] See for example Thomas Franck, 'Humanitarian Intervention', in *The Philosophy of International Law*, eds Samantha Besson and John Tasioulas (Oxford: Oxford University Press, 2010), 531–47.

[20] Michael Walzer, *Just and Unjust Wars: A Moral Argument with Historical Illustrations* (New York: Basic Books, 2000), 91–108.

between the government of a state and its population. Genocide against its own population cannot possibly be considered an expression of self-determination of a state. In such a case a state has clearly lost its internal legitimacy and is therefore no longer shielded from external intervention. Mere 'ordinary' incidental violations of human rights provide no real reason for intervention.

For Walzer, respect for cultural and political diversity among communities is paramount. It might well be that legitimacy in democratic states means that citizens can exercise their rights to freedom and political participation, but from this it does not automatically follow that non-democratic regimes in which such rights are not recognized lack legitimacy. Historically, many authoritarian regimes were accepted as legitimate by the population. Moreover, legitimacy is not an all or nothing issue, but rather it is a matter of more or less. But there are indeed also pragmatic or prudent reasons for not giving up the priority of self-determination too easily and to be cautious with regard to the right of intervention. If such an international 'right' of intervention were to exist, who would be able and willing to claim such a right? Every state on its own initiative, without any political or judicial adjudicating body? Looking back in recent history we may find a great number of states in which human rights are violated, sometimes in the most flagrant manner; we also find quite a large number of military interventions. But the two lists usually have rather little to do with each other. Intervention is often motivated by other considerations than humanitarian ones. If we were to apply the just war tradition's criterion of 'just intention', then there would turn out to be very, very few cases of humanitarian intervention. Even the interventions Walzer endorses – the intervention at the end of the nineteenth century of the United States in Cuba, then still under Spanish rule, and that of India in East Pakistan in 1971 – were motivated only partly by humanitarian concerns. The risk is that humanitarian intervention turns out to be a pretext for pursuit of strategic interests.

This leads us back to 'realism', the view that in international relations morality counts for nothing. Pleas for humanitarian intervention might then perhaps be considered as a (concealed) argument for the reintroduction, under another name, of the right to war. And if that is the case, then national interests would again be paramount, because in every war states put their soldiers in the most hazardous situations. Considering that a state has the duty to promote its own welfare and thus to protect the lives of its citizens, including those in the armed forces – this would even follow from Article 3 of the Universal Declaration – a state cannot take the decision to embark on war lightly. In historical practice it indeed turns out that states are very reluctant to commit their military forces for the sake of the welfare of the citizens of another state. Therefore, an intervention purely out of 'humanitarian' intentions is not an obvious course of action. Formulated differently, it also seems that soldiers – citizens in arms – are not prepared to risk their own interests, including their lives, unless the interest of their own political community is at stake, although this argument would not apply to mercenaries and professional armies.

A final but not unimportant argument against humanitarian intervention is the following. Such an intervention may be portrayed as reacting to a situation in which an innocent population must be rescued from the attacks of its own criminal regime. The expectation is that this regime can be removed by a military 'surgical' operation and that a normal order can be restored relatively easily. In reality, however, the situation 'on the ground' is often much more complicated than this. Often a variety of opposing and sometimes warring groups are involved, and intervention runs the risk of creating an even more chaotic situation, as in Libya after the 2011 intervention.

Nevertheless, the call for humanitarian intervention is understandable. It arises from the consciousness that persons are not only citizens of their own political community, but also 'members' of the cosmopolitan world community, on the grounds of the Universal Declaration, especially Article 28. Because of the arguments mentioned, this latter 'membership' does however not simply lead to a right to humanitarian intervention.

The Intervention in Kosovo

Just how complicated 'humanitarian intervention' is becomes apparent when we look back at the intervention by NATO on behalf of the people of Kosovo in 1999. Until then Kosovo had been an autonomous province within the Republic of Serbia, which itself had been part of the Republic of Yugoslavia. After the disintegration of that republic due to earlier tensions and violent secessions, Serbia restricted the autonomous status of Kosovo, which led to a demand of independence by (part of) the Kosovo population. This political demand was strongly rejected by the Serbian state, because it regarded (and still regards) Kosovo as an integral part of its territory. A bloody conflict ensued with numerous gross violations of human rights, which the international community tried to end by initiating negotiations between Serbia and Kosovo and by political and economic pressure. When these initiatives and pressures proved ineffective, the possibility of a military intervention was considered. But the Security Council would not authorize such an intervention and a resolution to this effect was vetoed by some of its permanent members. After that, in March 1999, NATO started an air campaign against Serbia without a clear legal, international mandate. After some time, the Serbian troops retreated from Kosovo and Kosovo became an independent polity, ruled initially by the UN. In 2008 Kosovo declared itself independent.

This military intervention in Kosovo has been the subject of heated discussion.[21] The elements that we encountered in this chapter come together

---

[21] The following articles published by two prominent scholars shortly after the intervention are considered very important: Bruno Simma, 'NATO, the UN and the Use of Force: Legal

here. For a start, the right of self-determination. Because Serbia considered Kosovo an integral part of its territory, it saw the intervention as a breach of its sovereignty and integrity, and thus as a violation of the UN Charter. The majority of the inhabitants of Kosovo rejected what they considered an occupation by Serbia, which then came to an end by means of outside intervention. From the perspective of Mill, however, independence should be the result of one's own effort, but the Kosovars would never have succeeded to gain independence on their own. Militarily they were not strong enough. Next is the element of the military intervention itself. According to one line of thinking, we should consider this intervention as an element in the transition from international law as primarily the law between states towards a cosmopolitan order in which human rights can trump considerations of state sovereignty. Such optimistic reading welcomes the change from the law of states to the law of world citizens, in which all human persons are considered as members of the same political world community, as announced in Article 28. Others, however, contested this rosy reading of the intervention; they argued that this flagrant violation of the prohibition on unilateral force in the Charter would endanger the prohibition itself and would set a dangerous precedent. Under the pretext of 'humanitarian' intervention every state or military alliance could from now on neglect the Charter and claim the right to go to war. This reading thus sees the Kosovo intervention as an erosion of the Charter and as a prelude to wars such as the one against Iraq in 2003 and that of the Russian Federation against Georgia in 2008 and against Ukraine in 2014.

So, was the Kosovo intervention a just war? As far as *ius ad bellum* is concerned, did NATO have proper authority? Was the cause sufficiently just and important? Was there proper intention on the side of the intervening force? Was it aimed at safeguarding humanitarian interests? Were all non-military alternatives exhausted and were the costs proportionate to the benefits? With regard to *ius in bello*, were the conditions of utility, proportionality and discrimination fulfilled? Surely, these questions can be answered only on the basis of an assessment of the facts and that is to a large extent an empirical matter. Those sympathetic to humanitarian intervention prioritize human rights over state sovereignty, but their opponents argue that the ultimate authority on war and peace should lie where the Charter placed it – with the Security Council. This may sometimes lead to a lack of action, but that is still preferable to a situation in which states, individually or multilaterally, decide for themselves whether resorting to military means is permissible. In a certain sense, NATO acted in Kosovo as prosecutor, judge and executor in adjudicating on the conflict between Serbia and the Kosovars. The rule of law would oppose anyone being a judge in their own case.

Aspects', and Antonio Cassese, 'Ex inuiria ius oritur. Are We Moving Towards International Legitimation of Forcible Humanitarian Countermeasures in the World Community?', *European Journal of International Law* (1999) 10: 1–22; 23–30.

Part IV
Duties and Virtues

16

Intermezzo II

Contrary to what is often thought, the Universal Declaration of Human Rights concerns not only rights and freedoms, but also duties and obligations. The final part of this book deals with these human obligations. That is appropriate because these obligations appear only at the end of the Universal Declaration. Article 29 says that everyone has duties to the community, not just for the sake of the community but also because a person cannot freely and fully develop their personality without a community. A human being is a creature that not only makes claims, but also on whom claims are made. The Universal Declaration then specifies this last aspect as follows: everyone is subject to the limitations determined by law in order to ensure the 'recognition and respect for the rights and freedoms of others' and the 'just requirements of morality, public order and the general welfare in a democratic society'. Finally, it is stated that no one may use their rights and freedoms in a way that is contrary to the purposes and principles of the United Nations. In other words, when someone makes use of their rights and freedoms, they ought to keep these purposes and principles in view. These consist, according to the Preamble of the Charter, of international peace and security and respect for human rights. In this way Article 29 anticipates final Article 30 on the basis of which no one may engage in any activity or perform any act aimed at the destruction of any of the rights and freedoms set forth in the Universal Declaration. The final two chapters shall argue that these duties indeed have a limiting and even moderating effect on (the claims of) human rights.

Rights and Duties

It seems appropriate that the Universal Declaration introduces duties. Remember Bentham's criticism of human rights as formulated in eighteenth-century declarations. His point was that attributing 'natural' rights to individuals without specifying corresponding duties and responsibilities would put the social order and stability into jeopardy. For that reason, Bentham regarded these 'natural' rights as encouraging anarchism. Moreover, he argued that natural rights might trump the common interest, privileging individual interests over general welfare. Similar criticism is found in Marx's view that human rights are really a form of egoism, because they privilege the rights of individuals over civic (and thus communal) interests.[1] According to Bentham and Marx, the axis of humans as individuals should not take precedence over the axis of humans as members of society. No society should therefore prioritize the interests of one individual over those of another simply because the first can claim their interests as a 'human right' and the other cannot. If various individuals make various claims on some societal arrangement, a decision must be made on the grounds of a criterion that applies equally to all, and in Bentham's view that criterion should be 'general welfare', not human rights.

A relatively recent legal case brings Bentham's point nicely to the fore. In 2001, the European Court of Human Rights decided in favour of a complaint by persons living close to Heathrow airport that the (new) regulation concerning noise during night flights violated their right to a private family life. The Court based its statement, obviously, on the European Convention, but in the framework of the Universal Declaration a similar right can be found in Article 12. The United Kingdom disagreed with the ruling of the Court and appealed against the decision, which was then overturned by the Grand Chamber of that same court.[2] Bentham would certainly have disagreed with the first ruling and would have welcomed the second ruling, but he would probably also have argued that the inconvenience for those living close to the airport caused by night flights should not stand in the way of the general economic interests of the United Kingdom and that this should not have been a matter for the courts to decide on the basis of abstract rights. In defence of human rights, however, Article 29 of the Universal Declaration can be invoked, because it holds, as we just saw, that exercising human rights can indeed be limited by general welfare 'in a democratic society'. Dworkin's well-known description of fundamental rights as trumping the ordinary process of democratic decision-making would not have been acceptable for Bentham.[3] After all, individuals have not only rights but also duties to contribute to the well-being of society. And no individual should count for more than another.

In the reception of the Universal Declaration, 'duties' have not played a major role, for at least two reasons. Certainly, it is understandable that in the beginning, attention was mainly given to the Declaration as a document of rights and that its duties were not emphasized. Stressing individual duties to the state did not have a particularly good name immediately after World War II. Recent totalitarian regimes had provided enough examples of the despicable and treacherous ways in which individuals were made subordinate to the state. In Stalinist communism the individual was first and foremost a member of a particular social class and the relationship between the classes was

---

[1]   An excellent collection of these texts can be found in Jeremy Waldron, ed., *Nonsense upon Stilts. Bentham, Burke and Marx on the Rights of Man* (London: Methuen, 1987).
[2]   See Case 36022/97, *Hatton and Others v The United Kingdom* [2003] ECHR.
[3]   Ronald Dworkin, *Taking Rights Seriously* (Cambridge, MA: Harvard University Press, 1977).

determined by the laws of the history of the class conflict. Under national socialism the individual was considered primarily a member of a particular race and a particular people, the motto being: 'Du bist nichts, dein Volk ist alles. ("You are nothing, your people are all').[4] The Universal Declaration's main idea was, as we saw, that a better new world could be brought about only by granting rights to individuals. Only this would enable them to be free from fear and want, and free to express their opinions and beliefs. Still, the history of the drafting of the Universal Declaration shows that including duties was a deliberate choice.[5]

Over the years there has been an enormous proliferation of human rights: the conventions established within the framework of the United Nations and that of the Council of Europe. We have already discussed many aspects of these rights, but has the promise of a better world been realized? It rather looks as if Bentham's fears could come to pass. Due to the great emphasis on individual rights, it seems as if the duties of individuals have been lost to sight. Only much later were there initiatives to pay more attention to 'duties'. In 1981, in the context of the Organization of African Unity, the African Charter on Human and Peoples Rights was established in which a whole chapter is devoted to human obligations. This was, sceptically, seen as an expression of African culture and as underpinning the autocratic structure of most African states. Another initiative was taken when the Universal Declaration was nearing its fiftieth anniversary. A number of prominent former statesmen and ex-politicians came together to establish a 'Universal Declaration of Human Responsibilities'.[6]

The reason for this initiative was the following. These elder statesmen feared that the continuous emphasis on claims of individuals would lead to social division and conflict rather than (international) co-operation and peace. In their view, the Universal Declaration of 1948 had not sufficiently led to an ethical basis of world-wide values by which political, religious and social differences could be overcome. This 'shared ethical basis' had not emerged at the time in which the organization of the United Nations had been established. Therefore, it was necessary, they thought, to take the initiative and address the human being's responsibility for the future of humankind as a whole. Now was the time, it was said, to emphasize solidarity and the obligations that bind humans together. Shortly after that, another declaration of duties and responsibilities was drafted with a similar ethical message, the so-called Valentia

---

[4] See, for example, Günther F. Klümper, *Du bist Nichts, Dein Volk ist Alles: Erinnerungen eines jugendlichen Zeitzeugen 1937–1941* (Baden-Baden: Aquensis, 2012); Martin Hirsch, Diemut Majer, and Jürgen Meinck, *Recht, Verwaltung und Justiz im Nationalsozialismus* (Baden-Baden: Nomos, 1997), 236–74 ('Das Volksgemeinschaftsprinzip', the principle of the community of the people).

[5] See Mary Ann Glendon, *A World Made New. Eleanor Roosevelt and the Universal Declaration of Human Rights* (New York: Random House, 2001), ch. 5.

[6] 'Universal Declaration of Human Responsibilities', Wikisource, last modified 8 March 2013, https://en.wikisource.org/wiki/Universal_Declaration_of_Human_Responsibilities.

Declaration.[7] Here too, it was argued that especially in view of important scientific and technological changes a reconsideration of human responsibilities was needed. New findings in biology and medical sciences made necessary a reflection on human nature and this would also require an emphasis on human responsibilities in domains such as economic expansion, environmental pollution, global warming and the exhaustion of natural resources. These challenges could not be faced by referring to individual rights of human beings but would demand a reconsideration of what it is to be human and of what every human being owes to himself and others. The basis of global ethics should not be unlimited free choice, but the principle of accountability.

The second reason why it took such a long time for the obligations of Article 29 to come into picture, is of a conceptual nature and lies in the concept of 'right' itself.[8] In its daily usage, 'right' can mean multiple things. It may refer to specific privileges that come with specific offices, often within institutional settings, such as that of a mayor of a city or a university professor, who respectively have the right to preside over the city council or to supervise PhD projects. In order to obtain these privileges, they must satisfy certain institutional conditions, such as being elected or selected. Having such privileges implies for this person certain institutional obligations. But if, say, a mayor has the right to legally conclude a marriage between two persons, it does not follow that any two persons have the duty to get married. It might well be the case that a mayor never has to make use of the right to conclude a marriage. Similarly, no promising student has to embark on a PhD project simple because there are professors who have the privilege of supervising PhDs. Also, the concept of 'right' can simply mean the freedom to do or not to do something. Think of an earlier example: on a fine summer day I have the right, one would say, to go cycling; but I don't have to do it, if I do not feel like it.

The concept of 'right' as used in 'human rights' is related to the meaning of privilege and freedom just mentioned, but it is also different. 'Right' as in human rights means a subjective claim which is correlated with an obligation on other persons. If I am the bearer of a specific right, I make the claim on everyone else to refrain from acting in such a manner that my right is violated or to act in such a manner that my right can be realized. To a right in this sense – a claim – there is a corresponding duty, and it is often said: no claim or right without a corresponding duty. Because of this correlation the question must arise on whom specific obligations rest and how far-reaching these obligations are. Take as an example everyone's human right, based on Article 3, to 'life, freedom and physical integrity'. What it means for a human being having the right to these goods, is that everyone else, in particular the state, has the obligation to respect this person's life, freedom and integrity. Initially this would imply the negative

---

[7] 'Declaration of Responsibilities and Human Duties', Globalization (2002), accessed 15 May 2019, http://globalization.icaap.org/content/v2.2/declare.html.

[8] Very loosely, I make use here of Wesley Newcomb Hohfeld, *Fundamental Legal Conceptions as Applied in Judicial Reasoning* (New Haven: Yale University Press, 1919).

duty of abstaining from acts that take these goods away. But it may also imply positive obligations. An effective protection of, say, the right to life would demand an apparatus to protect life and to prosecute possible violations of that right. Chapter 6 made it clear that the right to life is not simple at all but entails much more than just the negative obligation not to take someone else's life. This is certainly the case for the human right to a decent standard of living, as laid down in Article 25. Here too the question arises as to who bears the responsibility for making sure that this standard of living is attained. We saw in Chapter 14 how difficult it is to answer that question. It is also one of the reasons why this human right has a bad name: surely not every human being, as an individual, can be held to account for the fact that not every other human being has reached a decent standard of living? Therefore, it appears that this duty must lie with states and ordinary citizens would then have the obligation to pay their taxes in order to enable the state to honour its duties. Does this mean that the socio-economic rights, like that to a decent standard of living, merely imply positive duties? Certainly not: the right to a decent standard of living also implies the negative obligation not to deprive human beings of their means of livelihood, as happens for instance when a state deprives native populations of their lands.

The concept of 'rights' as in human rights implies corresponding duties, either negative duties to abstain from acting or positive ones to perform certain acts or both. Because it is often not very clear where negative duties stop and positive duties begin, some scholars argue that the distinction between positive and negative duties is not very helpful and would be better abolished and transformed in the following sense: a human right implies firstly the duty to refrain from any action that would infringe the interest which that right aims to protect, secondly the duty to protect that interest and finally the duty to realize that right.[9] In this line, Article 3 means not only that no one's life should be taken arbitrarily, but also that everyone's life should be protected and that everyone's life must be furthered. With such an understanding of the right to life, there is no longer a large gap between this right, originally understood as merely coming with negative duties, and the right to a decent standard of living as in Article 25, originally understood as implying 'positive' duties. This shading of the difference between negative and positive human rights also fits in very well with the way in which the Universal Declaration presents human rights, namely that they are indivisible. Article 2 explicitly says that everyone is entitled to 'all the rights and freedoms set forth in this Declaration'. The Universal Declaration has no preference for 'negative' rather than 'positive' rights.

Useful as these nuances may be, the fact remains that the concept of a right used in 'human rights' remains a claim-right. Within human-rights discourse, duties only appear in so far as they correspond to rights: without rights no

---

[9] The idea of a set of triple duties correlative to all basic rights stems from Henry Shue, *Basic Rights* (Princeton: Princeton University Press, 1996).

duties. Up to Article 29, the Universal Declaration only conceives of duties as the normative counterpart of rights. Article 29 is the only article that mentions human duties as an autonomous normative concept and conceives of human beings as bearers of duties that are not 'derived' from or do not correspond to rights. This is what Chapter 18 of this book will explore. Human beings do not only make claims to obtain something from others but are also obliged to give others their due.

One can put this point even a bit differently: Article 29 is a shift of perspective. Up to that point the Declaration emphasized claims, but now the attention is on what human beings ought to contribute to create a cosmopolitan society that fulfils the promise of human rights. This must be done – in the language of this Article – by simply obeying the law and fulfilling the demands made by the rights and freedoms of others, by meeting the demands of morality, public order and welfare. Human rights are thus no licence for disobedience, as Bentham feared. Chapter 17 will examine the important philosophical question of disobedience to the law. In Chapter 18 human beings will appear as primarily bearers of obligations. The next brief interlude will lead up to these themes.

Rights and Virtues

Chapter 1 stated that human rights are often regarded as the present-day embodiment of the idea of justice. As a concept, justice is connected to universality and to the promise of a social order in which the interests of all humans are guaranteed. This would be a good government for all. It has been suggested such a social order can only emerge if individual human beings do not only make claims on others but also meet their legal and moral obligations. Is this idea of justice enough for such an order to come about? Can a world free of 'barbarous acts' be achieved by appealing to this duty to justice only? Justice may well be a necessary condition of such a well-governed society, but is it also sufficient? A brief glance at the past suggests that this may not be the case.

One of the most famous visualizations of 'good government', the famous series of frescos in the Palazzo Pubblico of Siena's beautiful Piazza del Campo, suggests that not only rights and duties are needed, but also virtues. In the early fourteenth century the artist Ambrozio Lorenzetti painted the walls of the meeting hall of the governing body of the city state of Siena. In order to inspire them he sketched an allegory of good and of bad government. These frescos have become world famous not just because of their aesthetic qualities but also because they present us with an appealing view of what makes a government either good or bad. To start with bad government: it is headed by a tyrant who has surrounded himself with all sorts of vices such as divisiveness, quarrelsomeness, cruelty, miserliness and vanity and who tramples justice under foot. Such government leads to an impoverished and unsafe country, according to Lorenzetti. Good government on the other hand is led by a 'king' who is positioned between two rows of virtues, the cardinal ones (justice, modesty, generosity, wisdom and courage) and the theological ones (faith, hope and charity). According to the fresco, justice occupies a prominent place within good government, not only as a personal quality of the ruling king, but also as the institution which justly distributes goods and responsibilities and criminal punishments. Lorenzetti thus depicts justice twice: as the personification of one of the (cardinal) virtues (in the king) and as an institution. Justice as the most important quality of good government enables citizens to flourish, both within the city with its arts and crafts, and outside the city walls with agriculture and commerce. Good government leads to unity, prosperity and peace.[10]

Still, good government is according to Lorenzetti not the result of justice alone. Justice stands in need of being complemented by other virtues such as temperance, generosity, wisdom and courage. Lorenzetti seem to 'argue' that good government is made possible only when just institutions interact with citizens who behave not only justly, but also moderately, generously, wisely and courageously. This suggestion seems to fit rather well with the proposed interpretation of human duties at the end of the Universal Declaration. No one is allowed to emphasize his own rights and freedoms if that would conflict with the purposes and principles of the United Nations. Every human being ought thus to act moderately.

A similar message can be found at the very end of the Universal Declaration. According to Article 30 nobody – no state, no group, no single individual – may derive claims from the Universal Declaration if that would lead to 'the destruction of any one of the rights and freedoms' mentioned. No one may insist on their rights and freedoms in a manner that would cause damage to the Universal Declaration's purpose of establishing freedom, justice and peace in the world. For that reason, Chapter 18 will argue that the claims of justice are to be balanced with considerations of wisdom and especially moderation. This classical 'truth' is not only found in the work of Lorenzetti, but in ancient Rome as well, for example in Cicero's adage 'summa ius, summa iniuria' – the greatest justice leads to the greatest injustice.

Thus, the Universal Declaration concludes with a warning – human rights do not mean the absence of duties and exaggerated claims based on human rights are not permitted. Humans have human rights but they are not exempt from the duty to respect the laws of the society in which they live. They have to take each other's interests into consideration. Human beings have the duty to exercise their rights in a virtuous manner; what this might mean, is examined in Chapter 18.

---

[10] An extensive and illuminating interpretation of Lorenzetti's 'good government' can be found in Quentin Skinner, *Visions of Politics. Volume 2: Renaissance Virtues* (Cambridge: Cambridge University Press, 2002), esp. ch. 3, 39–117. See also David Miller, *Political Philosophy. A Very Short Introduction* (Oxford: Oxford University Press, 2003), 1–5, 74–5.

17

Everyone Has the Duty of Obedience

Are there human duties? The Universal Declaration of Human Rights says yes, but it mentions human duties in a very general and broad sense. On the basis of Article 29, clause 2, everyone is subject when exercising their rights and freedoms only to such limitations as are determined by law for the purpose of ensuring respect for the rights and freedoms of others and of meeting the just demands of morality, public order and the general welfare in a democratic society. Mentioning that 'everyone' is subject 'only' to these limitations seems like an understatement, since these limitations are very broadly formulated and spring from very diverse sources, both legal and moral. It is evident that Article 29 should make the rights and freedoms of others a limitation to my own rights and freedoms, and perhaps the same could be said of public order. After all, the declaration deals with the rights and freedoms of all human beings, and thus in principle they must be able to have all these rights and freedoms at the same time. This would certainly require a certain degree of regulation. Yet, making the demands of morality and general welfare grounds for limitations as well seems something entirely different. Is Article 29 antici-pating the utopian situation in which rights and freedoms are respected mutually and are in accordance with morality and general welfare? In the real world, however – both that of 1948 and in our days – human rights are frequently not respected, let alone could it be said that they can easily be harmonized with morality and welfare. Even positive law often does not embody the respect human beings are due. In the real world, public authority embodied in positive law often demands actions and entails obligations that seem to contradict human rights. Sometimes these rights merely seem to have the status of a moral claim.

How to deal with the tension between positive law and moral requirements, nowadays embodied in human rights, is and has been an important theme in legal philosophy. From where does positive law derive its claim to obedience if it violates morality? Traditionally, this conflict took the form of the tension between positive law or the command of a political authority on the one hand, and the conscience of an individual human being on the other. If such a conflict arises, which choice should be made? In the past, some authors have defended obedience of public order and positive law under all circumstances. The authority of the law trumps that of morality. Others have maintained that there cannot be a categorical obligation to obey positive law. The well-known, even famous words of Gustav Radbruch have already been mentioned, in Chapter 2: sometimes one encounters an 'intolerable tension' between legal commands and the requirements of justice, and this may then result in the duty to set aside the law as 'legal injustice'. In a famous legal case, from the days of the German occupation of the Netherlands, the justices of the Court in Leeuwarden ruled that they could not apply positive law in a particular criminal case. Doing so would bring them into conflict with their moral conscience. Also today many ordinary persons are confronted with conflicting obligations, for example when civil servants are supposed to cooperate with the deportation of migrants because these migrants are not entitled to residence, although they hold that their government's restrictive immigration policy is morally wrong. Here the obedience one owes to the law conflicts with one's moral and political views, or one's duty as a civil servant or as a private citizen is in conflict with one's personal responsibility. In legal philosophy, no consensus exists as to which obligations should have priority. Powerful voices maintain that the obedience to the law always weighs heavier than whatever moral views one holds dear.

The Importance of Obedience

The reason for adopting such a strict position is not difficult to understand: obedience or compliance is essential for the life of the law. Some philosophers, primarily those with a positivistic view, would even define law by means of such obedience. How to distinguish otherwise between law and morality? Legal rules can only be distinguished from other social rules, like conventional and moral rules or manners, by referring to a political authority as its origin and to the possibility of enforcement. Obedience or compliance is thus not a mere contingent matter in law, but it is essential for it to exist. Austin, the legal positivist mentioned in Chapter 1, emphasized indeed the fact that law is posited and can be enforced: it is not something which can be 'found' some-where, like moral rules, as some claim. It is established by the sovereign. Legal rules are the result of an issuing act by a person or a body, that is in the position to enforce obedience to what has been issued. If the sovereign is unable to enforce its legal commands, there would be no legal order but a mere collection of wishes or requests; law presupposes political power to enforce compliance. Law is essentially connected with power.

Nevertheless, others stress that no legal rule, even if it is merely a command, can do without a minimum of moral content. This is Fuller's position we have already encountered. His theory of the so-called internal morality of law holds that every legal order, in order to claim obedience, must fulfil some minimal requirements: the person or persons addressed by the order must be able to understand and comply, for no one can be obliged to do something which they do not understand or are unable to do. This is in line with the Roman adage, *ultra posse nemo obligatur.* Imagine for a moment the admittedly extreme legal 'command' to stop breathing. This can never be part of a legal order, because it is simply impossible for humans to comply. Therefore, all legal rules and regulations must take into account certain facts about human nature and about the environment in which humans live; a further requirement is that legal rules should be made known in advance: it is impossible to comply with an unknown, secret command. It also lies in the nature of the law that it is general, that is, addressed at a category of persons, and that different rules within the law should not contradict each other. Every legal system must consist of rules and commands that are internally consistent and do not continuously change qua content. These formal conditions form part of the 'nature' of the law. Fuller summarizes them as the 'internal' morality of law; Kant would perhaps call them the conditions of the possibility of law.

These 'formal' yet moral conditions of law must obviously be distinguished from an external and substantive morality of the law. Despite the internal morality of the law, much substantive injustice can still be part of the law. During the Apartheid regime in South Africa, many facilities were forbidden for the black population as indicated by signs such as '*slegs vir blankies*'. Such a legal prohibition of entrance would obviously violate the substantive morality of racial equality of all human beings, a starting point of the Universal Declaration which prohibits in Article 2 any distinction on the grounds of race or colour. But this prohibition does not contradict the internal morality of the law: racial discrimination can be promulgated in advance, can be general and prospective etc. It was possible for the members of the South African black population to comply with this prohibition.

Apart from such conceptual reasons that connect the law with obedience and compliance, there exist external grounds for obedience to the law – substantive moral reasons. In the history of legal and political thought, this issue has received serious attention, starting with the influential account of these grounds in Plato's famous dialogue *Crito*. The background of this dialogue is well-known: Plato's main character Socrates sits in prison awaiting the death penalty and his friends suggest that he should escape, in defiance of the sentence he has received from the Athenian court. Socrates refuses to accept this illegal proposal and argues that he should obey the law.[1] The background of the court case is also well-known. Socrates lived in the fifth century BCE, a time often called the golden age of Greek civilisation but also the time of the Peloponnesian War between the mighty cities of Athens and Sparta. In the heat of war, the Athenian democracy at times came under threat, when the aristocracy managed to seize power, but each time only for a brief period. After the restoration of democracy Socrates was arrested and accused of not having left Athens during the short period of aristocratic rule, and furthermore of have been fairly close to a number of prominent young

---

[1] Plato, *Crito*, 49e–52e.

aristocrats. This led to the following charges against Socrates: corrupting the youth, not respecting the gods of the city and introducing new gods. Before his judges Socrates denied all three charges, but he did so in such a challenging manner that the judges convicted him nonetheless and passed the severe sentence of death by drinking a cup of poison. While waiting for the sentence to be carried out Socrates remained in custody, when – as said – his friends seized the opportunity to search for some way to save his life. Speaking on behalf of these friends Crito suggested to Socrates that he should escape from prison and go into exile. Socrates rejected that offer because it was unjust. He was of the opinion that he had to obey the law, in his case to accept the death sentence of the Athenian court. What could he argue against 'the laws', when these would challenge him: Socrates, what are you doing, what are your intentions? Do you really want to destroy us, the laws, and with us the whole of society? Do you believe that a political society can survive when the laws have no force, when a criminal can escape his sentence at will and the law be overturned by individual citizens? The 'laws' would then, Socrates continued, argue that he owes everything to them and that he had had the possibility of leaving the city with his possessions, but that he had chosen not to do so. This implies, according to the laws, that there was a tacit agreement between him and the laws: they would take care of Socrates and he would obey them, even if they decided something that was against his interests: 'Socrates, was there not an agreement between you and us that you should acquiesce in the sentence passed by the community?'

In this dialogue, Plato presents us with a range of external moral reasons to obey the law. Without obedience to the law there is no social order, but anarchy. Therefore an ordinary citizen owes everything, in a sense, to the laws. This state of affairs is implicitly acknowledged by every citizen in their daily life by simply benefiting from the social order; by tacitly accepting the laws, one consents also to the obligations that these laws impose. For these reasons Socrates refuses to unlawfully escape from the prison and accepts without hesitation and without fear death by means of drinking poison.

The idea that the law as promulgated must be obeyed frequently appears in the course of the history of legal thinking. In the Middle Ages Thomas Aquinas was very wary of the thought that freedom from a tyrant could be won by disobedience and violence – even if the tyrant clearly had acted against the common good. Aquinas narrates the lovely story of an old woman who constantly prayed that the tyrant Dionysius would outlive her, while all the other inhabitants of Syracuse longed for his death. The reason she gave was that in a tyrannical system, it often happens that successor tyrants are more evil than their predecessors.[2] Despite the fact that in more modern times the social contract model of political authority became current, the argument that

---

[2] Thomas Aquinas, *De Regno ad Regem Cypri (On Kingship to the King of Cyprus)*, Book 1, ch. 7 (44).

disobedience to the law would threaten social stability remained and the argument that the disadvantages of a revolution against the established order would greatly exceed the disadvantages of an unjust authority. This is Hobbes's view: without social order, that is, in the natural condition of mankind, human life would be – and these have become famous words – solitary, poor, nasty, brutish and short. Because the situation of natural freedom is one of 'continual fear and the danger of violent death', it is advantageous for every human being to exchange this natural freedom for social security. A person who has agreed to the social contract – even tacitly – is bound to obey the law. Disobedience to the law would in the end lead back to the anarchy of the natural condition.[3] Despite his emphasis on human autonomy and human dignity, Kant accepts Hobbes's reasoning.[4] The state of natural freedom is one in which looms the war of all against all. Human beings can only escape from this dire situation by establishing a civil state which holds a monopoly of power. Kant considers all resistance to the legislative head of the state as inconsistent with that lawful condition; such a condition is only possible on the basis of the submission of all to the general will. Any form of sedition and even every attempt at rebellion has to be considered therefore as high treason and must be punished.[5] It would also be inconsistent to grant the people the right to judge whether the sovereign uses its power in a rightful manner, because the highest legislative power would then contain a provision to resist, which would mean that the highest legislation is not the highest and that would be self-contradictory. Allowing a right to disobedience would undermine the monopoly of power of the state and risk the disastrous return of the state of natural freedom. Kant merely allows every citizen to voice their protest publicly if in their view certain legislative actions of the state are unjust. But this freedom of publicity is not the freedom to disobey. In short: the main moral argument in favour of obedience is that it is in the interest of all human beings to have a stable social order, and that can be achieved only by obedience to the law.

Despite this impressive list of advocates of the duty of obedience, it is simply not true that the social order is threatened by occasional cases of disobedience. It is quite normal to find in every society instances of disobedience; the issuance of social rules limits the freedom of those subject to these rules. Even if these rules and the social order as a whole are fully justified and the outcome of a fair political process, there will always be some persons who seek advantages by breaking the rules. Think of a simple example like traffic regulations concerning speed limits. They are beneficial for social order and increase road safety and often no one is threatened by the odd breaking of a speed limit. Even those who regularly drive faster than the limit do not doubt the usefulness of these rules and will regard the rules in general as a good thing.

---

[3] Thomas Hobbes, *Leviathan*, 1.13–14.
[4] Even despite Kant's explicit rejection of Hobbes in Immanuel Kant, *Über den Gemeinspruch: Das mag in der Theorie richtig sein, taugt aber nicht für die Praxis*, AA VIII, 303–4.
[5] Immanuel Kant, *Metaphysik der Sitten*, AA VI, 320.

Yet, in special circumstances they make an exception for themselves. Others try to dodge paying their taxes, although they do not call into question the usefulness of taxation to finance public services. Such persons try to avoid paying too much tax and are disobeying the law as a sort of free-riders who are happy to benefit from public services paid for by others, without contributing to them. These are cases of ordinary disobedience, not motivated by moral concerns but by self-interest.

Obviously, these are not the sort of cases that worried Socrates, Thomas Aquinas, Hobbes and Kant. They were concerned by cases in which the validity of the law was challenged on moral grounds. That is not a case of selfish or self-interested disobedience, but disobedience as the result of a conflict between what is demanded of someone as a citizen and what is demanded of them as a human being. In that case someone considers a particular law or perhaps even the society as a whole as in conflict with some 'higher law' that stems from justice. This is a real conflict between posited law and the demands of morality. The authors mentioned so far are inclined to argue that preference should be given even then to the legal order, because that order is more important than what is demanded on the basis of some particular moral view. A threat to the legal order itself is to everyone's disadvantage – or that is at least the argument in favour of the duty of obedience.

The 'Right' to Disobedience

The social order argument is countered by an argument which has a long pedigree as well. In short it says that one should refuse obedience to laws or legal commands that are strongly opposed to what moral duty prescribes. If the law conflicts with morality, the latter must take precedence. In Chapter 1 we encountered Antigone, the heroine of the ancient classical tragedy of the same name. She famously refused to obey Creon, the ruler of her city, who had given her a command that was morally impossible for her to obey, namely to let her dead brother remain unburied.[6] According to Creon, disobedience was the greatest evil and would bring the city to ruins. Therefore, legal commands are more important than moral convictions, but many readers of this tragedy think that Antigone was right: 'I do not think your edicts strong enough to overrule the unwritten unalterable laws of God and heaven, you only being a man.'[7]

In the late Middle Ages, the group known as 'monarchomachs', opponents of the monarch, emphatically defended the right to oppose a tyrannical ruler. Monarchs rule by the grace of God, but this means that they must use their authority for the general interest. If they refuse to do so and ignores their

---

[6] A recent re-telling of Antigone is Kamila Shamsie, *Home Fire* (New York: Riverhead Books, 2017).
[7] Sophocles, *The Theban Plays*, trans. Edward F. Watling (Middlesex: Penguin, 1947), 138.

responsibilities to their subjects, the subjects have the right to revolt against them. This theory played an important role in the revolt of the Dutch provinces against the rule of the Spanish king in the sixteenth century.[8] In his famous *Second Treatise of Government*, at the end of the seventeenth century, Locke argued that Hobbes's view (and by implication that of Kant) was simply wrong. The trade-off between natural freedom and collective security would not, according to Locke, lead to an unconditional surrender to the sovereign, because, as mentioned before, 'this is to think that that men are so foolish that they take care to avoid what mischiefs may be done to them by polecats or foxes, but are content, nay, think it safely to be devoured by lions'.[9] Therefore the social contract should according to Locke be understood as a sort of mandate. Indeed, an exchange of obedience to authority takes place on the one side and the competence to rule on the other, but only on the condition that the ruler establishes rules that benefit those obeying them. The duty of obedience is therefore conditional and the ruler must abide by their mandate. According to Locke, the social contract is not a single event by which every person is thereafter bound – as Hobbes holds – nor should it be regarded as an idea of reason, as Kant claims.[10] It is a tacit agreement that must be renewed, as it were, by the citizens time and again, and they are bound by the agreement only when the state fulfils its proper function, namely to protect life, liberty and property. In contrast to Hobbes and Kant, Locke does not consider obedience self-evident. Since the reason human beings join society is for the preservation of their rights, it would be inconsistent to presuppose that the legislature should be obeyed if it abuses the societal power. When the legislators destroy the property of the people or reduce their status to slavery, they put themselves into a state of war with the people, who are thereby absolved from any further duty of obedience.

This important lesson of Locke's *Second Treatise* seems to fit well with the human rights perspective. The duty of obedience would only apply in a society in which individual rights are respected. Formulated a bit broader, the human duties of Article 29 would only come into play when a social order has been reached in which the rights and freedoms mentioned in the Universal Declaration are realized. When that is not the case or when the social order is deficient qua realization of human rights, there cannot be a broad duty of obedience, but there must be room for what is called civil disobedience: disobedience to certain legal rules because of moral or human rights concerns. A difficult point, as we will see, is determining exactly in which cases or at what point obedience can be withdrawn and when not.

The modern idea of civil disobedience is supported by famous historical examples. Especially in the nineteenth century one finds various cases of

---

[8] Ernst H. Kossmann, 'Volkssoevereiniteit aan het begin van het Nederlandse ancien régime', in *Politieke theorie en geschiedenis* (Amsterdam: Bakker, 1987), 59–92.

[9] John Locke, *Two Treatises of Government*, 2.93.

[10] Immanuel Kant, *Über den Gemeinspruch: Das mag in der Theorie richtig sein, taugt aber nicht für die Praxis*, AA VIII, 297.

non-violent resistance against injustices.[11] Leo Tolstoy, the author of the epic book *War and Peace*, set himself against the backwardness of feudal Tsarist Russia and the repression of the peasant population. He also turned against Russia's wars and regarded it his duty to honour the Christian message of peace and love of one's fellow men, even if it meant disobeying the law. Around the same time Henry Thoreau protested against the United States' war on Mexico and refused to pay his taxes for this reason, even though the decision to declare war was taken democratically. For him, the obligation to resist injustice was more important than a simple piece of democratic legislation. Perhaps the most appealing recent example of civil disobedience on the grounds of moral considerations is that of the black American preacher Martin Luther King, who became world famous because of his opposition to racial segregation in American society. He regarded the discriminatory laws in the southern states of the United States as a form of apartheid. This practice was not only contrary to the demands of justice and God's law, but also against human law. In 1954 the American Supreme Court – in the famous case of *Brown v. Board of Education*[12] – had decided that the discriminatory legislation in the southern states was in violation of the constitution that guaranteed that everyone had 'equal protection of the law'. King simply insisted that the constitutional decision should be applied and the practice of separate facilities for whites and blacks be stopped. One did not need to obey laws that were based on racial segregation. Indeed, in order to have those laws rescinded one had to break other laws so that attention would be given to this form of legal injustice.[13]

Civil Disobedience

Since there are apparently good arguments not only for but also against strict obedience to positive law, it seems best not to maintain that all laws must always be obeyed. The fact that a particular rule has a formal legal status does not mean that ordinary citizens cease to be humans who must decide on the basis of their own convictions and conscience whether or not to comply. Suppose a soldier receives an order that is evidently of a criminal nature, should they just obey and claim 'an order is an order'? Suppose that an immigration official must do something that they simply cannot reconcile with their conscience, must they then obey and claim that this action is simply part of their job? At the same time, it is clear that general obedience is needed for a stable social order. That is incompatible with everyone having the possibility to decide for themselves

---

[11] See for example Bob Blaisdell, *Essays on Civil Disobedience* (Mineola: Dover Thrift Edition, 2016).

[12] *Brown v. Board of Education of Topeka*, 347 US 483 (1954).

[13] Martin L. King, 'Letter from the Birmingham City Jail', in *A Testament of Hope: The Essential Writings and Speeches of Martin Luther King Jr.*, ed. James M. Washington (New York: HarperCollins, 1991).

whether or not to obey. Rawls tried to offer a solution to this dilemma – and thus to the difficulty presented by Article 29 – by establishing criteria or guidelines to determine when disobedience would be permissible and when not.

Rawls is an important philosopher whose work has already been used several times. Here too, his distinctions are helpful.[14] The first element of his answer is the nature of the society in which the question of obedience arises. It makes a great difference whether this question arises within a democratic society or not. One could argue that an individual citizen is less entitled to disobey in a society where the legislation is democratically legitimized than in a society in which citizens hardly have any say. That fits well with Article 29, according to which everyone is subject to limitations determined by law 'in a democratic society'. The more democratic a piece of legislation, the less justification for disobedience. Remember that this is also in a sense what 'the laws' said to Socrates: since in our state you had the opportunity to change the laws, you now owe them obedience. This does not mean that for Rawls no form of disobedience is permissible in a democratically organized society. The will of the majority does not automatically lead to justifiable rules. Majorities can make moral errors. Therefore, not every form of disobedience within a democratic state is automatically an expression of the unwillingness of members of a minority to accept democratic decisions. Legitimacy and democratic majority decisions are not always the same. In Chapter 12 we found that for this reason, many constitutions have set limits to the scope of the democratic majority rule. Majorities should respect fundamental rights and cannot simply deny minorities their minority religion, to mention just an example. Disobedience within a democracy is not by definition unjustified.

The second element of Rawls's answer focuses on the question under which condition disobedience is justified in a democracy. This question was triggered by a reflection on the problems of his time and his society: racial segregation and the Vietnam war. The answer Rawls gives us is based on his interpretation of social contract theory, namely that a society can be called 'just' when its guiding principles are chosen by persons who are in a position of impartiality. In such a position persons will choose two principles: society must give every member an equal right to the most extensive scheme of basic liberties compatible with a similar scheme for others and society must ensure not only that its positions and offices are open to all but also that social and economic inequalities are beneficial to all, including those least off in society. This we have seen before.

Imagine, Rawls continues, that a society starts out with these abstract principles. It has then to make things more concrete, by designing a constitution and by issuing laws and regulations. The more concrete these regulations become, the greater the chance of disagreement between citizens,

---

[14] See John Rawls, *A Theory of Justice. Revised edition* (Oxford: Oxford University Press, 1999), 319–43.

who will have different views as to what the principles of justice mean in a concrete situation. To give an example: should persons on the grounds of the right to equal opportunities receive compensation if they start from a societal position of disadvantage? Some would argue that positive discrimination is what justice requires, while others would disagree. Should a system of progressive taxation be introduced so that the least well off pay a smaller part of their income to the taxman than the rich? Citizens can reasonably disagree about this, if only because it is difficult to chart the effects of such measures for society as a whole and in the long run. In brief, in a society based on the two principles of justice, citizens will have different views on what justice requires in concrete legislation. Can some of them then disobey a particular piece of legislation, because they consider it unjust? When, in Rawls's view, is civil disobedience justified?

Rawls's answer is, in short, as follows. Civil disobedience can only be legitimized by reference to the principles of justice and not to moral principles that are not shared by all members of the society such as a presumed higher law, the Bible, the Koran or God. Because of the 'civil' and public nature of disobedience, it must not consist of clandestine or hidden actions, but take place in the open, as an appeal to all citizens of society that this particular piece of legislation is a violation of the principles of justice. A disobedient but conscientious citizen is also prepared to bear the consequences, in the form of penalties, of their disobedient actions. Civil disobedience is thus a protest against a particular law or legislative measure, but not against society as a whole. It is an appeal for a particular legislative measure to be repealed. Martin Luther King's protests against discriminatory legislation in the southern states is an excellent example of what Rawls means. This racist legislation was in violation of the prevailing principles of justice, which include 'equal protection of the laws'. It is thus clear that civil disobedience is different from the ordinary 'disobedience' of those who drive faster than the speed limit, evade taxes, and break into someone else's property for selfish reasons. It also differs from the radical disobedience when revolutionaries renounce all obedience to the society as such because they want to build society on a different set of principles.

Rawls thus sets the bar for civil disobedience relatively high. One cannot just resort to disobedience because one disagrees with the outcome of a process of democratic decision-making. Even if democratic outcomes do not automatically lead to legitimacy, a strong connection between the two exists. Therefore, Rawls holds that civil disobedience is only justifiable after first having made efforts to change the contested measure by democratic means. It should be used only as a last resort. Moreover, and this is important, civil disobedience can be justified only if it concerns laws and regulations that contain some obvious injustice, that is violations of the first principle of justice concerning equal rights to freedom of all citizens. Here Rawls follows the view of King too.

By means of civil disobedience to regulations that violate the equal rights of citizens, an appeal is made to the majority to repeal such unjust regulations.

With this understanding of 'civil disobedience' Rawls finds a middle ground between the arguments of Socrates and others who emphasize the importance of social order and stability, and the arguments of Locke and others who emphasize that the duty of obedience to the authorities should be conditional. While Article 29 of the Universal Declaration anticipates a utopian situation in which all rights and freedoms are realized, Rawls's position is realistic: persons may sometimes put their obligation to obedience aside if the principle of equal freedom is violated. Violations of the so-called difference principle (material inequalities are only permitted if they benefit those least off in society) are empirically so difficult to judge that they do not amount to the question of civil disobedience. Important to add here is that this priority according to Rawls not only applies to domestic democratic societies, but also makes sense within the realm of international relations.

International Disobedience

The question of obedience concerns not only citizens vis-à-vis their legislation but also states vis-à-vis each other and the international community. According to Article 29, 'everyone' has obligations to the community. The further explanation that fulfilling these duties is beneficial for the development of everybody's personality suggests that 'everybody' refers to natural persons. But this suggestion is not totally correct. The third clause of this Article says that rights and freedoms may not 'be exercised contrary to the purposes and principles of the United Nations'. Very few natural persons are so influential that they can thwart these purposes and principles. Moreover, the prohibition in Article 30 on 'any act aimed at the destruction of any of the rights and freedoms set forth herein [in this Declaration]' applies to individuals as well as to groups and states. It is clear then that the part of the Universal Declaration dedicated to duties also applies to states, but what could that mean? By mentioning the 'purposes and principles of the United Nations', states are obliged, as we saw in Chapter 15, to maintain international peace and security to which end the member states have to respect each other's political sovereignty and territorial integrity. For that reason, the United Nations does not have the authority 'to intervene in matters which are essentially within the domestic jurisdiction of any state'. Yet, the same Charter also affirms its 'faith in fundamental human rights' and sees 'the realisation of human rights' as one of its purposes.

Promoting international peace and stability and realizing individual human rights do not always lead to the same course of action. Therefore sometimes priorities will be needed. Those who place the greatest value on international stability will probably regard peace as paramount. We have already seen that Kant, for instance, did not acknowledge the right to intervene. Acknowledging such a right would undermine the establishing of international peace. Thomas Aquinas's recommendation to seek God's support if the people suffer under the rule of a tyrant may sound somewhat cynical, but suggests that he would agree with Kant.[15] The 'monarchomachs' and Locke take the opposite position and claim a right to rebel against tyranny. If such a right exists it would probably also be permitted for an outside state to protect an oppressed population from its tyrant through a humanitarian intervention. If citizens have the right to disobey and to revolt against a tyrannical regime, why would neighbouring states not be exempted from the duty to respect the political sovereignty and territorial integrity of that tyrannical state?

In a well-known essay on international law Rawls tries, again, to find a middle ground. In line with his position that civil disobedience can only be justified by violations of the principle of equal civil rights, he now defends that 'disobedience' on the international level and thus possibly the resort to war is justifiable only when gross violations of the most essential human rights take place within a tyrannical state. Because, according to Rawls, the list of human rights that now have international consensus is very limited, only the systematic violation of this 'special class of urgent rights', such as freedom from slavery, liberty of conscience and the security of an ethnic group from mass murder,[16] justifies disregard of the rule that states should mutually respect each other's sovereignty. The political significance of these urgent human rights is that they limit the sovereign powers of states. Only within the boundaries of these human rights can states use their right to self-determination. Genocide or the introduction of slavery cannot be regarded as an expression of the autonomy of a political community.

For Rawls, this does not mean that a violation of these urgent human rights should immediately be followed by a military intervention. The state that commits such violations of urgent rights need no longer be respected as a sovereign state. But before the question of a militarily intervention arises, other conditions have to be met. These are the conditions established in the just war tradition. A just cause alone is not enough. There must also be a reasonable chance of success and the costs of intervention in terms, for example, of civilian casualties, should not exceed the foreseeable benefits of removing the tyrannical regime. If these conditions are not met, the suffering population can do nothing more than follow Aquinas's advice and pray to God or Allah for help.

It is clear: there are no human rights without human duties. Human rights ought to be respected, to be protected and to be promoted. Only when these rights are guaranteed, can one agree with Article 29 that everyone is subject to the limitations that arise from the law and from public order. In our real world,

---

[15] Thomas Aquinas, *De Regno ad Regem Cypri (On Kingship to the King of Cyprus)*, Book 1, ch. 7 (51): 'for it lies in his power to turn the cruel heart of the tyrant to mildness'.

[16] John Rawls, *The Law of Peoples* (Cambridge, MA: Harvard University Press, 2000), 79.

human rights are frequently not guaranteed, so that obedience to human rights may easily lead to conflict with the prevailing legal and political order. The extent to which this conflict may lead to civil disobedience is widely discussed: the importance of a stable but imperfect legal and political order has to be balanced against the demands of the Universal Declaration. Emphasizing the importance of human rights should not lead to an underestimation of the importance of stability. In the international realm the existing consensus on urgent human rights is indeed important, as Rawls emphasizes. But with regard to non-urgent human rights, he would argue that their interpretation is basically a matter of domestic societies to decide. Here, outsiders should adopt an attitude of restraint and moderation. Outsiders are often unable to know how to apply these abstract rights in particular situations.

18

Everyone Has the Duty to Behave with Moderation

We have finally reached the last Article of the Universal Declaration. We encountered Article 30 in Chapter 16, but the issues that this Article raises deserve further exploration here. This is its text: 'Nothing in this Declaration may be interpreted as implying for any State, group or person any right to engage in any activity or to perform any act aimed at the destruction of any of the rights and freedoms set forth herein'. Interesting to note is that here again something is demanded of every human being, not merely from states and groups. Article 29 mentions duties of individuals too: duties that individuals have to the community in which they live. If indeed Article 29 mentions the duties of citizens, then it is plausible to read Article 30 as stressing duties individuals have to the community that is constituted by the 'rights and freedoms set forth herein [in the Declaration]'. We know that this community is not a world state, but 'merely' the cosmopolitan community that is envisioned in and by the Preamble. In that line, Article 1 obliges all human beings to behave in a 'spirit of brotherhood' vis-à-vis each other. The duty to contribute to the realization of all rights and duties of the Universal Declaration thus applies to everyone as a 'world citizen'. This 'division of labour' between Articles 29, duties of citizens, and 30, duties of world citizens, is 'mediated' by the third clause of Article 29: no one may use their rights and freedoms in a way that conflicts with the purposes and principles of the United Nations. These purposes and principles concern international peace and security, friendly international relations and respect for human rights, as spelt out in Article 1 of the Charter. In sum, the duties that human beings have on the basis of the Universal Declaration concern the political community to which they belong, and the human family, that is the community to which all political communities belong.

The impression that the Universal Declaration is concerned only with human rights and ignores human responsibilities and duties is thus incorrect. The related impression that the duties implied in human rights are merely duties for the state is also incorrect. Certainly, the state should respect and protect human life, should not torture anyone, should not arbitrarily strip humans of their property, should not exclude anyone from government and should protect cultural minorities – to name just a few of the issues that have been discussed. Often, and rightly so, it is emphasized that human rights limit the power of the state. Meanwhile it has become clear that human rights give rise to positive obligations for the state as well. To ensure, for example, that every human being can participate in government, elections need to be organized. Human beings can only be equal before the law if there are laws. Therefore, a clear distinction between negative and positive duties may not be very helpful and can better be replaced, as suggested by Shue, by three sets of obligations. Any human right implies firstly the duty not to act in a way that violates the interest which that right represents, secondly the duty to protect that interest, and finally the duty to enhance or realize that right.[1]

Not only states have obligations: so much is clear from Articles 29 and 30. Groups and individuals are urged not to abuse their rights and freedoms. One could perhaps say that the Universal Declaration closes with a warning addressed to groups and individuals: do not make unreasonable claims based on human rights; make use of one's human rights in a responsible manner. The European Convention on Human Rights makes a similar appeal in its (closing) Article 17: 'Nothing in this Convention may be interpreted as implying for any State, group or person any right to engage in any activity or perform any act aimed at the destruction of any of the rights and freedoms set forth herein or at their limitation to a greater extent than is provided for in the Convention.' Even the two international human rights conventions concluded between states contain this element of individual duties. The Preamble, identical in both conventions, says that individual human beings have duties to other individuals and to the community to which they belong.

The first implication of this duty to use one's human rights in a responsible manner was discussed in Chapter 17. Human rights do not obviate the prima facie duty of citizens to obey the laws of their society. They cannot, to mention one or two examples, simply refuse to pay taxes on the basis of their human right to property, or frivolously incite to violence or slander others on the basis of their human right to freedom of expression. The European Convention is clear about defamation. According to Article 10, clause 2 it is an abuse of one's freedom of expression to destroy another person's reputation, or to put one's national security in danger. According to some, the duty of obedience applies even if a particular state has little or no regard for human rights. The existence of a political order as such is considered more important than human rights. The acknowledgement of the duty of obedience within the Universal Declaration would probably remove Bentham's fear that human rights would lead to anarchy. Human rights are indeed not a licence for individual arbitrariness. If a citizen considers certain legal regulations as violating human rights, in principle they must use legal and political means to change these regulations.

The second, more indirect, implication of the duty to behave responsibly in respect of human rights is related to the view of humankind that this book

---

[1] Henry Shue, *Basic Rights* (New Jersey: Princeton University Press, 2007).

attributes to the Universal Declaration. On the basis of the first axis, a human being is an individual creature with a legitimate claim to their own space and to be free from certain sorts of treatment, such as torture and arbitrary detention. But besides being an individual creature, a human being is also a social being. The second axis tells us that human beings need certain social facilities, and their human rights therefore envision the respect for national, familial, cultural and religious identities. On the basis of this second axis a human being is not merely a claimant but also a person on whom claims are made. Kant captures these two axes neatly in the concept of a human being's 'unsocial sociability', as mentioned in Chapter 9. Human beings want, on the one hand, as individuals, to organize things in their own way and not to have things regulated by others. From this axis stems the desire for honour, power and possessions, and human beings can be ambitious, dominating and covetous.[2] But human beings are on the other hand also creatures that are born to others and grow up in all kinds of communities. Not only is everyone's identity determined by these particular communities, but almost all human beings have this great need to share their lives with others. Thus, humans simultaneously want to isolate themselves and to communicate with others and establish friendships. According to Kant, it is a good thing that both axes exist side by side, because without unsociability there is no autonomy, and without friendship and solidarity no good life. Kant does not claim that these axes can easily be brought together: too much emphasis on sociability is a threat to independence and autonomy, but unsociability alone puts the 'spirit of brotherhood', in the words of the Universal Declaration, under pressure.

Given the historic constellation, the Universal Declaration understandably emphasizes the first axis. While it gives room to the negative freedoms of the individual, it also acknowledges the human being's need to be a member of important communities. It even underlines the importance of the axis of humankind as a social being by emphasizing the duties of the individual to the community, in Articles 29 and 30. Article 1's 'spirit of brotherhood' should inform everyone's effort to bring about, in the words of the Preamble, 'a world in which human beings shall enjoy freedom of speech and belief and freedom from fear and want'.

Anthropological Worries

During the work of the commission, under the leadership of Eleanor Roosevelt, that had been commissioned by the United Nations to draft what would become the Universal Declaration, some cultural anthropologists were worried that the envisaged document on human rights would not give sufficient emphasis to the social nature of the human being and that it would focus too much on the axis of individuality, as supposedly common in western

---

[2] Immanuel Kant, *Idee zu einer allgemeinen Geschichte in weltbürgerlicher Absicht*, AA VIII, 21.

thinking. If that were to be the case, the new document would fail to be truly universal. For this reason, in 1947 the board of the American Anthropological Association published a public statement urging the committee to pay sufficient attention to the human being as a social and cultural creature.[3] This interesting statement still deserves attention for two reasons: it considers the human being as a bearer of duties, and it anticipates later criticisms of human rights as the embodiment of western individualistic values supposedly incompatible with the values of Asian and African cultures in which human communities play a much greater role.[4]

The AAA recommended the drafting commission to build on the scholarly findings within cultural anthropology, in particular by pointing to the fact that all cultures have certain ethnocentric tendencies. Cultures acknowledge the existence of other cultures, but generally speaking, they regard their own values as superior. There is a well-known example of this general habit, antedating the academic discipline of anthropology. In the fifth century BCE Herodotus, often considered the father of history, gave us the following example of regarding one's own culture as superior to that of others. When the Persian King Darius asked the Greeks for what price they would be prepared to eat their fathers' dead bodies, they replied that there was no price that could make them do so. When Darius subsequently asked the Callatiae whether they were prepared to stop eating the corpses of their parents and burn them instead, they cried aloud that he should not propose such a dreadful thing.[5] More recently, the sixteenth-century French philosopher Montaigne wrote in one of his famous essays that everyone calls 'barbarous' everything that is not in use in one's own country. Human beings seem to have no other level of truth and reason than the opinions and customs of the place where they live and they commonly find their own religion and government system the best there are. According to Montaigne, one should thus be reluctant to consider one's own views as superior and take into account that every human judgement is formed by one's culture.[6]

The habits and customs of a cultural group have, according to the American Anthropological Association, a great influence on its members. From the moment of birth these habits and customs, including language, determine

---

[3] The Executive Board, American Anthropological Association, 'Statement on Human Rights', *American Anthropologist*, New Series (1947) 49(4): 539–43; a recent challenge of the commission's effort to be universal (by invoking the help of a 'philosophers' committee) is Mark Goodale, 'The Myth of Universality: The UNESCO "Philosophers'Committee" and the Making of Human Rights', *Law & Social Inquiry* (2018) 43: 596–617.

[4] The debate on universal human rights and primarily 'Asian values' became prominent in the 1990s. See, for example, Xiaorong Li, 'Asian Values and the Universality of Human Rights', in *The Philosophy of Human Rights: Readings in Context*, ed. Patrick Hayden (St Paul: Paragon House, 2001), 397–408.

[5] *The History of Herodotus*, Book III, 38.

[6] Michel de Montaigne, 'Of Cannibals,' in *Essays*, trans. Charles Cotton (1580), http://essays .quotidiana.org/montaigne/cannibals/.

not only one's behaviour, but also one's thoughts, hopes, aspirations and even one's moral judgement. This cultural influence on each and every human being is so far-reaching and subtle that no one can become aware of it without long and thorough training. If a document on human rights were to overemphasize the respect for the personality of each individual human being, then – and this is the worry – it would insufficiently take into account the influence of cultural embeddedness. Therefore, respect for the diversity of cultures is as important as respect for individuals. Formulated differently, respect for the personality of each and every individual human being should include respect for cultural differences among human beings. Does this not lead to the problem that cultural embeddedness makes human beings consider their own ways of living to be best? Indeed, respect for cultural differences is not obvious and the acknowledgement of the importance of culture might lead to conflict rather than to respect. If one regards one's own culture as superior, one will look down on others, which will provoke antagonism.

This difficulty is however less troublesome – according to the anthropologists' advice – because human beings are often prepared to choose the tolerant attitude of live and let live, despite their cultural differences. Is this really the case? Look at the expansionist history of Western Europe and America, where the encounter with cultural differences lead to ideas of religious superiority and racial supremacy. As a consequence of this perceived superiority,[7] the West believed it also had the right and the duty to subject other so-called inferior cultures and nations to its rule in order to spread civilization. The doctrines of the 'white man's burden' and *mission civilatrice* were based on the distinction between developed and underdeveloped cultures and peoples. Therefore, the 'anthropological' advice given to the Roosevelt commission was that their document should not be a continuation of such doctrines by human rights means. It was really important to emphasize the equality of all human cultures; only such a recognition would ensure that the document would really be universal and applicable to all human beings. In sum, the American Anthropological Association advocated equal respect for all cultures, because it is impossible to prove the superiority of one culture over another. A truly universal document or declaration of human rights should contain no standards and values that are specific to one particular culture.

With this recommendation the American Anthropological Association adopted the position of cultural relativism: all cultures are equal and no particular individualistic culture may put its stamp on human rights. Relativism, in the philosophical sense, has a long pedigree, at least since Protagoras in Greek antiquity called man the measure of all things. It also has more modern advocates. In 1953, in his *Philosophical Investigations*, Wittgenstein defended the view that human beings interpret the world against

---

[7] A present-day example of this view is Roger Scruton, *The West and the Rest: Globalisation and the Terrorist Threat* (Wilmington: ISI Books, 2002).

the background of their 'forms of life'. These forms must be compared with games and there is no meta-game on the basis of which these games can be evaluated.[8] But relativism never had a good name, neither in Antiquity nor in our own times. Critics were and are always eager to point out the inconsistencies of relativism. First of all, suppose indeed that all standards and values are bound to the particular culture from which they originate. What then is the status of the recommendation that cultures should mutually respect and tolerate each other? There are two possibilities: either the 'recommendation' itself must be a standard that transcends the diversity of cultures, but then it cannot be relative and must be universal, or the claim of tolerance itself is only of limited value and is culturally determined. In the first option, the recommendation of mutual cultural respect contradicts relativism, and the second option does not explain why someone who is culturally inclined to intolerance should embrace the view that cultures must respect each other. In brief, relativism is either internally inconsistent or is itself a mere cultural view.

Critics are also eager to point out that respect for cultural differences is quite impossible to uphold in practice. To mention an example, should the cultural view of Nazi Germany, its genocidal racism, be respected? Or should burial practices be tolerated in which the widows of the deceased are burned along with their deceased spouses? What about female genital mutilation? It seems impossible to assert that all cultures are equal. Intolerant cultures or cultures that violate urgent human rights cannot be tolerated. A final and perhaps fatal objection against cultural relativism is that it suggests that human beings are imprisoned within their culture, or forms of life, from which there is no escape. But that is certainly not true; countless examples exist of human beings who leave their culture behind and adopt another culture, or of the mixing and blending of different cultures. Cultural relativism seems to lay an undue emphasis on the axis of humankind as a member of a community and to overlook that humans can and will break away from their cultural ties as individuals.

Even though these objections against the 'cultural relativistic' advice of the American Anthropological Association are valid, they seem at the same time to be beside the point. The advice was clearly intended to offer a counterweight to a one-sided emphasis on the human individual, as well as to warn against a document that would emphasize the superiority and supremacy of certain cultures and nations. In the past, similar views of superiority have led to horrible consequences. If there were to be a Universal Declaration, it should indeed be universal, and not a self-satisfied continuation of doctrines such as the 'white man's burden' and the *mission civilatrice*. Therefore, the Roosevelt commission was urged to be modest and to respect groups of human beings

---

[8] Ludwig Wittgenstein, *Philosophical Investigations*, trans. Elizabeth Anscombe (Oxford: Basil Blackwell, 1958). The famous Sapir-Whorf thesis, according to which the structure of one's particular language determines one's world view, is strongly influenced by Wittgenstein.

with different cultural backgrounds. Given the historical constellation, this was not an unreasonable demand. In 1947, western member states of the newly established United Nations, such as France, the United Kingdom and also the Netherlands, had every intention of taking back control of their old colonial dominions. The historical process of decolonization, as a result of which the number of member states of the United Nations would rise from a meagre 56 countries at that time to almost 200 today, had yet to begin. Therefore, the anthropological call for modesty with regard to western superiority was quite understandable.

Another point is also worth considering. Today, relativism has a bad name, but this was not the case during the period before the outbreak of World War II. In Chapter 11 we saw that two prominent defenders of the idea of parliamentary democracy presented 'democracy' as a relativistic doctrine. According to Kelsen, relativism is democracy's world view. If it were possible to reach 'truth' within the political or ethical domain, then it would not only be unjustified but also unreasonable to permit ordinary citizens to express their views and to enable them to form legislative majorities. Understandably, Plato was a fierce opponent of democracy, because he was convinced of the existence of absolute truth. According to Kelsen, the concept of 'truth' is only applicable to scientific facts and not to ethical, political or legal standpoints. Democracy exists therefore on the basis of the willingness of those participating therein to regard as equal every political view or conviction. Radbruch too considered democracy and relativism as closely connected. Precisely because there are no absolute ethical or political viewpoints, democracy presupposes a variety of opinions, viewpoints and values, and requires that human beings respect these differences.

Today the views of Kelsen and Radbruch are easily dismissed as naïve or inconsistent or both, for what would be their answer to political parties that make use of democratic procedures to gain a majority position and then start to implement their undemocratic policies, including abolishing democracy? In fact, this is what happened in 1933 when the Nazi party came to power in Germany. It ended democracy and introduced its own absolute values.[9] Is relativism not too weak a foundation for democracy, especially when it is under attack? Therefore, many now claim that democracy ought to be regarded as an absolute value and not as a relative one. Still, the view of Kelsen and Radbruch, and that of the American Anthropological Association, has its appeal. Suppose that there was some sort of 'evidence' or 'proof' that democracy or intercultural respect was indeed superior to all other possible forms of government or all other cultural attitudes. What sort of evidence or proof could this be? Would one be in a better position, armed

---

[9] Historically, the Nazi takeover was a complex historical process and it would be wrong to simply assert that the Nazis rose to power democratically. An excellent overview of these developments from a conceptual point of view still is David Dyzenhaus, *Legality and Legitimacy: Carl Schmitt, Hans Kelsen and Hermann Heller in Weimar* (Oxford: Oxford University Press, 1999), esp. ch. 1.

with such evidence or proof, to resist persons, movements or political parties that advocate another form of government or argue in favour of the superiority of their own culture? It seems that a democratic form of government and cultural pluralism can only flourish if a sufficient number of persons participating is prepared to qualify their sense of being right and to moderate their own political and cultural judgements. This is unlikely to be the result of some 'evidence' or 'proof', but rather to stem from a particular attitude that one could call virtuous.

Based on these considerations, the advice given by the American Anthropological Association makes sense. For a declaration to become truly universal, it should acknowledge cultural differences and everyone should adopt an attitude of a certain modesty with regard to one's own cultural pretentions and judgements. One should, following Articles 29 and 30, assert one's human rights with a certain degree of moderation. This is a call that finds support from the tradition of classical legal philosophy.

Classic Advice

It is unknown – at least to me – whether the anthropological worries had any influence on the text of the Universal Declaration. It is however clear that the emphasis on the axis of man as an individual is tempered by Articles 29 and 30. These Articles require one's obligations with respect to one's particular community and to human society as a whole to be taken seriously. In order to find out what such a proper attitude may be, it is helpful to return to the position adopted in Chapter 1: to write an introduction to legal philosophy on the basis of the idea of human rights as the embodiment of the modern idea of justice. For this reason, no modern state can claim to be just if it does not commit itself to human rights standards. States that do not are often called 'rogue states' and according to some commentators should no longer be entitled to political sovereignty and territorial integrity.

Is justice in the form of human rights capable of reaching the aims mentioned in the Preamble of the Universal Declaration, namely a world in which the four freedoms are realized, where the rule of law is respected and a decent standard of living for all is guaranteed? If too much emphasis is given to the axis of man as an individual being, then the answer is probably negative. Prioritizing individual rights might easily lead, according to Bentham, to a neglect of the general interest. Emphasizing individual rights may lead, according to Marx, to a society in which the interests of those who are socially and financially strongest will be promoted at the cost of the socially weak. Individual human rights do not lead to a connection between human beings, but to alienating them from each other. Therefore, Marx advocates a totally different social and political order, not based on human rights but on their community. Did Bentham and Marx exchange the emphasis on the individual human being for that on man as a social being? According to Rawls, this is

indeed the case: Bentham's utilitarianism does not give sufficient consideration to what he calls the 'plurality and distinctness of individuals'.[10] Utility can
in principle be aggregated over a plurality of persons in such a manner that
severe disadvantages for some can be compensated by advantages for others,
but according to Rawls this is unjust: individuals should not be considered
merely as elements of a calculus. Marx is also often accused of overestimating
the social nature of human beings as member of classes. All in all, Bentham and
Marx seem unable to find the right balance between humankind's sociability
and unsociability.

To Each Their Own

Therefore it is better to return to the classical definition of justice, 'to each their
own', that was mentioned in Chapter 1. In the modern understanding of justice
as 'human rights' this definition means that everyone has a claim to the rights
and freedoms of the Universal Declaration. The discussion of individual rights
and freedoms in the earlier chapters showed time and again that it is often
anything but clear to what an individual human being is entitled on the
grounds of the abstractly formulated human rights. Think back to some of
the examples: can someone claim a dignified death on the grounds of the right
to life or the right to privacy? Whilst no one may use the freedom of expression
in order to slander another person, when is an expression a case of 'slander'?
Everyone has the right to their own space, but how large should that space be?
Could the plans for a new runway for an important airport be thwarted
because of the right to private space of some of those affected? Everyone has
the right to take part in the government of their country, but how should this
be organized? Does it require referenda? Every member of a cultural minority
has the right to their own identity, but does the display of a religious symbol
such as the cross in state schools violate this right for religious minorities?

In the application of abstract human rights all kinds of conflicts lie in wait, in
particular when an individual thinks they have a particular claim based on
a particular human right, and the legal system does not agree to grant this
person their 'due'. In such a case there are two possibilities: the human right is
either understood too broadly by the individual or too narrowly by the legal
system. Many discussions about human rights revolve around this issue: where
to draw the line between what an individual is entitled to and what the legal
system is prepared to provide. Remarkably, the Universal Declaration seems to
understand the problem. While Articles 29 and 30 contain no magical formula
on how to solve such conflicting claims, they do state that individual human
beings are not allowed to make use of their human rights as if they had no
duties to the community. It is prohibited to use human rights in any manner

---

[10] John Rawls, *A Theory of Justice. Revised Edition* (Oxford: Oxford University Press, 1999), 26.

that is incompatible with the respect for human rights for everyone or with the aims of the Universal Declaration.

The Universal Declaration thus cannot be read as a 'Magna Carta' of individual liberty rights or as a liberal philosophical tract that recognizes only individuals and not communities. A proper use of human rights shows the 'spirit of brotherhood', as required by Article 1. In order to clarify this a little further, I suggest we return again to the definition of 'justice' as 'to each their own'. Whilst in modern times 'human rights' seem to constitute the content of 'their own', it is important to note the important difference between such modern understanding and its classical interpretation. In brief, the difference boils down to the following: justice in the classical sense means that everyone must give everyone else 'their own', while justice in the sense of human rights means that everyone may claim 'their own' from everyone else. Classical justice is defined from the perspective of the agent who acts in order to give to everyone that to which they are entitled. Modern justice gives centre stage to the recipient as the person who claims their due from everyone else. From a classical point of view, a 'just' individual gives others what is 'theirs', whereas 'just' individuals in the modern sense claim that others provide them with what is 'their own'. 'Justice', thus, is seen either from the perspective of the agent or from the perspective of the recipient.

For this reason, the classical view holds the 'duty to justice' as central, whereas the modern view, in contrast, is all about the 'right to justice'. Justice means either the duty to grant everyone else 'their own', or the right to receive 'one's own' from others. In both cases justice means 'to each their own', but there is a great difference. The modern idea of justice considers a human being first of all as the bearer of (human) rights and therefore stresses the axis of man as an individual. By emphasizing 'my' right to be given by others what is mine, the axis of humans as social creatures disappears into the background. In the classical interpretation the reverse is the case. Justice is all about the duty to provide others with 'their own' and the axis of humans as individuals becomes less important.

It is very interesting to note that this classical formula 'to each their own' is often accompanied by two other formulae. These three are found together in the work of the Roman jurist Ulpian in the third century CE and were adopted by Kant in his eighteenth-century doctrine of law.[11] 'Each their own' (*suum cuique tribuere*) is preceded by two other formulae, namely '*honeste vive*' (be an honourable human being) and '*neminem laede*' (do not wrong anyone). Together, these three are, in Kant's view, fundamental legal duties. Herewith, Kant does not deny that everyone can make claims on others based on their humanity. According to him, the innate human right of freedom of the one person indeed means a claim whereby all others are placed under the obligation not to treat that person in any way that infringes this freedom. But

---

[11] Immanuel Kant, *Metaphysik der Sitten*, AA VI, 236–7.

a human being is for Kant not merely the bearer of this right, but also the bearer of these three legal duties. Justice means for Kant that one is both the holder of a human right and the bearer of those human duties. An individual human being has simultaneously rights and duties.

Remarkably, the first of these legal duties concerns the proper attitude of a person to themselves: be an honest or an honourable person (*honeste vive*). According to Kant, this duty consists in asserting one's worth. It urges everyone to preserve their dignity in relationship to all other human beings so that no one shall make themselves – in agreement with the formulation discussed in Chapter 4 – a mere means for others. Everyone has a duty to consider themselves as an end in itself. The second legal duty then prescribes the proper attitude of each person to all others: 'do injustice to no one' (*neminem laede*), which means that no one may wrong another person. Finally, Kant mentions 'to each their own' as the third legal duty. But here too, the duty should not be seen from the perspective of the recipient but from that of the agent: the duty is on all of us, to 'give others their due' (*suum cuique tribuere*).

This classical view of justice can be understood as a clarification of what a proper attitude towards human rights may mean. 'Each their own' teaches us that justice is the source not merely of human rights, but also of human duties. According to Kant, each individual can claim certain behaviour of others on the basis of the human right to freedom, but each individual also has, on the basis of justice, the fundamental duty to treat themselves and others in a particular manner – to live as an honourable human being, not to wrong others and to give others their due. Every person has to uphold their dignity, not to wrong others and to respect them, when making claims on the basis of their own right to freedom. In this way Kant combines the axis of (the right of) the human being as an individual and the axis of (the duty of) the human being as a social creature. The claims that individuals can make on others on the basis of their rights are balanced by their legal duties.

This surely clarifies Articles 29 and 30 even further. Because the claims that one can make are 'tempered' by these duties, the human rights of the Universal Declaration are not the rights of isolated, unembedded individuals, but of the members of a variety of communities within 'the human family' as the ultimate community. By taking the interests of these communities into consideration, the Universal Declaration cannot be accused of the solipsism or egoism that Marx levelled at the eighteenth-century understanding of human rights. Human beings are not to regard each other as hindrances to individual freedom, but as the source of (mutual) duties.

Cardinal Virtues

We encountered Lorenzetti's visualization of good government in the town hall of Sienna in Chapter 16. Building on, among others, the classical philosophies of Plato, Aristotle and Thomas Aquinas, Lorenzetti presented good government as the outcome of justice's cooperation with other virtues, such as temperance, fortitude and prudence. These are known as the cardinal virtues, because they are central to a virtuous life. From them, all other virtues can be derived, as the Latin *cardo* means lynchpin or hinge.

It is not so remarkable that justice, even if it takes the form of 'human rights', is brought into connection with these other virtues. According to Plato, 'justice' is nothing other than the quality which makes the presence of the other three virtues possible and which sustains them.[12] Temperance, fortitude and prudence are the appropriate ways in which human beings deal respectively with their physical cravings and desires, their psychological or mental condition and finally their ability to reason. The person who exercises these virtues is a just person. In a just society, according to Plato, cravings and desires are tempered, dangers and challenges are faced with courage and the leadership of the society is placed in the hands of those who are wise.

It goes almost without saying that prudence or practical wisdom has to play a major role, not only in the drafting of human rights but also in the application of those rights within concrete situations. The Universal Declaration as one of the most important documents of the twentieth century not only aimed to offer an answer to the problems and challenges of its time, but it also took the human condition of unsocial sociability into account. It did not formulate an unachievable utopia but reflected on human possibilities and limitations. Articles 13 and 14 – discussed in Chapter 12 – are a nice example. These Articles strive for a good balance between the right of a political community to decide on the composition of its population and the interests of foreigners who seek protection from persecution. Maybe the right balance has not (yet) been struck, but it seems in any case prudent that the Universal Declaration does not argue in favour of an unlimited right of migration which would require the abolition of state borders. The virtue of prudence is also needed when national and international lawmakers have to translate human rights into legally binding constitutional rights and when judges have to answer the question whether a concrete human right has been violated, as in the *Lautsi* case discussed in Chapter 13.

The virtue of fortitude or courage is historically connected to the defence and protection of the political community against external threats and therefore it takes the form of a proper middle between cowardice and recklessness. Fortitude would also be an adequate name for someone who defends their convictions against fierce opposition. It is not difficult to see how fortitude plays a role in justice as human rights. Respect for human rights is not self-evident in many situations, certainly not in the case of emergencies. Chapter 7 discussed the difficulty of safeguarding the 'absolute' right not to be tortured when torture might appear to be the only way in which a threat can be neutralized. It also takes

---

[12] Plato, *Republic*, 433b: (Socrates speaks) 'I think that this is the remaining virtue in the state after our consideration of temperance, fortitude and prudence, a quality which made it possible for them all to grow up in the body politic and which when they have sprung up preserves them as long as it is present.'

courage to uphold human rights standards when these rights or their application go against the will of a democratic majority. For that reason, Chapter 11 argued that the idea of human rights accords better with a material concept of democracy than with a formal, statistical view. When the axis of the human being as a social creature is likely to overshadow the axis of the human being as individual, justice must be supported by fortitude.

In light of the above, the link between justice as human rights and the virtue of temperance is obvious as well. In the classical view this virtue is concerned with humankind's proper attitude with regard to (bodily) cravings and desires. Anyone who allows themselves to be ruled by these physical elements, becomes immoderate, greedy and self-indulgent. Anyone who neglects the satisfaction of their desires becomes unfeeling. Temperance requires finding and keeping a good balance between too much and too little. As we have just seen, the claims on the basis of human rights should be tempered by the human duties as formulated by Ulpian and Kant. Cicero too stresses that moderation plays an important role when considering what justice requires.[13] The virtue of temperance prescribes an attitude of self-constraint. Whereas justice bids us not to wrong others (*neminem laede*), the virtue of temperance tells us to treat others with respect. This is important for these others, but also for oneself and one's status within the political community. Given Cicero's influence, it is unsurprising that Kant too recommends moderation with regard to one's claims on others. Someone who does not behave moderately displays egoism or arrogance,[14] and that is a violation of the duty of the *honeste vive*.

Therefore, justice must be 'supported' by moderation. It would be wrong if justice in the form of human rights were to lead to a situation in which each and every 'I' would demand what is 'theirs' without consideration of what is due others. Then human rights would indeed be egoistical rights. Claims on the basis of human rights should steer clear of the immodesty of an arrogant refusal to consider the interest of others. 'Each their own' implies not only claims for oneself, but also giving others their due. This moderation is but a small price readily to be paid for the respect that is due to one's self and to others.

Temperance and Human Rights

It turned out that the idea of human rights is indeed a good starting point for an introduction into legal philosophy. The emergence of human rights in the modern era led to a transformation in thinking about the relationship between human beings and the law. But this transformation should not mean a complete break with the past. Classical counsel on justice is essential for a proper understanding of the idea of human rights. By acknowledging legal duties and the virtue of

---

[13] In *De officiis*, Cicero dedicates a large part of the first book to *Temporantia* (1.37–151; especially in 88, Cicero emphasizes the importance of moderation in applying criminal justice).

[14] Immanuel Kant, *Metaphysik der Sitten*, AA VI, 465.

temperance as parts of the idea of human rights the problems indicated by Bentham and Marx can be overcome. In the eighteenth-century declarations of human rights, too much emphasis was given to the axis of man as an individual, and the axis of man as a social creature was neglected. The Universal Declaration, in particular in its Articles 29 and 30, helps restore the balance between the axes. Individual human rights should not thwart the intention of the Declaration, namely to set a 'common standard of achievement for all peoples and all nations' which can only be realized in a 'spirit of brotherhood'.

Perhaps it is surprising that an introduction in legal philosophy on the idea of human rights ends with 'temperance', a theme that is not often connected to human rights. Temperance or moderation does not fit within the framework of human rights if it is all about claims that can or cannot be legally enforced. Some may even see 'temperance' as part of an old-fashioned conservative discourse on the virtues rather than as part of a progressive discourse on human rights. However, this is a false impression. One could point out the interesting doctrine of the 'margin of appreciation' that the European Court of Human Rights has developed in its case law.[15] Without going into any detail, this doctrine enables the Court to grant its member states a wide competence to decide for themselves what is demanded by the European Convention on Human Rights. Perhaps some commentators will argue that the Court has given too much room to the interpretation of the member states of what individual rights entail. Others argue the opposite: the Court has allowed too little space for member states to uphold their view of what human rights require, and in that case the Court has overstepped its legal competences.[16] Whoever is right in this debate, one thing is clear: the Court does not regard human rights as enshrined in the European Convention as 'one size fits all', but it rather treats them as a standard which must be applied with prudence and moderation. Abstract human rights need interpretation and this should primarily be done at the level of the member states and against the background of the social values that are current there.

Finally, temperance also accords well with the anthropological worries. It acknowledges the 'human, all too human' tendency to regard one's own views and one's own culture as superior and all else as barbarous. Moderation resists a facile complacency with regard to human rights that deplores and exaggerates shortcomings elsewhere and ignores its own failures or covers these under the cloak of love. The Bible warns against this. 'And why beholdest thou the mote that is in thy brother's eye, but considerest not the beam that is in thine own eye?'[17]

---

[15] Janneke Gerards, 'Pluralism, Deference and the Margin of Appreciation Doctrine', *European Law Journal* (2011) 17: 80–120.

[16] This is defended in Lord Hoffman, 'The Universality of Human Rights' (lecture, Judicial Studies Board Annual Lecture, 19 March 2009).

[17] Mt. 7: 3.

Bibliography

Alexy, Robert. *Begriff und Geltung des Rechts*. Freiburg/München: Alber, 1994.

Alexy, Robert. *Mauerschützen: Zum Verhältnis von Recht, Moral und Strafbarkeit*. Hamburg: Vandenhoeck & Ruprecht, 1993.

Aly, Götz. *Hitler's Beneficiaries: Plunder, Racial War and the Nazi Welfare State*. Translated by Jefferson Chase. New York: Holt, 2008.

Anderson, Benedict. *Imagined Communities: Reflections on the Origin and Spread of Nationalism*. London: Verso, 1983.

Arendt, Hannah. *Eichmann in Jerusalem: A Report on the Banality of Evil*. London: Penguin Classics, 1992.

Arendt, Hannah. *The Origins of Totalitarianism. New Edition with Added Prefaces*. New York: Harcourt Brace Jovanovich, Publishers, 1973.

Aristotle. *Politics*. Available from http://classics.mit.edu/Aristotle/politics.1.one.html.

Arrigo, Jean Maria. 'A Utilitarian Argument against Torture Interrogation of Terrorists'. *Science and Engineering Ethics* (2004) 10: 543–72.

Austin, John. *The Province of Jurisprudence Determined*. Indianapolis: Weidenfeld & Nicholson, 1954 (orig. 1832).

Barnard, David. 'In the High Court of South Africa, Case No. 4138/98: The Global Politics of Access to Low-Cost AIDS Drugs in Poor Countries'. *Kennedy Institute of Ethics Journal* (2002) 12: 159–74.

BBC. 'Torture intelligence criticized'. Last modified 11 October 2004. http://news.bbc.co.uk/2/hi/uk_news/3732488.stm.

Beard, Robert, trans. *1936 Constitution of the USSR*. Lewisburg: Bucknell University, 1996, www.departments.bucknell.edu/russian/const/36cons04.html.

Beccaria, Cesare Bonesana di. *An Essay on Crimes and Punishments: By the Marquis Beccaria of Milan, with a Commentary by M. de Voltaire. A New Edition Corrected*. Albany: W. C. Little & Co., 1872, http://oll.libertyfund.org/titles/beccaria-an-essay-on-crimes-and-punishments.

Berlin, Isaiah. 'Two Concepts of Liberty'. In *Four Essays on Liberty*. Oxford: Oxford University Press, 1969.

Bingham, Tom. *The Rule of Law*. London: Penguin Books, 2006.

Blackstone, William. *Commentaries on the Laws of England (1765–69)*, https://lonang.com/library/reference/blackstone-commentaries-law-england/bla-414/.

Blaisdell, Bob. *Essays on Civil Disobedience*. Mineola: Dover Thrift Edition, 2016.

British Library. 'English Translation of Magna Carta'. Published 28 July 2014, www.bl.uk/magna-carta/articles/magna-carta-english-translation.

Carens, Joseph. 'Aliens and Citizens: The Case for Open Borders'. *The Review of Politics* (1987) 49: 251–73.

Cassese, Antonio. 'Ex inuiria ius oritur: Are We Moving towards International Legitimation of Forcible Humanitarian Countermeasures in the World Community?' *European Journal of International Law* (1999) 10: 23–30.

Cassirer, Ernst, Kristeller, Paul Oskar and Randall, John Herman Jr. *The Renaissance Philosophy of Man*. Chicago: University of Chicago Press, 1948.

Cassirer, Toni. *Mein Leben mit Ernst Cassirer*. Hamburg: Felix Meiner, 1981.

Cesarani, David. *Eichmann: His Life and Crimes*. London: Vintage, 2004.

Chatterjee, Deen K. *The Ethics of Assistance and the Distant Needy*. Cambridge: Cambridge University Press, 2004.

Cicero. *On Duties*, edited by M. T. Griffin and E. M. Atkins. Cambridge: Cambridge University Press, 1991.

Cohen, Hendrik Floris. *The Rise of Modern Science Explained: A Comparative History*. Cambridge: Cambridge University Press, 2015.

Coetzee, John Maxwell. *Diary of a Bad Year*. London: Vintage Publishing, 2007.

Commission for Looted Art in Europe. 'Washington Conference Principles on Nazi-Confiscated Art'. 3 December 1988, www.lootedartcommission.com/Washington-principles

Constant, Benjamin. 'The Liberty of the Ancients Compared with That of the Moderns (1819)'. In *Constant: Political Writings*, edited by Biancamaria Fontana. Cambridge: Cambridge University Press, 1988.

Danner, Mark. 'Torture and Truth: America, Abu Ghraib, and the War on Terror', *New York Review of Books* (2004).

Dershowitz, Alan. 'Tortured Reasoning'. In *Torture: A Collection*, edited by Sanford Levinson. New York: Oxford University Press, 2004.

Doyle, William. *The French Revolution: A Very Short Introduction*. Oxford: Oxford University Press, 2001.

Drèze, Jean, and Sen, Amartya. *Hunger and Public Action*. Oxford: Oxford University Press, 1989.

Dworkin, Ronald. 'Do We Have a Right to Die?' In *Freedom's Law: The Moral Reading of the American Constitution*. Oxford: Oxford University Press, 1996.

Dworkin, Ronald. 'Introduction: The Moral Reading and the Majoritarian Premise'. In *The Moral Reading of the American Constitution*. Oxford: Oxford University Press, 1995.

Dworkin, Ronald. *Taking Rights Seriously*. Cambridge, MA: Harvard University Press, 1977.

Dworkin, Ronald. 'The Morality of Abortion'. In *Life's Dominion: An Argument about Abortion, Euthanasia, and Individual Freedom*. New York: Random House, 1993.

Dworkin, Ronald. *The Philosophy of Law*. Oxford: Oxford University Press, 1977.

Dworkin, Ronald. 'Why Must Speech Be Free?' In *Freedom's Law: The Moral Reading of the American Constitution*. Oxford: Oxford University Press, 1996.

Dyzenhaus, David. *Legality and Legitimacy: Carl Schmitt, Hans Kelsen and Hermann Heller in Weimar*. Oxford: Oxford University Press, 1999.

Erasmus, Desiderius. 'Complaint of Peace'. In *Collected Works of Erasmus*, Vol. 27, edited by Anthony Herbert Tigar Levi. Toronto: University of Toronto Press, 1986.

Executive Board, American Anthropological Association. 'Statement on Human Rights'. *American Anthropologist*, New Series (1947) 49(4): 539–43.

Feinberg, Joel. *The Moral Limits of Criminal Law*. 4 vols. Oxford: Oxford University Press, 1984–90.

Foucault, Michel. *Discipline and Punishment: The Birth of the Prison*. New York: Random House, 1978.

Franck, Thomas. 'Humanitarian Intervention'. In *The Philosophy of International Law*, edited by Samantha Besson and John Tasioulas. Oxford: Oxford University Press, 2010.

Fraser, David. *Law after Auschwitz: Towards a Jurisprudence of the Holocaust*. Durham, NC: Carolina Academic Press, 2005.

Freedom House, 2018, https://freedomhouse.org/.

Frowe, Helen. *The Ethics of War and Peace: An Introduction*. London: Routledge, 2016.

Fuller, Lon. *The Morality of Law*. London: New Haven, 1964.

Gellner, Ernest. *Nations and Nationalism*, 2nd edn. Oxford: Blackwell, 2006.

Gerards, Janneke. 'Pluralism, Deference and the Margin of Appreciation Doctrine'. *European Law Journal* (2011) 17: 80–120.

Glendon, Mary Ann. *A World Made New: Eleanor Roosevelt and the Universal Declaration of Human Rights*. New York: Random House, 2001.

Globalization (2002). 'Declaration of Responsibilities and Human Duties'. Accessed 15 May 2019, http://globalization.icaap.org/content/v2.2/declare.html.

Goodale, Mark. 'The Myth of Universality: The UNESCO "Philosophers' Committee" and the Making of Human Rights'. *Law & Social Inquiry* (2018) 43: 596–617.

Griffin, James. *On Human Rights*. Oxford: Oxford University Press, 2008.

Grimm, Dieter. 'Does Europe Need a Constitution'. *European Law Journal* (1995) 1: 282–302.

Gross, Oren. 'The Prohibition of Torture and the Limits of the Law'. In *Torture: A Collection*, edited by Sanford Levinson. New York: Oxford University Press: 2004.

Habermas, Jürgen. *Between Facts and Norms: Contributions to a Discourse Theory of Law and Democracy*. Cambridge, MA: MIT Press, 1996.

Habermas, Jürgen. 'On the Internal Relation between the Rule of Law and Democracy'. In *The Inclusion of the Other: Studies in Political Theory*. Cambridge: Polity Press, 2005.

Habermas, Jürgen. 'Remark on Dieter Grimm's Does Europe Need a Constitution'. *European Law Journal* (1995) 1: 303–7.

Habermas, Jürgen. 'The Concept of Human Dignity and the Realistic Utopia of Human Rights'. *Metaphilosophy* (2010) 41: 464–79.

Habermas, Jürgen. 'The European Nation-State: On the Past and Future of Sovereignty and Citizenship'. In *The Inclusion of the Other: Studies in Political Theory* Cambridge: Polity Press, 2005.

Hart, Herbert Lionel Adolphus. 'Positivism and the Separation of Law and Morals'. *Harvard Law Review* (1958) 71: 593–629.

Hart, Herbert Lionel Adolphus. *Punishment and Responsibility: Essays in The Philosophy of Law*. Oxford: Oxford University Press, 2008.

Hart, Herbert Lionel Adolphus. *The Concept of Law*. Oxford: Oxford University Press, 1994 (orig. 1961).

Hathaway, Oona A. 'The Promises and Limits of the International Law of Torture'. In *Torture: A Collection*, edited by Sanford Levinson. New York: Oxford University Press, 2004.

Hazareesingh, Sudhir. 'Haughty Dirigistes'. *London Review of Books*, 23 May 2019.

Hegel, Georg Wilhelm Friedrich. *Phenomenology of Spirit*, edited by Terry Pinkard. Cambridge: Cambridge University Press, 2018.

Hegel, Georg Wilhelm Friedrich. *Philosophy of Right*. Translated by Thomas Malcolm Knox. Oxford: Oxford University Press, 1952.

Hirsch, Martin, Majer, Diemut and Meinck, Jürgen. *Recht, Verwaltung und Justiz im Nationalsozialismus*. Baden-Baden: Bund Verlag, 1997.

Hobbes, Thomas. *Leviathan*. Adelaide: The University of Adelaide Library, 2016. https://ebooks.adelaide.edu.au/h/hobbes/thomas/h68l/.

Hoffman, Lord. 'The Universality of Human Rights'. Judicial Studies Board Annual Lecture, 19 March 2009.

Hohfeld, Wesley Newcomb. *Fundamental Legal Conceptions as Applied in Judicial Reasoning*. New Haven: Yale University Press, 1919.

Hollis, Aidan and Pogge, Thomas. *The Health Impact Fund. Making New Medicines Accessible for All*. Incentives for Global Health, 2008.

Holmes, Oliver Wendell. 'The Path of the Law'. *Harvard Law Review* (1897) 10: 457–78.

Honderich, Ted. *Punishment: The Supposed Justifications*. London: Pluto Press, 2006.

Hopgood, Stephen. *The Endtimes of Human Rights*. Ithaca: Cornell University Press, 2015.

Hunt, Lynn. *Inventing Human Rights: A History*. New York: W. W. Norton & Company, 2007.

Jaspers, Karl. *Die Schuldfrage: Von der politischen Haftung Deutschlands*. Zürich: Lambert Schneider, 1946.

Joas, Hans. *Die Sakralität der Person: Eine neue Genealogie der Menschenrechte*. Frankfurt am Main: Suhrkamp, 2011.

Kant, Immanuel. *Immanuel Kants Schriften*. Ausgabe der Preussische Akademie der Wissenschaften (AA). Berlin: De Gruyter, 1902.

Kant, Immanuel. *Political Writings*, edited by Hans Reiss. Translated by Barry Nisbet. Cambridge: Cambridge University Press, 1991.

Kant, Immanuel. *Practical Philosophy*. Translated and edited by Mary J. Gregor. Cambridge: Cambridge University Press, 1996.

Kavanagh, Aileen and Oberdiek, John, ed. *Arguing about Law*. London: Routledge, 2009.

Keay, Douglas. Interview with Margaret Thatcher. *Woman's Own*, 23 September 1987.

Kelsen, Hans. *Introduction to the Problems of Legal Theory*. Translated by Stanley L. Paulson and Bonnie Litschewski Paulson. Oxford: Clarendon, 1996

Kelsen, Hans. 'The Rule against Ex Post Facto Laws and the Prosecution of the Axis War Criminals'. *The Judge Advocate Journal* (1945) II: 8–12.

Kelsen, Hans. *The Value and Essence of Democracy*. Translated by Brian Graf, edited by Nadia Urbinati and Carlo Invernizzi Accetti. Lanham: Rowman Littlefield, 2013.

King, Martin L. 'Letter from the Birmingham City Jail'. In *A Testament of Hope: The Essential Writings and Speeches of Martin Luther King Jr.*, edited by James M. Washington. New York: HarperCollins, 1991.

Kinsella, David and Carr, Craig L., ed. *The Morality of War: A Reader*. London: Rienner Publisher, 2007.

Klümper, Günther F. *Du bist Nichts, Dein Volk ist Alles: Erinnerungen eines jugendlichen Zeitzeugen 1937–1941*. Baden-Baden: Aquensis, 2012.

Kossmann, Ernst H. Volkssoevereiniteit aan het begin van de het Nederlandse Ancient Regime. In *Politieke theorie en geschiedenis*. Amsterdam: Bakker, 1987.

Kramer, Matthew H. *Torture and Moral Integrity: A Philosophical Enquiry*. Oxford: Oxford University Press, 2014.

Lancaster, John. 'Marx at 193'. *London Review of Books*, 5 April 2012.

Leroi, Armand Marie. *The Lagoon: How Aristotle invented Science*. London: Bloomsbury, 2014.

Lessig, Lawrence. *The Future of Ideas: The Fate of the Commons in a Connected World*. New York: Vintage, 2002.

Li, Xiaorong. 'Asian Values and the Universality of Human Rights'. In *The Philosophy of Human Rights: Readings in Context*, edited by Patrick Hayden. St Paul: Paragon House, 2001.

Locke, John. *A Letter Concerning Toleration (1689)*, edited by Kerry S. Walters. Peterborough: Broadview Editions, 2013.

Locke, John. *Two Treatises of Government*, edited by Peter Laslett. Cambridge: Cambridge University Press, 1988.

Luban, David. 'Fairness to Rightness. Jurisdiction, Legality and the Legitimacy of International Criminal law'. In *The Philosophy of International Law*, edited by Samantha Besson & John Tasioulas. Oxford: Oxford University Press, 2010.

Marx, Karl. 'On the Jewish Question'. www.marxists.org/archive/marx/works/1844/jewish-question/.

Marx, Karl. *Critique of the Gotha Programme*. Moscow: Progress Publishers, 1970. www.marxists.org/archive/marx/works/1875/gotha/.

Marx, Karl and Engels, Friedrich. *Manifesto of the Communist Party*. Translated by Samuel Moore. Moscow: Progress Publishers, 1969. www.marxists.org/archive/marx/works/1848/communist-manifesto/.

Mayer, Jane. 'Whatever It Takes. The Politics of the Man Behind "24"'. *New Yorker*, 19 February 2007. www.newyorker.com/magazine/2007/02/19/whatever-it-takes.

Mazower, Mark. *No Enchanted Palace: The End of Empire and the Ideological Origins of the United Nations*. Princeton: Princeton University Press, 2009.

McCrudden, Cristopher. 'Human Dignity and Judicial Interpretation of Human Rights'. *The European Journal of International Law* (2008) 19: 655–724.

McMahan, Jeff. *Killing in War*. Oxford: Oxford University Press, 2009.

Mertens, Thomas. 'Memory, Politics and Law – The Eichmann Trial. Hannah Arendt's view on the Jerusalem Court's Competence'. *German Law Journal* (2005) 6(2): 407–24.

Mertens, Thomas. 'Radbruch and Hart on the Grudge Informer. A Reconsideration'. *Ratio Juris* (2002) 15: 186–205.

Mill, John Stuart. *On Liberty* (1859). www.utilitarianism.com/ol/five.html.

Mill, John Stuart. *On Liberty, Utilitarianism, and Other Essays*, edited by Mark Philip and Frederick Rosen. Oxford: Oxford University Press, 2015.

Miller, David. *Political Philosophy: A Very Short Introduction*. Oxford: Oxford University Press, 2003.

Milward, Alan. *The European Rescue of the Nation-State*. London: Routledge, 2000.

Minder, Raphael. 'Court Rules Spanish Museum Can Keep a Painting Seen as Nazi Loot'. *New York Times*, 1 May 2019. www.nytimes.com/2019/05/01/arts/design/court-rules-spanish-museum-can-keep-a-painting-seen-as-nazi-loot.html

Montaigne, Michel de. 'Of Cannibals'. In *Essays*. Translated by Charles Cotton (1580). http://essays.quotidiana.org/montaigne/cannibals/.

Müller, Ingo. *Hitler's Justice: The Courts of the Third Reich*. Translated by Deborah L. Schneider. Cambridge, MA: Harvard University Press, 1992.

Nadler, Steven. *A Book Forged in Hell*. Princeton: Princeton University Press, 2011.

Nietzsche, Friedrich. *Thus spoke Zarathustra*, edited by Robert Pippin. Translated by Adrian Del Caro. Cambridge: Cambridge University Press, 2006.

Norrie, Alan. *Crime, Reason and History: A Critical Introduction to Criminal Law*. Cambridge: Cambridge University Press, 1993.

Nozick, Robert. *Anarchy, State and Utopia*. New York: Basic Books, 1974.

Nussbaum, Martha. 'Duties of Justice, Duties of Material Aid: Cicero's Problematic Legacy'. *The Journal of Political Philosophy* (2000) 8: 176–206.

Nussbaum, Martha. 'Justice for Women!'. *New York Review of Books*, 8 October 1992. www.nybooks.com/articles/1992/10/08/justice-for-women/.

Nussbaum, Martha. 'Kant and Stoic Cosmopolitanism'. *The Journal of Political Philosophy* (1997) 5: 1–25.

Nussbaum, Martha. 'Sodomy Laws: Disgust and Intrusion'. In *From Disgust to Humanity: Sexual Orientation & Constitutional Law*. Oxford: Oxford University Press, 2010.

Orford, Anne. *International Authority and the Responsibility to Protect*. Cambridge: Cambridge University Press, 2011.

Owen, James. *Nuremberg: Evil on Trial*. London: Headline Review, 2006.

Pauer-Studer, Herlinde and Fink, Julian, eds. *Rechtfertigungen des Unrechts: Das Rechtsdenken im Nationalsozialismus in Originaltexten*. Frankfurt am Main: Suhrkamp, 2014.

Paulson, Bonnie L. and Paulson, Stanley L. (translation) 'Statutory Lawlessness and Supra-Statutory Law (Radbruch, 1946)'. *Oxford Journal of Legal Studies* (2006) 26: 1–11.

Paulson, Stanley L. 'Classical Legal Positivism at Nuremberg'. *Philosophy and Public Affairs* (1975) 4: 132–58.

Paulson, Stanley L. 'Lon L. Fuller, Gustav Radbruch and the "Positivist" Theses'. *Law and Philosophy* (1994) 13: 313–59.

Pierik, Roland. 'Mandatory Vaccination. An Unqualified Defence'. *Journal of Applied Philosophy* (2018) 35: 381–98.

Piketty, Thomas. *Capital in the Twenty-First Century*. Translated by Arthur Goldhammer. Cambridge, MA: Belknap Press, 2017.

Pinker, Stephen. *Enlightenment Now: The Case for Reason, Science, Humanism and Progress*. New York: Viking Press, 2018.

Plato. *Laws*. Available from http://classics.mit.edu/Plato/laws.9.ix.html.

Pogge, Thomas. *Politics as Usual: What Lies behind the Pro-Poor Rhetoric*. Cambridge: Polity Press, 2011.

Pogge, Thomas. 'The International Significance of Human Rights'. *The Journal of Ethics* (2000) 4: 45–69.

Pogge, Thomas. *World Poverty and Human Rights*. Cambridge: Polity, 2002.

Pope John XXIII. *Pacem in Terris*. 1963. www.papalencyclicals.net/john23/j23pacem.htm.

Purdy, Jedediah. *After Nature: A Politics for the Anthropocene*. Cambridge: Cambridge University Press, 2015.

Radbruch, Gustav. 'Der Relativismus in der Rechtsphilosophie'. In *Gesamtausgabe*, edited by Arthur Kaufmann, vol. 3. Heidelberg: Müller, 1990.

Radbruch, Gustav. 'Gesetzliches Unrecht und übergesetzliches Recht'. *Süddeutsche Juristenzeitung* (1946) 1: 105–8.

Rawls, John. *A Theory of Justice: Revised Edition*. Oxford: Oxford University Press, 1999.

Rawls, John. *Justice as Fairness: A Restatement*. Cambridge: Harvard University Press, 2001.

Rawls, John. *Political Liberalism*. Cambridge, MA: Harvard University Press, 1993.

Rawls, John. *The Law of Peoples: With the Idea of Public Reason Revisited*. Cambridge, MA: Harvard University Press, 2001.

Rawls, John. 'Two Concepts of Rules'. *The Philosophical Review* (1955) 64: 3–32.

Raz, Joseph. 'Human Rights without Foundations'. In *The Philosophy of International Law*, edited by Samantha Besson & John Tasioulas, 321–38. Oxford: Oxford University Press, 2010.

Rejali, D. *Torture and Democracy*. New Jersey: Princeton University Press, 2007.

Robert H. Jackson Centre. 'Opening Statement before the International Military Tribunal'. www.roberthjackson.org/speech-and-writing/opening-statement-before-the-international-military-tribunal/.

Robertson, Geoffrey. *Crimes against Humanity: The Struggle for Global Justice*. London: Penguin Group, 2006.

Rosen, Michael. *Dignity: Its History and Meaning*. Cambridge, MA: Harvard University Press, 2012.

Rousseau, Jean Jacques. *The Social Contract and Other Later Political Writings*, edited by Victor Gourevitch. Cambridge: Cambridge University Press, 2012.

Sandel, Michael. *What Money Can't Buy: The Moral Limits of Markets*. New York: Farrar, Straus & Giroux, 2012.

Sandel, Michael. *Justice: What's the Right Thing to Do?* London: Allen Lane, 2009.

Sands, Philippe. *East West Street: On the Origins of Genocide and Crimes against Humanity*. London: Knopf Publishing Group, 2016.

Satz, Debra. *Why Some Things Should Not Be for Sale: The Moral Limits of Markets*. Oxford: Oxford University Press, 2010.

Schirach, Ferdinand von. *Terror: Ein Theaterstück und eine Rede*. München: Verlagsgruppe Random House GmbH, 2016.

Schmitt, Carl. *The Crisis of Parliamentary Democracy*. Translated by Ellen Kennedy. Cambridge, MA: MIT Press, 1985.

Scruton, Roger. *The West and the Rest: Globalisation and the Terrorist Threat*. Wilmington: ISI Books, 2002.

Sen, Amartya. *Poverty and Famines: An Essay on Entitlement and Deprivation*. Oxford: Oxford University Press, 1981.

Seneca. *Letters from a Stoic*. Translated by Robin Campbell. London: Penguin Books, 1969.

Seneca, *Moral Letters to Lucilius*, available from https://en.wikisource.org/wiki/Moral_letters_to_Lucilius.

Sensen, Oliver. 'Kant's Conception of Human Dignity'. *Kant-Studien* (2009) 100: 309–31.

Shah, Mustafa. 'Islamic Conceptions of Dignity: Historical Trajectories and Paradigms'. In *Dignity: A History*, edited by Remy Debes. Oxford: Oxford University Press, 2017.

Shamsie, Kamila. *Home Fire*. New York: Riverhead Books, 2017.

Shue, Henry. *Basic Rights*. Princeton: Princeton University Press, 1996.

Simma, Bruno. 'NATO, the UN and the Use of Force: Legal Aspects'. *European Journal of International Law* (1999) 10: 1–22.

Singer, Peter. 'Affluence, Famine and Morality'. *Philosophy and Public Affairs* (1972) 1: 229–43.

Singer, Peter. *One World: The Ethics of Globalisation*. New Haven: Yale University Press, 2002.

Singer, Peter. *The Most Good You Can Do: How Effective Altruism Is Changing Ideas on Living Ethically*. New Haven: Yale University Press, 2015.

Skinner, Quentin. *Visions of Politics: Volume 2: Renaissance Virtues*. Cambridge: Cambridge University Press, 2002.

Sophocles. *The Theban Plays*. Translated by Edward F. Watling. Middlesex: Penguin, 1947.

Spinoza, Baruch. *Theological Political Treatise*, edited by Jonathan Israel. Cambridge: Cambridge University Press, 2007.

Sussman, David. 'What's Wrong with Torture'. *Philosophy and Public Affairs* (2005) 33: 1–33.

Tebbit, Mark. *Philosophy of Law: An Introduction*. London: Routledge, 2005.

Tesón, Fernando. *Humanitarian Intervention: An Inquiry into Law and Morality*. New York: Transnational Publishers, 1988.

Trebilcock, Michael. 'The Case for a Liberal Immigration Policy'. In *Justice in Immigration*, edited by Warren Schwartz. Cambridge, Cambridge University Press, 1995.

Twining, William L. and Twining, P. E. 'Bentham on Torture'. *North Ireland Law Quarterly* (1973) 24: 307–56.

Unger, Peter. *Living High and Letting Die: Our Illusion of Innocence*. New York: Oxford University Press, 1996.

United Nations. 'United Nations Development Programme'. Accessed 15 May 2019. www.undp.org/content/undp/en/home.html.

Vatican. 'Catechism of the Catholic Church'. www.vatican.va/archive/ccc_css/archive/catechism/ccc_toc.htm, no. 1700

Vermeulen, Ben. 'The Freedom of Religion in Art. 9 of the European Convention on Human Rights: Historical Roots and Today's Dilemma's'. In *Freedom of Religion*, edited by Bram van de Beek, Eddy van der Borght and Ben Vermeulen. Leiden: Brill, 2010.

Waldron, Jeremy. *Law and Disagreement*. Oxford: Oxford University Press, 1999.

Waldron, Jeremy, ed. *Nonsense upon Stilts: Bentham, Burke and Marx on the Rights of Man*. London: Methuen, 1987.

Waldron, Jeremy. *The Harm in Hate Speech*. Cambridge, MA: Harvard University Press, 2012.

Waldron, Jeremy. 'What Are Moral Absolutes Like?' *The Harvard Review of Philosophy* (2012) 18: 4–30.

Walzer, Michael. *Just and Unjust Wars: A Moral Argument with Historical Illustrations*. New York: Basic Books, 2000.

Walzer, Michael. 'Political Action. The Problem of Dirty Hands'. In *Torture: A Collection*, edited by Sanford Levinson. New York: Oxford University Press, 2004.

Walzer, Michael. *Spheres of Justice: A Defence of Pluralism & Equality*. Oxford: Blackwell, 1983.

Wansbrough, Henry, ed. *The New Jerusalem Bible: Reader's Edition*. New York: Doubleday, 1990.

Weber, Eugen. *Peasants into Frenchmen, The Modernisation of Rural France 1870–1914*. Stanford: Stanford University Press, 1972.

Weiler, Joseph. 'Does Europe need a constitution? Demos, Telos and the German Maastricht Decision'. *European Law Journal* (1995) 1: 219–58.

Weiler, Joseph. 'Freedom of Religion and Freedom from Religion: The European Model'. *Maine Law Review* (2013) 65: 760–8.

Weiler, Joseph. 'The Transformation of Europe'. In *The Constitution of Europe*, 10–101. Cambridge: Cambridge University Press, 1999.

West, Ed. *1215 and All That: Magna Carta and King John*. New York: Skyhorse Publishing, 2017.

Wikipedia. 'Health Impact Fund'. Accessed 5 April 2019. https://en.wikipedia.org/wiki/Health_Impact_Fund.

Wikisource. 'Universal Declaration of Human Responsibilities'. Last modified 8 March 2013. https://en.wikisource.org/wiki/Universal_Declaration_of_Human_Responsibilities.

Wittgenstein, Ludwig. *Philosophical Investigations*. Translated by Elizabeth Anscombe. Oxford: Basil Blackwell, 1958.

World Inequality Lab. 'World Inequality Report 2018'. Accessed 19 May 2019. https://wir2018.wid.world/.

Zürn, Michael. 'Democratic Governance beyond the Nation-State'. *European Journal of International Relations* (2000) 6: 183–221.

Treaties

Council of Europe. Convention for the Protection of Human Rights and Fundamental Freedoms. 4 November 1950. ETS 5. www.coe.int/en/web/conventions/full-list/-/conventions/rms/0900001680063765.

Declaration des Droits de l'Homme et du Citoyen. Paris. 26 August 1789. https://fr.wikisource.org/wiki/Déclaration_des_Droits_de_l'Homme_et_du_Citoyen.

Declaration of Independence. Philadelphia. 4 July 1776. www.archives.gov/founding-docs/declaration-transcript.

Declaration of the Rights of Man and Citizen. Paris. 26 August 1789. www.conseil-constitutionnel.fr/sites/default/files/as/root/bank_mm/anglais/cst2.pdf.

European Union. Treaty Establishing the European Community (Consolidated Version). Rome Treaty. 25 March 1957. www.refworld.org/docid/3ae6b39c0.html.

European Union. Treaty of Lisbon Amending the Treaty on European Union and the Treaty Establishing the European Community. 13 December 2007. 2007/C 306/01. https://eur-lex.europa.eu/legal-content/EN/TXT/?uri=celex%3A12007L%2FTXT.

UN General Assembly. Convention against Torture and Other Cruel, Inhuman or Degrading Treatment or Punishment. 10 December 1984. United Nations. Treaty Series, vol. 1465, p. 85. www.ohchr.org/en/professionalinterest/pages/cat.aspx.

UN General Assembly. International Covenant on Civil and Political Rights. 19 December 1966. 2200A (XXI). www.ohchr.org/en/professionalinterest/pages/ccpr.aspx.

UN General Assembly. International Covenant on Economic, Social and Cultural Rights. 16 December 1966. Treaty Series, vol. 993, p. 3. www.refworld.org/docid/3ae6b36c0.html.

UN General Assembly. Universal Declaration of Human Rights. 10 November 1948. Resolution 217A. www.un.org/en/universal-declaration-human-rights.

United Nations. Charter of the United Nations. 24 October 1945. 1 UNTS XVI. www.un.org/en/sections/un-charter/chapter-i/index.html.

Jurisprudence

International

Case 18984/91, *McCann and others v. The United Kingdom* [1995] 21 ECHR 97 GC

Case 2668/07, *Dink v. Turkey* [2010] ECHR

Case 48939/04, *Öneryildiz v. Turkey* [2004] ECHR

Case 2364/02, *Pretty v. The United Kingdom* [2002] ECHR

Case 1948/04, *Salah Sheekh v. The Netherlands* [2007] ECHR

Case 66069/09, 130/10, 3896/10, *Vinter and others v. The United Kingdom* [2013] ECHR

Case 31322/07, *Haas v. Switzerland* [2011] ECHR

Case 22978/05, *Gäfgen v. Germany* [2010] ECHR

Case 30814/06, *Lautsi v. Italy* [2011] ECHR

Case 36022/97, *Hatton and Others v. The United Kingdom* [2003] ECHR

Case 34044/96, 35532/97, 44801/98, *Kessler and Krenz v. Germany* [2001] ECHR

Case 36376/04, *Kononov v. Latvia* [2010] ECHR

Case 26/62, *NV Algemene Transport- en Expeditie Onderneming van Gend & Loos v. Netherlands Inland Revenue Administration* [1963] ECR 1; [1963] CMLR 88

Case 15375/89, *Gasus Dosier- und Fordertechnik GmbH v. The Netherlands* [1995] ECHR

Prosecutor v. Furundzija, IT-95-17/1

Advisory Opinion on Minority Schools in Albania (1935), PCIJ Reps. Ser. A/B, No. 64

Case concerning Barcelona Traction, Light and Power Co. (*Belgium v. Spain*), ICJ Reports 1 1970

Germany

BVerfG 1 BvR 357/05, www.bverfg.de/e/rs20060215_1bvr035705en.html.

BVerfG 2 BvR 578/07, www.bverfg.de/entscheidungen/rk20081007_2bvr057807.html

BVerfG 89/155, *Brunner v. European Union Treaty*

Holland

District Court Rotterdam, 7 April 2004, ECLI:NL:RBROT:2004:AO7178

District Court The Hague, 14 October 2005, ECLI:NL:RBSGR:2005:AU4347; ECLI:NL: RBSGR:2005:AU4373.

Hoge Raad, 17 September 2002, ECLI:NL:PHR:2002:AE6118

Israel

Public Committee against Torture in Israel v. Israel, 38 I.L.M. 1471 (1999)

United Kingdom

A *Local Authority v. E* [2012] EWHC 1939 (COP)

R *v. Bow Street Metropolitan Stipendiary Magistrate, ex parte Pinochet Ugarte (No 3)* [2000] 1 AC 147

United States

Roe v. Wade, 410 US 113 (1973)

Filártiga v. Peña-Irala, 630 F 2d 876 (2nd Cir. 1980)

Laurence v. Texas, 539 US 558 (2003)

Obergefell v. Hodges, 576 US _ (2015)

Hustler Magazine Inc. v. Falwell, 485 US 46 (1988)

Brown v. Board of Education of Topeka, 347 US 483 (1954)

Subject Index

Name Index